W9-APM-282

25
NON-ROYALTY
ONE-ACT PLAYS
for ALL-GIRL CASTS

25 NON-ROYALTY ONE-ACT PLAYS *for* ALL-GIRL CASTS

Compiled by

BETTY SMITH

Yale Drama School and University of Michigan; Sole Critic-Judge, North Carolina State Drama Tournament; Play-Reader, Federal Theatre; Play-Reader and Editor, Dramatists Play Service; Rockefeller Fellow in Playwriting; Rockefeller-Dramatists Guild Fellow in Playwriting; Avery Hopwood Award in Playwriting; Author of Fifty Published One-Act Plays.

With an Introduction by

KENNETH T. ROWE

NEW YORK

GREENBERG : PUBLISHER

CAUTION

The plays in this volume are fully protected by copyright law. All rights, including professional, amateur, motion picture, recitation, television, public reading, radio broadcasting, and the rights of translation into foreign languages are strictly reserved.

NOTICE FOR AMATEUR PRODUCTION

Any strictly amateur group not charging admission, may produce on the stage or as a non-commercial radio broadcast, without permission or royalty payment, any of the plays contained in this volume. **And permission is granted to any amateur group to make copies of any play in this book for use as acting scripts for its own amateur production.**

NOTICE FOR PROFESSIONAL PRODUCTION

For any form of non-amateur presentation (professional stage or commercial radio), permission must be obtained in writing from the publisher. Inquiries regarding royalty fees should be addressed to Play Department, GREENBERG: PUBLISHER, 400 Madison Avenue, New York, N. Y.

First Printing, August 1942
Second Printing, January 1943
Third Printing, March 1944

MADE IN THE UNITED STATES OF AMERICA

TO

KENNETH THORPE ROWE

My first playwriting teacher

TO THE LADIES

Here is a book of which I am proud to be the compiler. For many years I have been alive to the widely felt need for a collection of good, up-to-date one-act plays for all-girl casts. I can safely say this book fills the bill. And handsomely too, since virtually every play included has been tested on the stage and greeted with applause. Many have won prizes, and among the authors are numbered some of the outstanding playwrights in the one-act field—Josephina Niggli, Noel Houston, Robert Finch, Tennessee Williams, and Spranger Barry, to mention a few. Equally important, each of these plays may be performed by amateur groups without payment of any royalty fees at all.

The twenty-five plays you will find on the following pages represent every type of drama under the sun—or, rather, behind the footlights. They comprise comedy, farce, folk drama, satire, romantic drama, biographical plays, tragedy, social drama. With the exception of *Cakes for the Queen,* which is meant for dance groups, they will suit most talents. They take place in locales all over America, with one in France and another in Jerusalem. Their casts run from two to nine or more characters. Besides being good theatre, they make good reading and study material as well.

I should like to call out from the wings a number of nice people to whom I am under obligation. First, thanks in general to my kindest friend and best critic, Barrett H. Clark, whose practical help over the years has kept me at the typewriter; and to Professor Frederick H. Koch, whose affectionate friendship has smoothed my writing way these past five years. Specifically, I want to thank the following people for their invaluable help and encouragement: Professor Kenneth T. Rowe, of the University of Michigan; Professor Walter P. Eaton, of Yale; Henry T. Netherton, head of the Berkeley Playmakers; and Dr. George Savage, of the Dramatic Department, University of Washington.

I should like also to thank C. Seymour Thompson, Librarian of the University of Pennsylvania, for help in the matter of the play *Constantia.* In this connection, I am indebted also to Josephina Niggli and Marian Gleason, who called this play to my attention.

BETTY SMITH

Chapel Hill
North Carolina

CONTENTS

Miracle at Blaise — Josephina Niggli — 1
A Miracle Play (6 characters)

She Writes a Roof — Noel Houston — 22
A Comedy (4 characters)

The Return — Robert Finch — 35
A Play of the West (3 characters)

Lucy — Ida Drapkin — 48
A Christmas Play (5 characters)

At Liberty — Tennessee Williams — 60
A Drama (2 characters)

Lady Rosa — Maud Merritt — 68
A Comedy Drama (5 characters)

Graveyard Day — Susie Smith Sinclair — 84
A Folk Play (6 characters)

December Seventh — Dorothy Clifford — 109
A Drama (7 characters)

Angel of Mercy — I. Dyer Kuenstler — 122
A Biographical Play (6 characters)

Girls *Must* Talk — Paul T. Gantt — 136
A Comedy (6 characters)

The Blue Tie — Beulah Jackson Charmley — 146
A Drama (3 characters)

The Project — Lorraine Bagley — 158
A Satirical Comedy (7–9 characters)

Gander Sauce — Betty Smith — 173
A Comedy (3 characters)

The Woman Along the Road — E. Harriett Donlevy — 185
A Holy Week Drama (5 characters)

The Three-Timer — James F. Stone — 196
A Farce (6 characters)

A Hint of Lilacs — Ruth Welty — 214
A Social Drama (6 characters)

Squaw Winter — Frances Langsdorf Fox — 230
A New England Tragedy (5 characters)

The Bayfield Picture — Spranger Barry — 248
A Drama (3 characters)

Little Immortal — Elisabeth Wehner — 258
A Portrait Play (4 characters)

The Faces of Deka — Michael Morgan — 270
A Futuristic Play (9 characters)

Little Strangers — Mary Thurman Pyle — 291
A Comedy (6 characters)

Culcha — Walter Carroll — 305
A Negro Comedy (10 or more characters)

Tomorrow Is the Day — Jameson Bunn — 317
A Tragedy (6 characters)

Cakes for the Queen — Lealon Jones — 337
A Pantomimic Comedy (8 characters)

Constantia — Charles Stearns — 348
A Romantic Drama (7 characters)

INTRODUCTION

This book means something to me personally. I do not keep a classified card file of the scores of requests that come to me each year as a teacher of playwriting and drama to suggest plays for production. Most of these requests carry specifications: *a community theatre may want a comedy, entertaining but not too light, preferably with some social significance; not more than three sets, preferably one, and they must be simple, adapted to staging with limited equipment and finances; there can be parts for two good women and one good man, but the other parts must be such as can be handled by inexperienced actors, and not more than twelve in all.* As easy as that! There are requests for plays for high school students, for college drama courses, for rural audiences, for small-town audiences, for city audiences, for tragedy, comedy, and social drama, for experimental plays, for regional plays—and the hardest of all to meet have been those with the one simple specification: *an all-women cast.*

Without the card file, I am still willing to commit myself, on impression, that the largest single demand is for those all-women plays. In the General Federation of Women's Clubs there are approximately 14,500 clubs with around 3,000,000 members; in college circles there are 1,155 national Greek-letter sorority chapters, with around 350,000 members. Aside from the specific drama groups, the occasional plays that a large proportion of such organizations want to do, call for a considerable feminine dramatic literature. The membership of college play-production courses and in amateur acting groups averages two women to one man. This overflow of feminine acting talent has been confronted with the ironical situation that plays of mixed casts average two parts for men to one for women, and that, with many plays for all men readily available, there have been very few for all women. I am sure that I experience only a fair sampling of a great national need. The simple fact is that girls and women want to act and to produce plays; and playwrights, editors, and publishers have treated them in niggardly fashion. For years I referred requests for women's plays to Frank Shay's *Treasury of Plays for Women;* but that book was published in 1922, and eighteen plays cannot last forever. There came a time when the letters were likely to include, "We have done plays from the *Treasury of Plays for Women,* but . . ." For some years I have just evaded the problem. Now I can refer every request for a no-man play with confidence to Betty Smith's *Plays for All-Girl Casts.*

Here are twenty-five one-act plays, and not a man among them. They are all new, fresh plays that belong to the drama moods and idioms of today. The change since the old *Treasury of Plays for Women* seems to me a natural and healthy one. The early Little Theatre movement tended to be naïvely, self-consciously cultured; art and beauty were often identified with delicate and exotic fancies apart from a crass and sordidly material American background. The literature of one-act plays which it produced abounded in pretty fantasies and poetic plays of imagined Oriental and Renaissance settings—plays of Zanab and Bishara, of Mario, Guido, and Bianca. Beauty in this new collection of plays is hardier fare, dug out of life. The selection of plays will be welcomed for its variety, in contrast to the earlier one-act play literature. For the most part, the plays are natively American and close to life, and that is a richer source of variety than fancy. The inclusion, as the closing play of the book, of *Constantia,* written for women in 1798 by the Reverend Charles Stearns, not only adds the distinction and interest of an exceedingly rare play, but is an appropriate signature; remote as the play seems now in some respects, it was indigenous to the America, and the Massachusetts, of its writing.

The editorship of these plays for girls and women represents a most happy conjunction of talent, personality, and experience for such a book. Betty Smith commenced her career of playwriting in my one-act-play course at the University of Michigan characteristically by writing *two* one-act plays, each of which was so good that there was nothing to do but to include them both—instead of the usual one play per author—in the published volume of Michigan plays for that year. Since then she has had over fifty one-act plays published. I have lost track of the number of drama prizes she has won, seven at my last count, but there have been other prizes available since then. She has twice been awarded a Rockefeller Fellowship in Drama. She has acted in summer theatre and on Broadway, engaged in varied critical and editorial activity, had experience in community theatres, and has been associated for a number of years with the Carolina Playmakers. Working from the University of North Carolina, she has been fortunately situated in one of the most distinguished centers of playwriting activity for finding her authors and plays. Miss Smith's practical acquaintance with the theatre and familiarity with amateur production are evident throughout the selection and editing of these plays.

KENNETH ROWE

Ann Arbor, Michigan

MIRACLE AT BLAISE

A Miracle Play

BY JOSEPHINA NIGGLI

THE CHARACTERS

MADELEINE GIRAUD.
BERTHE, *her sister-in-law.*
GABRIELLE MORTIER, *a young girl from the Village.*
NICOLE LACROIX, *a secret visitor.*
TABITHA, *a stranger.*
VÉRONIE VIDEAU, *a woman of the Village.*

PLACE. The Village of Blaise in occupied France.
TIME. Christmas Eve, 1941.

MADELEINE GIRAUD'S *kitchen in the small French village of Blaise, in occupied France, is general living quarters for the house; serving as bedroom, living-room and dining-room as well. In the right wall—on a raised hearth—is a fireplace which is also used for cooking. Downstage of it is a door which leads into the extra bedroom. On the back wall is a hanging cupboard, holding a milk jug, dishes, pots, pans, etc. Also in this back wall, at the left, is a door leading outside. In the left wall is a window and below it is the table where Madeleine and her sister-in-law, Berthe, eat. There is a large chair, well cushioned, and with shawls thrown over it, drawn up at the fire. At either end of the dining table are two straight chairs. Although the room is sparsely furnished, there is an air of comfort and good living in it.*

As the play opens, the room is empty. Then the door at the back opens and Madeleine enters. She is about forty years old; a big, strong, earthy woman dressed in peasant clothes. In one hand she carries a bucket of milk. As she puts it on the dining table, the whining voice of her sister-in-law, Berthe, calls from the next room.

BERTHE (*calling*). Madeleine.* Madeleine! Is that you?

MADELEINE. Yes, Berthe.

BERTHE. I have been calling and calling. Why don't you answer me?

MADELEINE. I did answer you, Berthe. (*She goes to bedroom door, opens it.*) Do you want to sit in here for a little while?

BERTHE (*wailing*). It is too cold.

MADELEINE (*gently*). Not by the fire, Berthe.

BERTHE. Do you expect me to walk in there by myself?

MADELEINE (*going into the bedroom*). Of course not, Berthe. (*After a moment, she returns supporting Berthe. Berthe is one of those delicate, small-boned women that it would take a cyclone to kill. She has capitalized on her fragility for ten years. Madeleine guides Berthe over to the big chair.*) I tell you, it is a pitiful sight in the village. There is not one tinseled star to show that it is Christmas—not one candle in a single window.

BERTHE. These Nazis—I could kill them.

MADELEINE. On Christmas Eve?

BERTHE. On any day. (*Sharply.*) There is a draft, Madeleine. I tell you, I feel a draft.

MADELEINE (*wrapping Berthe in the shawls*). The window and doors are tight shut, Berthe. You will be warm in a moment.

BERTHE (*gesturing toward the bedroom door*). That door is still open.

MADELEINE (*going to it and closing it*). But I am closing it now, Berthe.

---

* Madeleine's name is pronounced in the French fashion: Mad-lain, save when Tabitha couples it with her American surname, "Royal." It is then pronounced in the American fashion, the final syllable rhyming with "tin."

BERTHE. If I did not watch you every moment, you would be the death of me. I think you want me to die.

MADELEINE (*wearily*). Oh, Berthe!

BERTHE. Ever since my brother brought you to this house fifteen years ago, you have been waiting for me to die. Oh, I've known it, you and your high and mighty ways.

MADELEINE (*goes to the cupboard and gets dishes, a cloth, and flat-ware to set the table. She then goes to the table, puts the milk bucket on the floor, and begins to set the table for supper. This action continues through the speeches*). Oh, Berthe, must we have that argument again?

BERTHE. In fifteen years not one word of where you came from nor where my brother found you. How do I know you were ever married to him?

MADELEINE (*sharply*). You have seen the marriage documents many times.

BERTHE. Forgeries. All forgeries.

MADELEINE. I will have no more of this!

BERTHE. Ha! And now you're the fine lady again. Well, my brother is dead. The Nazis killed him in this terrible war. For all I know, you helped to kill him.

MADELEINE (*stopping her work and turning sharply*). What do you mean by that?

BERTHE. You know well enough what I mean.

MADELEINE (*going over to her*). I asked you a question, Berthe. Answer me!

BERTHE (*scraping up her rat's courage*). You're a fifth columnist, that's what you are.

MADELEINE (*looks down at her in silence for a moment, then reaches out and slaps her*). You are never to say that again. Do you hear me? Never!

BERTHE (*begins to cry*). I knew this day would finally come. I knew you'd hit me. I knew you'd beat me.

MADELEINE. Quiet your tongue, woman!

BERTHE (*wailing*). You are evil, evil! Everyone in the village knows how evil you are.

MADELEINE. I have always been a good neighbor.

BERTHE. This is only to fool the people that you have betrayed. The mayor and his family, prisoners of the Nazis!

The blacksmith, a prisoner! The baker, a prisoner! And why? Because you betrayed them! Next, you'll betray me! And then you'll have this fine farm all to yourself . . . you'll own all of it as you've always wanted to own it!

MADELEINE. I've never told you the truth, but now I will. The farm is mine, all of it. Your brother left it to me in his will. You have lived here on my charity, and you will live here until you die. On my charity, mine!

BERTHE. That is not true. The farm is part mine. My brother told me it was.

MADELEINE (*turning back to her work*). Do you never tire of lying?

[*There is a knock at the back door.*

BERTHE. Who is that? It is the Nazis come to take me, Madeleine!

MADELEINE (*going to the door*). Don't be a fool! (*She opens the door, and Gabrielle Mortier enters. Gabrielle is a shy, plain young woman of about twenty.*) Enter. Enter this house, Gabrielle Mortier, and God's blessings on you.

GABRIELLE. God's blessings on you, Madeleine Giraud, and on you, Berthe.

BERTHE. What are you doing here?

GABRIELLE. My mother is ill again. The doctor says she must have milk. I have been to the Nazis, Madeleine, but they say. . . .

MADELEINE. That a dead Frenchman is a good Frenchman, I know.

GABRIELLE. I have been to three houses in the village, but they have no milk to spare. They have children, and the Nazis have taken all that is left over.

MADELEINE. You can have ours and welcome, Gabrielle. (*She lifts the milk bucket and starts to pour some into a pitcher.*)

BERTHE. No, she cannot! I am a sick woman, too. I have to have milk.

MADELEINE. It won't hurt you to go one day without it.

BERTHE. I won't give up my milk. I won't. I will die if I don't get it. I know I will.

GABRIELLE. Oh, Madeleine, I don't want to take. . . .

MADELEINE. Here, I have divided it fairly. A fourth for

Berthe, a fourth for you, and a half for the Nazis. Return every day for my portion until your mother is better.

GABRIELLE (*catching Madeleine's hand and kissing it*). Oh, Madeleine, how can I thank you?

MADELEINE (*without embarrassment*). Nonsense. You would do the same for me.

GABRIELLE. My little hen laid an egg this afternoon. I hid it away from the Nazis. I will bring it to you for your breakfast in the morning, Madeleine, as a Christmas gift.

MADELEINE (*laughing as she goes to the door with the girl*). Give the egg to your mother, Gabrielle, and pretend that it is my gift to her.

GABRIELLE (*pulling her shawl over her head and going out the door*). God's blessing on your house, Madeleine Giraud.

MADELEINE (*standing in the door and calling after her*). And on yours, Gabrielle Mortier. (*Turns back into the room and goes back to setting the table.*) Now, there is a good daughter.

BERTHE. You would give away everything in this house if I didn't watch you.

MADELEINE. Nonsense. (*She drops a knife to the floor.*) Ah, a knife on the floor, a visitor at the door. (*She picks it up, polishes it on her apron, and puts it back on the table.*) A nice, sharp knife. Does that mean a sharp visitor?

BERTHE. How are you going to eat the next few days? This milk and a bit of cereal is all you have.

MADELEINE. Cereal without milk is not bad after you get used to it. Perhaps I shall even come to like it very much. (*She bends forward to look through window.*) There goes Véronie Videau. (*Waves her hand and calls.*) God's blessing, Vér . . . eh, she didn't hear me. (*Looks up at sky.*) It is growing dark. Soon it will be the hour of curfew.

BERTHE (*snapping*). Curfew! And after curfew bell no Frenchman dare walk the street! These devil Nazis having the impudence to tell good Frenchmen when they can walk abroad.

MADELEINE. This is the war, Berthe. They are the conquerors.

BERTHE. In the last war it was different. One Christmas there were Americans quartered in this village, and what a laughter and singing and flowing of wine there was that night, I can tell you.

MADELEINE (*still looking through the window*). Americans. Think of it, Berthe, that same evening star up there in that green twilight sky will be shining on America to-night, just as it is shining here.

BERTHE (*not paying any attention*). These Nazis, they take away our food. They close the doors of our church. And then they expect us to be happy because they are here. They would even tear Christmas out of our hearts if they could.

MADELEINE (*softly to herself*). Christmas, And laughter in the streets and the boat-whistles on the Mississippi.

BERTHE. What's that you say?

MADELEINE. Nothing. I was just remembering when I was a little girl. We used to have a great party, Berthe. And everyone would come in fancy dress. And there was a puppet show, and dancing, and ice cream.

BERTHE. What is that . . . this ice cream?

MADELEINE. It is twenty years since I have tasted it, and yet it is as clear in my memory as though I had just finished licking the spoon. (*She goes over and sits on the hearth-stone near Berthe.*) So sweet and so creamy and so cold against the tongue. Do you know what I would like for Christmas, Berthe? A dish of ice cream.

BERTHE. Yes, I thought so. Selfish as always. You want some-thing for yourself. Me . . . I want a miracle.

MADELEINE (*smiling gently*). A miracle? In this village of Blaise?

BERTHE. Why not? Is this not Christmas Eve? This is the time for miracles to happen.

MADELEINE. What kind of a miracle, Berthe?

BERTHE. I want all the Nazis driven out of France, and all the food they have stored away put here in the center of this room for me to eat. That is what I want for Christmas.

MADELEINE (*laughing. She goes back to the table and to work again*). You know, Berthe, when I was a little girl an old colored man told me, "If you're gonna wish, you might just as well wish big." And you've certainly wished big this night, Berthe.

BERTHE. When you were a little girl. Where were you a little girl? Where?

MADELEINE (*abruptly serious*). That is my business.

BERTHE. I am your sister-in-law. I have the right to know.

MADELEINE. Stop nagging at me! (*She lights a candle and puts it in the window.*) I'm sorry, Berthe. I didn't mean to yell at you.

BERTHE. What are you doing?

MADELEINE. Putting a candle in the window. It is Christmas Eve.

BERTHE. You can't leave it there. The Nazis will tear our house down if we show a light in the window.

MADELEINE. Curfew bell hasn't rung yet! I'll put it out then.

[*There are three short knocks and one long one at the back door.*

BERTHE. Who is it? Who knocks like that?

MADELEINE (*half under her breath*). The victory knock!

BERTHE (*terrified*). Who is it, Madeleine? Who is it?

[*The knock is repeated. Madeleine suddenly goes to Berthe and pulls the woman upright.*

MADELEINE. Go into your bedroom!

BERTHE. But what is it?

MADELEINE. I don't know. But whatever it is, it is better for you not to know.

BERTHE. It is your friends, the Nazis, coming to learn more news—more families to arrest.

MADELEINE (*in a cold, hard voice*). I slapped you the last time you said that, Berthe. I will kill you the next!

BERTHE (*shrinking back from her*). Madeleine!

MADELEINE. I mean it, Berthe. (*Knock is repeated.*) Now go into the bedroom and shut the door.

BERTHE. I hear you. I hear you! (*She hobbles to door, where she turns for a final thrust.*) I will not live in this house with you any more.

MADELEINE (*indifferently*). Do as you please about that, but get out. (*Berthe goes into bedroom. Madeleine goes over to her door and listens, then goes to back door, opens it and steps aside.*) You can enter now. (*Nicole Lacroix enters. She is a capable, decisive young woman of twenty-seven. She wears a tailored suit and a crushed felt hat, both of which will be stylish as long as women wear clothes.*) I am sorry I had to make you wait. My sister-in-law was here.

NICOLE. You are cautious, and that is a good thing. (*Goes to fire and holds out her hands to warm them.*) I was afraid I wouldn't get here before curfew.

MADELEINE. Something has happened.

NICOLE. Is it written all over me, then? (*Pulls off her hat and tosses it aside.*)

MADELEINE. I can tell. You are like my husband. When things went wrong, his body was like a coiled spring. A little breeze would set it vibrating.

NICOLE (*sitting on the hearth*). Can anyone overhear us?

MADELEINE. Just a moment. (*She opens the bedroom door and goes out for a moment, then returns.*) There is no one here but Berthe, and she is cowering in her bed with the cushions over her face. She could not hear it thunder.

NICOLE. Good. Listen to me, Madeleine. I have very little time. The radio station was located tonight.

MADELEINE. Saints in Heaven! Was anyone caught?

NICOLE. Jean-Baptiste, and Armand.

MADELEINE. Oh, the brave young men.

NICOLE. But before the raid a bit of news came through. The British are planning to bomb the field where the Nazis have hidden their planes.

MADELEINE. Good.

NICOLE. Not good enough. A fire must be lighted in the field to give the English a target.

MADELEINE (*calmly*). You want me to light the fire, is that it?

NICOLE. Certainly not. (*She stands and begins to pace about the room.*) You are too valuable as a post office. No one suspects you. We can not risk losing you.

MADELEINE. Who will do it then?

NICOLE. I will do it myself.

MADELEINE. But how? It will soon be curfew and then. . .

NICOLE (*sharply*). You must get me a curfew pass.

MADELEINE. Where will I get such a thing?

NICOLE. I don't know, but I must have one. (*She sits near the table.*) If this were not so important, I would risk running the curfew, but I dare not chance being arrested. (*She sees the lighted candle, then snatches it up and blows it out.*) You fool! What is this candle doing in your window?

MADELEINE. It is Christmas. I was just going to leave it for a little while.

NICOLE. And risk pulling the Nazis in on us? Where are your wits? (*She pulls the curtains at the window, shutting out all light but the light from the hearth.*) Light your lamp.

MADELEINE (*as she obeys, lighting the lamp on the table near the hearth, the left side of the room is left in soft shadow*). For once I am afraid I was not thinking of France, but just of Christmas.

NICOLE. This is no time for superstitious nonsense. (*Madeleine jerks her head aside and Nicola suddenly goes to her.*) I am sorry, Madeleine. I, too, once lighted candles. But France is in darkness now.

MADELEINE. I know. It is all right. But where am I to get the curfew pass? That is the important thing.

[*There is a knock at the back door and Gabrielle calls from outside.*

GABRIELLE. Madeleine. Madeleine!

MADELEINE (*snatching up the shawls from Berthe's chair*). Sit here. Cover yourself with these shawls. (*Nicole runs over and cowers down in the chair. Madeleine helps to cover her while she calls out.*) One moment, Gabrielle. (*In a low voice to Nicole.*) She will think you are Berthe. (*She goes to door and opens it.*) Come in, Gabrielle Mortier. Is your mother worse?

GABRIELLE. Oh, Madeleine, I am so frightened. (*She comes quickly into the room.*) She keeps calling for you. Will you come, please?

MADELEINE (*with a quick glance at Nicole*). But, Gabrielle—I cannot leave Berthe here alone.

GABRIELLE. I will stay here.

MADELEINE (*too quickly*). No! (*Seeing Gabrielle's surprised expression, she adds hastily.*) She would be terrified without me.

GABRIELLE (*going over to the chair*). Please, Berthe. It would be only for an hour.

NICOLE (*in a muffled voice*). What of the curfew?

GABRIELLE (*kindly*). You are so hoarse, Berthe. Have you a cold?

MADELEINE. A very bad cold. You must stay away from her, Gabrielle, or you will catch it.

GABRIELLE (*beginning to cry*). Oh, please, Madeleine. Only for an hour. Please.

MADELEINE. But Berthe is right, Gabrielle. How can I come back through the curfew?

GABRIELLE. We can borrow old Véronie Videau's pass. She will lend you hers.

MADELEINE. Old Véronie has a curfew pass? Are you sure?

GABRIELLE. Of course. She is now cooking for that Captain Werner. The fat captain.

MADELEINE. Are you certain you can get me that pass?

GABRIELLE. I think so.

MADELEINE. Wait outside for me, Gabrielle. (*Taking the girl aside.*) I must argue this out with Berthe alone. She is very peculiar, but I know how to handle her.

GABRIELLE (*clutching Madeleine's arm*). You will hurry?

MADELEINE. Yes, Gabrielle. I will hurry. (*Pushes her toward the door. Just then a bell begins to toll in the distance. They both instinctively stop.*) The warning bell!

GABRIELLE. Oh, Madeleine, hurry!

MADELEINE. Listen, Gabrielle, you go and get that pass now. By the time you return, I will be ready.

GABRIELLE. Yes, that is best. (*She hurries through the door. Madeleine runs to the door and closes it securely, as Nicole flings aside her cocoon of shawls and stands.*)

NICOLE. You will have to take care of that girl when she returns.

MADELEINE. It is a miracle, Nicole, getting the pass so easily. Oh, the good God is on the side of freedom-loving people. I know it.

NICOLE. Get me a change of clothes. (*She picks up her hat.*) I can't go through the streets in this outfit. They will know I am a stranger in the village, and arrest me regardless of the pass.

MADELEINE (*showing her into the bedroom*). You will find what you need in here. In the closet. Pay no attention to the wailing of Berthe. She is a fool.

NICOLE (*going through the door*). Fools are dangerous.

MADELEINE (*speaking through the door to her*). Not this one. I can handle her. (*There is a knock at the back door.*) There is Gabrielle now. She must have run all the way and back. (*She goes to the door and opens it.*) Come in, Gabrielle.

[*Tabitha enters. She wears the traditional French peasant dress, and over her hair lies a dark shawl which she has caught up under her chin with her hand. Other than that, she is a woman without definite age and without definite nationality.*

TABITHA. Good evening. God's blessing on this house.

MADELEINE (*giving way before her*). Who—who are you?

TABITHA. My friends call me Tabitha. It is not a French name but it should not be difficult for your American tongue.

MADELEINE (*shocked*). My American . . . what do you want? What are you doing here?

TABITHA (*going to the fire*). You know the law . . . that no one shall be out after curfew. Listen. (*She raises her hand and, as she does so, the great curfew bell begins to toll.*) I had nowhere to go, and when I saw the candle in your window, I knew that this was a friendly house and charitable to strangers.

MADELEINE (*turns and looks at the window*). But the candle isn't there. It was put out.

TABITHA. The memory remains.

MADELEINE. I'm sorry, but you can't stay here . . . not tonight. I'm sorry.

TABITHA (*laughing softly and sitting in the big chair*). Would you turn me out to be arrested by the Nazis . . . I, who have been your friend for so long?

MADELEINE. I never saw you before in my life.

TABITHA. But I have been beside you for all these fifteen years in this village of Blaise. When you sat three days and nights without sleep beside the little sick daughter of the blacksmith, I kept your vigil with you. When you walked through the great storm to help Odette Ferrand have her man-child, I walked with you. When you gave up your milk ration to the mother of Gabrielle Mortier, I felt your hunger.

MADELEINE (*shrinking back against the table*). Who are you?

TABITHA. I told you, Madeline Royal. I am Tabitha.

MADELEINE. Madeline Royal! I have not been called that for twenty years.

TABITHA. But that was your name. In New Orleans, that was your name. (*She sits up in the chair as though it were a throne.*) Or so I've been told. I didn't know you then.

MADELEINE. New Orleans!

TABITHA. You must have been very beautiful in New Orleans. Men lost their heads over you, didn't they? And then the death of young Oliver Warren . . . the police still think you killed him, don't they? The American police.

MADELEINE. It was an accident. He said he would kill me if I didn't marry him. We struggled. The gun went off.

TABITHA. But he was the fourth to die. The other three were suicides, weren't they?

MADELEINE. I couldn't help it—they. . . .

TABITHA. You might have been a little kinder to them. But you were too proud of your power over the hearts of men. New Orleans was well rid of you, Madeline Royal, when you ran away to drift through every sinkhole port in the world until, after five years, you came at last to Marseilles.

MADELEINE. That is all done and forgotten.

TABITHA. But what of your husband, Madeline Royal? What of Henri Giraud, who found you in that cheap café on the Marseilles waterfront? He loved you.

MADELEINE. I made him a good wife.

TABITHA. You did, my dear. You did. And you have been good to Berthe, your sister-in-law; the whining, selfish Berthe.

MADELEINE. She is sick. She doesn't mean what she says. She doesn't realize how it sounds.

TABITHA (*laughing gently*). You need not defend her to me. I know all about Berthe. Just as I know all about you—and all about Nicole.

MADELEINE (*looking at the bedroom door*). Nicole. Yes—Nicole.

TABITHA. You had forgotten her for a moment, eh, Madeline?

MADELEINE. You cannot stay here. When Gabrielle comes with the pass, I must. . . .

TABITHA. She will not come. (*She raises her hand and seems to be listening.*) Her mother has just died. Gabrielle and old Véronie are in front of Gabrielle's house now. A neighbor is calling to Gabrielle to enter the house. Gabrielle goes in.

MADELEINE (*half screaming*). Stop it! I can't stand any more!

TABITHA. Are you afraid, Madeline? Madeline Royal was never afraid of anything, except dying. Are you afraid of dying?

MADELEINE. The pass. I must have that curfew pass.

TABITHA. Do you think Véronie Videau, who has the pass, will stay in a house of death? Even now she is walking down a cobbled street toward this house. A Nazi sentry is stopping her. She is telling him that she is coming here. She is telling him something else.

MADELEINE. What?

TABITHA. You will discover that for yourself. Now he has stepped aside. She is coming this way.

MADELEINE. I must get ready. (*She takes a half-step towards the bedroom door.*) I must warn Nicole.

TABITHA. Wait. I am not finished.

MADELEINE. There is no time.

TABITHA. I have only to raise my hand . . . so . . . (*She raises her right hand slightly.*) and all time stops. Even the beating of the heart and the drawing of the breath. In this moment there is no movement anywhere in the world save in this room.

MADELEINE. I am afraid. I am afraid!

TABITHA. Because of you four men died, Madeline Royal. Are you ready to face your punishment?

MADELEINE. Not tonight! Not now!

TABITHA. Yes. Now.

MADELEINE. But I have work to do! Important work. I am not asking this for myself. Believe me.

TABITHA. Tonight you will hold a life in your hands. What you do with that life will balance the deaths of those four men. Your own destiny is in the balance of the Mighty Justice. See that you decide well. (*Rises and goes to bedroom door.*) You are a free soul, Madeline Royal. May God have mercy on you.

MADELEINE (*shuts her eyes and leans heavily on table*). That is what the judge says when he pronounces death sentences. *May God have mercy on your soul.* (*While she is speaking, Tabitha goes into bedroom and shuts door quietly behind her. Madeleine opens her eyes. A knock sounds on back door, to which she pays no attention.*) Where are you? Where are you? (*Runs to bedroom door and flings it open.*) Tabitha!

NICOLE (*comes to door although she cannot be seen*). Stop screaming, you fool, and let that girl in with the pass.

MADELEINE (*drawing back from door*). But you—you haven't changed your clothes.

NICOLE. How could I? I just came in here. Open the door or the Nazis will be wondering what is wrong here.

MADELEINE. You just—went in there? Are you sure?

NICOLE. Have you lost your wits, woman? Do you know what it means to destroy that air base tonight? The Nazis are planning to bomb another English town as they bombed Plymouth. It means the death of thousands of innocent people . . . thousands of children and babies. Now pull yourself together for the sake of the merciful Jesus who was born on Christmas night.

MADELEINE. I'm sorry. (*She brushes her hand across her face.*) I must have been dreaming. Yes . . . of course . . . dreaming. (*She turns and goes quickly to bedroom door, shutting it, then opens back door.*) Enter Gabrielle, and you too, Véronie Videau.

[*Véronie Videau comes in. She is a sly, wizened woman with a habit of dry-washing her hands. She is really very little older than Madeleine, but where the latter has remained upright and strong as a tree, Véronie has shrunk closer to the earth. She is the same size as Nicole, but there the resemblance ends. Her voice is sleek and hateful, just as she is foul and wicked.*

VÉRONIE. Just Véronie Videau. Not Gabrielle, my friend.

MADELEINE (*almost afraid to ask the question*). Where is Gabrielle?

VÉRONIE. Haven't you heard? It is so sad. Her mother died this evening. As we passed her house, they called her in.

[*Madeleine sways and almost falls. Véronie catches her.*

VÉRONIE. Madeleine, you are ill?

MADELEINE (*jerking away from her*). No. I am all right. Leave me alone.

VÉRONIE (*smiling maliciously*). Always the fine lady. You are too good for this village of Blaise, Madeleine Giraud.

MADELEINE. You talk like Berthe. (*Trying to control herself.*) Come to the fire and warm yourself, Véronie.

VÉRONIE (*as she goes to the fire*). Yes, it is cold out. Cold and still. No one in the streets at all.

MADELEINE. Not even Nazi sentries?

VÉRONIE (*whirling to face her*). What do you mean by that?

MADELEINE. Nothing. I was just asking a plain question.

VÉRONIE. I tell you I saw no one in the streets.

MADELEINE. You are lying!

VÉRONIE. How dare you speak to me like that?

MADELEINE. You saw a Nazi sentry. You spoke to him. You told him something about this house.

VÉRONIE. How do you know that?

MADELEINE. What did you tell him? What lies were you whispering to him?

VÉRONIE. You were there in the street. You saw me.

MADELEINE. I was not there.

VÉRONIE. Then how did you know whom I was talking to?

MADELEINE (*turning away from her*). I don't know.

VÉRONIE. Hah! I've caught you out at last, my fine lady. Do you know what the Nazis do to people who break the curfew? (*Catches Madeleine's wrist.*) They stand them up against the wall and shoot them . . . that's what they do.

MADELEINE (*twisting her wrist free*). But *you* have a pass. You can go where you like.

VÉRONIE (*producing the pass from a pocket in her skirt and shaking it in Madeleine's face*). Here it is. Look at it. The pass of Véronie Videau. I can go anywhere I like in this village. Anywhere. While you, my fine lady, must cower at home by your little fire.

MADELEINE (*coaxingly*). Let me hold it in my hands, Véronie.

VÉRONIE. Oh, no. (*She thrusts it back into her pocket and begins to mince around the room.*) I've waited years for this moment . . . years when I could prove to you that I was greater than you.

MADELEINE. Why do you hate me, Véronie?

VÉRONIE (*whirling on her*). Why should I not hate you? Henri Giraud was my man. We were to be married in the Church of St. Pierre. And then what happened? He went off to Marseilles and brought you back with him . . . you . . . the woman from nowhere. The woman without a past. And here you've lived for fifteen years, lording it over everybody . . . helping your neighbors as though you were a great lady from the hill coming down into the village to be kind to the peasants. Well, I'm tired of being a peasant. Now I am the strong one. And you are finished.

MADELEINE. What do you mean . . . I am finished?

VÉRONIE. I have told the Nazi that you are a member of the Underground.

MADELEINE. You can't prove that.

VÉRONIE. I told them about the mayor and about the blacksmith. You know what happened to them.

MADELEINE. You did that? You?

VÉRONIE. And now I have told them about you. I told them to give me an hour and I would prove it to them.

[*As she says this, bedroom door opens and Tabitha enters. She quietly shuts door and goes to dining table. In her hand is a Bible. She sits down. Neither of the women sees her.*

MADELEINE. How can you hope to prove such a monstrous story?

VÉRONIE (*holds up curfew pass*). I told them that you had sent Gabrielle Mortier to borrow my pass—that you meant to steal it from me—to use it to pass an underground spy through the curfew.

MADELEINE (*moving away from her*). You mean all the sentries know this stupid story of yours?

VÉRONIE. Oh, it isn't so stupid. The pass isn't enough. There is also a password that is changed every day.

MADELEINE. What gave you the idea I would try to send a spy through on your pass?

VÉRONIE. The story came to me as in a dream.

MADELEINE (*clasps her hands and looks beseechingly at bedroom door*). A dream. A dream—a too-true dream.

VÉRONIE. Of course I know there isn't really any spy, but I am going to burn the pass, and then when they come and find it gone, they will shoot you.

MADELEINE (*goes to table and picks up a knife without seeing Tabitha*). How clever you are, Véronie.

VÉRONIE. I have had a long time to learn how to be clever. Fifteen years is a long time, Madeleine.

MADELEINE (*concealing knife in the folds of her skirt*). But you're not clever enough. You don't think I believe that silly story about a password, do you?

VÉRONIE (*filled with her own superior knowledge*). You think there is no password?

MADELEINE. I certainly don't.

VÉRONIE. Then say, "Berlin is my destiny" to the Nazi who arrests you, and feel the slam of his hand across your mouth.

MADELEINE. I don't believe you!

TABITHA (*gently*). She is telling you the truth, Madeline.

MADELEINE (*gasps, but does not turn to look at Tabitha*). You here?

VÉRONIE. What did you say?

MADELEINE. I said—I said you must hate the people of Blaise to betray them so to the Nazis.

VÉRONIE. I'm no fool. I know which side of my bread is buttered. And I have no use for weaklings.

MADELEINE. Véronie, listen to me. I never realized that I had done you any wrong.

VÉRONIE. It's too late, now, for soft speeches. I am going to burn this pass now, and you will die for it.

MADELEINE. Not only me, but Berthe, too. What of Berthe? She has never harmed you.

VÉRONIE. What do I care about Berthe? What do I care about anything, but one thing? And when they stand you up to shoot you, I am the one who is killing you. I am pulling the triggers of those guns. I—Véronie Videau! (*Shakes pass at Madeleine.*) Look at this pass well, Madeleine. It is your life that is burning!

[*She flings pass on hearth. As she does so, Madeleine leaps at her. There is a brief struggle—Madeleine's arm with the knife rises and falls. Véronie gives a muffled scream and collapses to the floor as Madeleine springs across her and pulls the precious pass out of the fireplace, brushing off the ashes and examining it to see that it is safe.*

TABITHA (*softly*). Four men dead, and now a woman, and all because of you, Madeline Royal.

MADELEINE (*not turning toward her*). I had to do it. I had to.

TABITHA. Four men dead and now a woman.

[*Nicole, dressed in peasant garb, enters from the bedroom. Berthe stumbles in behind her. Neither one notices Tabitha.*

NICOLE. I heard a struggle. What happened?

BERTHE (*gives a strangled shriek*). What have you done?

MADELEINE (*facing them*). I've killed her. (*Takes a step towards Nicole.*) I had to. She was going to burn the pass so that she could betray me to the Nazis. Yes, and Berthe, too . . . Berthe, who never did her any harm.

BERTHE (*sobbing*). Me? She was going to betray me? That wicked woman. And now they will kill us all. All!

NICOLE (*whirls and slaps her face*). Shut up, you fool. (*Berthe collapses on the hearth ledge, sobbing. Nicole turns to Madeleine.*) But you saved the pass?

MADELEINE (*extending it*). Here it is. When the sentry stops you, show him the pass and say, "Berlin is my destiny." He will let you through. Luckily, you look enough like her to fool them in the dark.

NICOLE. When they find her dead, they will execute you.

MADELEINE. I know. But what is one woman or even two

against . . . what was it you said . . . a thousand innocent people . . . a thousand laughing children?

NICOLE (*goes to her and takes her hand*). God's mercy on you, Madeleine Giraud. (*Kisses Madeleine's cheek, then slips quietly out of the back door.*)

BERTHE. How could you do such a thing? Now the Nazis will kill us both. How could you do such a thing to me . . . your own sister-in-law?

[*A light suddenly streams down on Tabitha and shines on the Bible that is open in front of her. As she reads, Berthe's hand goes up to her mouth in terror, and Madeleine goes down on her knees as though she were praying.*

TABITHA (*reading*). *Now there was at Joppa a certain disciple named Tabitha, which, by interpretation, is called Dorcas: this woman was full of good works, and alms deeds which she did. And it came to pass, in those days, that she was sick and died, whom, when they washed, they laid her in an upper chamber. And for as much as Lydda was nigh to Joppa and the disciples had heard that Peter was there, they sent unto him two men, desiring him that he would not delay to come to them. Then Peter arose and went with them. When he was come, they brought him into the upper chamber, and all the widows stood by him weeping, and showing the coats and garments which Tabitha made while she was with them. But Peter put them all forth and kneeled down and prayed, and turning him to the body, said, "Tabitha, arise," and she opened her eyes, and when she saw Peter, she sat up, and he gave her his hand and lifted her up; and when he had called all the saints and widows, presented her alive. And it was known throughout all Joppa; and many believed in the Lord.* (*Tabitha stops reading and looks at the two women.*) Madeline Royal, are you ready for your judgment?

MADELEINE. You need not tell me. I know what it will be. The Nazis will come and find her dead body. They will look in her pocket and find the pass gone. (*She stretches out her hands pleadingly.*) Can't you save Berthe? She had no hand in this. She is innocent. But the Nazis will not believe that. Please, will you save her?

TABITHA. Look in the pocket of the woman who is dead.

MADELEINE. No. No. I cannot touch her.

BERTHE. I will look. (*She bends over Véronie and thrusts her hand in the pocket. Then she gives a gasp.*) Why, here is the curfew pass.

[*There is a heavy banging at the back door. It is loud and strong, but, as Tabitha raises her hand, it suddenly stops.*

MADELEINE. They have stopped knocking.

TABITHA. It is only a little pause in time. Have you forgotten, Madeline Royal, that this is Christmas Eve? Have you forgotten that someone wished for a miracle in this house?

BERTHE (*sharply*). I wished for it. It was me!

TABITHA (*rising so that the light falls around her like a shawl*). Once in Joppa I, too, died for a little while, and Peter drew me back into life. And since then, at Christmas, I walk the little alleys of the world.

MADELEINE. You gave me my chance and I threw it away. I killed her.

TABITHA. A thousand innocent lives . . . a thousand laughing children. . . . You saved your soul, Madeline Giraud, when you thought you had lost it.

MADELEINE (*too dazed to understand*). But I killed this woman!

TABITHA (*stretching out her hands*). On Christmas Eve, dead souls should walk softly to God, as did the mother of Gabrielle Mortier. But this woman, this Véronie Videau, is not yet ready for the judgment of God. You say you killed her. I say she has only been asleep. (*In a clear, rich voice.*) Véronie, arise!

[*For a moment, there is silence, then Véronie slowly sits up, her hands pressed against her face. Gradually she pulls herself upright, and, as she does so, the light shining down on Tabitha goes out.*

BERTHE (*awed*). A miracle. A miracle!

[*The loud knocking starts in again at the door.*

TABITHA. Give this woman her pass, Berthe.

BERTHE. Here. (*She thrusts it into Véronie's hand, who stares down at it dazed.*)

TABITHA. Open the door, Madeline Giraud. What have you to fear?

[*Madeleine, proud as a queen, rises to her feet and walks to the door as . . .*

THE CURTAINS CLOSE

SHE WRITES A ROOF

A Comedy

BY NOEL HOUSTON

CHARACTERS

HETTIE CLARK, *an author.*
INEZ BROWN, *her daughter.*
BERGAL, *her maid.*
MISS GARBER, *her secretary.*

PLACE. A typical American town.
TIME. The present. Mid-morning.

HETTIE CLARK *does all of her writing in an upstairs study. A large window C. in rear wall is covered with draw curtains. The walls are cheerful where shelves of books do not occupy wall space. A large desk, with an armchair behind it, is at L. C. Next to desk is a straight chair. R. C. is an easy chair with an upholstered stool near by. The carpeted floor is littered with crumpled papers. Doors are U. of R. and D. at L.*

As the play opens, Hettie is writing at her desk. She is a determined, white-haired lady wearing a gay smock. Hettie lives to write, and is fierce and emotional when the fire of inspiration is upon her, as it is at the present moment.

HETTIE (*lifts paper and reads*). Now, let's see. "And so proud youth goes marching on toward the goal." (*Rises, walks back and forth using pencil as indicator.*) X a x a x a x a x a x a. No. That's six. Now, let's see. "And so proud youth goes marching *to* the goal." Ah! X a x a x a x a x a. That's five, and right. Sounds even better, more the miracle. (*Sits behind desk.*)

BERGAL (*comes in timidly from R. Not pretty, she may be Swedish, although she has no accent. She carries a dust cloth*). Good mornin', ma'm. Am I disturbin' your writin', ma'm?

HETTIE (*airily*). 'Tis but a trifle, beautiful princess. Pronounce your desire and it shall be done.

BERGAL. Please don't make fun of me, ma'm. Your daughter wants to see you, ma'm. Says she had somethin' she wanted to see you about, ma'm.

HETTIE. Indeed? Then why, pray, couldn't she beard the lion in the den herself, rather than send an emissary. (*Bergal giggles, Hettie smiles.*) What is her command—her command, my innocent emissary?

BERGAL (*giggling*). You're trying to cast reflections on me.

HETTIE. Has the sweet compliment of innocence then become an accusation? (*Rises and declaims.*) Ah, fast-rotating world, that in every century views itself from a different angle, and condemns that which it once praised. (*Seizes pencil, scribbles.*) Say, that's pretty good.

BERGAL. I don't know about that, ma'm. But your daughter looked for you in the music room and, when she couldn't find you there, she didn't feel like climbin' the stairs, so she asked me to look here. And I don't know, ma'm.

HETTIE. You don't know what?

BERGAL. What her command is, ma'm.

HETTIE. Oh.

BERGAL. Although she did look a little upset, ma'm. Just a little upset, ma'm.

HETTIE. That so? Well, tell her I'll be down presently. Tell her I'm writing a short poem. Very short.

BERGAL (*turning to go R.*). Yes, ma'm.

HETTIE. And, Bergal, will you open the curtains and the window and let some of the morning in? Like a good girl?

BERGAL (*turning to window*). Yes, ma'm.

HETTIE (*hurrying over her last line*). X a x a x a. . . .

BERGAL (*wheeling U. C.*). Esnay, am-may.

HETTIE. What?
BERGAL. What did *you* say, ma'm?
HETTIE. Why, x a.
BERGAL. Ixnay?
HETTIE (*going to her*). Ixnay? No. X a.
BERGAL. X a?
HETTIE. Yes. X a.
BERGAL. Oh. I thought you said ixnay.
HETTIE. Oh. No, you see, I was counting the meter in this poem. X stands for the unaccented syllables and a for the accented ones. There must be five in each line.
BERGAL (*blankly*). Oh, I thought you said ixnay, ma'm. That's pig latin for nix. I thought you wanted me to nix on something.
HETTIE. Do you talk pig latin?
BERGAL. Me and the chauffeur next door talks to each other a lot in it. Not that we're sayin' or doin' anything wrong, ma'm.
HETTIE. I'm sure not. (*Bergal turns to open curtains, but pauses as Hettie goes on.*) You know, Bergal, you've been worth your weight in gold to me as characters in stories. Nearly everything you say or do is worth printing. (*She sighs and sits on edge of desk.*) If only everyone were like that. Now, this pig latin business. I shall put that in my next. It's really funny. (*Fright grows on Bergal's face.*) Tell you what I'm going to do, Bergal. I'm going to write a story with you as the heroine. The hero is going to be the chauffeur next door.
BERGAL (*coming C.*). Oh, please, ma'm!
HETTIE. You two are going to be sweethearts and get married. Now, what do you think of that?
BERGAL (*twisting her dust cloth*). I wish you wouldn't do that, ma'm. I don't like being in your stories.
HETTIE (*amazed*). What's that?
BERGAL. It's embarrassin'. You always poke fun at me. And if you make me marry that chauffeur, I'll just die. *He'll* poke fun at me, or think me pertinent.
HETTIE. I never heard of such a thing. You mean you don't want to be a heroine? There aren't many people I'd make

heroines. Come now. Think! A moonlit evening. The moon is coming over the garage, you two sitting on the steps of the servants' quarters. Vines and the peach trees. He tells you of his plans for the two of you.

BERGAL. Oh, please, ma'm. I'd just die if he read that. I just couldn't stay, ma'm.

HETTIE (*incredulously*). You're joking.

BERGAL (*as forceful as it is possible for her to be*). I mean it, ma'm.

HETTIE (*walking around her desk*). Well, I. . . . Listen, Bergal. There are probably a hundred thousand maids in this country. And how many do you think get to be heroines in stories?

BERGAL. I don't know, ma'm.

HETTIE. How many do you think would like to be? (*Hettie advances on Bergal, who retreats before her.*) Why, to be a heroine is their dream! You say and do things just like those they'd say and do, and when I tell them about you, they imagine it's themselves. I bring them their dreams through *you!*

BERGAL (*backs against easy chair and falls into it*). Well! I'd rather you'd bring 'um to 'um through someone else, ma'm. I just couldn't.

HETTIE (*going to desk, Bergal following*). That's enough, Bergal. I'll write the story nevertheless. By the way, where is my secretary? Have you seen her?

BERGAL. I think she's in the bedroom, ma'm, addressin' the beckonin's to your daughter's party.

HETTIE. Very well. Tell Mrs. Brown . . . tell my daughter I'll be down presently.

BERGAL. Yes, ma'm. (*At door.*) But if you write that, ma'm, I'll have to go. (*She goes out R.*)

HETTIE (*sitting behind her desk*). Confound that girl. (*To her paper.*) "And so proud youth goes marching to the goal. Undaunted by Adversity's. . . ." (*She writes a moment and then surveys the lines.*) Now if only I haven't read this someplace.

[*Inez Brown enters from R. carrying a magazine. Tall, cultivated, smart-looking, Inez is not quite so sophisticated as she fancies herself to be. She is of too good breeding to give way to tantrums, but at the moment she is having difficulty maintaining her poise. So she takes refuge in a haughty dignity. This scene is played brightly and crisply.*

INEZ (*frigidly*). Mother dear.

HETTIE (*pulling the smock collar up around her ears*). When I hear that "Mother dear" instead of plain "Mother," I know the wind blows not from the south but from the north.

INEZ. You might have come down, Mother.

HETTIE. Perhaps I should have hidden deeper.

INEZ. Don't joke, Mother, please. Not now. (*She lays the opened magazine on desk.*) I've just read your latest triumph, "Girl in Despair."

HETTIE. Ah, it's here. Looks rather nice, doesn't it? The "lead" story, too. I should have received more money. (*Holding out magazine and regarding story approvingly.*) Nothing is more astounding and satisfying than one's own writing in print. Well, how does the story go, Inez?

INEZ (*sarcastically*). Beautifully. I like particularly that illustration on the next page of the girl and her mother. And the line underneath reading, "I can't *make* Joe ask me for a date. What shall I do?"

HETTIE (*turning to it*). Yes, that *is* nice. Fredericks is the illustrator. Nice.

INEZ (*icily*). Nice.

HETTIE. What is it, my dear? You like the story, don't you?

INEZ. On the contrary, I think it the most disgraceful thing I ever read.

HETTIE. Eh?

INEZ. Tell me. Was that particular line original with you, or did you hear someone say it?

HETTIE. Well now—you know how it is. Stories are written . . . well . . . from our experiences.

INEZ. Isn't that line something you overheard your granddaughter, my daughter, Evelyn, say to me some six months ago?

HETTIE. Well, yes, I think so. As a matter of fact, I got the idea for the story out of the incident.

INEZ. Incident? Tragedy!

HETTIE. Oh, you exaggerate. I prefer to call it an incident.

INEZ. And I prefer to call it a tragedy.

HETTIE. Very well, if it will make you more miserable.

INEZ. You got more than an idea from your eavesdropping, didn't you? Completely and cruelly, you have set down there an analysis of Evelyn's whole romance with Joe Stewart as ruthlessly as if you were a reporter on a tabloid.

HETTIE (*calmly sitting at her desk*). Oh, no. The incident was only the basis for the yarn.

INEZ. Yet, not content with what actually happened, you have added a parade of imagined details which everyone will accept as true.

HETTIE (*mumbling over her poem*). X a x a x a x a. . . .

INEZ. You have revealed to the world a secret of your granddaughter. And you call this exposé nice.

HETTIE. Dear Inez, aren't you getting yourself rather up over nothing? After all, we're not likely to be ostracized because of a story I've had accepted by the editors of an excellent magazine as the best story they publish this month.

INEZ. If only you would cease to be an author long enough to realize your responsibilities as the head of this family, and think in personal terms. . . .

HETTIE (*laughing*). Your accusations are certainly most personal, Inez. (*She looks at story again.*) At least I'm thankful you don't attack the story itself. I couldn't permit that. My temperamental vanity, I suppose.

INEZ. Please, Mother. I've come to plead with you.

HETTIE. To plead with me?

INEZ. To *beg* on my knees, if necessary.

HETTIE. Beg?

INEZ. You know your stories are closely read by everyone in the community. They have come to know that if they read a story of yours in which a wife has been deserted by her husband, that the wife referred to is me. And they know when they read it that what I told everybody . . . that Henry and I decided quietly to separate, wasn't true . . . that he left me because, well, your story said it was because I objected to his habit of sniffling his nose . . . and everybody believes that.

HETTIE. Well, it was true, wasn't it? (*She smiles.*) Henry left you and you had to come back and live with me because you raised such fury about such a trivial thing.

INEZ. That's beside the point. The point is, you told the *world* about it. And if in a story of yours a woman complains because she doesn't have enough clothes, everybody knows you and I had a tiff over it. If they read in a story of yours that a woman refused to go to a dinner-dance because of another woman who was to be there, then they know I didn't go to the Bretto Fon dance because Mrs. Farrell was to be there.

HETTIE. Oh, now, Inez. . . .

INEZ. And they know it was Mrs. Farrell because you take pains to describe her so accurately. If you tell about a girl who had to leave boarding school because she stayed out after curfew, then they know why Evelyn didn't go back to the Academy despite what I have told people to the contrary.

HETTIE. Serves you right. Why didn't you tell the truth? It wasn't bad of Evelyn. I thought it rather cute of her.

INEZ (*melodramatically*). There are no walls to your house, no privacy in our affairs. Our innermost thoughts are broadcast for the world to laugh over.

HETTIE (*somewhat taken aback by Inez's dramatics*). Dear Inez, I had no idea you felt that strongly about it. You've never even mentioned. . . .

INEZ. I didn't want to mention it. You don't intentionally hurt my daughter and me, I know. But all the time you keep writing about both of us. Not biographies, but twisted pictures that unfortunately have not been so twisted that they are unrecognizable. They have been caricatures.

HETTIE (*seeking a defense in theory*). To select from that about us and present it attractively—that is art.

INEZ (*shaking her head*). Even when I was a child you wrote about me. I've always hoped that, as you became established, you would no longer do it. (*She takes a deep breath.*) Apparently, it shall always go on. And this . . . this story is too terrible.

HETTIE. I hardly know what to say. This sudden attack on

my writing. You break in on me so melodramatically. (*She sits on footstool before Inez and pats her affectionately.*) Why, you're almost amusing. (*Inez rises and stands in back of chair.*) Really now, aren't you exaggerating? Our friends don't know of Evelyn's breakup with young Joe.

INEZ. Evelyn knows! And Joe knows!

HETTIE. There's no reason for taking it as anything but pure fiction.

INEZ. There wouldn't be if you hadn't laid a precedent by *always* writing about your family. That makes it plain.

HETTIE. Confound it, the story is laid in the West. The girl's description doesn't fit Evelyn. The story has a different ending from what really happened.

INEZ. But the essence is true and recognizable.

HETTIE. Rot. Why, even Evelyn wouldn't recognize it.

INEZ. You think not? You think she wouldn't recognize herself and Joe in this story?

HETTIE (*hesitantly, weakening*). No-o-o. Not unless she purposely hunted it, or. . . .

INEZ. Perhaps she was looking for it. Perhaps she *knew* that you would write a story about it and has been searching every magazine for weeks in fear of finding it.

HETTIE. Why, Evelyn and I have been together. We went for a walk only yesterday. She never told me. . . .

INEZ. She feels that to you she is only a specimen; to be pried into, experimented on, and the findings published.

HETTIE. Nonsense!

INEZ. She saw this story before I did, poor girl. She brought it to me in tears. (*A little sniffle.*) She's leaving this afternoon, she says.

HETTIE. What? Why, Evelyn can't leave. (*Attempting a short laugh.*) She has no money.

INEZ. I told her that. She said she won't need money; that she is going to get a job as secretary or airline hostess or something.

HETTIE. Adventuring girl against the world. I envy her.

INEZ. Mother! Don't you know she may never come back?

HETTIE. Yes, I know. It may be for an absurd reason, but if

Evelyn has made up her mind—I know that granddaughter of mine. She may not come back. I should regret that. *I* love her, too.

INEZ. Then, for my sake—for our sakes—won't you stop writing about Evelyn and me and Bergal? Bergal told me on the stairs just now that she, too, is leaving.

HETTIE. Bergal leaving? Why, I'm going to make her my hero. . . . (*She checks herself.*)

INEZ. There are so many things in the world to write about. Save us for yourself, Mother. Don't tell everyone about us, down to our table manners. Write about *anything* else.

HETTIE (*with a touch of regret as she goes to her desk*). I don't know anything else.

INEZ (*standing in front of desk*). But others write about China and Africa and India and the North. Why can't you too, Mother? You know about those places.

HETTIE. Those writers have been there. I haven't. I was going, yes. I was going to all of them. But your father died, and I had to stay right here and work my fingers to the bone, raising you; giving you an education. And then you married Henry, and he could never find work and I had to support both of you. And then, when he left you, I had to support you and Evelyn. I've just been stuck here.

INEZ. You're blaming me? (*She draws back.*)

HETTIE. Do you think I enjoy this twaddle I write about us? I don't want to write about you, over and over. But you're all I know. I'm tied here, hand and foot.

INEZ. You're cruel to say that.

HETTIE. Haven't you been cruel? You've told me that the only thing I'm able to do is distasteful to you. Is it that you want me to stop writing altogether?

INEZ. No, Mother. Only to stop writing about us.

HETTIE. That means to stop it altogether. I should never dare to write of something I don't know.

INEZ. Well, then, why not stop just for a while? Can't you? Can't you afford to, I mean?

HETTIE. So that's it. I tell you I will never stop writing. Even if I could, I wouldn't. Now that I've approached a measure of success, and expect my daughter and her daughter to enjoy it with me—and compliment me for what I've done, I find them both turned against me.

INEZ. I haven't turned against you. It's just. . . .

HETTIE. The world likes my stories. That's why I can sell them. Thousands read my stories because I make you look like themselves. They recognize themselves in you. They are delighted that I know so much against their souls and their minds.

INEZ. Don't raise your voice so, dear.

HETTIE. You say they read in a story of mine that you and I had a spat over your clothes. The money from that story bought the very fur coat you were wanting. They read that you didn't go to the Bretto Fon dance because of Mrs. Farrell. That story bought the evening gown you wore to the Millards' reception last month. They know why Evelyn didn't go back to boarding school, yes. But do they know that story bought the roadster she flings herself around town in? She pleaded for that car for weeks while I searched my wits for something to write about and finally thought of the school incident.

INEZ. But, Mother, to know that the food we eat is bought with the paragraphs about how we eat it!

HETTIE. But you *do* want to eat, don't you?

INEZ. Then you won't stop?

HETTIE. I have a family to support. Even now, the roof over us must be repaired. When you came in, I was dallying with a little poem, clearing my mind so I could think of something to write about to fix the roof.

INEZ. And you'll take our souls and stretch them over for a roof.

HETTIE. A stark but rather poetic way of putting it. And since you put it that way—I will. If only I can find something to write about. Nothing but commonplaces has happened around here for so long that—hmmm. (*Struck with a sudden thought, Hettie stands motionless, then walks D. L. and stands there, thinking half aloud.*) Tell me what . . . no. Wait a minute. Hmmmm. Yes, by heavens! But the ending . . . hmmmm . . . the ending. (*She faces*

Inez.) My dear, you came here because of a story I had written, didn't you?

INEZ. Yes.

HETTIE. You came to plead with me to stop writing about my family, didn't you? To cease humiliating and embarrassing it.

INEZ. But I don't. . . .

HETTIE. Bear with me. So far no decision, no climax has been reached. We are right where we were at the moment I realized what you wanted me to do, and you realized I wouldn't do it. Now *what* is the next move?

INEZ. I don't follow you.

HETTIE. You've said I must stop my kind of writing and I've told you I won't. Now that you know I won't, *what* . . . now think carefully . . . *what* are you going to do about it?

INEZ. There is only one thing I can do. Leave this house.

HETTIE. *Capital!*

INEZ. *What?*

HETTIE. I didn't think you had the courage to say it. But you had. So that's the way I'll end it.

INEZ. End what?

HETTIE. The piece I'm going to write about what's happened here between us! It's never been done before. Entirely new and logical. (*Excited with inspiration, she paces up and down.*) Say, it might go better as a play. Sure! (*Dramatically.*) Family revolts against author who exposes it to world!

INEZ (*aghast*). Mother!

HETTIE (*jubilantly*). It'll pay for the roof. I though of it just now. Only the ending stuck me. But you've fixed that.

INEZ. Haven't you any human feeling?

HETTIE. You can cool off now, my dear. You've done your share.

INEZ. I mean what I said, Mother. If you write that play, I'll. . . .

HETTIE (*laughing happily*). No, you won't. Oh, no.

INEZ. Bergal is leaving, Evelyn is leaving, and I swear I am leaving you too.

HETTIE. Bergal is a housemaid and Evelyn is young, but you, my pet, are neither. You never did a day's work in your life. (*In high spirits.*) You must have a roof over your head, my sheltered daughter, and I'll provide it for you. Now, where is my secretary? Oh, yes. In the bedroom, addressing invitations to your big dinner-dance—to be paid for with the story I wrote about the way she scatters bobby-pins everywhere—a habit to which you so strongly objected.

INEZ. You're like a woman gone mad.

HETTIE (*with a touch of exasperation*). Do you think I'm going to let us starve? If you want me to write nice things, then *be* nice. I can write nothing but you. You make my stories, not I. They are only a mirror of you and Evelyn and Bergal and the rest. Try to improve yourselves if you would be better pleased with what I write.

INEZ. What good does it do to plead with you?

HETTIE. None. You had better go lie down. (*Inspired again.*) I'm going to make a roof! (*Calling off L.*) Miss Garber! (*Inez wheels, starts for door, then stops.*) You're *not* leaving my house, are you?

INEZ (*capitulates with a gesture of "what's the use?" and sits on upper arm of easy chair, back to audience*). I'll stay. You know that. Where could I go? I'm tied here, too.

HETTIE. Nicely put. (*She kisses Inez's hair.*) I'll use that.

MISS GARBER (*attired in dark, tailored suit, wearing glasses, enters rapidly from L. with notebook and pencil*). You called?

HETTIE (*very businesslike*). Sit down. (*Miss Garber primly sits in straight chair.*) Miss Garber, we're going to write a play; about an author who writes only about her family because it's the only way she knows to coax pennies into the bank. The principal scene will be between the author and her daughter. The daughter announces she is leaving, but finally admits she is tied by her own incompetency and cannot.

INEZ (*rising and throwing up her arms in despair*). Why, oh, why did I ever have a writer for a mother? (*Goes out R.*)

[*Hettie is so wrapped in thought she does not see Inez go.*

Miss Garber writes rapidly in shorthand as Hettie paces, dictates and gesticulates vigorously.

HETTIE. Describe this room for a setting. The characters are the writer, her maid, her daughter and her secretary. (*Miss Garber springs to her feet to protest.*) Be quiet! I *will* put you in it. (*Miss Garber sits abruptly.*) Make a note about a comedy opening. Between the author and the maid. She's writing a—just jot down x a. That'll recall it to me. I want to get into the dramatic part. The maid exits, threatening to leave. The daughter enters. Begin the dialogue, please. (*Hettie acts out the parts in rapid melodrama.*) Daughter: Mother, dear. Author (pulls smock collar about her ears): When I hear that Mother dear, instead of plain Mother, I know the wind blows not from the south but from the north. (*The curtain begins to fall.*) Daughter: You might have come down, Mother. Author: Perhaps I should have hidden deeper. Daughter:
[*But* . . .

THE PLAY IS OVER

THE RETURN

A Play of the West

BY ROBERT FINCH

CHARACTERS

ADDIE.
MRS. SHAW.
ROSE SHAW.

PLACE. Ruby Valley, Montana.
TIME. Early evening. Autumn. The present.

THE SHAW *ranch house is an old log house, comfortable, warm and livable. It has been carefully built and well preserved. The ceiling of the living room is low but the room itself is large. In the right wall is a door leading to the bedroom. Right of center, in the rear wall, is a heavy outer door. Left of door is a low couch with a colorful blanket and cushions on it. Downstage, in left wall, is a massive stone fireplace. Long, heavy logs repose on the andirons. A large, heavy easy chair faces the fireplace, and there is a low rocker near by. At right center is a large hand-made table of heavy wood, and on it is a kerosene lamp with a large, dark-colored lamp-shade which throws its light down in a golden pool about the table. There are several plain, sturdy chairs about the table. Smaller oil lamps are at either end of the mantlepiece. Above it hangs a picture of a young man in frontier clothes. Elsewhere on the walls are hung bright, heavy-textured decorative woven blankets. A huge animal skin serves as a hearth rug. There is a low, wide window, prettily curtained in faded chintz, above the couch. It looks out over the broad valley and the distant Ruby Mountains. The mountains are purple and gold and their snow-capped peaks gleam in the light of the setting sun.*

As the play opens, the lamps are unlighted. The mountains are shadowed against the setting sun. Mrs. Shaw, a frail, sweet woman of fifty, is closing a suitcase standing on the couch. Her hat lies near by. Addie, a neighbor, is watching her sympathetically. Addie is a strong, quiet-looking spinster of thirty-five. She has a strength and a dignity that make her almost handsome in spite of her plain dress. Mrs. Shaw snaps the lock on the suitcase, sighs and looks out of the window.

ADDIE. You shore hate to leave the Valley, don't you, Miz Shaw.

MRS. SHAW. I've lived here thirty years. Ever since I was married. (*She sighs.*) I wish. . . .

ADDIE. I know. You wish I hadn't written to your girl, Rose, telling her how sick you was last winter. Then she wouldn't be coming here to take you away. I thought she'd come back here to stay. Instead. . . .

MRS. SHAW. You meant well—writing to her.

ADDIE (*truculently*). If *I* didn't want to go, I *wouldn't.*

MRS. SHAW. But Rose worries so much about me being here alone, winters, that it interferes with her work.

ADDIE. Seems like she could come back to the Valley to live with you.

MRS. SHAW. She hates the Valley. Ever since she was old enough to start school, she's been fighting to get away from it. She's tried and tried. . . .

ADDIE. Seems like she's won out. She's been five years away. (*With quiet astonishment.*) I'd die if I were away from here so long.

MRS. SHAW (*listening*). I thought I heard a car. The train came in fifteen minutes ago. She should be here.

ADDIE (*after listening*). I don't hear anything 'cepting Tom chopping the logs for that cabin of his.

Mrs. Shaw. Dear Tom. He'll be hurt again.

Addie. Did Rose write she *wouldn't* see him?

Mrs. Shaw. She won't be staying long enough. Mr. Houston is going to drop her off here, go to his house for a bite of supper and then come back to pick us up to make that seven o'clock train.

Addie. Half an hour to say goodbye forever to the valley where she was born. There are things about Rose that I can't understand.

Mrs. Shaw. She'll be nervous from the trip. She wouldn't want to be upset by a lot of goodbyes.

Addie. Tom brought her pony over. Maybe she'd like to ride through the Pass with him once more.

Mrs. Shaw. She wrote especially that she didn't want to see Tom.

Addie. I told Tom that. He just laughed and said, "That means it's time I was getting that log house finished for Rose and me."

Mrs. Shaw. But don't tell her he said that. That will make her so angry.

Addie (*hurt*). Ain't every girl my brother would build a house for. 'Specially a girl he ain't seen in five years; a girl who just sends a letter or a post card when she takes a notion.

Mrs. Shaw. I didn't mean—I mean I'd rather have Tom for a son than anyone else I know. It's just that Rose thinks we're all working to get her here and keep her here.

Addie (*putting her hand on her arm*). I know, Miz Shaw. I told Tom he was a fool, but—(*Sighs.*) For some men there's just one girl. Can't see any other. If they can't have her, they don't want any.

Mrs. Shaw. Please, Addie dear, don't speak of Tom or the house. Don't tell her how Tom's been taking care of her pony. She didn't want to come here—wanted me to meet her at Butte. But I promised there wouldn't be any talk. . . .

Addie. Wonder she just didn't send you a ticket to New York and let you fight your way east alone.

Mrs. Shaw. She's been in California all summer. It's just as easy for her to go back this way. Besides, she didn't want me to take that long trip alone. My heart. . . .

ADDIE. New York ain't going to do your heart any good. Doctor said the mountains are better for you.

MRS. SHAW. Don't tell Rose that the Doctor said I haven't much more time. (*Pleadingly.*) Don't tell her. She might think that she *has* to stay here with me.

ADDIE. She's shore got you stampeded, ain't she? (*Kindly.*) Don't worry, Miz Shaw. I won't say anything. Only. . . .

MRS. SHAW. Listen!

ADDIE (*after listening*). I don't hear anything, 'cepting Tom's stopped work.

MRS. SHAW. I hear a car.

[*They listen. Sound of approaching car is heard.*

ADDIE. Shore 'nough. That Houston's Model T, all right.

MRS. SHAW (*happily*). Rose is home.

ADDIE. For a few minutes. (*Goes to door right.*) I'll fix her some supper.

MRS. SHAW. There won't be time. (*Goes to door right.*) I'll make her a cup of tea. You stay here to greet her, Addie. I'm afraid I'll break down and cry if. . . . (*She starts to weep and hastily goes out through right door.*)

[*Addie, with folded arms, stands watching center door. Car comes up loud, stops, starts up again and fades away. The door opens and Rose enters. She is about twenty-four. Very pretty and restless. She wears a becoming dark traveling suit and silk shirt. She has no luggage.*

ROSE. Addie darling!

ADDIE (*melts and takes her into her arms*). Rose, baby, it's good to see you again.

[*They embrace.*

ROSE. Where's Mother?

ADDIE. Fixing you some tea.

ROSE. How is she?

ADDIE. Packed and ready to leave.

ROSE. No. I mean, you wouldn't have written me if you weren't worried about her.

ADDIE. She went through a bad time here last winter—sick and all alone here. I thought you ought to know.

ROSE. You did right. She mustn't be left alone.

ADDIE. But I didn't think you were fixing to take her away. I though you would come and stay here with her.

ROSE (*pulling off her gloves petulantly*). Now, Addie, I've not been traveling night and day to get here just to have you lecture me.

ADDIE. I always feel like I'm your older sister. Maybe I do take liberties.

ROSE (*with a quick change of mood*). You're a dear. It's just that I'm upset by all this traveling. . . .

ADDIE. Why don't you stay—just a few days—and rest up?

ROSE (*explosively*). No!

ADDIE (*quietly*). Afraid the Valley will cast its spell on you?

ROSE (*with an involuntary look at the mountains seen through the window*). Of course not.

ADDIE. Afraid to see your old friends again?

ROSE. Nonsense! There isn't time. (*Casually.*) How *is* Tom?

ADDIE (*bitterly*). You ain't caring. You ain't caring how he's been eating his heart out for five years—waiting. . . . waiting. . . .

ROSE (*walking around impatiently*). Where *is* Mother? We haven't much time.

ADDIE. I'm sorry, Rose, I guess I talk too much.

ROSE. Oh, forget it. (*Pause.*) Mr. Houston told me that Tom's building a house.

ADDIE. Yes, he's working on a cabin for his homestead just at the head of the Valley. Going to leave his father's ranch. Have his own place.

ROSE (*too casually*). Does that mean he's getting married?

ADDIE. *He* thinks he is.

ROSE (*too offhand*). Anybody I know?

ADDIE (*with meaning*). The girl he loves would be a stranger to you—now.

ROSE (*shrugs*). I hope he'll be happy.

ADDIE. Tom will always be happy—living in the Valley with the mountains around him.

ROSE (*suddenly*). Addie, tell me before Mother comes in. Did the Doctor say she *had* to stay in this altitude? He didn't say the change would be bad for her?

ADDIE (*looking steadily at Rose*). The Doctor said—(*She pauses and looks at kitchen door. She speaks dully.*) No. Won't make no difference where she lives.

ROSE. Good!

[*From the distant canyon, the long-drawn-out wail of a coyote is heard. Rose shivers. Addie closes the back center door which has been standing opened since Rose's entrance.*

ADDIE. Just a coyote. They're always crying this time of evening. (*Sitting down.*) But I guess you forgot—being away so long.

ROSE. I haven't forgotten. (*Pacing restlessly.*) I wish I could. It's a lonely sound. As lonely as death. (*Faces Addie and speaks with suppressed emotion.*) It's lonely and cold. And I never liked it here.

ADDIE. You'll be leaving it soon—you and your mother. And this time there'll be no coming back for either of you.

ROSE. I wouldn't have come back this time excepting for Mother.

[*Mrs. Shaw comes in with a tray on which is a cup of tea and some small cookies. She sees Rose and her hands tremble.*

ROSE. Mother! (*She takes tray from her, sets it on table and then kisses her mother.*)

MRS. SHAW (*not being able to control her tears.*) My baby is home again.

ROSE (*smiling*). Only for a few minutes. Remember, you promised.

MRS. SHAW. I know. (*Making an effort to smile.*) But you could sit down for those few minutes—take off your hat and have a cup of tea.

ROSE (*pulling off her hat*). I'm not hungry.

MRS. SHAW. To please me. A last meal in your old home.

ROSE. Since you're so sentimental—(*Sits at table and tastes the tea. Smiles.*) You know, Addie's been working on me—trying to get me to stay.

MRS. SHAW (*reproachfully*). Addie, you promised!

ADDIE. But it's so pretty here. It's a nice Valley to have a home in. (*Simply.*) I like it better than any place I've ever been in.

ROSE. Sure. It's fine if you like never seeing anyone from one week to the next—hearing nothing but the wind and the coyotes and the bawling of the cattle. I should think you'd hate it, Mother.

ADDIE (*hotly*). She loves it here. Everything she loves is in this Valley. And there's your father buried on the hill above the ranch.

ROSE. Yes—there's Father. Sometimes it seems as if he planted our roots so deep they can never be torn up.

ADDIE. I'm like he was. And your mother's that way, too. When we die, we'd like to rest on a hill looking over the Valley. (*Sternly.*) And you're not to forget that, Rose Shaw.

ROSE (*angrily*). All this talk of dying. People live out here just to die.

ADDIE (*offended*). I'm sure they die in New York, too.

ROSE. Maybe. But they're not always talking about it. There's too much else to do. All the wonderful things—theatres, art galleries—wonderful stores—Something to do every minute. (*Impulsively.*) You'll love it, Mother. I have the cutest apartment. Steam-heated. You'll never have to worry again about getting the wood split. And when the temperature goes down, you'll never know it, except when you look out the window and see the snow falling over the East River.

MRS. SHAW. For thirty years I've been looking out of that window and seeing the Ruby Mountains. (*Looks out of window.*)

ROSE (*startled*). Thirty years here? It's incredible.

MRS. SHAW. I was just your age when I married and came here to live in this house that your father built for me.

ROSE (*with a little laugh*). Like Addie's brother is building for his wife. Valley men don't change much, do they?

MRS. SHAW. I remember how pretty it looked when we rode up the Valley—white against the green pine trees. (*Smiles wistfully.*) Your father had trained a wild little calico pony for me to ride.

ROSE. I know. You told me so often that he was the grandfather of my pony. (*Suddenly.*) How *is* Major?

ADDIE. Tom's been taking. . . .

ROSE (*jumping up*). Oh, never mind. Mr. Houston will be here in fifteen minutes. All packed, Mother?

MRS. SHAW. All packed. (*Her eyes go to the picture over the mantelpiece.*)

ROSE (*gently*). Take Father's picture if you want to. We can make room for it in the apartment.

MRS. SHAW. No. I want it to stay where it has hung since the day we married. I don't want a thing in this room changed. I trust you, Addie, you and Tom, to keep it this way always for me.

ADDIE. Oh, we will, Miz Shaw. (*Wipes a tear away with a corner of her apron.*)

MRS. SHAW. Rose, your father made every piece of furniture in this room with his own hands. That rug—(*She indicates the fireplace rug.*) He killed that bear. I wove these carpets. My two babies were born in that room. (*Inclines her head to door, right.*) There are marks on the kitchen wall showing how much my children grew. My son's mark stopped when it was so high. (*Holds her hand about four feet from ground.*) That other baby lies buried out there on that hill. (*Again looks at window.*)

ADDIE (*weeping*). It's the cruelest thing I ever heard of—tearing your mother up by the roots like that. And her with less than a year to. . . .

MRS. SHAW (*imperatively*). Addie, please!

ADDIE. Excuse me. (*She takes tea tray from table and exits by door, right.*)

ROSE (*pacing*). Mother, I know how you feel. Believe me, I know. But don't—don't keep working on me. I can't stay. I have a good job. It took me five years to get where I am. I'm young. I want to be where there's life and fun.

MRS. SHAW. I know.

ROSE. But I've been worrying about you. My work has suffered. Can't you see, Mother, it will all be for the best? You'll be happy in New York with me. We'll be together. And I need you, Mother. I get lonely sometimes, with nobody. . . .

MRS. SHAW. I'm glad to go with you, Rose. I love this Valley.

But I want to be with my own, when—(*She stops suddenly.*)

ROSE (*turning suddenly*). When? Tell me. When, Mother?

MRS. SHAW. When—winter comes again.

ROSE. That's sensible. Winter comes too quickly here. The snows start to come down from the mountains in September, and May is nearly over before spring comes.

MRS. SHAW. Somehow, the spring is sweeter for being so reluctant.

ROSE. What good is spring and summer here? Too short a time, really, for anything to grow, excepting the sage and the grasses.

MRS. SHAW. Your father planted a wild rose bush near the doorstep the day you were born.

ROSE. And it's short and stunted and never did bear a rose.

MRS. SHAW. Rose's bush, he called it. (*She smiles.*) No, it never did grow high. But its roots are deep in the ground. No one can ever pull them up.

ROSE. A rose bush without roses. So typical of everything in the Valley.

MRS. SHAW. Your father said it would come to bloom when you came back to stay.

[*Rose starts noticeably.*

ROSE (*after a pause*). That's a very pretty thought. But if I've got to stay here to make it bloom, it can go roseless. And that's that. (*Looking at her watch.*) I wonder what's keeping Mr. Houston?

[*Addie enters with a deerskin divided riding skirt over her arm and a fringed deerskin jacket.*

ADDIE. I've fixed us a little supper.

ROSE (*shortly*). Thank you, but we're eating on the dining car. (*Looking at her.*) What in the world have you there?

ADDIE. Your riding clothes.

ROSE (*takes coat, holds it up and laughs*). Wouldn't I look silly cantering through Central Park in this outfit.

MRS. SHAW (*happily*). Oh, then you still ride?

ROSE. Of course. Only I have a tailored habit.

ADDIE. Your father dressed these skins and your mother spent a long time sewing on them.

ROSE (*handing coat back to her*). Maybe I'll send for it some day when I move into a bigger apartment and have more storage space. But put it away now, Addie.

ADDIE (*timidly*). I though you'd like to take one last ride through the Valley.

ROSE (*angrily*). The Valley! The Valley! Always the Valley! I hate it, I tell you. I hate it! (*Furiously she pulls the curtains across the window, shutting out the view of the mountains.*)

MRS. SHAW. Somehow, it seems dark when you can't see the mountains no more. (*She goes to the table and lights the lamp.*)

ADDIE. Tom brought your little pony over.

ROSE (*happily*). Oh, where is he?

ADDIE. Just outside the kitchen door. I knew you'd want to see Major again. And Tom has him all saddled.

ROSE. I'll thank Tom and you to mind your own business, Addie.

MRS. SHAW. Addie meant it kindly.

ROSE. I'm sorry, Addie. But you and Tom went to a lot of trouble for nothing. I wouldn't have time for a ride, even if I wanted to. Mr. Houston will be here in a minute.

ADDIE (*eagerly*). You'll have time. I phoned when I was out in the kitchen. Told the Houstons I didn't think you were leaving tonight. He'll come by tomorrow, same time.

ROSE (*furiously*). How dare you! How dare you! I didn't want to come back. I knew there'd be some trick to keep me here.

ADDIE (*with dignity*). I didn't mean to trick you. I just can't understand why anybody that was born and brought up here wouldn't want to stay here.

MRS. SHAW (*gently*). Addie, I promised Rose I'd go with her. And I'm going.

ADDIE (*pleadingly*). But one day longer won't make any difference.

MRS. SHAW. You're not making it any easier for me, Addie. I want to go now. I couldn't stand saying goodbye to the house and the Valley again.

ADDIE. All right, Miz Shaw. I'll go tell Tom. . . .

ROSE. No!

ADDIE (*continuing coldly*). To ride over and get one of the Jackson boys to take you to the train. They've got a fast car. You'll catch your train all right.

ROSE. Phone the Jacksons.

MRS. SHAW. They have no phone.

ADDIE. Don't worry. Tom will get word to them in three minutes. (*Going to right door.*) I'll put these away. (*Indicates riding clothes.*) I'll go out through the back door. (*Exits right.*)

MRS. SHAW. Light the lamps on the mantelpiece, dear.

ROSE (*impatiently*). But, Mother, we're leaving soon.

MRS. SHAW. I don't want to leave the house dark. Besides, Addie and Tom will be eating their supper here.

ROSE. All right, Mother. (*Reaches up to light the lamps.*)

MRS. SHAW. I remember when you were little. Every day you'd ask your father, "When will I be big enough to light those lamps?"

ROSE. And I remember how proud I was when I was finally allowed to do so. I was thirteen and felt so grown up.

MRS. SHAW (*taking a letter from her purse. She is sitting on the couch*). You must bear with me if I'm sentimental about it all. But when I was packing, I read your father's letter again—the one that made me decide to come out here. (*Unfolds letter.*)

ROSE (*distressed*). Please, Mother. . . .

MRS. SHAW. Let me read it aloud for the last time. It's saying goodbye to him.

ROSE. If you won't cry. . . .

MRS. SHAW. I promise. Sit down, dear. (*Rose sits in chair near fireplace. Mrs. Shaw reads.*) "Dearest Mary." (*She pauses to steady her voice.*) "It will be weeks before this reaches you." (*Looking up.*) The mail went by stagecoach in those days. (*Reading.*) "And months before we meet. Yet, you're already here, it seems. You will like our home. I remember when I first saw the place. It was early morning when I crossed the Pass and rode into the Valley. It was the first real day of spring. The sky was deep blue. Above the Valley, the sun broke through and the prairie grass was shimmering gold for miles along the stream. The air was fresh and warm, and I loved this valley from the first."

ROSE. Is that the letter in which he told you about the fawn? (*Silently, Mrs. Shaw hands her the letter. Rose holds it under the table light and reads.*) "I saw a deer and her fawn in a little aspen grove along the trail, and, above them, the sage shone dewy and green in the early sun. The trout leaped in the deep dark pools and the water was clear and cold where I stopped to drink. All day I rode up the Valley along the little streams till, just at sunset, I came to this grove of pines, a spring and a meadow waist-deep with wild grass below a rocky hill. Dearest Mary, if you'll come. . . ."

[*Rose's voice chokes with emotion. She hands letter back to Mrs. Shaw and runs out door right. Mrs. Shaw sits staring at the letter for a while.*

MRS. SHAW (*continues the reading in a low voice*). "This is the place. This is where we'll live all the rest of our lives together. The house I've built is warm and as pretty as I could make it for you." (*Mrs. Shaw sits staring at the letter for a long time.*) "It's only a cabin, of course, but I tried to build it in a way that would please you." (*Door, center, opens and Addie comes in quietly. She has a bunch of sage-brush in her hand.*) "From the big window, you can see clear across the Valley. There aren't any flowers. They're hard to grow. But I'll plant some and they'll *have* to grow for you. I'll make them." (*Looking up.*) And when you came, dear, we named you Rose. You were our flower. . . . (*Sees that Rose isn't there.*)

ADDIE (*stepping forward*). Tom's gone over to the Jackson's.

MRS. SHAW (*wearily*). Yes. I want to get it over with now.

ADDIE (*handing her the sage*). I picked some sage for you to take with you. The smell will stay for a long time. Might help you when you're homesick.

MRS. SHAW (*taking sage*). Thank you, Addie. (*Carefully puts it in letter, returns letter to her purse.*)

ADDIE (*excited*). And Miz Shaw, you'll never believe me, but. . . .

MRS. SHAW. What, Addie?

ADDIE (*in awe*). You know that bush by the steps?

MRS. SHAW. Rose's bush?

ADDIE. It's—it's going to bloom!

MRS. SHAW. Not this late in the fall?

ADDIE. I couldn't believe it myself. But look!

[*The two women step out of the door. They return almost immediately. Mrs. Shaw is carrying a small rose not yet opened.*

MRS. SHAW. Her father said—(*She stares at the rose.*)

ADDIE. We better not tell Rose. She'll think. . . .

[*Rose enters from door right. She is wearing the divided skirt, her silk shirt and the fringed jacket. She wears cowboy boots and carries a black flat-crowned sombrero by the string.*

MRS. SHAW. Rose! (*Gently, Rose reaches up and takes off her mother's hat.*) The bush by the door. (*Holds out the rose.*)

ROSE (*taking it*). I know. (*Quietly.*) I saw it was blooming when I came. I didn't want to mention it. (*Thrusts rose through the band of her hat.*) Addie, do you still want to get us some supper? (*Puts her hat on.*)

ADDIE. It's almost finished.

ROSE (*pulling on her gauntlets*). Set an extra place. (*Going to door.*) We'll be back. (*As she goes out.*) I think I'll ride over and see how Tom's cabin is coming along. (*She goes out, closing the door after her.*)

ADDIE (*rushing to door, opens it and calls out*). But Mr. Jackson. . . ?

ROSE (*her voice fading*). Ask him to pick up my bags at the station.

ADDIE (*slowly closes door and stands with her back to it*). We've won, Miz Shaw, you and me and Tom!

MRS. SHAW (*goes to her and takes her two hands*). Not us, Addie, dear. She heard the Valley calling . . . the Valley. . . .

[*Mrs. Shaw goes to window and pulls back the curtains. It is nearly dark, but a moon is coming up behind the mountains. The two women stand facing the window, looking out. Everything is deep in silver . . . and peaceful. . . .*

CURTAIN

LUCY

A Christmas Play *

By IDA DRAPKIN

THE PEOPLE

MOTHER FOSS, *"Gramma."*
GRACE, *her daughter-in-law.*
LUCY, *her granddaughter and Grace's niece.*
MRS. MARTIN, *Grace's friend.*
MRS. STONE, *a visitor.*

PLACE. A little New England town.
TIME. A sunshiny afternoon, about a week before Christmas.

GRACE'S *kitchen is as neat and sunshiny as only a good New England kitchen can be. There are two large windows upstage, curtained in starched white dimity. Bright red geraniums stand in clay pots along the sills. Through the windows there is a view of hazy blue mountains and dark, old pine trees with snow-laden branches. Right of windows is a wide, white-painted door which leads to the outdoors. Downstage in right wall is a door leading to other rooms of house. Upstage of door are rows of white-painted shelves, holding pink willow-ware dishes with the cups hanging on little hooks. Crisp shelf-paper edges the shelves. In center of left wall is a well-polished coal range. Copper or shining aluminum pots and pans hang in a neat row over the stove. Upstage of stove and over to right is a Boston rocker. Downstage of stove is a carpet-covered*

* Also suitable for any time of the year.

hassock. There is a table between the two windows on which are tea things, daintily made sandwiches and a large glass of orange juice. There is a larger table, center, slightly upstage. It is covered with a fresh, starched, red-and-white-check cloth. On it stand several iced cakes, still uncut, a loaf of nut bread, a knife and other things.

As the play opens, Mother Foss, a kindly woman of sixty, is sitting in the Boston rocker, knitting. She is putting the finishing rows on a pair of long brown stockings. Grace, her daughter-in-law, a rather good-looking, well-dressed, capable woman of thirty-five, is looking over the refreshments.

GRACE. I guess everything's about ready. I hope the chicken stays moist in the sandwiches. It was a very good chicken, wasn't it? (*Doesn't wait for an answer.*) The roast we had this week, too. I've always liked marketing at the Hansom's. They do well by us.

GRAMMA. Lucy's cooking helped a lot, too. She certainly has a knack, that child.

GRACE. It's not surprising, Mother Foss. She's had enough practice cooking at that wretched home of hers.

GRAMMA. I wouldn't say wretched, Grace.

GRACE. I'm sorry. Lucy's mother *is* your daughter, after all. but the truth. . . .

GRAMMA. She is also your husband's sister.

GRACE. Why, Mother Foss! There is no comparison between Ed and Ellen.

GRAMMA. They are both my children. Ellen is as dear to me as Ed. Ellen's had misfortunes. . . .

GRACE. I'm sure I did the right thing. I took Lucy here to live with us. Why—why I treat her like my own—

GRAMMA (*quietly*). It was kind of you, Grace.

GRACE. You know, it's unbelievable, but I don't think Lucy's happy here.

GRAMMA. Do you think she wants to go back to her parents?

GRACE. She'd be selfish enough to leave us; to think of herself first. After all we've done for her since September!

GRAMMA (*looks up and speaks significantly*). We?

GRACE. I suppose she finds this house too clean and too quiet. She's used to children running wild and noise. I can't imagine anyone missing Lucy's brothers and sisters; those filthy little beggars.

GRAMMA (*in mild reproof*). Grace!

GRACE. Perhaps you think I've been hard on Ed. I know I've insisted that he stay away from his sister's. (*Walking around the room.*) But, to tell the truth, Mother Foss, I'm afraid he'll catch something up there.

GRAMMA (*smiling*). Now, Grace—

GRACE. Everybody says I've been very generous, offering his oldest niece a home with us. I treat her like a daughter, get real attached to her, and then—have you noticed?

GRAMMA. Yes, I've noticed.

GRACE. She's been different ever since Ed took her Christmas shopping, day before yesterday. He said she was awfully excited about having hot chocolate in Estelle's—it was the first time she'd ever eaten out. (*She touches cake icing with her finger-tip to see if it is hard.*) She talked a blue streak, he said. You *know* how quiet she usually is.

GRAMMA. She isn't quiet with Ed or me.

GRACE (*firmly*). She's a quiet child, Mother Foss. I may not have children of my own, but I know children from reading and from my friends.

GRAMMA. And you think that qualifies you to run for the school board as well.

GRACE (*on the defensive*). I'd accept the responsibility only out of community spirit. I'm swamped with work as it is.

GRAMMA. It will mean getting your name in the paper that much more. I'm afraid I'll never understand why people want things their heart's not in—just for their pride. (*Goes back to her knitting.*)

GRACE. Mother Foss, sometimes you provoke me! You simply refuse to understand. I suppose you think I asked Lucy to live with us just so people would say what a kind and loving aunt I was! (*Goes to window and rather viciously pinches a withered leaf off one of the plants.*)

GRAMMA (*patiently*). It's the Christmas season, Grace, and

I have a certain feeling this time of year. I want to hold it. Let's not quarrel. You have good qualities; my son wouldn't have married you otherwise. You're one of the few women I know who keeps herself neat as her house, and that's saying something.

GRACE (*pleased*). I don't mind telling you I said some very nice things about you, too, to Mrs. Stone. She's the new doctor's wife. She's coming today.

GRAMMA. Weren't we speaking of Lucy?

GRACE. Really, Mother Foss, I'm worried about Lucy. Ed said, that at Estelle's, she suddenly stopped talking and he couldn't even get yes or no out of her after that. (*Suddenly.*) She can't hear us, can she?

GRAMMA. No, she's too busy in there getting things ready.

[*Grace goes to door, D. R., opens it a crack, peers out and closes door cautiously.*

GRACE (*crossing to Gramma*). Mother Foss, I *know* she's thinking of going home again—to her shiftless parents and those six children.

GRAMMA. Shiftless! Lucy's father is a very sick man.

GRACE. He could work if he made up his mind to! He imagines a lot of his symptoms. People do, you know—make regular invalids of themselves.

GRAMMA. According to Dr. Brennan, Lucy's father hasn't got long to live.

GRACE. Dr. Brennan's the old-fashioned calamity type of doctor. I wish Dr. Stone would see him. He might have a different story. (*Puts her hand on Gramma's shoulder.*) But you won't say a word to Lucy, will you, about her father?

GRAMMA. Why not?

GRACE. She might exaggerate its importance. She'd run off home and people would say I hadn't treated her well. *People* are apt to imagine a lot of things, too.

GRAMMA. And you're afraid you won't be elected to the school board?

GRACE. Nonsense! (*She turns away from Gramma and goes to table by window.*) I've just bought her a winter coat, too. (*Lifts slice of bread and examines a sandwich.*)

GRAMMA. I wish you had let me put a few dollars towards it. I know she'd have liked some fur.

GRACE (*wheeling around angrily*). Mother Foss, I'm going to bring Lucy up my way. You must understand that.

GRAMMA. No catering to her vanity, eh?

GRACE. It's a good, warm coat. Any child would be happy to have it. Did you see the coat she brought with her? (*Comes down to Gramma and speaks firmly.*) I let you buy oranges for her afternoon snack. (*Nods her head in direction of glass of orange juice.*) Although I don't approve of eating between meals; especially when they're as well planned as the meals I serve.

GRAMMA. I notice your club ladies don't hesitate to stuff themselves when they come here. There's food enough on those tables for an army.

GRACE. That's different. You use a lot of energy playing bridge. (*Crosses her arms and walks to D. R. door.*) Ed would spoil her, too. (*Cautiously opens door, looks in, cautiously closes it. Goes back to Gramma. Speaks secretively.*) She didn't need that hot chocolate after a hearty lunch.

GRAMMA (*sighs*). All I can say is, this is a hard time for her. It's the Christmas season and she's homesick.

GRACE (*indignantly*). But—

GRAMMA (*holding up her hand to forestall the interruption*). But there are things that will keep her here. She's a sensitive child. She appreciates the clean linen and the warm house and the pink willow ware.

GRACE. They've put her a grade ahead in school, too. She's in the sixth, now.

GRAMMA. And she's made friends. She's gained since she came. And she thinks the world of you and Ed.

GRACE (*looking over her shoulder at D. R. door*). She's a deep one. I don't like children to be deep. They're likely to be sly.

GRAMMA. It's loyalty, with Lucy. Loyalty to her own. It's up to you, Grace, whether she stays or not.

GRACE. Well, nobody can say I haven't been a mother to her and an example in the finer ways of life. (*Door D. R. opens and Lucy enters quietly. Grace assumes a quick smile and a singing voice.*) Oh! All done, dear?

[*Lucy is a thin, sensitive-looking child of twelve or thirteen. She wears a dark, serviceable dress and an apron.*

LUCY. Yes, Aunt Grace. There are enough chairs now, and I've filled all the candy and nut dishes.

GRACE. Did you put the Queen Anne cloth on the refreshment table?

LUCY. Yes, and I changed the lamps. I thought you'd like to have the six-way one by your chair.

GRACE. That's fine. You might make up some more of those ginger marmalade sandwiches on nut bread. The ladies liked them so much the last time. (*Goes to D. R. door.*) I'm going upstairs and rest till they come. Show them in and take their things. Don't cut the cake till just before you serve the refreshments. I think that's all. (*She goes.*)

[*Lucy begins to slice a loaf of nut bread.*

GRAMMA. Sit down and rest a little, Lucy. (*Lucy smiles warmly at her.*) There's plenty of time, you've more than enough sandwiches already. (*Lucy stops cutting and glances at sandwiches on other table.*) You've been buzzing around like a bee all day. Fine school vacation you're having. Get your orange juice and come here where it's warm.

LUCY. Thank you, Gramma. (*Goes to table, picks up glass of orange juice and holds it up to let the sun shine through it.*) Orange juice is pretty with the sun shining on it. (*Takes glass over to Gramma.*) But it's neat and cold, the way everything is here. (*Shyly.*) Except you, of course, Gramma. You're the sun.

GRAMMA. Nonsense. (*Smiling with pleasure.*) You're just trying to get on the good side of your old gramma, the way they all do. Even Grace. Telling Mrs. Stone about me! I can well imagine what she said. Now sit down and rest.

LUCY. Do you think Aunt Grace will mind? (*She sits on the hassock.*)

GRAMMA. I'll be responsible. There. Now relax a little. I don't like your mouth. You had a good report from school, didn't you?

LUCY. Yes.

GRAMMA. Did you lose your dog?

LUCY (*laughing*). I haven't got a dog.

GRAMMA. I saw you walking with a girl the other day. She has a real sweet look. Who is she?

LUCY. Marian Bradley.

GRAMMA. John Bradley's girl?

LUCY. Yes, her father's president of the mill.

GRAMMA. Did you and she have a little tiff?

LUCY. Oh, no. She invited me over to her house.

GRAMMA. There! You got promoted, you made a good friend. Everybody likes you. Your Aunt Grace was saying just before you came in, she thinks you're real handy around the house.

LUCY (*eagerly*). Aunt Grace said that?

GRAMMA. Don't say a word, but I know they'll adopt you if you stay.

LUCY. Uncle Ed is awfully good to me. But I don't think Aunt Grace—

GRAMMA. It's her way. She doesn't wear her heart on her sleeve. But she means well. We'll be honest with each other, Lucy. We'll talk like two grown women. What is there for you at home? Missing school day after day, spoiling the younger children by doing all the work for them, driving yourself beyond your strength.

LUCY. But Gramma—

GRAMMA. Here, you'll get clothes and schooling. You're bright and I know you can see it will help them if you stay.

LUCY. Help . . . ?

GRAMMA. I don't mean what they save at home not having you there. I mean later.

LUCY. Oh, Gramma, I wish I was grown already; I wish I could work. I wouldn't care what it was. Just so I could give them a home like this—and clothes like I wear—and good food. And we'd have a nurse for Papa, so Mom could have a rest from waiting on him.

GRAMMA. You will, one day. You stay here and get your schooling. Fit yourself for a good job. Now finish your orange juice. You've hardly touched it. (*Lucy sets her glass on the floor and runs the back of her hand across her eyes.*) Child, you're crying! What will the ladies think?

LUCY. It was so pretty downtown, Gramma. It gets dark early, they light the colored lights in the windows, and the toys move around and talk like real people. The trucks go by with Christmas trees. I kept wishing I could bring it all to Papa. Why, they even have to take his meals in to him now.

GRAMMA. Yes, it's always pretty at Christmas. There's a different feeling in the air. You love everybody, you want to go up and kiss them, even strangers. The world is like a big church with its walls taken down. Its windows are blue sky and snow. People talk in carols. Their good wishes and giving are music God loves to hear. The pews reach so far, these chairs are part of them, and a couple of rows away is your father. We're all together, Lucy, in the same big place, all happy together.

LUCY. *That's* how it is. How nice you say it, Gramma. Your heart just chokes up, it's so grand. You don't feel an outsider any more, you feel like you *belonged*. (*She smiles wistfully.*) We always had such fun at home Christmas, Gramma. There were plenty of odds and ends around the house to make presents out of. And the church sent a basket. It will be a proper and a cold Christmas at Aunt Grace's, with real presents that those who get them don't like and a turkey bought with money out of the budget.

GRAMMA. That's no way to talk; at Christmastime, too.

LUCY. I'm sorry, Gramma. I'm wicked and ungrateful. I don't deserve to be treated nice. Please forgive me.

GRAMMA. There now, don't take it so to heart. You're a good girl. But you haven't told me. What's drawing that pretty mouth of yours down, and making your eyes sad? Are you afraid the baby at home has colic? All babies do and they get over it. Do you think the frost has cracked the window panes? They'll be fixed. What is it, Lucy?

LUCY (*after a while*). Well, the day I was having hot chocolate with Uncle Ed in the restaurant, I looked out. And across the street was Danny and Tom. They were looking in the window at the toys.

GRAMMA (*stops knitting, looks quickly at Lucy, then resumes her knitting but works faster than before*). Oh!

LUCY. Danny had on the big leather coat the Welfare gave him; it's big enough to allow for growing, but it don't seem like he'll ever grow up to it. It lets all the cold in. There was a big hole in his pants.

GRAMMA. And Tom?

LUCY. Tom had a cold. He kept wiping his nose with his hand. I wanted to run out and give him my handkerchief. He never has one. They looked so hungry and frozen, and I was drinking hot chocolate I didn't need after a big lunch. The girls aren't looking after them right. I know the boys walked all the way down from the Center, the whole eight miles, and then they had to walk back in all that snow and dark.

GRAMMA. Did you speak to your Uncle Ed about it?

LUCY. I wanted to. But Aunt Grace said now I was in *her* house I mustn't always be looking back, like Lot's wife.

GRAMMA (*grimly*). If Grace is quoting scripture these days, you can tell her I'll show her some passages that are a lot more fitting.

LUCY. I don't know what to do, Gramma. (*She stands up.*) I'm all mixed up. I don't know what to do.

[*Mrs. Martin and Mrs. Stone pass in front of the windows. Gramma turns when a shadow falls in the room, and sees them.*

GRAMMA. Isn't that somebody coming around by the back door? (*Lucy picks up glass of orange juice, sets it on table near the window and looks out.*) Probably don't want to mess up the front hall. Snow's a pesky thing.

LUCY. It's Mrs. Martin and a strange lady. They're looking at the mountain. (*Runs to door, D. R., opens it and calls softly.*) Aunt Grace?

GRAMMA (*twisting around to look at windows*). If she's looking at the mountain, she's a stranger, all right. I don't know what these folks from away see in a mountain. (*Resumes her knitting.*) Must be Mrs. Dr. Stone.

LUCY (*opening back door*). Hello, Mrs. Martin.

[*Mrs. Martin and Mrs. Stone enter. They are a little older than Grace and well dressed. They are clad warmly against the cold.*

MRS. MARTIN (*stepping in*). Hello, Lucy. (*Mrs. Stone follows her. Lucy closes door.*) Hello, Mother Foss. This is Mrs. Stone. (*The ladies acknowledge the introduction.*) I was showing her what a lovely view Grace has from the kitchen window and where the garden is in summer.

GRACE (*entering from D. R.*). Hello.

MRS. MARTIN (*turning*). Hello, Grace. We came around the back. You don't mind? I wanted Helen to see why you're such a good housekeeper—because you have the best view in town from your kitchen.

MRS STONE. She's just joking, Mrs. Foss. A housekeeper is good because she's good and that's all there is to it. But a nice kitchen like this certainly helps. (*Smiles at Lucy, who smiles back.*) Is this your little girl? (*Extends her hand.*)

GRACE (*too quickly and with a shocked sound in her voice*). Oh, no! She's not my daughter.

[*There is an awkward pause. Mrs. Stone, ill at ease, withdraws her extended hand.*

MRS. MARTIN (*embarrassed*). This is Lucy, Grace's niece.

MRS. STONE (*ill at ease*). How do you do, er—Lucy.

LUCY (*hastily*). Won't—won't you let me take your things, Mrs. Stone, Mrs. Martin? (*Mrs. Stone stares at her. Lucy twists her hands in her apron. She talks breathlessly while the ladies slip out of their coats.*) I was just having orange juice. (*With an anxious look at Grace.*) Aunt Grace *always* has orange juice for me in the afternoon.

MRS. MARTIN (*as Lucy takes her coat*). Thank you.

MRS. STONE (*the same*). Thank you.

MRS. MARTIN. You'll find Grace has many other talents besides housekeeping. She's in about *everything,* and does a wonderful job, too. The town's first lady. What will it be next, Grace? The school board?

MRS. STONE (*looks at Lucy, then at Grace, then back at Lucy. She sounds relieved*). Oh! Then you *do* like children?

GRACE (*after a quick look at Lucy*). Why, whatever made you think—(*Hurriedly.*) Do come into the next room. There's a good view from the front of the house, too.

[*Grace goes out D. R., followed by Mrs. Martin. Mrs. Stone is last. She turns to look at Lucy before she follows the other two. The door is closed.*

GRAMMA. That was very tactless of Grace. She didn't mean anything by it. (*As if to herself.*) But how quickly a stranger can grasp the way things are.

LUCY (*going to D. R. door*). I'd better take these things up to the bedroom. And finish the sandwiches. (*She stops and turns to face her grandmother.*) No!

GRAMMA. Child. . . .

LUCY (*her face radiant*). I know now, what I must do.

GRAMMA. You know she wouldn't take you again if you went home.

LUCY. I know.

GRAMMA. We have to put up with little inconveniences if we want to get anywhere in this world. The way isn't all smooth; pebbles keep getting into our shoes, or snow. We can't be too sensitive. You must believe me. I'm older than you.

LUCY (*slowly, as she lays the coats over the back of a chair*). She was ashamed of me. Did you hear her? (*With a wry smile.*) Oh, no! This isn't my daughter. (*Slowly.*) I don't blame her, Gramma. How can she love me when I'm not faithful to my own?

[*There is a long pause. Finally Gramma breaks the yarn off, lays the completed stocking with the other, and smooths them both.*

GRAMMA (*sighing deeply*). That's done.

LUCY. You've finished them. (*Runs to Gramma and strokes the stockings.*) They're so soft and warm. Who are they for?

[*Bell rings offstage.*

GRAMMA. They're for you, dear. It's a long walk and the drifts are high on the Center road. (*Taking her hand.*) You're a brave girl. Your gramma was wrong.

LUCY (*drops to her knees and kisses the old woman's hands*).

You couldn't ever be wrong. You're so good to me. I love you so much.

[*Bell rings again.*

GRAMMA. You'd better answer the door. Grace won't want her friends staying out in the cold.

LUCY (*lightly*). They can come around the back like Mrs. Martin. I haven't much more time with you.

[*Bell rings again.*

GRAMMA. Go along, now! No sauce! (*Spanks her lightly as Lucy, laughing, jumps to her feet.*)

LUCY (*halfway to the D. R. door, stops, turns, looks at Gramma. Gramma smiles at her*). Oh, Gramma! (*Rushes back to her, throws her arms about her neck as . . .*)

THE CURTAIN FALLS

AT LIBERTY*

A Drama

BY TENNESSEE WILLIAMS

CHARACTERS

GLORIA LA GREENE.
HER MOTHER.

PLACE. Blue Mountain, Mississippi.
TIME. The present. September. 2:30 A.M.

GLORIA LA GREENE *is not very proud of her home. It may be seen why when a spotlight reveals a section of stage to represent the corner of an antiquated living-room. A middle-aged woman in a dingy wrapper is seated stoically on a red-plush sofa. Beside her is a table supporting a red-globed oil lamp with a fringe of glass pendants. The outside door and a window are in the right wall; inner door to the left. There is an oval mirror, gilt-framed, and a large "glamour photo" of Gloria La Greene. (This is her stage name. Her real name is Bessie.)*

As the play opens, the window is streaming with slow September rain. The woman sits rigidly as in a daguerreotype picture. A noise in the hall indicates Gloria's return. The door is pushed slightly open and the mother stiffens still more at the sound of an altercation.

GLORIA (*off*). No, that's enough, that's enough! Charlie, don't tear me to pieces.

---

* First published in *American Scenes*, John Day Company, Inc.

[*Mother clears her throat and sits up very straight.*

GLORIA. Shhh! (*Closes door from outside. There is a short silence; then a man's laugh.*) Good night, Charlie, and thanks for a marvelous time!

[*She enters. Gloria is a thin, feverish-looking blond whose stage experience is stated with undue emphasis in her makeup. She wears a soiled white satin evening dress, part of an "excellent wardrobe," and carries a copy of* Billboard *which she throws on the table.*

GLORIA. Well! The Reception Committee!

MOTHER. What was the trouble between you?

GLORIA (*going straight to the mirror*). The usual trouble.

MOTHER. He wasn't a gentleman?

GLORIA (*feverishly inspecting herself in the mirror*). Hmmm?

MOTHER. They never are, these picked-up acquaintances; men you meet in hotels.

GLORIA. I wouldn't expect them to be.

MOTHER. Then why do you go out with them, Bessie?

GLORIA. Hmmm? (*Suddenly turns from mirror.*) Oh, God in the Kingdom of Heaven, I wish you'd. . . .

MOTHER. *Why* do you go *out* with them?

GLORIA. Because, if I didn't, I'd have to stay in with you! Isn't that a pretty good reason?

MOTHER. Your voice is hoarse.

GLORIA. I know it, it's always hoarse!

MOTHER. Then is it wise to go out?

GLORIA. Yes, yes, it's wise! Infinite wisdom, that's me! The Sphinx of Egypt, I've got a job as her stand-in.

MOTHER. You're feverish.

GLORIA (*removing the rabbit-skin cape*). Am I?

MOTHER. I can tell by the way you're talking. You broke an engagement with Vernon. He was over. He stayed and had a talk with me.

GLORIA (*inspecting cape*). This lining is rotten.

MOTHER. He told me that you made yourself a. . . .

GLORIA (*furiously*). A what?

MOTHER. A subject for talk in a hotel barbershop!

GLORIA. Well, that's marvelous. I'm delighted to hear it! Why should I *hire* a press agent?

MOTHER. He said that you pick up with strangers, transients at the Delta Planters' Hotel.

GLORIA. Indeed!

MOTHER. Tonight, he said you were out with a man that the Vigilantes had warned to stay out of Blue Mountain.

GLORIA. He's lying, he's—out of his mind!

MOTHER. No. You're out of *yours.*

GLORIA (*rips the torn lining out of the cape*). I will be, soon —if I don't get out of this stifling atmosphere.

MOTHER. Where would you be otherwise, jobless, in your condition?

GLORIA. Oh—the Miami Biltmore! It's two-thirty.

MOTHER. I know what time it is. I've done nothing but watch the clock.

GLORIA. When I was out on the road all those times, you didn't know where I was, you didn't know who I was out with!

MOTHER. No.

GLORIA. But you slept, didn't you?

MOTHER. No.

GLORIA. The way you look, I believe you. Mother, you look like death.

MOTHER. So do you—like death at a masquerade party!

GLORIA (*unconsciously facing the mirror*). I've had lots of compliments on my appearance lately.

MOTHER. No doubt. (*With a short laugh.*) Sarcastic remarks from people who laugh at you privately?

GLORIA (*with a sudden, imploring desperation*). Why should anyone laugh?

MOTHER (*relentlessly*). You give them occasion to, Bessie.

GLORIA. Naturally, after ten months cooped up sick in this jerk-water town, I'm—not the radiant creature I once used to be.

MOTHER. Forget that radiant creature and come down to earth.

GLORIA. *Drag* me down—if you can.

MOTHER. I also talked to the doctor. He was shocked when I told him how much you're running around. (*Gloria looks frightened.*) He mentioned the X-ray pictures. They're not too good.

GLORIA (*hoarsely*). What did he say about them?

MOTHER. He said the lung-tissues can heal if you give them a chance.

GLORIA. I'm restless, I have to go out, I can't stay in all the time.

MOTHER. Your energy's feverish, Bessie. You feel like doing more than you're fit for.

[*Gloria sinks upon sofa beside her mother. She sits very rigidly. Neither looks at the other. There are several inches of space between them.*

GLORIA. I can't just sit here and wait for something to happen. Polish my nails and curl my hair and wait for Christ's Second Coming! Is that what you and the doctor would recommend for me?

MOTHER. No, Bessie.

GLORIA. I'm glad of that!

MOTHER. Vernon is. . . .

GLORIA. Yes! Vernon *is!* And that's absolutely *all!*

MOTHER. I believe he would still marry you if you came to your senses.

GLORIA. Vernon does not represent the future I plan for myself.

MOTHER. I remember you said the same thing ten years ago.

GLORIA. Well, it's still true.

MOTHER. There's quite a difference between the future and the past.

GLORIA. I know that.

MOTHER. The past keeps getting bigger and bigger at the future's expense! (*Pause.*)

GLORIA (*with a desperate effort to shake off despair*). We drove into Meridian and bought a copy of *Billboard.* It has my ad in it. (*Rises quickly and snatches up magazine.*) Look here, listen to this! (*Reads aloud in a high, excited voice. Trembling and drunkenly, she crouches toward the table lamp for a better light.*) "At Liberty." (*She pauses to cough.*)

MOTHER (*ironically*). Yes—at liberty!

GLORIA (*going on breathlessly*). "Leads, ingénues—27, blond, attractive—"

MOTHER. Huh!

GLORIA. "5 ft. 2, 114 lbs., singing, dancing, specialties—" (*The mother makes a stiff, fretful gesture. Gloria reads with rising excitement, panting breathlessly.*) "Quick study, versatile—Excellent wardrobe—Write! *Wire!*—Gloria La Greene—Blue Mountain—" (*Here suddenly the enthusiasm dies out and she looks at her mother with a frightened expression.*) Blue—Mountain—Mississippi. . . . (*Coughs.*) How do you like it?

MOTHER (*grimly*). It's full of misrepresentations.

GLORIA. Oh, it is not!

MOTHER. It *is!* Can't you even distinguish between a truth and a lie? You're not twenty-seven, Bessie, you're thirty-two.

GLORIA. I don't *look* it.

MOTHER. You *do!*

GLORIA. Nobody else says I do.

MOTHER. Why should they?—Shout it across the street at you?

GLORIA. You want to destroy my confidence! Make me feel utterly hopeless. (*Sobbing a little.*) I've had bad times, no breaks, like everyone else in show-business. But I'm not—*through!*—Do you think?

[*The mother stares at her implacably.*

GLORIA (*slowly*). Oh—So you think I *am?* (*Her voice rises almost to a scream.*) You sit on that old threadbare sofa, night after night, waiting there for me, like Mrs. Doomsday in person! Honest to God, your eyes, they're like a tape-measure, taking my size for a coffin! But I'll—I'll cheat you out of it, though!

MOTHER. Bessie!

GLORIA. Don't Bessie me! (*She coughs and shudders.*)

MOTHER. You're drunk and you're sick, your face is burning with fever! Look at your dress, how it's torn!

GLORIA. What if it is? I don't care. (*Pause. She turns to the mirror.*) Where is it torn?

MOTHER. The seam is ripped out at the waist.

GLORIA. That can be mended.

MOTHER. Yes, but other things can't.

GLORIA. Everything can be mended, it's only a matter of time.

MOTHER. Ah! Such sublime optimism.

GLORIA. Sure. When people are starving, they take optimism and stuff it into their stomachs. Like water, like grass! It gives the illusion of having had a big dinner. (*Lifts her head stubbornly.*) I'm not discouraged. I never will be discouraged. Driving home in the rain, I thought to myself. . . .

MOTHER. That tomorrow you'd be laid up.

GLORIA. No!

MOTHER. What *did* you think?

GLORIA. That tomorrow I'd be—(*Suddenly smiles.*) Cast for a marvelous part in a Broadway production! You see, I'm an artist, Mother! I want to cry out, don't stifle the passion in me!

MOTHER. What kind of expression is that?

GLORIA. A cry from the soul. (*She turns to window abruptly and pulls it open. Pause.*) The weather-bird says—the rain will continue forever.

MOTHER. Put down that window.

GLORIA. No.

MOTHER. You're exposing your chest.

GLORIA. To think I was born in this place, Blue Mountain, Mississippi. How do they get the mountain? It's as flat as a board! But Christ in Chicago, they certainly picked the right color!

MOTHER (*throws the cape over Gloria's shoulders*). There's actually one other light still burning. Upstairs at the Bassett's. Mrs. Bassett is dying.

GLORIA. I might have known it. Death is the only thing they'd leave the lights on for, in this fabulous city. There was only one boy here that I ever liked and that was Red Allison, Mother.

MOTHER. Fell off the back of a freight car and lost both his legs. (*Pause.*)

GLORIA. Better than what I lost.

MOTHER. Yes? What did you lose?

GLORIA. Wings on my dancing shoes.

MOTHER. You're talking absurdly, Bessie.

GLORIA. I lost 'em not all at once, but gradually. They melted away in the sun like that Greek boy who wanted to fly so badly. Or maybe it was the rains they melted in. I don't remember. (*She sits down.*)

MOTHER. You're running a temperature. (*Sits down as before.*)

GLORIA. Red and I had a club composed of two members, him an' me. We invented a rebel yell. Yes, and a constitution! The first rule in it was never to stop moving forward. Poor Red! He's broken the rule.

MOTHER. I wouldn't be joking about it, a thing like that. A wild, irresponsible boy, but the end that he came to was tragic.

GLORIA. We used to swim jay-bird together at Sikeston's Creek.

MOTHER. Did you indeed!

GLORIA. Oh, nothing was wrong about it, we were just kids. I went to Cheyenne when I heard. He was already dead. I got there ten minutes too late, they'd pulled the sheet over his head. It wasn't quite long enough, though. His hair stuck out, as loud as the Fourth of July! It was sort of—impertinent looking! Congratulations, I said, you don't need legs any longer.

MOTHER. Who did you say that to?

GLORIA. Nobody. Myself. (*Gets up tiredly.*) I practiced my dance routine this morning at the Elk's Social Hall. My wind's kind of bad but otherwise I'm okay.

MOTHER. You can't expect a complete return to health, Bessie.

GLORIA. Can't I?

MOTHER. No. You've had hemorrhage, Bessie. The tissues can heal but. . . .

GLORIA (*wildly*). STOP IT! (*In her cry there is all the tortured passion for life that a human heart can contain.*) Stop it, Mother! (*Pause.*) There's only one lie contained in this advertisement. At Liberty—that's the lie!—I am not at liberty, Mother, I'm caught in a trap!

MOTHER (*closing her eyes*). So am I.

GLORIA. Oh, but I'm not discouraged! No, it's just that I haven't had such good luck to brag about lately. . . . (*She turns and enters the door, left.*)

[*The mother sits stiffly waiting. After a moment, a burst of hysterical sobbing is heard through the door. The mother leans over slowly and turns down the lamp.*

MOTHER. Yes, and—neither have I.

THE PLAY IS ENDED

LADY ROSA

A Comedy Drama

BY MAUD MERRITT

CHARACTERS

DORIS, *known as "Doddy," engaged to Ivan.*
MAY, *her friend and roommate.*
JULIA, *another friend and roommate.*
MRS. ANGELA, *the janitor's wife.*
ROSA LADOYEVITCH, *Ivan's mother.*

PLACE. New York City.
TIME. Saturday afternoon. Spring. The present.

DODDY'S *apartment is a small two-room-and-bath affair which she shares with May and Julia. There are two long, narrow windows in upstage wall. Between them is a gate-legged table on which is a pretty lamp and some books and magazines. There is a door upstage in left wall which leads to other rooms. Downstage of this door is a wide, low couch with a pretty covering and a coffee table before it. In center of right wall is a door which leads to the hall. Downstage of door is a straight chair. Upstage is a pretty chest of drawers with a small mirror hanging above it. There are one or two armchairs about. The couch has cushions, there are some nice prints on the wall, a flowering plant on the window sill, and other touches which the girls have added in order to make the place a home.*

As the play opens, May, in a pretty housecoat, is standing before the mirror tweezing her eyebrows. Julia enters from left in lounging pajamas. The girls are young and pretty.

MAY. I wonder why each one of these dinky little hairs hurts so much? (*Pulls.*) Ouch!

JULIA (*picks up pair of silk hose from couch, throws them down again in disgust*). Every darned stocking I own has a snag in it just about to run.

MAY. There's a pair in my drawer. You can have them for what I paid for them. (*Julia gets stockings from bottom drawer of chest.*) Ouch! (*Surveys her face in hand mirror.*) Don't tell me we're not descended from the apes. (*Back to plucking.*) I saw a baboon in the zoo last week with eyebrows exactly like mine.

JULIA. How much longer are you going to be? I've had a bath, done my nails. Look! (*Kicks off a mule and holds out one foot.*) That's what I call a swell job.

MAY. Carmine polish on your toenails in September! What a waste.

JULIA. It isn't every day that I meet up with royalty.

MAY. I should hope not. You're positively jittery.

JULIA. Oh yeah? And I suppose you're as cool as a cucumber.

MAY (*crossing to sit in armchair with polish which she applies to her nails*). At least I don't spend time polishing my *toenails*. You don't suppose Lady Ladoyevitch will ask to see them, do you? (*She laughs.*)

JULIA (*pulling on a stocking*). I don't know that it's any funnier than your straightening up all the bureau drawers. And I didn't by any chance see you put on your best undies, did I?

MAY. It gives me more confidence, having things all right underneath as well as on the outside.

JULIA. Exactly how I feel about my feet. Now I can break my leg and not worry. (*Regards her toes thoughtfully.*) Wish she could see them. They do look grand. I almost think I *will* sprain my ankle.

MAY. I wouldn't bother. This is just a hail-and-farewell for you and me. We're just Doddy's friends, and Lady Ladoyevitch will probably say—(*Imitates affected voice of an aristocrat.*)—"Thumbs down, my dear, on those impossible roommates of yours."

JULIA (*angrily*). Oh, she will, will she?

MAY. Maybe, maybe not. But she's not coming here to see you nor me. She's coming to see Doddy. You and I—we're just background. It's Doddy's show and we mustn't spoil it by talking too much or getting in the way.

JULIA (*after a pause*). May, honest, don't you wish it was you who was going to marry Ivan?

MAY. Oh, I don't know, Julia. Having to live up to someone can be an awful strain. Imagine having to dress for dinner every night. Imagine having a butler behind your chair all the time, watching you eat. Imagine if it was asparagus, corn on the cob or oysters. Suppose an oyster slipped.

JULIA (*waving a stocking*). That would be nothing. He'd be trained for that. He'd just pick it up and say, "Madame, your oyster!" (*Sighs.*) But I wish I were marrying money, or what have you. No more worrying about getting sick or old or losing your job. And to have someone as crazy about you as Ivan is about Doddy! (*Sighs in ecstasy.*)

MAY (*softly*). It would be wonderful, wouldn't it? But I wouldn't want to be in Doddy's shoes today, meeting my mother-in-law for the first time.

JULIA. Don't you worry about Doddy. Doddy's okay. Doddy isn't you or me.

MAY. But, Julia, suppose she doesn't like her?

JULIA. Doddy likes everybody, the dumbbell. And don't forget this Lady Ladoyevitch is Ivan's mother.

MAY. Listen. I mean, supposing she doesn't like Doddy? Doesn't want her for a daughter-in-law?

JULIA (*angrily*). I'd throw her out on her ear!

MAY. Well, then, suppose she likes Doddy all right, but not you or me. Suppose she turns her nose up at us? Doddy wouldn't stand for that, you know.

JULIA (*pulling on other stocking defiantly*). Mrs. Lady Ladoyevitch better not turn up any of her noses at me! I'm too good a saleswoman to have anything like that pulled on me.

MAY (*grimacing*). Then why did you polish your toenails?

JULIA. And why are you wearing your best panties? (*Whimsically answering her own question.*) Because neither of us cares a hoorah for royalty.

MAY (*putting nail polish in drawer*). Come on. Let's have this room straightened up when Doddy gets home.

JULIA (*getting up as May removes cosmetics from chest top and places them in drawer*). Poor kid! Wouldn't you know old Puddingface would keep her after hours today? You'd think he'd have some heart about Saturday afternoons. (*She punches a cushion into shape.*)

[*For a while they are busy, not talking, occupied with their thoughts as they straighten up the room.*

MAY. Ever hear about trying to make a silk purse out of a sow's ear?

JULIA. I've heard it can't be done.

MAY. Well, *we're* trying to do it. Look, Julia, what is it about Doddy that makes her different from us?

JULIA. You tell me.

MAY. But what makes her that way? Her folks are poor, just like ours. She didn't go to college or boarding school any more than we did. She hasn't half our style, and yet. . . .

JULIA. I don't know what it is, but she has it.

MAY. Doddy said her grandfather used to tell her, when she was little, that there were three ways to know a lady: By the way she walked, by the way she laughed, by the way she drank her tea.

JULIA. And your laugh, my pet, resembles at times, the hyena's.

MAY. And your walk, my love, is a one-wheel waddle.

JULIA (*complacently*). It gets me where I'm going. As for this tea-drinking stuff, I'll take coffee. Just the same, I wish Doddy would come. I'm all covered with duck bumps. You finish dressing, May, while I finish in here.

MAY. Okay. (*Goes into bedroom left, leaving door open.*)

[*Julia, in pantomime, tries to imitate a lady, pacing back and forth in front of the mirror, first mincing, then striding, turning her toes out, turning them in. Finally, in disgust, she flops into a chair, picks up a vase from the table and pretends to drink from it, her little finger first sticking out straight, then curled up. As she sips, she experiments with her laugh. She jumps guiltily when the doorbell buzzes. She presses button at right door.*

MAY (*calling from bedroom*). There's Doddy at last. Push the button, Julie. The infant has forgotten her key again.

JULIA. I did. We'll have to tie that key around her neck. I've seen people in love before, but Doddy wins by a neck.

MAY (*dreamily*). Mustn't it be wonderful to feel that way?

[*Doris rushes in breathlessly with a long white box under her arm. She is a very pretty girl. She wears a simple tailored business dress with white touches.*

DORIS (*breathlessly*). I thought I'd never, never get away. Those letters simply had to go out tonight. Mrs. Angela will be up in a few minutes. Julie, you were marvelous to think of having her for our maid this afternoon. (*Pulling off her hat.*) What time is it anyway?

JULIA. Quarter past three.

DORIS. Heavens! Ivan's mother will be here at three-thirty. Where's May?

JULIA. Still gilding the lily.

MAY (*coming out of bedroom, fully dressed*). Flowers in the box, Doddy?

DORIS. Ivan sent them. (*Opens box, takes out enclosed envelope and tucks it away in her dress.*) The boy was just delivering them when I came in. (*She buries her face in the box and then passes it to Julie and then to May.*) Gorgeous?

JULIA. Delirious!

MAY. They're lovely. But aren't you going to read the letter?

DODDY. Oh, no. I'll save that for when I go to bed.

JULIA. Maybe Ivan's. . . .

MAY. Love is love.

JULIA. Aren't you going to change, Doddy?

DORIS. Ivan said not to. I'll just wash and brush my hair. My, but I'm tired. Can anyone tell me why being nervous about anything like this should tire me more than a full day's work?

JULIA. Here. Give me those flowers. I'll put them in water for you. (*Takes them, goes out left.*)

MAY (*following Julia*). I'll fix the flowers. You make yourself decent for human consumption. One look at you, and

Ivan's mother. . . . (*Her voice trails off as she goes out to the kitchen.*)

DORIS (*crosses to table, picks up framed picture of a handsome young man. Kisses it*). Thanks for the flowers, darling. Thanks for everything. I love you, Ivan dear. . . . (*Puts picture down as May enters with flowers in the vase.*)

MAY (*showing them to her*). All right?

DORIS. The magic touch. Thank you. (*Puts flowers next to picture.*)

MAY. How do I look?

DORIS (*turning her around*). Mrs. Ladoyevitch will be sorry Ivan isn't marrying you instead of me. Perhaps I *ought* to change.

MAY (*kissing her*). Sweet and simple. That's your line, Doddy. Stay the way you are. Julie and I will see that you two are left alone some of the time.

DORIS. Isn't it silly, May? I'm scared. Yet, if Ivan loves me, why shouldn't his mother like me too?

MAY (*patting her arm*). You just keep thinking about Ivan and that she's his mother and everything will be all right. You've nothing to be scared about. You're a good kid, Doddy. You've been straight and honest with everybody. And you're kind, not a couple of hard-boiled eggs like Julia and me. If the lady wants more than that in her son's wife, then it's just too bad!

DORIS. Oh, May, you're such a comfort, and you look so terribly nice. I wish we could pretend it was you Ivan was going to marry. Just while she's here.

MAY. Don't be a nut.

JULIA. Who's a nut? (*She is dressed.*)

MAY. You.

JULIA. Not little Julie. You should have seen the sale I pulled off this morning.

DORIS (*looking at her searchingly*). You didn't do anything foolish?

JULIA. Go comb your hair. (*Looks at her wrist watch.*) You have exactly three minutes.

DORIS. Good heavens! (*Rushes into bedroom.*)

JULIA. You know I'm apt to get a raise?

MAY (*sinking on divan*). I suppose I've got to hear it. (*Resigned.*) What wonderful thing did you do? (*Briskly.*) And make it short.

JULIA (*sitting next to her*). I made a sale this morning that will go down in history.

MAY (*yawning*). All by your little self?

JULIA. Practically. Although Doddy's Ivan was a big help.

MAY. You mean he bought something for Doddy?

JULIA. No. Early this morning a foreign-looking woman—you could tell she didn't know anything—came in and asked for me. Baker brought her over. This woman said Ivan had told her I'd take care of her.

MAY (*grimly*). And you did, I expect.

JULIA. Ivan was sweet to send her to me . . . so's I could make a sale. Or so I thought. Then I found out she didn't want to spend much . . . she didn't know a thing about clothes and . . . well. . . .

MAY. Well?

JULIA (*a little ill at ease*). Well, there was this sample model that Baker had brought back with her from Paris, when Paris was still Paris. Well, that coat has been a smootch on Baker's pride. She and the boss have had bitter words about it. Three times it sold and three times it bounced back. But it *was* a Paris coat.

MAY. So you sold it to Ivan's friend.

JULIA (*getting up and walking about*). Good heavens, May, she wasn't a friend of his . . . a relative of one of the servants, perhaps.

MAY. Well, you sold her a coat. So what?

JULIA. But such a coat! You never saw so many buttons. Right straight down the front, up the sleeves. Seams, pockets, everything . . . buttons. So this foreign woman. . . .

MAY (*shocked*). Jule! You didn't. . . .

JULIA (*shrugging*). She wanted the latest style . . . at a price. After I sold her the coat, I went with her to get a hat. There was one, a beautiful flame red; a little stepsister of a hat. No one had been able even to get it on a woman's head for a try-on. (*Proudly.*) It was a cash sale and no returns because it was such a bargain.

MAY. Now we've got it.

JULIA. What?

MAY. The difference between Doddy and us. Doddy would starve first before she pulled a trick like that on a poor woman. (*Indignantly.*) And after Ivan was nice enough to send you a customer.

JULIA (*shamed but flippant*). Well, a girl must eat, mustn't she?

MAY (*sighs*). I suppose so. Well, that's one problem solved for Doddy. Marrying money. And he's good-looking too. By the way, what are we to call Ivan's mother? Madame, Lady, or just Your Highness?

JULIA (*shrugging*). Search me. Wonder if she smokes? (*Arranges ashtrays.*)

MAY. All Europeans smoke like chimneys.

JULIA. Is Serbia in Europe?

MAY. It was.

JULIA. I wish I had gotten some long ones. (*Gets package of cigarettes from table, opens it and places them in cigarette box on table.*) Well, she'll just have to take 'em or leave 'em.

DORIS (*enters, drying her hands on a towel*). It's long after half past. I wish she'd come.

JULIA. May wants to know what we're to call her.

DORIS (*hesitantly*). Why, just Mrs. Ladoyevitch, I guess. Ivan calls her Lady Rosa. But we couldn't do that. He says all the people who've worked for her adore her. Ivan's crazy about her. He says she's beautiful and kind. Ivan says. . . .

JULIA (*holding her head in her hands*). Ivan says! Ivan says! And Ivan says! Oh Lord, what a theme song.

[*There is a knock. All run around nervously. Doris throws her towel behind the couch. May primps before the mirror. Julia, making an attempt to walk like a lady, goes to door right.*

DORIS (*whispering*). But it can't be her! She'd have rung the bell.

[*Julia opens the door. There stands Mrs. Angela in a black-*

and-white checked dress and a little white apron. Her hair is slicked down and a white cap rides it jauntily.

MRS. ANGELA (*hesitantly looking from one to the other*). I look all right, no?

JULIA. Perfect. The perfect cartoon of the maid.

MRS. ANGELA (*pleased*). Thank you, Miss Julia. I try.

DORIS. You look very neat and nice.

MRS. ANGELA (*to Doris*). What I do? You tell me what I do.

DORIS (*taking a long breath*). When I buzz the dumb-waiter bell three times. . . .

MRS. ANGELA. Like when you want I should get the garbage?

DORIS. Yes. Only you go to the front door. A lady will ask for me. You show her up here. If she has a bag of any kind, you carry it for her.

MRS. ANGELA (*putting her hand on her heart*). Not so heavy a bag, maybe?

DORIS (*laughing*). Oh, no. Just a little bag, if any. Then you stand in the doorway and say like this—(*Illustrates.*)—"Madame Ladoyevitch."

JULIA. You'd better have a dress rehearsal.

DORIS. Try it.

MRS. ANGELA (*as if she were a street huckster calling strawberries*). Madame Ladoyevitch!

DORIS. No, no! Please! Not so loud.

MRS. ANGELA. Sure. Sure. (*Loud whisper.*) Madame Ladoyevitch.

MAY. The villain approaches.

MRS. ANGELA (*disappointed*). Not right?

JULIA. Look! Say it like you were telling me that Mrs. Maloney was here with the wash.

MRS. ANGELA (*her head bobbing up and down*). Sure. Sure. Madame is here with the wash.

DORIS (*sighs*). Oh well. Just do the best you can.

MRS. ANGELA. I do. I do for your feller. That Ivan, he's one nice man. He send my boy to place on Long Island where he gets nice job with the vegetables. Nice. . . .

DORIS. Now if you'll go down and be ready. . . .

MRS. ANGELA. Sure. Sure. (*She goes door right.*)

JULIA (*looking at her watch*). Four o'clock!

MAY. Did you read her letter right? Is this the day? I never could go through this again. Never!

DORIS (*gets letter from table, reads it*). She does write beautifully. Ivan said she studied right along with him. Ivan says. . . . (*Julia and May groan.*) She read all of his schoolbooks. I thing he must have had a tutor or something. Although he really never speaks much about. . . .

[*The bell rings. All are petrified and stand looking at each other. Doris pushes the button three times. The girls scurry about fixing things and themselves. Then they stand in the middle of the room, waiting. The door opens. Mrs. Angela enters. Her arms are filled with paper sacks from the tops of which vegetables protrude. Her cap is askew. A figure follows her into the room. May and Julia gasp. The woman with Mrs. Angela is a short, stocky woman in a black coat, covered with buttons and a flame-red hat!*

MRS. ANGELA. Madame Ladoyevitch! (*Suddenly a bag bursts. Cabbages, onions, and tomatoes flood the room. Mrs. Angela stoops to retrieve them. A plucked chicken falls from another bag.*)

JULIA (*in a terrible voice*). Where did you get those?

MRS. ANGELA. Miss Doris . . . she said carry lady's bags and. . . .

DORIS. That's all right. (*Coming forward.*) I'm Doris, Madame Ladoyevitch. (*Takes her hand and draws her into the room. Mrs. Angela has gone to kitchen and returns with a dishpan in which she gathers up the vegetables.*) Julia. May. This is Ivan's mother. (*To Lady Rosa.*) These are the friends I live with.

LADY ROSA (*as Julia stares at the coat and hat*). We have met before. (*Doris looks surprised.*) You were so good to me when I come in your store to buy this hat and coat. You are surprised, no?

JULIA. And how! (*Quickly.*) I mean, yes, indeed. (*Doris looks at Julia.*)

MAY. How do you do, I'm sure.

LADY ROSA. It is so nice to have friends to live with. Yes?

DORIS (*looking steadily at Julia*). Yes.

LADY ROSA (*taking both of Doris' hands in hers*). It is sweet for you to let me come see you. I ask Ivan how you look and he laugh and say, "Like no other girl in the world." So I know for sure he love you.

DORIS. Thank you. Er—let me take your hat and coat.

[*Slowly Lady Rosa takes off the red hat and the coat. There is a startling change in her appearance. She is quite lovely in a gray dress with white collar and cuffs. Her gray hair is smooth and neatly parted in the middle.*

DORIS (*involuntarily*). Oh!

LADY ROSA. Something is wrong. Yes? No?

DORIS (*leading her to divan*). Oh, no.

MAY. The vegetables, you know. So unexpected.

LADY ROSA (*as she sits on divan with Doris*). Those. (*To girls.*) My Ivan he tell me always in the hurry you are. No time for the shopping of the good vegetables. So I bring.

JULIA (*affectedly*). Very good of you, I'm sure, to go to the trouble. . . .

LADY ROSA. No, no, no. No trouble. These things I grow on my farm. I will send you some more if you can use.

MAY (*murmuring*). How nice.

LADY ROSA. The ladies in the big houses where I go to sell my vegetables, they say, "Rosa, nobody grows things like you." (*Smiles.*) I get a big head.

MRS. ANGELA (*who has piled all the spilled vegetables in the dishpan, now rises and rushes over to Lady Rosa. She is excited*). Lady Rosa! (*To girls.*) Why you no tell me it is Lady Rosa? That's where my Sam works. On Lady Rosa's farm. I hear always from him, Lady Rosa she good. Lady Rosa she kind.

LADY ROSA (*kindly*). Well, you must be Dina. All the time Sam he talk about his mother, Dina. Sam is a good boy.

MRS. ANGELA (*beaming, as she backs through door left*). I take vegetables in the kitchen. See you later, Lady Rosa. (*Draws herself up.*) You no pay me, Miss Doris. I wait on Lady Rosa free.

JULIA (*after a wink at May, passes the cigarettes to Lady Rosa.*) Smoke?

LADY ROSA (*declining*). In Serbia the old ladies smoke pipes.

JULIA. I can run down to the corner and get you one.

LADY ROSA (*laughing and more at ease than the others*). Na, na. I am not that old.

MRS. ANGELA (*stands in doorway holding head of Chinese cabbage*). Miss Doris, she no go in icebox.

DORIS (*getting up*). I'll fix it.

LADY ROSA (*getting up*). The kitchen, you will let me see?

DORIS. Of course. (*Smiles.*)

LADY ROSA (*as she and Doris exit door left*). Of all rooms, the kitchen it is the best, no? (*They are out.*)

MAY (*angrily pacing*). I could choke that Ivan and bury him in quicksand. Why didn't he give us some idea that his mother ran a truck farm?

JULIA (*viciously grinding out her cigarette*). Why not make it hot oil? You bet he got Doddy's promise to marry him before he let her see his family. Smart, wasn't he?

MAY. We better be careful. I saw Doddy watching us. She's sunk, poor darling. All her big hopes! (*Shrugs.*) And now look at the darn things.

JULIA. I'm glad I sold her that ghastly coat and hat—now.

MAY. Sh!

LADY ROSA (*as she and Doris re-enter*). Is small the kitchen, but nice. (*As she and Doris sit on divan.*) In Serbia is kitchen big as whole house. (*Speaking to them all.*) I tell Ivan's Doris about my Serbia. (*Spreads her hands and sounds very homesick.*) It can be so beautiful, my Serbia. The hills so blue, the grass so green, and so many willow trees by the streams, you would not believe. And someday it will be like that again when there is peace. But ah! It is beautiful!

JULIA (*pertly*). The old U. S. A.'s not so bad.

LADY ROSA (*quickly*). Is beautiful and wonderful here. And my Ivan is now an engineer. A good engineer. In Serbia, peasants like us do not have engineer sons. (*She fumbles in bag and hands Doris a picture.*) I show you Ivan's father.

MAY. If you'll excuse us, we'll bring in the tea. (*Nudges Julia as a signal. Both stand up.*)

LADY ROSA (*quickly*). No trouble, please.

JULIA (*abruptly*). No trouble. (*They go out door left.*)

LADY ROSA (*looking over Doris' shoulder*). Yes, this is Ivan's father. He went to another war, and he did not come back, and so Ivan and I come to America. Here is that boy, Ivan. (*Hands Doris another picture.*)

DORIS (*taking it hungrily*). He's sweet.

LADY ROSA (*shaking her head*). He does not look as if he grow up big and strong. He work with me in the fields, even when he is so little. But soon he is stronger than me. Yet why do I tell you all this? You know. Ivan has told you.

DORIS (*slowly*). No, he did not tell me. He told me some things. They sounded different. . . . (*Crying out.*) Oh, I'm all mixed up.

LADY ROSA (*surprised*). You thought we were of the higher class?

DORIS (*embarrassed*). Well, he always called you Lady Rosa. He spoke of your place on Long Island. I didn't know.

LADY ROSA. He makes fun, that Ivan. Lady Rosa's the name the farm hands give me. (*Fumbles in her capacious bag again.*) I brought you some lace. Orange blossom lace. Ivan's Tante Maria made it long ago and sent it for Ivan's bride. He was only twelve. How we did laugh. (*She smiles.*)

DORIS (*takes lace, but lets it drop in her lap without looking at it*). Oh, thank you. It's lovely.

[*Julia and May come in with the tea. It is a service for only two people. They place it on low table before divan and draw table up before Doris. Then they go out again, casting looks of compassion at Doris behind Lady Rosa's back.*

LADY ROSA (*looks up, catches them, but pretends not to notice*). Thank you. It is so nice.

DORIS. Will you have cream or lemon?

LADY ROSA (*still smiling*). Could I have first a glass of water? Would it be too much trouble? Some boys I asked where your street was, told me wrong. I walked far and it is very warm.

DORIS (*glad to escape for a moment*). Of course. I'll get it right away. (*Jumps up, the lace falls to the floor unheeded. She goes out door left, leaving it open.*)

[LADY ROSA, *her face sombre, picks up the lace and folds it slowly. She pauses, however, when she hears voices from the kitchen.*

MAY (*off*). Doddy! You're as white as a sheet.

DORIS (*off*). No, no. I'm all right.

JULIA (*off*). That boy-friend of yours had some nerve! Making you believe his mother was near royalty. If he had to lie, he might at least have warned you in time.

DORIS (*off*). Please! Please don't talk so loud.

JULIA (*off*). A guy who can lie like that before he's married would sure be a little Lulu with practice.

MRS. ANGELA (*off*). Why you not let me wait on Lady Rosa?

MAY (*off*). We served the tea ourselves. Things aren't the way we thought they were.

MRS. ANGELA (*her voice rising*). Ha! I know. You think Lady Rosa not good enough to be serve by maid.

DORIS (*off*). Please! All the doors are open.

[*Kitchen door, off, slams shut. Lady Rosa rises to her feet slowly. She puts lace on table and picks up her coat and hat. She looks at them, then slowly replaces them on divan. She picks up her bag, forgetting the lace and pictures. She leaves quietly by door right, closing it gently after her. Doris enters with glass of water. Looks around. Places glass on table, runs to door right, flings it open and looks down the hall. Then she calls out.*

DORIS. Julia! May! She's gone! (*She throws herself on the divan and weeps bitterly.*)

JULIA (*running in with May*). Doddy, what's the matter?

DORIS (*sobbing*). She's gone. Oh, she's gone.

MAY. She must have heard us. But she'll be back. She left her coat.

JULIA (*kneeling down beside Doris*). Look, kid, that's the best thing that ever happened to you.

MAY (*smoothing Doris' hair*). Listen, honey. Don't cry. It's all over.

DORIS (*frantically*). What will I do? What will I do?

MAY. You won't be home when your friend Ivan calls. That's all.

DORIS (*leaning up on one elbow*). I just can't understand why Ivan went out of his way to deceive me. He always seemed so honest.

JULIA. That's the kind to keep your eye on.

DORIS. If he had told me, left me to decide whether I'd marry him after I knew, I could have understood and respected him. (*Throws herself down and weeps again.*) I loved him so terribly. But he shouldn't have fooled me. Now I don't know what to think. I don't know! I don't know! (*Buries her face in the cushion.*)

JULIA (*beckoning to May*). We've got to make her laugh. Now's the time to make her see it's got a funny side. Run get a bouquet of vegetables from the kitchen. (*May runs out door left. Julia drapes lace over her head. May returns with Chinese cabbage, a bunch of beets and a bunch of carrots which she holds over her arm like a bouquet. Julia grabs the Chinese cabbage, holds it like a bridal bouquet. May falls in line behind Julia. They parade up and down before Doris, humming the wedding march.*) Tum-t-tum-t. Tum-tee-tum-tee.

DORIS (*looks up. They grin at her. Doris gets to her feet*). How can you be so *mean.*

MAY (*discarding bouquet*). Listen, Doddy. Maybe it's not so bad. Maybe he explained in that note that came with the flowers.

DORIS. The note! (*Takes it from pocket and reads aloud.*) *Dearest: This will reach you before my mother does. That she is a peasant, will not matter to my Doris when you see her. It seemed unfair to prejudice you in any way before you met her. She is all the things I have told you and more. She is a true lady—Lady Rosa.*

JULIA. I suppose he thinks that makes everything just ducky.

[*There is a knock on the door. The girls look at each other, then May opens the door. Lady Rosa enters with dignity.*

LADY ROSA. You will excuse? I forgot my husband's picture and my boy's. (*May hands her pictures. Lady Rosa looks at Julia.*) And the lace of Ivan's bride.

JULIA (*shamed, removes lace from her hair*). I'm so sorry. (*Gives her lace. Lady Rosa turns to go.*) Wait! you forgot your hat and coat.

LADY ROSA. Those, I wish no longer. I do not like.

JULIA. Then why did you buy . . . ?

LADY ROSA. Ivan, he tell me how good you are; how hard

you work. I am sorry when I see how hard you try to sell these. (*Indicates coat and hat.*) So I buy.

JULIA (*ashamed*). Oh! (*Sits on divan holding the rejected hat.*)

LADY ROSA (*turns to Doris*). Poor little girl. The sea of life is so rough for her. You are hurt. Ivan will be hurt. To love largely is wonderful. To be disappointed in that love is terrible. I would not have it so, but it is something I cannot help.

[*Lady Rosa goes out with dignity, leaving the three girls staring after her. Doris recovers first.*

DORIS (*running to door*). Wait! Wait! Please don't go.

MAY (*holding her*). Maybe it's better this way, Doddy. You may be sorry.

DORIS (*shaking her off*). No! (*Calls again.*) Lady Rosa! Lady Rosa!

LADY ROSA (*in doorway*). Did you call me—(*With infinite tenderness.*)—my child?

DORIS (*in a whisper*). Oh, Mother.

[*Lady Rosa holds out her arms. Doris goes to her and kisses her.*

JULIA (*shamefacedly*). Look! I can't do a thing about the hat. But you'll get a refund on the coat, or else—(*All stare at her for a moment. Then Lady Rosa begins to laugh. One by one, and hesitantly, the others join in.*) You know, that will be the fourth time that coat bounced back. Gosh!

[*All are laughing heartily as . . .*

CURTAIN

GRAVEYARD DAY

A Folk Play

BY SUSIE SMITH SINCLAIR

THE FOLKS

VIRGIE FISHER, *prominent church member.*
IRMA JACKSON, *her gentle-hearted friend.*
RUBY RUSSELL, *recently married.*
ELLA CRAWFORD, *always looking for trouble.*
FLORINE RANSOM, *willing to help find it.*
MARGIE ANDREWS, *who is outside the fold.*

PLACE. Western North Carolina.
TIME. Late in August. The present.

FRIENDSHIP CHURCH, *in the mountains, is having its clean-up day. This is the climax of their church activities, when they meet to clean up the cemetery. The graves occupy two acres of ground on one side of the church. Once a year, the members meet there to pull weeds, rake and burn leaves and to straighten the rows of rocks that mark the lines between the family lots. At noon they will stop work, open the baskets which they have brought, and a huge banquet will be spread on the long table in the church-yard under the oak trees. When they have eaten all they can hold, they will rest a while under the trees. Then they will come into the church for a prayer-meeting. For most of the afternoon they will sing, pray and testify. Then they will hurry home to be in time for the "milkin'."*

The church, inside, is small, dusty and neglected-looking. It has two sections of seats, the aisle between them extending from the front door to the platform.The aisle is parallel to the footlights, and thus the home-made varnished benches are placed ends to audience. There is a door L. and platform R. Steps and platform are covered with dingy carpet. On platform is a Bible stand covered with an embroidered, fringed velveteen cover hanging crookedly. Also on platform is a table holding a glass pitcher and a dingy tumbler and a vase of tightly bunched bright-red paper flowers. R. of platform is a small reed organ with its gaudily fringed stool. Songbooks and Sunday School quarterlies are piled in disorder on top of organ. Against R. wall is a set of three shelves containing discarded books, pamphlets, etc. This rubbish is concealed by drawer curtains. Along wall, center back, are three uncurtained and unshaded windows. The hot August sun streams in, revealing the dust on everything. Two or three cheap pictures of vividly colored Bible scenes hang on the walls.

As the play opens, two mountain women enter. Virgie Fisher is tall, big-boned and fifty. She wears a faded but clean starched gingham dress and apron and a dingy black straw hat trimmed with soiled flowers. All the women respect Virgie, who does not hesitate to express her opinions. She is down on sin and sinners. Irma Jackson is younger, but looks worn and tired. There is a wistful sweetness about her face. She wears a brightly colored house dress, a decent-looking hat and steel-rimmed glasses.

VIRGIE (*as they enter and walk down the aisle*). Hit jist takes a cemetery cleanin', Irma, to make me realize I'm gittin' 'long in years.

IRMA. Hit's the truth, Virgie. They hain't any of us gittin' no younger.

VIRGIE. I'm that wore out, I jist natch'ly had to come in the church an' rest my bones. (*Sits heavily on first bench and fans herself with her apron.*)

IRMA. Hit was a plumb relief when you stopped rakin' leaves an' ast me didn't I want to step this way with ye. (*Goes to window and peers out.*)

VIRGIE. Why don't ye set an' rest, then?

IRMA. I was jist lookin' out. You know, hit struck me all of a suddent that there warn't hardly no young folks at the cemetery cleanin' this year.

VIRGIE. Law, you jist now thinkin' that? Two-three year ago it come to my mind. When our generation passes to our reward, there won't be nobody to so much as pull a weed from out'n the middle of our graves.

[*Sound offstage of old-model car horn blowing violently. They turn and look toward door.*

VIRGIE. Now who could be blowin' that horn in sich a fashion right under the nose of the church?

[*Horn again.*

IRMA. Sounds like John Russell's car he bought over at Asheville last spring when he sold his cow.

VIRGIE. Yes, that's hit. That contraption of his'n is the least car an' most noise I ever saw hooked up together.

[*Horn again.*

IRMA. He does love to blow that horn.

VIRGIE. Yes, an' I wisht he'd stop. Hit's might' near splittin' my ears.

IRMA. Seems like a pity fer a man to trade a cow fer a car. 'Specially a fresh cow.

VIRGIE. That's a man fer ye.

IRMA. Still an' all, hit mus' be nice to have a car.

VIRGIE. Maybe so, but ye cain't milk one.

[*Ruby Russell enters from L. She is twenty and pretty. She wears a mail-order silk-print dress, runny silk stockings, high-heeled slippers and a cheap and becoming hat. Although young, she is religious and means to give her marriage a good start by going to church and taking her husband with her. Right now, though, she is annoyed as she comes down the aisle carrying a large basket.*

VIRGIE. I'll declare if hit ain't Ruby Russell. How air ye, Ruby?

RUBY (*placing basket on bench and approaching women*). I'm tol'ble, Miz Fisher. But I will say men can be the beatin'est things. Soon as we got here, John jist hopped outer that car an' grabbed hisself a rake an' left me settin' there. I blowed and blowed fer him to come back an' set this here basket of dinner out fer me, but he never heered me.

VIRGIE. He must be gittin' deef young if he never heerd that horn.

RUBY. I had to lug this basket in here by myself. (*To Irma, who is still standing at window.*) How you, Miz Jackson?

IRMA. I'm as peart as common, I reckin, Ruby.

RUBY (*to Virgie*). You feelin' well, Miz Fisher?

VIRGIE. I'm middlin', thank ye, Ruby. Whyn't ye jist leave the basket settin' in the car till time to spread dinner?

RUBY. I was feared somebody might tamper with hit. I thought hit would be safer in here.

IRMA. Us's dinner is settin' out there on the big table in the yard. I don' reckon nobody will bother hit.

RUBY. Maybe not. But since I got mine in here, I'll leave it. You 'uns ain't through cleanin' up the cemetery yit, air ye?

VIRGIE. Hit ain't quite finished yit. But I've done ever' lick I mean to. I ain't as young as I used to be.

RUBY. Well, I better git along out there an' he'p 'em finish up or they'll be sayin' I jist come to eat. Hit makes me so mad, gittin' here so late.

IRMA. Was you 'uns hindered some way, Ruby?

RUBY. John jist couldn't git the car started. I set there on the front seat and watched him push down on the starter and yank an' jerk till I was ready to cry. But hit was too late to try to git here with the mule, so I couldn't do nothin' but set an' wait.

IRMA. Well, you got here in time to spread dinner, so hit's all right now.

RUBY. I'll go out an' he'p 'em work. You 'uns watch that basket fer me if ye aim to set in here.

VIRGIE. All right, Ruby, we won't let nobody bother it. (*Ruby runs out. Virgie looks after her, shaking her head.*) She's a quare one. Settin' out there blowin' that horn for John to come tote that basket in here.

IRMA. Wonder why she didn't want to tote it in by herself?

VIRGIE. She's always had quare notions. She not only makes John saw an' cut the firewood, but she makes him tote it in, too.

IRMA. She ain't sickly, is she?

VIRGIE. Her? She's as spry as a yearlin' calf.

IRMA. What does John do her work fer, then?

VIRGIE. They hain't been hitched long. (*Smiling.*) He'll git over it.

IRMA (*with a deep sigh*). Yeah. Most men does. Well, I'm glad her an' John came. They're purt' nigh the only young folks on the place.

VIRGIE. Hit makes me plumb sad to think of it. Now, when I was a girl there warn't nothin' I looked fo'ward to, like graveyard day.

IRMA. Hit's the truth.

VIRGIE. Ever'body, young or old, come out. Nobody wouldn't miss hit.

IRMA. Don' seem like the young people know how to have a good time no more. Don' seem like they keer much about graveyard day no more.

VIRGIE (*sighing*). I don' know what in the world the world's comin' to!

IRMA (*looking out of window*). Florine Ransom's out there rakin' off her ma's grave.

VIRGIE (*with interest*). I wisht I felt like gittin' up an' watchin' her. Is Ella Crawford close by?

IRMA (*leaning over to get a good view*). Yes. Yes, sir. There comes Ella now.

VIRGIE. And I'm too pyore tard to git up an' hear 'em. I hain't missed one of their rows since Florine's ma was buried.

IRMA. An' that was fourteen-fifteen year ago.

VIRGIE. Ever' bit of it. An' she hadn't no more'n been put in the ground till the Crawfords claimed the Ransoms had buried their ma part on the Crawford lot. They claim that the line between the two lots run smack thoo the middle of old Miz Ransom.

IRMA. Ella an' Florine has started wordin' it now.

VIRGIE. I'd like to hear it, but I already know what they'll say when they git started. They bin sayin' the same thing ever since the fuss started.

IRMA (*turning away from window*). I don' see how they keep up a family feud about a pore dead body in a grave.

VIRGIE. Ella says hit's the principle of the thing. She says if they lets the Ransoms git by with buryin' half their ma on the Crawford lot, they's no tellin' who might be tryin' it next.

IRMA. That's what the Ransoms say too. Jist the principle of the thing. Well, as long as they both take it out in talkin', there ain't no harm done, I reckin.

VIRGIE. No, I reckin not. But they'll be spattin' off an' on all day.

IRMA (*looking out window again*). Say, Ella's headin' this way.

VIRGIE. Comin' in the church?

IRMA. I believe she is.

VIRGIE. Git away from that winder then. I don' want her to think we been pryin' in her business.

IRMA. Gracious, no. I hain't got no mind to meddle. (*Sits next to Virgie.*)

VIRGIE (*innocently*). Hit's jist like I says, Irma, this has been one of the best years fer fattenin' hogs. A uncommon lot of acorns in the woods.

IRMA. An' they was a sight of faulty apples fell off the trees this year, too.

ELLA CRAWFORD (*enters. She is stout, red-faced, forty and fiery-tempered. She wears a cotton dress and big straw hat. Walks angrily down the aisle*). I'm so hot an' tard an' mad!

VIRGIE. Set down an' rest a spell, Ella. You shore mus' be tard. You been here since 'fore I come an' I'm plain tuckered myself.

ELLA (*as she sits with them*). Hit ain't the work that tuckers me. I love to clean up the graves. But I get so bilin' mad ever' year, I'm purt near made up my mind not to come nex' year.

IRMA. Now, Ella, git that notion out'n yore mind. Ever' year somebody drops out, an' the way hit's goin' there soon won't be nobody left.

ELLA. The church can har somebody to come clean up.

VIRGIE. Don' you dare put no sich idee in words in no church meetin'. First thing you know we'd all vote fer hit.

IRMA. We like cemetery cleanin's.

VIRGIE. Clean-up day is about the only social life we got left at Friendship Church.

ELLA (*calmer*). I know an' I don' aim to do nothin' to break hit up; but them Ransoms know they put half their ma on our side but they wouldn't own it fer the world.

IRMA. I reckin they sorta hate to think of a boun'ry line right slap thoo her middle.

ELLA. We don' mean no disrespect, but hit's our land an' we don' aim to let no trespassin' git by.

[*Irma, again at window, sees something.*

IRMA. All your chillun well, Ella? (*She is trying to change the subject.*)

ELLA. All tol'able, thank ye. I left the oldest ones home to take care of the youngest ones. I jist brought the fryin'-size ones along with me.

FLORINE RANSOM (*enters. She is thin and tired. She is fanning herself with her hat*). Howdy.

VIRGIE. Set down an' git yore breath, Florine. Looks like all of us is 'bout to give out.

FLORINE (*as she walks down the aisle*). I been wonderin' where you got to, Virgie. I 'lowed to Jake that you'd jist 'bout had one of yore heart spells an' had to go home.

VIRGIE. No, Florine, I ain't missed a cemetery cleanin' fer thirty year. An' I don't aim to miss one till you 'uns will be puttin' flowers on my grave.

FLORINE. That'll be many a year yit, Virgie. (*Sits and turns to Irma.*) Hain't it time to git dinner spread?

ELLA (*spitefully*). I don' wonder ye're hungry, Florine. Been workin' so hard cleanin' up a lot that don' belong to ye.

FLORINE. I jist been pullin' weeds an' rakin' trash from my ma's grave.

ELLA. If some folks was as respectful of their ma like they claim, they would have her took up an' put in land that belongs to them so's she could rest in peace without trespassin'.

VIRGIE. Now, Ella, for goodness' sakes, remember yore in the house of the Lord.

IRMA. Law, yes. Let's don' have no wordin' in here. (*Again at the window.*) I wonder ain't they all thoo an' ready to eat. No, they's still some men workin' on the Morrison lot.

ELLA. Yeah. Since Gil Morrison got killed down to Fort Bragg, ain't nobody left in the family to look after their lot.

IRMA. Well, the neighbors don' begrudge keepin' it clean. Gil was one of the nicest boys hereabouts.

FLORINE. They's still some human kindness left in the world, although it is seldom in this day an' age.

ELLA. Yes, kindness is seldom. They's fer too many that don' think nothin' but to grab what don' belong to them.

IRMA (*quickly changing the subject*). Since we're in here, looks like we might straighten things up a little. (*Begins to straighten books on the organ.*)

VIRGIE. Reckin we might. (*But she doesn't move.*) I've wondered why we don' do more fer the looks of this church nohow.

ELLA. We do sorter neglect the inside of the church, don' we?

IRMA. Well, hit's the outside of the church that most folks see, so I reckin hit's best to put most our work on the graves, where the results make a show.

ELLA. Yeah. (*Rising.*) But I think Virgie's right. We ought to clean up inside too. (*Goes to cabinet, pulls back curtains and begins to throw the accumulated rubbish on the floor.*) Jist look at this stuff. I bet hit's been here ten year.

IRMA. Or longer. (*Picks up an old quarterly.*) 1926! Look at that now.

ELLA (*picking up old songbook*). What's this? (*Reads.*) "Songs of Praise." Don' you 'uns remember? That's the songbook we had the split-up about.

FLORINE. Split-up?

VIRGIE. The time that young Evangelist from Georgia come here to hold a revival. The young squirt brought his own songbooks with him.

IRMA. Hit comes back like yistiddy. Hit split the membership of Friendship Church wide opener than a sardine can.

VIRGIE. Hit shore did! Look at it! (*Shakes book violently.*) He might as well tried to sell us a Chinee book. Round notes! Couldn't nobody sing out'n 'em.

ELLA (*contentiously*). Some of us could.

VIRGIE. Humph! Nobody cain't read round notes.

ELLA. I said then, an' I still say, shape notes is behind the times. An'. . . .

[*The sudden entrance of Ruby interrupts this threatening conversation. Ruby walks in excitedly, holding up a bottle which is half full of a colorless liquid.*

RUBY. Miz. Fisher, look here!

VIRGIE. What ails ye, Ruby?

ELLA. Why, Ruby Russell, I didn't know you was here.

RUBY. I'm here an' I want you 'uns to look what I found.

IRMA. For gracious sakes! A liquor bottle!

FLORINE. What's a thing like that doin' at the church?

RUBY. That's what I mean to find out. (*Shaking bottle.*) Look! It's half full.

IRMA (*timidly*). Maybe hit's jist water.

RUBY. Take a whiff of hit. Water! (*Uncorks bottle, flourishes it under Irma's nose.*)

IRMA (*backing away*). Oh, don't! I never could stand the smell of the stuff.

VIRGIE. Where'd ye git hit?

RUBY. Found it hid under that hy-geranium bush on the Gibbs' lot.

IRMA. I always did think that there hy-geranium was the purtiest think in the cemetery.

ELLA. An' ye found that bottle of whiskey hid there?

RUBY. Yes, I did.

IRMA. Seems like a pity to bring the stuff in the house of the Lord.

FLORINE. Think of hidin' liquor in the cemetery!

VIRGIE. I know who it belongs to.

RUBY. Who?

VIRGIE. Ole Man Newman's been bringin' liquor to Clean-Up Day fer many a year, an' ever' one of ye ort to know it.

IRMA. I don' reckin he means no harm.

VIRGIE. You 'uns shore muster noticed that when the rest of us comes in to prayer meetin' in the afternoon after clean-up, he goes off. When he turns up ag'in, he's higher'n Cat Head Mountain.

ELLA. Why hain't he never been churched for hit?

VIRGIE. Nobody ever wanted to start hit, I reckin.

ELLA. Hit's time somebody started somethin'. An' if anybody starts hit, hit's gonna have to be us women.

IRMA. We hain't got no proof he put hit there.

RUBY. Proof's easy enough to git.

ELLA. How do you mean, Ruby?

RUBY. I aim to put this here bottle back. After we git thoo eatin' dinner, we can sorter watch till we see him go git hit.

ELLA. Then we can face him with the facts.

IRMA. What'll you do with him?

ELLA. Make him come to prayer meetin' this afternoon an' make acknowledgment.

IRMA. How can you make him if he don' want ter?

ELLA. We can see that he's turned out'n the church. Hidin' liquor in the cemetery!

RUBY. Hit's disrespect to the dead.

IRMA. But the dead don' know the diff'unce.

ELLA. I wouldn't be s'prised if they knows as much as some folks I could name.

RUBY. I'll put the stuff right back where I found hit.

ELLA. I'll go with ye. We cain't let a chancet like this go by. Who knows but what he might be converted this very day on ercount of us ketchin' up with him. (*She and Ella go to door.*)

RUBY. One of us'll have to keep a eye on the hy-geranium bush.

[*They are gone.*

VIRGIE. Now they'll be another church row.

IRMA. The church has been gittin' along peaceable fer two years. Seems a pity to start anything now.

FLORINE. Ella Crawford hain't happy fer a minute less'n she's in the middle of a quar'l.

VIRGIE. She's got an incline in that direction. Ruby is sorter snappy too. Course, she means well.

FLORINE. Seems like folks that means well is always stirrin' up trouble, 'specially in the church.

IRMA. You reckin pore Ole Man Newman will come in church an' make acknowledgment?

VIRGIE. Not a chancet. He knows too much 'bout the rest of us to git up there an' humble hisself.

IRMA (*walking to window*). Must be near time to lay out the dinner.

VIRGIE. Did ye bring one of yore sweet tater pies?

IRMA. No. We done our first tater-grubbin' last week an' they hain't had time to sweeten up yit. Seems like they jist hain't got no meanin' to 'em yet.

VIRGIE. Hit jist natch'ly takes time to flavor a sweet tater.

IRMA. Florine, come here. (*Florine hurries to window.*) Is that shore 'nough Margie Andrews trudgin' this way?

FLORINE. Yes, sir. So help me Hannah! It is.

VIRGIE. Has she got the baby with her.

IRMA. Yes.

FLORINE. Well, she's brassy, hain't she?

VIRGIE. I don' know. I've always claimed that when a girl gits herself in trouble, the best thing she can do is jist to brass it out.

FLORINE. But that baby hain't a month old yit. Seems like she coulder kept it home. She hain't got no call to come to Clean-Up Day. She hain't got no folks buried here.

IRMA. You reckin Margie could be comin' to clean up Gil Morrison's grave? She claimed he was her baby's daddy.

VIRGIE. She shore wouldn't have the cheek! Hit was the boldest thing I ever heered of—blamin' it on a dead man. Gil was such a quiet-seemin' boy too.

FLORINE. Hit was kinder lucky fer her that Gil Morrison fell off that army truck an' got killed. He didn't live to deny her story.

IRMA (*apologetically*). She claims they was married.

FLORINE. Look! She's turnin' in here.

VIRGIE. You mean comin' in the church? With that baby?

IRMA. I reckin she's 'bout tuckered, walkin' all them miles luggin' the young 'un.

VIRGIE. She don' know there's anybody in here. Git away

from the winder, Florine, you an' Irma. Let's don' be watchin'.

IRMA (*sitting down near Virgie*). I hain't got no grudge ag'in the girl. She hain't the first one to go wrong. Of course hit was wrong, tryin' to put the blame on a pore dead boy, but—

VIRGIE. Sh!

[*Margie Andrews enters. She is a thin girl of eighteen. Her face shows suffering and grief. But there is also the sweet tenderness of young mother-love. She is dressed in her Sunday best: a cheap faded rayon dress, scuffed and scarred slippers, no stockings and a misshapen hat. But her pretty hair hangs softly about her face. She carries a blanket-wrapped bundle: her baby. Suspended from her arm is a white flour bag half full of clothing, etc. The bag is fastened together at the top with a strip of cloth. Margie's arm is through one of the loops of the bow. When she sees the women, she hesitates.*

MARGIE. I—I didn't know anybody had come in yit. It hain't time fer prayer meetin' yit, is it?

FLORINE (*indifferently*). Not yit. We was jist restin' 'gin time to lay out dinner.

MARGIE. I think I'll set down. I didn't know I was so weak. (*Sits wearily, holding baby close.*) I jist come here to put somethin' on Gil's grave. (*Sets the flour bag on the bench beside her.*)

VIRGIE (*indignantly*). Put somethin' on Gil Morrison's grave?

FLORINE. You neen'ter bothered. The men is cleanin' the Morrison lot. Gil's grave will be looked after.

MARGIE (*smiling*). That's shore kind of 'em. I wouldn'ter hardly had the strength to do it all.

FLORINE. You wouldn'ter, eh?

MARGIE. I don't seem to be mendin' like I ort. But I jist had to come today. I brought a piece of August lily to plant on his grave. He told me oncet he thought August lilies was purty.

VIRGIE. He did, huh?

MARGIE (*with a slow smile*). I had one in my hair. He said it smelled sweet. So I brought a root of one.

IRMA (*sympathetically*). August lilies do stink sweet fer a fact.

FLORINE. An' ye mean to plant one on Gil's grave?

MARGY. Hit's so little I can do. But I couldn't let the day go by without takin' note of it. Fer his sake, ye know. (*She bows her head and wipes away a tear.*)

VIRGIE (*more kindly*). Hit won't hurt fer ye to put a August lily on Gil's grave. (*Pause.*) How's yore pa, Margie?

MARGIE (*looking up, pleased with her interest*). 'Bout the same. He still putters 'round a little.

FLORINE. Hit's a burden on a ole man like him to have this baby on his hands to raise.

MARGIE. Yes, an' that worries me right smart. That's why—(*Stops suddenly.*) But he loves my baby. He talks baby-talk to her—that is, when he's feelin' well.

VIRGIE. Reckin that hain't none too often.

MARGIE (*sadly*). No.

IRMA. Hit's sorter hard on ye, havin' a sickly pa to look after, ain't it, Margie?

MARGIE. I hain't complainin', Miz Jackson. If it wasn't fer the baby, I wouldn't mind. I've looked after Pa as fer back as I can remember. I'm kinder used to hit. But with her—(*Looks fondly into baby's face.*)

IRMA. What's its name?

MARGIE. Marguerite Gilbert Morrison.

FLORINE. That's a long handle fer sich a little thing.

MARGIE (*smiling*). I reckin it is. But I named her fer me an' Gil both. My name's Marguerite. I sorter wisht folks had called me that 'stid of jist Margie.

FLORINE. I reckin Margie is good enough to be called by.

MARGIE. But I want my baby to be called Marguerite.

IRMA. Folks gin'lly calls a young 'un whatever hits ma says.

MARGIE. Yes, but—(*She hesitates, looking at the women searchingly.*) I was 'fraid folks might fo'git what I called her. I mean—(*She stands up.*) I believe I got my breath now. I'll take the lily out there now, so's I can git away 'fore dinnertime. I never brought nothin' to spread. I—(*She lays baby gently on bench.*) She's asleep. She'll be quiet now fer a spell. There's a bottle milk fer her in this flour poke. (*As she talks, she takes paper-wrapped sprig of lily root from bag.*)

VIRGIE. You talk like you was leavin' her fer the rest of the day, 'stid of jist steppin' out to set a root.

MARGIE (*smiling crookedly*). Hit does sound silly, I reckin. I—jist wanted to be sure she hain't gonna be no bother. There's clothes in the poke, too.

VIRGIE. If she needs changin' ye can do hit when ye git back.

MARGIE. Yes, of course. I—I jist—(*Almost breaks down. Kneels beside baby and lays her head against it. She gets up, tries to smile.*) You won't mind watchin' her?

FLORINE. She won't be no bother to nobody till you git back, I reckin.

MARGIE. Thank ye, Miz Ransom an' Miz Fisher. (*Turns to Irma.*) She won't be no trouble, Miz Jackson. She's a good baby. (*Turns suddenly and hurries out. The women stare after her.*)

FLORINE. Don' she beat all!

IRMA. Seems like she hated to leave the baby with us even fer a little time.

VIRGIE. I reckin a girl with a baby like that does hate to put it eround fer others to have to look after.

IRMA. Hit won't hurt nobody layin' there.

FLORINE. She don' act 'shamed, does she?

VIRGIE. I was jist stud'in 'bout that. I never saw nothin' like it. She acted like there warn't nothin' to be 'shamed of. Jist like Gil *was* her lawful husband.

IRMA. She's awful peak-ed lookin'. I sorter feel sorry fer her. She's had a tough time, lookin' after Ole Man Andrews all her life. An' now the baby.

VIRGIE. She's got herself to thank fer the baby.

FLORINE. Yes, an' we cain't count'nance no such girl.

VIRGIE. No. Human nature bein' what it is, church members has to condemn sin an' sinners. If we don', there hain't no limit to what some folks would do.

ELLA (*enters, walking backward, peering out door*). I cain't hardly believe my eyes! Wasn't that Margie Andrews jist walked past me?

VIRGIE. Warn't nobody else.

ELLA. What a nerve she's got. (*Starts to sit down.*)

IRMA. Be careful! Don' set on the baby!

ELLA (*jumping up quickly*). The baby? Did she leave it here?

VIRGIE. Ye see it, don' ye?

ELLA. Well, of all the—

VIRGIE. Did ye an' Ruby git the liquor bottle planted, Ella?

ELLA. Yes. Right dab where she found hit. Me an' her is gonna take turns erwatchin' hit.

IRMA (*going to cabinet*). We started straightn'in' this mess. Let's finish hit. (*Begins picking up books, quarterlies, and stacks them neatly on shelves.*)

FLORINE (*helping*). Ye mean to say all this clutter stays in this thing all the time?

IRMA. I reckin so.

FLORINE (*picking up small Bible from floor*). Now where'd this Bible come from? (*Reads haltingly from flyleaf.*) Reverend Troy Stevens. (*Looking up.*) Why, that's that young preacher from eround Asheville.

VIRGIE. He pastored us ten-twelve year back.

IRMA. An' his Bible's been here all this time! Wonder did he ever miss hit.

FLORINE (*pulls out slip of paper from between leaves*). He's got somethin' scribbled all over this here paper. See can ye make out what it says, Irma.

IRMA (*timidly as she takes paper*). Ye reckin I should ort to read what he wrote out an' put in his Bible?

VIRGIE. Hit ain't gonna do nobody no harm after twelve year.

IRMA. Well, let me see. (*Turns paper around and looks at it over the top of her spectacles, then peers under her spectacles.*) Oh, shucks, I'll have to take these specs off so's I can see to read. (*Does so.*) Now this is—well, what do you reckin? You know what this is? (*Impressively.*) Hit's sermon notes!

VIRGIE. Sermon notes! I recollect now. That's what we had the stir-up about.

FLORINE. Yes, sir! He's the one that—

VIRGIE. He was a Pharisee! He would write off what he had

to say and would slip them notes in his Bible an' look at 'em on the sly when he was preachin'.

ELLA. I remember him. Hit never took nobody long to ketch on to him, though.

VIRGIE. Law, no! Inside of three preachin' Sundays after he started here, ever' man, woman and child in the church knowed he was a hypocrite.

ELLA. Any preacher who hain't got faith enough to depend on the Lord to put the right words in his mouth hain't got a real call to preach. Read what it says, Irma.

IRMA (*looking closely at page*). He's got some scripture wrote down. (*Reading.*) *First John 4:7 and 8.* (*Very slowly.*) *Beloved, let us love one another, for love is of God, and everyone that loveth is born of God. He that loveth not, knoweth not God. For God is love.*

[*There is a pause. Irma looks at the paper in her hand.*

ELLA. What's the last line ag'in, Irma?

IRMA (*slowly*). *He that loveth not, knoweth not God. For God is love.* An' then he's got some more things writ down. (*Reading.*) *Brethren in the church must have: First, understandin'; second, sympathy; third, forgiveness.* I don't see no use in readin' on. Seems like I shouldn't be readin' 'em nohow.

FLORINE (*thoughtfully*). It muster been a good sermon he preached from sich a text.

VIRGIE (*doubtfully*). But it couldn'ter come from the heart if he had to write it down to remember it. Anyhow, the church took an' turned 'im off fer usin' 'em.

IRMA. You reckin *we* coulder been wrong?

ELLA. If we was wrong, our intentions was right. The Lord can read our hearts an' fo'give our mistakes.

IRMA. But sometimes our mistakes hurt other people.

FLORINE. Say, this baby of Margie's is stirrin'. What if it wakes up an' starts squallin'?

IRMA. She'll be back in d'rectly. Hit don' take long to set out a root of August lily. Here, Florine, he'p me finish this mess of songbooks an' things. What about us settin' here, preachin' Sunday after preachin' Sunday, ever' month fer years, with all this rubbish here under our noses an' us never knowin' hit.

RUBY (*enters fanning self with hat*). Whew! It's got so hot out there, hit's hard to stand it.

FLORINE. Is the work finished out there, Ruby?

RUBY. Jist 'bout. The men has gone to the creek to wash. I reckin hit's time to spread dinner.

VIRGIE. I shore feel like eatin'. Ruby, did ye see that Margie Andrews headed this way from Gil Morrison's grave?

RUBY. I seen her go kneel by the grave a few minutes, then she got up an' sorter staggered off.

ELLA. Which way did she go?

RUBY. She went t'wards the Mitchell woods. Why?

IRMA. Oh, Ruby, she left her baby.

RUBY. Her baby? You mean—is that her baby?

ELLA. Whose you reckin' hit is?

IRMA. She's jist gone to set an' rest an' ponder a little. She'll be back d'rectly.

ELLA (*going to window*). Well, hit's quare. (*Looking out window.*) She hain't in sight.

VIRGIE. Look ag'in, Irma.

IRMA. She hain't out there, Virgie. You reckin she—

FLORINE. Yes, sir! I bet she has!

IRMA. Has what?

FLORINE. Gone off an' deserted this baby.

RUBY. Oh, Lord, no! You mean, gone off an' left it fer us to—

VIRGIE. That's what she meant when she said them things. That's why she went to all the trouble to tell us about its milk an' clothes. She never meant to come back.

FLORINE. An' she wanted one of us to take the young 'un to raise.

ELLA. Hain't we got troubles enough?

IRMA. I reckin she was drove to it. The baby's frettin'. (*Approaches baby hesitantly.*) It hain't the little thing's fault—hits mother runnin' off an' leavin' it. (*Picks up baby indifferently, looks at it and her face softens.*) Hit's a cute little thing. (*Cuddles it.*) There, there. Hit's quietenin' already.

ELLA. We ort to go tell somebody to follow the girl an' bring her back. She shouldn't be 'lowed to jist off like that an' leave her responsibilities fer other folk to look after.

IRMA (*sitting with baby in her arms*). Don' send nobody after her. Course hit's wrong what she done. But this pore little thing—Margie cain't give it a good home. Hit's a cute little thing. I—I could take hit home with me. It's sorter sweet to feel a baby in my arms ag'in.

FLORINE. Irma, ye mean to—to—(*Goes to Irma.*) Let me look at her. (*Irma lifts blanket from baby's face.*) Well, well! I'll declare! Hit is sweet, hain't it?

VIRGIE. Irma, put it in my lap a minute while you look in that there flour poke an' git that bottle of milk.

IRMA (*smiling as she rises*). Ye jist want an excuse to hold her. Well, here she is. (*Lays baby in Virgie's lap.*)

VIRGIE (*looking at baby*). Well, well! Hello, darlin'. Say, Irma, did ye notice this—well, look at her nose an' that mouth. Who does she put ye in a mind of?

IRMA. I thought of that, too. She's a lot like—

VIRGIE (*slowly, firmly and with meaning*). She's like her daddy, Gil Morrison.

IRMA. I reckin yore right.

VIRGIE. Now git that bottle of milk.

[*Irma unties strings and gets milk bottle from flour sack.*

ELLA. Couldn't I hold her a little bit, Virgie?

VIRGIE. What fer? You got eight of yore own.

ELLA. I know. That's what makes me feel so kind of teched. The little thing's daddy's out there cold an' dead in the cemetery, an' hits mama's gone off an' left hit.

VIRGIE. She knowed she was leavin' hit in good hands. (*She rocks baby gently on her knees.*)

IRMA. Here's the milk. (*Gives bottle to Virgie.*) What's this? (*Peers into flour sack.*) Virgie, here's somethin'—(*Pulls out a note.*)—wrote on a piece of paper.

VIRGIE. The pore girl left us a letter.

ELLA. We know how to take care of a baby 'thout her writin' an' tellin' us how.

FLORINE. Read what hit says, Irma.

IRMA. All right. (*Looks at paper closely.*) Oh, these blamed specs of mine! Sometimes I wonder do I need 'em. I cain't see a thing till I take 'em off. (*Takes glasses off and reads letter.*) *Dear Ladies: I am writin' this to you because I know some of you will be at the church, today bein' Clean-Up Day. I know all of you are good Christian women. Please try not to blame me too much fer what I am doin'. I don't want my little baby ever to think her mother didn't love her. I love her so much is why I'm doin' it. I cain't give her a decent raisin', an' I want one of you to take her an' be a mother to her.*

ELLA. She planned hit all—gittin' rid of her baby as easy as that.

FLORINE. She's right, though. (*Pause.*) The baby'll have a better chancet with me.

ELLA. Is that so! Who says *yore* gonna be the one to git her? One more baby in my home wouldn't be no trouble.

VIRGIE. Girls, let Irma finish the letter.

IRMA (*reading*). *I am puttin' our marriage papers in the clock on the far-board at home, where Pa can find them easy. I'd kindly like fer the baby to have them.* (*Looking up.*) Her marriage papers! Her an' Gil *was* married!

ELLA. If they was, whyn't she say somethin' 'bout them papers sooner?

VIRGIE. Maybe she didn't know anybody doubted it. Go on, Irma.

IRMA (*reading*). *Me an' Gil slipped off to Greenville to marry. We didn't mean to tell nobody till later, because he was drafted an' had to go to Fort Bragg. When I found out about the baby comin', I never wrote him because I didn't want to bother him. Then he got hurt an' died without ever knowin'.*

FLORINE. Hain't that the pitifulest thing!

VIRGIE. Go on, Irma.

IRMA. Hit's hard to read. Seems like my eyes is sorter bleary.

ELLA. Put yore specs back on.

VIRGIE. No, she don' want her specs. Finish it, Irma.

IRMA (*reading*). *I ain't had no heart to draw a breath since the day I heerd about Gil, but I had to go on livin' till little Marguerite come. Now she's here an' she's like Gil, an' I don't want to leave her, but she will have a better chancet. I can never be no good to her.*

FLORINE (*wiping her eyes*). Hit makes me so ashamed. I ain't been 'bout that girl to do her a turn while she was needin' somebody.

VIRGIE. None of us ain't.

ELLA. No. We taken it fer granted she had sinned.

VIRGIE. Even if she had, we didn't have no call to treat her so low. The pore, motherless girl!

IRMA. The text of Brother Stevens is comin' home to roost.

ELLA. What we gonna do?

VIRGIE. We're gonna find the pore child an' bring her back an' be good to her.

FLORINE. You mean we won't git to keep the baby?

VIRGIE. No. I aim to see that Margie an' her baby gits a few comforts out'n life. My old man an' me has raised our family an' wouldn't like nothin' better than to do fer the two of 'em.

ELLA. Somebody's gonna have to look after Margie's pa.

VIRGIE. He ain't half as helpless as he thinks he is. Margie's spoiled him all her life. But she muster knowed he could look out for hisself or she wouldn'ter gone off an' left him like she's done.

FLORINE. Hit'll do him good to do fer hisself.

VIRGIE. Some of ye better start after Margie. She cain't be far away. I'll stay here with the baby.

ELLA. Come on, Ruby. Me an' you can ketch up with her. We're spryer'n the rest.

RUBY. I 'spec she's headin' fer the Hendersonville Road. Means to go off an' git herself a job. We can cut thoo the lane an' head her off.

VIRGIE. Tell her we all want her to come back an' be one of us. Tell her we—

IRMA. Tell her we love her like Brother Stevens' text said.

VIRGIE. We'll all prove we love her after we git her back. You 'uns git 'long now. Go ketch up with her.

IRMA (*again looking at letter*). Oh! Oh!

VIRGIE. What's the matter?

IRMA. I didn't read all. They's more. Hit says—(*Her hands are trembling.*)

VIRGIE. Fer the Lord, Irma, what ails ye?

IRMA. I cain't hardly see this, but—but—hit looks like it says—

ELLA. Go on 'fore I have a nervous breakdown.

IRMA (*reading*). Bury me next to Gil. Plant a August lily on my grave too. (*Silence.*)

[*With a great effort, Virgie gets to her feet.*

ELLA. B-b-ury? Did she say bury?

FLORINE. Oh, Lord, that means she's gonna—

VIRGIE. Shut up, all of ye. Run git the men to go to the river. She's headed fer there. If they hurry, they may git there in time.

ELLA (*as she and Ruby rush to the door*). Lord, let us git there in time.

VIRGIE. Ruby, call John, an' you an' him drive to the river.

RUBY. Lord, no, Miz Fisher! We cain't be bothered with that car at sich a time. (*She and Ella go out.*)

FLORINE. What if she didn't mean the river?

IRMA. The Lake. She mighter had that in mind.

FLORINE. I'll run git some of the men started to the Lake. (*Runs out.*)

IRMA. We'll stay in here with the baby, Virgie, an' pray, pray, pray.

[*Virgie stands holding baby close to her breast. Irma stands near her. They seem to be whispering a prayer. Then Virgie sits down, her lips still moving, and rocks baby gently in her arms. Irma goes to cabinet and picks up Preacher Stevens' Bible. She opens it.*

IRMA (*reading as if praying*). *Beloved, let us love one another, for love is of God.* (*Pauses.*) *For God is love.* (*She closes book slowly, sets it down gently and comes to sit next to Virgie.*) Oh, Virgie, we didn't love enough. We was so self-righteous. If God lets that pore girl come to her death, it will be on us.

VIRGIE. That pore girl all these years in our midst, 'thout no mother, with a no-'count father. Her gonna have a baby, her sweetheart—her husband, I mean—dead an' gone. An' we never went to see about her.

IRMA. 'Stid of cleanin' up the cemetery, we ort to clean up our hearts.

VIRGIE. Pray God it ain't too late.

IRMA. If they don' find her in time, we'll be guilty of—

VIRGIE. Whether they find her in time or not, we're guilty jist the same of not havin' love. Preacher Stevens' sermon was meant fer me, even if it *was* wrote down in his notes.

IRMA. We'll make it up to the baby, won't we?

VIRGIE. I reckin this precious baby will have love showered on her from ever' woman that's been here today. But that hain't puttin' us right. Hit'll take bitter tears an' repentance to ever git fo'giveness.

[*There is a sound at the door. Both women look up. Margie is standing there. She comes down the aisle and looks at the place where she left the baby.*

MARGIE. My baby! My baby! Where is she? (*Sees baby in Virgie's arms.*) Oh, give her to me! Give her to me, I say.

VIRGIE (*gently giving baby to Margie*). Margie! Oh, thank the Lord!

MARGIE (*in a broken voice as she sits on bench and hugs the baby close*). Oh, darlin', I couldn't leave you. I tried. But I couldn't. (*Whispers.*) My baby!

VIRGIE. You've come back, Margie. Praise the Lord!

IRMA. We're shore glad ye changed yer mind, Margie.

MARGIE (*fiercely*). Yes, I reckin ye air glad. Ye couldn't be bothered with her. I started to the river but I kep' seein' how you 'uns looked at me when I come in here with her.

VIRGIE. We jist didn't know no better, Margie.

MARGIE. I was wantin' her to have a better bringin'-up than I could give her. But all the way thoo the woods I could see yore eyes, an' the cold way you looked. An' I kep' rememberin' that nary a one of ye had ast to look at her. Her a new baby, an' not a one even wanted to look at her!

IRMA. May the Lord fo'give us.

MARGIE. I saw her little face as last I looked at her. I saw her here, lyin' on this bench in the church, an' I knowed not a one of ye would want her. So I turned eround an' come back. I cain't give her a decent raisin', maybe, but I can love her. An' that's somethin' nobody can do but me—her own mother.

VIRGIE (*gently*). Ye must ca'm yoreself now, Margie honey, or ye'll be too sick to look after her.

IRMA. Let me hold her fer ye while ye rest an' collect yoreself a little.

MARGIE. No! No! I cain't let nobody else have her—ever.

IRMA. We love the little thing, Margie. An' when we thought ye'd run away, we all wanted her. I was goin' to take her home with me.

MARGIE. You was goin'—you mean you did l-look at her an' love her?

VIRGIE. Yes, Margie. Hit's shore a good thing you come back. We'd er had a church split 'bout who was goin' to git the baby. We was ever' one determined.

MARGIE (*frightened*). What I started to do—hit was wrong. Hit was awful! They won't try to take her away from me 'count of it, will they?

IRMA. Nary a bit of it. They ain't nobody in the world can give a baby as decent a raisin' as its own mother can.

MARGIE. I know. I know. Hit was jist that I was discouraged 'bout ever'thing. Without Gil to he'p me, I didn't see ahead. I still don' know how zactly I'll make it, but I will, some way or other.

VIRGIE. Hit won't be so hard with all the women in Friendship Church he'pin' you, Margie.

MARGIE. I—I—I don' know why I though you 'uns looked hard an' mean. But I did. I hope the Lord will fo'give me fer my wrong thinkin's.

IRMA. We've all got a lot to be fo'give fer.

ELLA (*comes in, in great excitement, followed by Ruby and Florine*). They say she headed back this way.

FLORINE. Towards the church. Maybe she'll—

VIRGIE (*pointing to Margie, whose head is bowed over the baby*). There she sets.

ELLA. Praise God from whom all blessings flow!

RUBY. Oh, Margie, I'm so glad you come back. Ye give us all

sich a skeer. Let me go tell 'em all. (*Ruby runs out calling.*) Here she is! John! John! All you 'uns out there! She's safe. She's safe. (*Ruby's voice dies away as she runs out.*)

FLORINE. I never was so thankful to see anybody settin' in church since the time my oldest boy, Bert, come in an' was converted.

MARGIE (*looking up and smiling through her tears*). I'm sorry I made so much trouble. I hope you 'uns won't hold it ag'in me.

FLORINE. Lord bless ye, Margie, ye've put somethin' in my heart that's been missin' fer a long time.

ELLA. I know what ye mean, Florine. Me too. I been spiteful fer these years back an' I thought it was kinder funny to be bossy. I'm gonna try to change my ways. Hit'll be hard at my age, but I mean to try.

FLORINE. Ye ain't the only one, Ella. Seems like I see myself now. An' I don' like the looks of myself, neither.

ELLA. Will ye fo'give me, Florine, fer them mean things I said 'bout yore ma's grave bein' on our side?

FLORINE. They's fo'giveness to be had on both sides, Ella. I—

[*They look at each other and then put their arms about each other.*

VIRGIE (*to Margie, who is giving the baby her bottle*). Ye've brought them two together, Margie, an' they been feudin' fifteen year.

IRMA (*wiping her eyes*). We all had a baptism of love. (*Briskly.*) Well, I reckin we'd better git out there an' spread dinner. The men an' chillun will be gittin' impatient.

RUBY (*entering*). Ever'body's ready to eat. Come on! (*Picks up her basket.*)

VIRGIE (*smiling*). Shouldn't ye ort to make John come git it an' lug out that basket for ye, Ruby?

RUBY (*laughing*). I'm a full-grown woman, now.

IRMA (*smiling*). Time ye was watchin' that hy-geranium bush, Ruby.

RUBY. Huh? Oh, that! Well, now, hit plum' slipped my mind. An' if hit's the same with the rest of ye, I'll jist let Ole Man Newman come git his bottle—undisturbed.

VIRGIE. Ye know, I feel so revived, I want to shout an' sing.

FLORINE. Ye do look happy, Virgie. I purt' nigh believe ye could git music out'n a round-note book.

VIRGIE. I could. No doubt 'bout it.

IRMA. At the prayer meetin' after dinner, we'll have a reg'lar ole-time 'sperience meetin'.

[*All start walking to the door as they talk. Margie hesitates.*

RUBY. Come on, Margie.

MARGIE. I reckin I better start on home. I never brought nothin' to eat, an'—

VIRGIE. Home, nothin'. Yore gonna eat with the rest of us an' I'm gonna hold the baby while ye eat.

ELLA. I was in hopes I'd git to hold the baby.

IRMA. I reckin we'll have to take turns.

[*Sound of auto horn blowing.*

RUBY. John's blowin' the horn fer us to hurry, I reckin.

VIRGIE (*as they go out*). Men folks mus' eat even come Jedgment Day.

RUBY. Ain't hit the truth!

[*They go out, Ella and Florine leading. The others follow. Virgie and Margie are last. As Margie hesitates, Virgie puts her arm around her. The two women, Margie holding her baby and smiling happily, are the last to leave the church.*

CURTAIN

DECEMBER SEVENTH

A Drama

BY DOROTHY CLIFFORD

THE CHARACTERS

JANET RANKIN, *an American resident of Honolulu.*
MERIKO, *her Japanese-American maid.*
JEAN RANKIN, *her six-year-old daughter.*
ELIZABETH, *her four-year-old daughter.*
BESS, *her close friend and next-door neighbor.*
BARBARA, *another friend and neighbor.*
MRS. STONE, *the air-raid warden.*

PLACE. Waikiki Beach, Honolulu, T. H.
TIME. Early morning. Sunday, December 7th, 1941.

JANET RANKIN'S *cottage at Waikiki has a very pretty, sunny breakfast room. There is an archway, left, which leads to living room and a door, right, which leads to kitchen. Downstage of R. door, is a long, narrow table on which stand a table radio and a telephone. There are children's toys scattered about the floor. Upstage center, are three large windows, prettily curtained, which look out on the trees in the backyard. The early morning Hawaiian sunshine streams in through these windows. A small, round table, partially set for breakfast, stands before the windows. There is a high chair drawn up to it and two other chairs. One or two wicker chairs, gayly cushioned, are scattered about.*

As the play opens, the stage is empty. Immediately are heard four or five dull explosions in the distance. Janet, a pretty woman of twenty-seven, enters hurriedly from archway. She is in housecoat and slippers. As she is halfway across the room, another dull explosion is heard. She stops and listens.

JANET (*calling*). Meriko!

MERIKO (*a Japanese girl of twenty, comes from kitchen. She, too, wears a housecoat. Her speech is thoroughly American. No accent*). Yes, Mrs. Rankin.

JANET. Did the noise wake you up? Those explosions, I mean.

MERIKO. I was awake already, but I got up to see what they were.

JANET. Did you see anything?

MERIKO. No. But I heard airplanes.

JANET. I'll call Mr. Rankin at the paper. He may know.

[*She goes to phone. Another dull explosion. Jean and Elizabeth enter. They go to Meriko when they see their mother at phone. Both are in pajamas and bare feet.*

MERIKO. Look who's up so early.

JEAN. What's the noise for, Meriko?

MERIKO. Did it wake you up, Jean?

JEAN. Uh-huh. 'Lizabeth heard it, too.

ELIZABETH. Boom. Boom.

MERIKO (*sitting and taking Elizabeth up on her lap*). You'd better have some slippers on your feet. You go get them, Jean.

[*Jean runs out through archway.*

JANET (*at phone*). Bob, this is Janet. What's happening? (*Listens at phone.*)

MERIKO (*playing with Elizabeth's toes*). This little pig went to market. This little pig. . . .

JANET (*at phone*). All right, I will. But let me know when you get back, won't you?

MERIKO. And this little pig went wee, wee, wee.

ELIZABETH. Wee, wee, wee.

JANET. Goodbye, darling. (*Hangs up, stands looking at phone a moment. Turns and sees Elizabeth.*) Elizabeth, you go find Jean.

[*The child slides off Meriko's lap and goes out through archway.*

MERIKO (*rises, looks at Janet with dread in her face*). Yes?

JANET. The trouble we expected has come, Meriko.

MERIKO. Oh, no, Mrs. Rankin, not—

JANET. Yes. Mr. Rankin said planes were bombing Pearl Harbor. He's going out to cover the story.

MERIKO (*holding her side as if in pain*). I don't want to think about it.

JANET. This is something that must be faced.

MERIKO. Are they coming this way?

JANET. Mr. Rankin didn't say anything more. He said to turn on the radio for special bulletins about what to do. (*Goes to radio and turns it on.*)

JEAN (*enters, followed by her sister. Both are wearing slippers*). 'Lizbeth put her own slippers on.

[*Elizabeth smiles proudly and sticks out a slippered foot.*

JANET. Sure. She's a big girl now. I think maybe you children should get dressed.

JEAN. So early?

JANET. Why not? As long as we are all awake we might as well stay up. Meriko, will you help them get dressed?

MERIKO. Certainly. Come on, kiddies.

[*They go out through archway.*

RADIO VOICE. Ladies and gentlemen, the sounds you have just heard are coming from the vicinity of Pearl Harbor. It is hard to tell accurately, but a large number of airplanes appear to be dropping bombs on the fortifications there.

JANET (*as if to herself*). It's here. This is the day.

RADIO VOICE. Keep tuned to KGU. Do not use the telephone. We will announce orders to civilian defense units. That is all.

BESS (*calling from outside*). Janet! Yoo-hoo!

JANET. In here, Bess. Come in.

BESS (*a young woman, enters from kitchen. She has on a light sports coat over her pajamas*). Did you hear? You know. . . ?

JANET. I called Bob at the paper.

BESS. Does he have any more news—other than what we know?

JANET. Not yet. He's on his way to Hickam Field.

BESS. Aren't you afraid for him?

JANET. No. It's his job to be where the news is.

RADIO VOICE. Attention, civilian defense workers! All air-raid wardens report for duty. First-aid units 11 to 21 report to posts immediately.

BESS. What will you do about the children when they call our first-aid unit?

JANET. Go, of course.

BESS. And leave them?

JANET. I knew that I'd have to go when I joined the unit.

BESS. But would you leave them with—(*Raises her eyebrows significantly in the direction of the archway.*)

JANET. Why, certainly. Meriko loves them as if they were her own.

BESS. But she's Japanese.

JANET. What of it?

BESS. Do you think it's safe to leave your children at a time like this with a Japanese maid?

JANET. Really, Bess, you don't mean you think Meriko would do anything to harm the children?

BESS. You can't tell what they might do, when their country is at war.

JANET. Bob said the planes hadn't been identified yet.

BESS. Have you *any* doubt?

JANET (*slowly*). No doubt at all.

BESS. Well, I know what I'd do if I had any children.

JANET (*sighs*). I faced all this when I started with the Red Cross.

BESS. You've always been sure in your own mind about things, Janet. I admire you for it even if I can't see it your way.

JANET. Why, Bess, you know Meriko has always been like one of the family.

BESS. I've been wondering lately how much we ought to trust any of these Japanese.

JANET. Why, she's lived with us all the time she was going

to the University. She was born on American soil. Her parents are American citizens. By birth, upbringing, and education, she is as much American as we are.

BESS. Well, we never know how much that means. Race ties might be stronger than country ties, you know.

JANET. Oh, nonsense, Bess. Don't let the war fever get you.

BESS. I'd think about it pretty seriously if I were you—before I'd go off and leave the children with her.

JANET. And I told you I have thought about it. (*More cheerfully.*) How about some coffee? Wouldn't you like a cup?

BESS. Oh no, thanks. I think I'll run across home and get some clothes on in case we're called out.

JANET. Well, if they do call us, stop by for me.

BESS. Okay, I'll do that. 'Bye, now.

JANET (*walking to kitchen door with her*). And get rid of those scarehead notions.

[*Bess motions Janet to be quiet as Meriko enters through archway with children. The children and Meriko are dressed. Meriko wears a fresh house dress. Bess noticeably draws back from Meriko.*

JEAN. Hello, Bess.

MERIKO. Good morning, Mrs. Keller.

[*Bess ignores her greeting. Meriko realizes the slight, but Janet doesn't seem to.*

BESS. Hello, Jean and Elizabeth. My, you're dressed bright and early.

JEAN. Yes, Meriko helped us.

BESS (*still ignoring Meriko*). And now you can have a good breakfast.

JANET. That's right, Will you start breakfast, Meriko?

MERIKO (*who has withdrawn behind a mask*). Yes, Mrs. Rankin. (*As she goes to the kitchen, she has to pass Bess, who obviously backs away from her.*)

BESS. I don't like your having her here.

JANET. Why, how silly. You know she's wonderful to have around. Look how she helped us with that British Aid tea at your house last week. We never could have swung it without her.

BESS. Well, if anything happens, don't say I didn't warn you. (*Goes to kitchen door.*)

JEAN. Where are you going, Bess?

BESS. Home, to get dressed myself.

JEAN. Then we can go to the beach?

JANET. Oh, I think we'll play here this morning.

BESS (*about to exit kitchen door, changes her mind*). I think I'll go out this way. (*Crosses to archway.*) See you later. (*Exits.*)

JANET. I have a new game for us to play.

JEAN. Oh, goodie, what is it?

JANET. I'll tell you. Cover your eyes, both of you, while I hide some things. (*They run to corner and stand holding their hands over their eyes. Janet is collecting some small objects.*) Then you can look for them. Whoever finds the most will get to hide them next. Are you eyes shut tight?

JEAN. Mine are, Mummy.

ELIZABETH. Yes, Mummy.

JANET (*hides several cubes of sugar from bowl on table, pencil from near phone, several of the smaller toys, etc.*). Now play fair. Keep your eyes shut until I tell you to start. Are you ready?

JEAN. Yes, Mummy.

ELIZABETH. Yes, Mummy.

JANET. All right. Begin!

[*Children start looking in breakfast room and adjoining living room.*

RADIO VOICE. Attention, civilians. Stay indoors. Do not use the telephone. You will be notified of further precautions by your air-raid wardens.

JEAN. I found it. I found it.

JANET. What? (*She has forgotten the game.*) Oh, what did you find?

JEAN. Your pencil.

ELIZABETH (*happily*). Pencil.

JANET. So you did. Now, Elizabeth, you must look hard to find something, too.

[*Knocking at outside door.*

MRS. STONE (*outside*). Mrs. Rankin, Mrs. Rankin. Are you awake?

JANET. Yes. (*Hurries through archway.*) Just a minute.

MRS. STONE (*off*). I'm Mrs. Stone. I'm air-raid warden for this section.

JANET (*off*). Come in, Mrs. Stone.

MRS. STONE (*enters with Janet. She is a capable, middle-aged woman*). Is Mr. Rankin here?

JANET. No, he works at night on the paper. He's not off yet.

MRS. STONE. In case the planes come this way, the sirens will sound at the fire station.

JANET. Should we stay indoors?

MRS. STONE (*shaking her head*). These cottages aren't very strong. We've been instructed to tell you to go out in the grove of trees in back of the house. (*Turns to leave.*)

JANET. Thank you. I have to leave shortly, but I'll tell Meriko before I go.

MRS. STONE (*stops, surprised*). You're leaving?

JANET. I expect my first-aid unit will be called.

MRS. STONE. Who will be in charge here? I'm supposed to speak to the person in authority in every home.

JANET. Oh, I see. (*Calls.*) Meriko!

MRS. STONE. Your maid?

JANET. Yes.

MRS. STONE. Is she reliable?

JANET. Oh yes. She's been with us for years.

MERIKO (*enters looking as though she expected to be hurt, but trying to cover it up*). Yes, Mrs. Rankin?

JANET. Meriko, this is Mrs. Stone, the air-raid warden. I told her you will be in charge here when I go with the Red Cross.

MRS. STONE. Surely, Mrs. Rankin, you're not thinking of leaving your children with a—a—(*She is embarrassed but feels that she must say it.*)—a—Japanese!

[*Meriko recoils as if struck. She sees her world crumbling about her.*

JANET (*gasps*). Why, Mrs. Stone! Meriko is as much American as you or I.

MRS. STONE. I don't like to hear you talk like that. Of course, it's none of my business, but I don't think it's the thing to do.

JANET (*gently but firmly*). I'm afraid you are presuming on your position, Mrs. Stone. Please give Meriko the instructions you have for her.

MRS. STONE (*sniffs*). Very well. (*Recites, not looking at Meriko.*) In case you hear the sirens blow at the fire station, take these children into the grove of trees in back of the house and all of you lie flat on your faces until the raid is over. Three short blasts will signal the "all clear." Do you understand? (*Looks at Meriko as though she were an enemy. Meriko says nothing, bows her head slowly and raises it.*) I must be going. I still have the rest of this block to cover. But I want to tell you, Mrs. Rankin, that I feel this is a case to be reported to the authorities. Good day. (*Goes out through archway.*)

JANET. Mrs. Stone! (*Hurries out after her.*)

[*Meriko stands there, stunned. She can hardly realize what is happening to her life.*

JEAN (*showing Meriko the things she has found*). Look, Meriko. We're playing treasure hunt.

MERIKO (*smiling at the child*). What a lot of treasures you have found.

JANET (*coming back into the room*). That woman got away before I could tell her what I think of her.

MERIKO (*finding it difficult to say*). Mrs. Rankin, I'm afraid for—for you.

JANET. For me?

MERIKO. Don't antagonize all those people on my account.

JANET. Oh, Meriko. (*Goes to her.*) Just because that woman has some fool notions and doesn't know when to keep her mouth shut—

MERIKO. It isn't just this Mrs. Stone. Even Mrs. Keller—

JANET. Bess! Why, how ridiculous! She just had a lot on her mind. Don't give it another thought. Isn't breakfast nearly ready?

MERIKO. Nearly. I'm just ready to make the toast.

JANET. Good. I'll get the children ready.

[*Meriko exits into kitchen.*

JEAN. Mummy, 'Lizbeth found more than I did but I've got more.

JANET. How is that, darling?

JEAN. 'Cause hers were sugar an' she ate 'em.

JANET (*smiling at Elizabeth*). Oh, Elizabeth, did you eat your treasures? (*The child nods, her mouth full.*) You two go wash your hands because breakfast will soon be ready.

[*They put down their treasures and exit through archway.*

RADIO VOICE. Attention, civilian defense workers! First-aid units 1 to 10 report for duty. Units 1 to 10 report immediately.

JANET (*calls.*) Meriko! (*Hurries toward kitchen.*)

MERIKO (*in doorway*). Yes?

JANET. My first-aid unit has just been called.

MERIKO. What about your breakfast?

JANET. You can pour out a cup of coffee for me while I'm getting into my uniform.

JEAN (*calling from offstage*). Barbara's here, Mummy.

JANET (*calling*). Come on in, Barbara.

BARBARA (*a young woman of Janet's age, enters in her Red Cross uniform*). I simply couldn't stand it to stay home alone, so I thought I'd wait over here until they called us.

JANET. The order just came over the radio.

[*Meriko, who has been waiting to see if Barbara will notice her as she usually does, now sees that Barbara is ignoring her. She returns to kitchen.*

BARBARA. What are you going to do about the children?

JANET. They'll be as safe here as any place. That is, until we know whether they decide to evacuate us.

BARBARA. Oh, Janet, why didn't you go home last year?

JANET. This is my home. I have no relatives back in the States, unless you want to count Bob's parents.

BARBARA. But you could have gone to them.

JANET. I wouldn't leave Bob here. As long as he has to stay, the children and I will share his risks.

BARBARA. But don't you think *now* that your duty is to your children—to stay with them? Wouldn't Bob expect you to look after them first?

JANET. Meriko can look after them all right. There are injured people for me to look after.

BARBARA. That may be, but I think I'd stay with them. There are lots of first-aid workers.

JANET. But suppose all of them took that attitude? Where would our defenses be?

BARBARA. What if the evacuation order is given while you are away?

JANET. Then Meriko can take them to the hills. She has looked after them ever since Jean was two years old.

BARBARA. Well, they're your children, Janet. Why should I tell you what to do? Just the same. . . .

JANET. Don't say any more, Barbara. They are my children. I must do what I think is best for all of us.

RADIO VOICE. Attention, citizens of Oahu. Evacuation plans are being completed to remove all women and children from danger zones as soon as the first raids have stopped. Everyone should begin preparing for evacuation. That is all.

BARBARA. Oh, Janet, you can't go off and leave them with that Jap girl. I know you think a lot of her. But your children—

JEAN (*entering with her sister*). We washed our hands all by ourselves.

JANET. Jean, I'm going away for a little while this morning. You and Elizabeth are to do whatever Meriko tells you.

JEAN. Where're you going?

JANET. To the Red Cross.

JEAN. In the morning? But you never go till afternoon.

JANET. This is special, today. Now go out and tell Meriko to give you your breakfast in the kitchen.

JEAN. All right. Come on, 'Lizbeth.

[*Hand in hand, they go out to the kitchen.*

JANET. I'll get into my uniform. I'll be ready in a moment. (*Goes out through archway.*)

MERIKO (*entering from kitchen door*). Mrs. Rankin. . . . Oh, good morning. (*Waits, sees Barbara isn't going to speak to her. Draws into herself.*) I beg your pardon. I thought Mrs. Rankin was here. (*Takes high chair from table and carries it into the kitchen.*)

BARBARA (*coldly, as Meriko goes*). She's gone to dress.

MERIKO. Thank you. (*Exits.*)

BESS (*comes through archway in uniform*). Come on, Janet. Let's go. (*Sees Barbara.*) Oh, hello, Barbara. Is Janet ready?

BARBARA. Hi, Bess. She's getting ready.

BESS. What do you think about her going off and leaving the children?

BARBARA. I've just been telling her I don't think it's right.

BESS. Especially leaving them with that. . . .

BARBARA. Yes, she's Japanese, you know. Even though she doesn't act like one.

BESS. Janet refused to recognize the danger of it when I talked to her.

BARBARA. It isn't that she doesn't know all about it. It's just that Janet has always had high ideals about serving her country.

BESS. You know how she was when she first came—doing volunteer social service work.

BARBARA. Yes, and there was that business girls' club she organized at the Y. W. She went on with that after Jean was born.

BESS. She's never stopped doing things and in a lot of ways I admire her for it.

BARBARA. You've got to hand it to her. She hasn't let herself become tied down at home.

BESS. That's one reason she's such an interesting friend.

BARBARA. Bess, all these things are fine in peace-time, but this is different.

BESS. I know it. It's swell to have a community spirit in ordinary times, but how do we know what will happen now?

JANET (*enters slowly. She wears a summery dress and carries her uniform over her arm*). You girls go on.

BESS. You're not coming with us?

BARBARA. You're. . . .

JANET. Not now. Maybe later. (*Hangs uniform over chair.*)

BESS. You're smart to look after the children first.

JANET. I don't know. . . .
BESS. Come on, Barbara. Let's be off.
BARBARA. Keep an eye on my house, Janet, if anything happens.
BESS. Mine, too. 'Bye, Janet.
JANET. Good luck, gals.

[*They go. Janet sits down thoughtfully at the breakfast table.*

MERIKO (*entering*). There's something I want to say to you, Mrs. Rankin, before you go.
JANET (*trying to stop her*). But, Meriko. . . .
MERIKO (*intent on her own thoughts*). I just wanted you to know how much I appreciate your faith in me, to leave the children with me. I mean, at a time like this.
JANET. Why I'm. . . . not go—
MERIKO. I'm just as loyal an American as you are, Mrs. Rankin. I was born on American soil and educated in the American way. There are thousands of loyal Americans on these islands, who, while they may look like our enemies, have the interests of America at heart and hate everything that the people of Japan do. These loyal Americans should not be discriminated against.
JANET. I know that you. . . .
MERIKO (*sighs*). Yes, it's going to be hard on some of us Americans right now, on account of our race. We feel the same as you but we can't change our outside appearance. That's why it means so much to me . . . to have you accept my loyalty without question.
JANET (*feeling her faith in the girl returning*). It is hard to know what to do at a time like this. After my friends spoke to me this morning. . . .
MERIKO (*quietly*). You always know what's right to do.
JANET. Thank you, Meriko. (*Rising to her feet with decision.*) I've always trusted you but it helps to hear you say that now. (*Putting her hand on the girl's shoulder.*) I'm the one who's lucky . . . to have someone like you to leave the children with.
MERIKO (*with deep feeling*). Thank you, Mrs. Rankin.
JEAN (*calling from the kitchen*). Meriko.

ELIZABETH (*the same*). 'Riko.

MERIKO (*happily*). Coming, darling. (*She runs out as the radio comes on.*)

RADIO VOICE. Ladies and gentlemen, KGU, the *Honolulu Advertiser,* brings you an eye-witness account of the bombing of this island. Bob Rankin of the *Advertiser* staff has just returned from Hickam Field. (*Janet runs over and hangs breathlessly over the radio.*) Come in, Bob.

BOB (*over the radio*). Thank you, Joe. Military restrictions prevent me from telling you in detail what I have been able to see. But I want to urge the people of Oahu to be strong and brave. Stick to your posts. There is urgent need for civilian defense units and first-aid workers to respond whole-heartedly. (*Janet crosses to chair and picks up her uniform. She holds it over her arm and smooths it.*) This is the time to protect your homes by protecting your country. The Army and Navy are helping you. Show them your appreciation. Report to your posts. . . .

JANET (*in a whisper*). Yes, Bob.

BOB (*over radio*). . . . And stay there until the work is done.

JANET. Yes, Bob. I'm on my way.

[*She starts to run out of the room through archway, the uniform over her arm, and starts to unbutton the top button of her dress, as. . . .*

QUICK CURTAIN

ANGEL OF MERCY

A Biographical Play

BY I. DYER KUENSTLER

CHARACTERS

CLARA BARTON, *angel of mercy.*
AUNT ROSE, *her old friend.*
GRANNY MARTIN, *in charge of supplies.*
AMY MARTIN, *her granddaughter.*
MARTHA, *a charwoman.*
MRS. HAMILTON, *a wealthy and influential lady.*

PLACE. Worcester, Massachusetts.
TIME. During the Civil War.

CLARA BARTON *has taken over an empty warehouse as temporary headquarters. A crude table is used as a desk. It has a straight chair behind it. There are other chairs and a bench about the room. The entire right wall has wooden boxes of supplies stacked against it. The boxes are of varying sizes. On other tables and on the floor, stand bundles of sheets, blankets, clothing and baskets of food. The windows are high, narrow and dusty. The door at left leads to the street. A door at right, with packing boxes piled on either side, leads to the workshop where women are making bandages and other articles needed for the wounded.*

As the play opens, Granny Martin is emptying a basket of preserves. She is a little, white-haired lady, becomingly dressed in a dark blue gown of the period. There is a knock on door left.

GRANNY (*not stopping her work*). Come in.

AMY (*enters left*). Granny! (*She is a pretty girl of twenty. She wears a pink dress of the period and carries a beribboned picture hat. She seems worried.*)

GRANNY (*looking up*). Amy, my dear.

AMY. Oh, Granny, is there any news?

GRANNY. Not yet, dear.

AMY. I'm so worried about Walter. (*Paces agitatedly.*)

GRANNY. Now, now, don't worry. Miss Barton has gone down to the docks to meet the wounded soldiers when the transports come in. She promised to inquire about Walter right away.

AMY. But she has so much to do. She may forget.

GRANNY (*slowly*). Miss Barton never forgets.

AMY (*impatiently*). When do you expect her back?

GRANNY. There's no telling. (*Holds up a glass of jelly.*) Isn't the color pretty?

AMY (*impatiently*). Yes, yes. Granny, she's been gone for hours.

GRANNY. There is much to be done.

AMY (*not listening*). There must be lots more wounded men this time. They say it was one of the bloodiest battles of the war.

GRANNY. Try to put your mind on something else, dear.

AMY. I can't. I can't.

GRANNY. Think of Miss Barton—all the work she does.

AMY. I do and it makes me ill. (*Going to Granny.*) Granny, they say she washes their wounds—herself.

GRANNY. Why, yes, she does. She does everything she can to make those poor boys more comfortable.

AMY (*shudders*). *I* couldn't. The very thought of looking at a wound makes me sick.

GRANNY. I don't believe the soldiers like their wounds any more than you do. But someone has to tend to them.

AMY. But a lady like Miss Barton. . . .

GRANNY (*stopping her work*). Clara Barton's heart is full of nothing but compassion for those poor men. By the time they are brought here from the battlefields, some of them are too far gone to help. Miss Barton is trying to get permission to work right on the field of battle. Then there won't be so much time lost. Many more lives may be saved.

AMY. A lady on the battlefield? They'll never give her permission. Besides, she might get killed.

GRANNY. Miss Barton never thinks about herself. She hasn't time. (*Resumes unpacking.*)

AMY (*sitting on a packing case*). Granny, do you know what day this is?

GRANNY. Tuesday, isn't it?

AMY. Today was to have been my wedding day.

GRANNY (*looks at her pityingly*). I had forgotten. One doesn't think about weddings these days.

AMY. And now Walter—

GRANNY. Walter is a very brave young man. You should be so proud of him for volunteering.

AMY. I am. I am. In fact, I insisted that he go. It seemed kind of glorious then. But now I've changed my mind. I think war is horrible. There's nothing glorious about it.

GRANNY. You would not love him if he shirked his duty.

AMY. Granny?

GRANNY. Yes, dear.

AMY (*going to her and speaking with a catch in her voice*). Granny, suppose he is— What will I do if he doesn't come back?

GRANNY. Now, now, that's no way for a brave girl to talk.

AMY. But I'm not brave, Granny. I'm terrified all the time. Sometimes I dream I see him lying wounded on the field —dying—and no one near to comfort him. Then I cry in my sleep.

GRANNY (*pityingly*). Poor Amy!

AMY (*hysterically*). Thousands of men are being killed every day.

GRANNY. And thousands live to fight on the morrow.

AMY. Walter won't be killed, will he, Granny? God won't let him be killed, will He? Tell me He won't!

GRANNY (*putting her arm around her*). Don't talk like that, child! It won't help you—or Walter.

AMY (*clinging to her and sobbing*). I can't help it. I can't help it. If he doesn't come back, I want to die too.

GRANNY. I had three sons in this war. Two of them will never come back. (*Sighs heartbrokenly.*) I try to forget by helping the sons of other mothers. (*Gently, as she pats Amy on shoulder.*) And you would try to carry on in the same way.

AMY (*sobbing quietly*). But I love him so. I love him so.

GRANNY (*quietly*). I loved my sons.

AMY (*consoling her*). I know, dear. Forgive me. (*She draws away from her and paces nervously.*) But I can't help it. I'm crazy with worry. All this waiting—waiting—day after day, week after week, and no word from him. Oh, I hate war and the suffering that it brings. (*Goes back to Granny.*) I want to be happy—to look at beautiful things—to have gay friends around me. That isn't wrong, is it, Granny?

GRANNY. It's natural to want to be happy. (*Sighs.*) Busy people are the happiest people these days. (*Handing her a pencil.*) Suppose you check over these supplies that just came in? It'll keep your mind from worrying.

AMY. Yes, Granny. (*Listlessly takes her grandmother's place at the table.*)

GRANNY. I want to see how the women are getting on with the bandages in the other room. (*Starts for right door. There is an imperative knock on left door. Granny turns and goes to left door.*) I'll see who that is. (*Opens it.*)

MRS. HAMILTON (*enters*). Your pardon. Miss Barton advertised in the *Worcester Spy* for supplies for the wounded soldiers. Is this *warehouse* her headquarters?

[*Mrs. Hamilton is an aristocratic lady with an arrogant and condescending manner. She wears a fashionable gown and bonnet. She carries a basket of food with a few apples on the top. She looks around haughtily, as thought she had expected to find a better place. Amy stares at her curiously.*

GRANNY. Yes, madam. For the present.

MRS. HAMILTON (*condescendingly*). I'm Mrs. George Hamilton. (*Places basket on table.*) I have brought some preserves and some fresh fruit.

GRANNY. Thank you, Mrs. Hamilton. We have very little fresh fruit.

MRS. HAMILTON. I surmised as much. Kindly tell me what you are most in need of.

GRANNY. We need old sheets for bandages—blankets, shirts, socks and any cast-off clothing.

MRS. HAMILTON. I presume Miss Barton could use a gift of money?

GRANNY. Oh yes, indeed.

MRS. HAMILTON. I will mail her a cheque immediately. (*As she crosses to left door.*) And I'll look over my linens. If there are any worn sheets, I'll send them to you. Good afternoon. (*Bows condescendingly.*)

GRANNY. Good afternoon, and thank you, Mrs. Hamilton. (*Mrs. Hamilton exits left. Granny smiles as she lifts an apple from the backet.*) What nice rosy apples. (*Puts it back.*) Check this basket, too, Amy. (*Exiting right.*) Call me if you need me.

AMY. I will, Granny (*Amy starts counting apples. She isn't much interested in the work. She makes mistakes and has to start over. There is a knock at left door. Amy looks inquiringly at right door, then towards left door and finally calls.*) Come in.

MARTHA (*entering timidly*). Please, Miss— I wonder if I've come to the right place. Is this Miss Barton's headquarters? (*She is middle-aged and tired-looking. She is shabby and there is a ragged shawl around her shoulders.*)

AMY. Why, yes. Supplies are received here and women make bandages and do other work out there in that room. (*Nods to right.*)

MARTHA. I haven't anything to give to Miss Barton, but I heard that she needed helpers.

AMY. I believe that she does. But you'll have to speak to my grandmother, Mrs. Martin. She's in charge. Please sit down. I'll go get her. (*Martha sits on packing box. Amy goes off right.*)

[*There is a knock on left door. Martha looks around but does not get up. The knock is repeated. Then the door is opened and Aunt Rose comes in. She is a pleasant, buxom woman, fond of bright colors. She wears a full skirt of bright red and a bright blue blouse. She carries a large market basket on one arm and her other arm holds a large bundle of sheets. She pants as she staggers in under her load.*

AUNT ROSE. Hello, there! (*Looks around.*) What, nobody here?

MARTHA. Er—the young lady went to call someone.

AUNT ROSE. I'll wait. (*Sets her bundles down.*) Whew! I reckon I ought to get thin after that. (*Sits on nearest packing box but jumps up as it creaks ominously.*) That will never hold me up. (*Tries out another box gingerly. It is satisfactory. She sits down. Fans herself with her handkerchief.*) Gracious! That was hot work. I suppose you have some relatives at the front? (*Sociably.*) Everyone has, you know.

MARTHA. Yes, ma'am. Both my boys are fighting. I kind o' wish George hadn't gone. He's just turned seventeen.

AUNT ROSE (*kindly*). Why, he's just a baby. Have you heard from them lately?

MARTHA. Not since their cousin was sent back here wounded. He said my boys was all right then.

[*Amy and Granny come in. Amy goes back to checking. Granny greets Rose.*

GRANNY (*pleased*). Why, Rose! How are you?

ROSE. Good and warm. (*Looks at Granny.*) My, you're looking fine. (*Lugs basket up on table and takes out a large jar of preserves.*) I brought six crab-apple and some apple butter, cheese, flour and a few other things.

GRANNY (*looking into basket*). That's wonderful!

ROSE (*poking into other basket*). Who brought all this? Gracious! Fresh fruit is *so* scarce.

GRANNY. A Mrs. Hamilton.

ROSE. Not *the* Mrs. George Hamilton that leads the society here! Well! (*Sits on wrong box, jumps up.*) My gracious! (*Looks for stronger box.*)

GRANNY (*to Martha*). You wished to see me?

MARTHA. Yes, ma'am. I'm Martha Reed. I'm a widow and I ain't got nothin' to give Miss Barton, but I'd like to help some way.

GRANNY. We need workers.

MARTHA. I'll do anything, ma'am.

GRANNY. We need help down at the docks. Can you stand the sight of wounded men? Some of the men are in a terrible condition by the time they get here.

MARTHA. I know. And I'd like to help them poor soldiers.

GRANNY. If you'll wait until Miss Barton gets here, I know she'll be glad to tell you what to do.

MARTHA. I'll wait. (*Sits down again.*)

ROSE. Where *is* Clara?

GRANNY. Down at the docks.

ROSE. I declare, Clara used to be so sensitive and retiring. It beats me how she got used to so much suffering.

GRANNY. Then you knew her when she was a girl?

ROSE. Gracious, yes. My nephew Stewart used to play with her. She called me Aunt Rose, too. She was a queer child, afraid of everything. I guess she's changed, now.

AMY. Listen! I thought I heard Miss Barton. (*All listen.*)

CLARA BARTON (*off left*).Thank you. We can never have too many supplies.

[*Clara Barton enters carrying a bundle which she sets on the table. She pulls off her bonnet. She is a vivid, dark-haired woman. She wears her hair parted in the middle and coiled becomingly at the nape of her neck. Her dress is plain but in good taste. Her expressive eyes sweep about the room. Her voice is rich and low, she speaks slowly but with decision.*

AMY (*going to her impulsively*). Oh, Miss Barton, is there any. . . . (*Granny silences her with a gesture.*)

CLARA BARTON. Why, Aunt Rose! I am glad to see you. (*Holds out her two hands.*)

ROSE (*taking them*). How are you, Clara?

CLARA BARTON. I've been thinking of you. In fact, I've been talking to your nephew. He is *Sergeant* J. Stewart Brown now. Did you know?

ROSE. Yes. But if you saw him, he must have come on the transport. That means—he's wounded. (*Clara Barton nods.*) Oh, how *is* he, Clara?

CLARA BARTON. Now, now, it's nothing serious. He will recover.

ROSE. I'm so glad. Stewart has been like a son to me.

CLARA BARTON. Yes, I remember. Oh, it was so good to talk to him again. (*Her voice serious.*) I saw two sons of people I used to know. Poor fellows. Both are fatally wounded, I fear.

GRANNY. Miss Barton. (*Signs to Martha.*) Mrs. Reed has been waiting to see you.

[*While Clara Barton talks to Martha, there is a knock on door left. Granny admits Mrs. Hamilton, who has returned with a bundle of sheets. Granny takes bundle from her, pantomiming that she must be quiet until Miss Barton finishes talking. Mrs. Hamilton first waits impatiently, then becomes increasingly interested in the conversation.*

CLARA BARTON. I'm so sorry you had to wait.

MARTHA (*respectfully*). If you please, Miss Barton, I'd like to help down at the docks, if you'll let me.

CLARA BARTON. We need help there badly, but I'm afraid—the work is very strenuous and—(*Sighs.*)—heart-breaking. There are sights that will twist your heart. Men who. . . .

AMY (*coming forward*). Are the men so horribly disfigured, Miss Barton?

CLARA BARTON. Why, yes, some of them are. But I wasn't referring to that.

AMY. You mean then. . . . (*She whispers.*) That they suffer so?

CLARA BARTON. Unbearably. It is unbelievable how much they do suffer. No, you can't believe it until you work among them. Nothing—absolutely nothing is done for the men as they lie wounded on the battlefield. They bleed and suffer until the stretcher-bearers get to them. Then they are brought here. Often it is too late. Their wounds . . . the tedious journey. . . .

AMY (*shuddering*). No. No! You can't mean that they bleed to death.

CLARA BARTON. Some do, on the battlefield. Then death comes as a merciful release. You see, child, if a soldier is too far gone, they leave him to die where he has fallen. There is no room on the transports excepting for those who stand a chance of survival.

AMY. How terrible!

CLARA BARTON. Yes, and many a poor fellow dies on the journey, too. Those that reach here . . . how they survive, that is one of God's miracles. I've seen them with their wounds covered with blood and mud dried and baked on as hard as a turtle's shell.Their screams of agony when they are touched are almost inhuman.

AMY (*putting her hands over her ears and backing away*). No! No!

MRS. HAMILTON (*stepping forward*). That's horrible! Such neglect should not be permitted.

CLARA BARTON. The neglect is not intentional. Nevertheless, needless death and unspeakable suffering will continue unless relief can be given directly to the wounded men where they have fallen on the field of battle.

MRS. HAMILTON. I had not thought things were like that. (*Sits in chair and thinks.*)

AMY (*frantically*). Miss Barton, Miss Barton, I've got to know. I've just got to know. *Is* there any news of Walter?

CLARA BARTON (*looks at her a long minute before answering*). Yes, Amy.

AMY (*grabbing her arm*). Is he wounded? Did he come on the transports? (*Rushing to door left.*) Oh, I must go to him.

CLARA BARTON (*compassionately but firmly*). Amy! (*Amy stops and waits without turning around.*) He was shot as he assisted a wounded comrade to safety.

AMY. Then he *is* here. (*Going to Miss Barton.*) Tell me what I must do. I'll do anything . . . anything to help him.

CLARA BARTON (*gently*). He doesn't need help now, dear.

AMY (*backing away from her, her hand to her mouth*). No! No! He's not dead! He's not dead, I tell you. No!

CLARA BARTON (*sorrowfully*). My poor child.

[*Amy places her hand to her mouth to stifle a scream. Granny goes to her but Amy turns from her and throws herself on a bundle of blankets in a dark corner. All regard her compassionately. Granny tries to comfort her, but she pushes her away. Later, Rose sits beside her and by degrees draws her head into her lap.*

MARTHA (*coming forward*). Please, ma'am, I've two boys . . . and I thought maybe you could tell me. . . .

CLARA BARTON (*taking a long list from her pocket*). What are their names?

MARTHA. Tom and George Reed of the 15th Massachusetts.

CLARA BARTON (*runs her finger down the list. Stops suddenly when she comes to a name. Folds list slowly, looks at Martha*). Mrs. Reed, I wish there were some way of putting words together to. . . .

MARTHA (*quietly*). You mean they're dead. (*Clara Barton lowers her head.*) Both of them?

CLARA BARTON (*her arm about her shoulder*). Oh, I wish I had better news for you. Your son, Tom, is among the missing. He may be alive. I sincerely hope so. But George died . . . very bravely.

MARTHA (*sobbing quietly, her back turned*). Not Georgie, my baby. He was only just seventeen.

[*Clara Barton holds in her arms the bent figure wracked with sobs.*

MRS. HAMILTON (*hesitates, then comes to them. Clara Barton smiles her slow, sweet smile at her, relinquishes Martha and indicates that Mrs. Hamilton take over. Mrs. Hamilton touches her arm awkwardly*). My good woman, we are proud of your sons. They fought and died for their country. Such men are heroes. Is that not so, Miss Barton?

CLARA BARTON. Yes, madam. That is true. They are called heroes. But that thought brings little comfort to the broken hearts of wives and mothers. (*Looks at Amy.*) And sweethearts. (*There is quiet for a while, broken only by the quiet sobbing of Amy and Martha.*) Ah, yes, no matter how righteous the cause, war is always cruel. It crushes the fair forms of our most promising men—the young men, the strong men. It costs millions of times more, in anguish and suffering, than the whole world is worth.

MRS. HAMILTON. We are at war, Miss Barton, and you use strong words.

CLARA BARTON (*quietly*). No. You see, I've been in the midst of it. Other people hear the fine speeches, the eulogies over the heroic dead. I do not hear. Because I have seen the blood, the tears, the broken bodies, the horrors.

ROSE. Yes, if anybody has seen those things, Clara has.

CLARA BARTON. In times like these, we must fight for our country and our convictions. We know what is right and we are fighting for the right. That must be. On the other hand, we must not blind ourselves to the horrors of war. Only by facing these things squarely can we help and prevent needless loss of life.

MRS. HAMILTON. How can we, as women, do more than we are doing?

CLARA BARTON. Somehow, we must get to the front lines, reach the men soon after they are wounded . . . when quick help might be the means of saving lives.

MRS. HAMILTON. We? (*She is amazed.*) You refer to yourself, Miss Barton? (*Clara nods.*) Surely, you, a frail woman, would not venture on the battlefields?

CLARA BARTON. I have worked and worked to bring that about. And now it seems that at last. . . .

MRS. HAMILTON. Aren't you afraid? You might be killed.

CLARA BARTON. I have seen death in too many forms ever to fear it.

MRS. HAMILTON. But the horrible, bloody sights. . . . (*She shudders.*)

CLARA BARTON. Those, too, I am accustomed to seeing.

MRS. HAMILTON. But, Miss Barton, the soldiers . . . while we honor them and all. . . . (*She seems embarrassed.*) I mean that army life is rough. A woman alone . . . unprotected. . . .

CLARA BARTON (*quietly*). I have no fears. I know soldiers. Some are rough, as you say, and many are profane. But all were sweet young boys once, and underneath the dirt and mud and the profanity, there is always this little-boy sweetness.

MRS. HAMILTON. I'm sure society wouldn't sanction it.

CLARA BARTON. Then society is too silly even to be considered in this thing.

ROSE (*leaves Amy and comes to Clara. Amy stirs, sits up and starts to take an interest*). But, Clara, while your heart and spirit are willing, your body is frail. You couldn't stand the stench . . . the crude way of living. Your health will break down under exposure.

CLARA BARTON. I have considered all these things. Strength will be given me.

ROSE. You speak as though everything was settled. Are you really making plans to go?

CLARA BARTON. My plans are all made. I have been promised a mule-team to carry my supplies to the front lines.

MRS. HAMILTON (*horrified*). No! A lady like you. . . .

CLARA BARTON (*quietly*). I am needed on the battlefields.

MRS. HAMILTON (*smiling*). I am concerned needlessly. Of course they will never give you passports.

CLARA BARTON. So I feared at one time. I met with blank refusal everywhere. But at last General Rucker has seen things my way. I may now hope for success.

GRANNY (*pleased*). Oh, that's wonderful, Clara! I know how much that means to you.

MRS. HAMILTON. That's all very well, Miss Barton. If you wish to sacrifice only *yourself,* that is your affair. But you cannot do the work alone. You must need help. Do you have the right to ask other women to go into danger? You have a high purpose. It will see you through. But ordinary women. . . .

CLARA BARTON. Women have courage that is not dreamed of. They have given their sons and husbands and sweethearts. They have sacrificed to give clothing and supplies. They will not hesitate to sacrifice themselves if need be. I shall recruit an army of . . . soldiers of mercy.

GRANNY. I want to go with you, Clara. But I'm afraid I'm too old.

CLARA BARTON. Grandma Martin, your place is here. I'll need you here to keep the flow of supplies moving from here to the battle front. In fact, I'll need you even more than I do now. You will be my right hand at home.

MRS. HAMILTON (*thoughtfully*). You are a brave woman, Miss Barton. I have been waited on hand and foot all my life. I'd be worse than useless . . . as . . . as . . . a soldier of mercy. (*She smiles.*) But I know I could induce my friends to help you financially. I myself will give all that I am able.

AMY (*coming forward*). Miss Barton, if you will take me, I . . . I want to be the first soldier in your army of mercy.

CLARA BARTON. Hadn't you better think it over first, Amy?

AMY. I have made up my mind.

GRANNY. Now, child, you're upset, hearing about Walter and . . . why don't you sleep on it?

AMY. It is because of Walter that I want to go. I think of him dying alone, where he fell . . . his wounds. . . . (*She starts to weep but controls herself.*) If I only knew that there had been some kind woman there, to comfort him in his last moments—to take messages for his loved ones—I could stand my grief better. I want to do for other poor men what I wish someone had done for him.

CLARA BARTON. Poor Walter! If he had received immediate help, he might not have died.

AMY (*quietly*). I thought of that, too. That's why I want to go.

[*Clara Barton takes her hand.*

MARTHA (*coming forward and speaking brokenly*). I'll go with you too, ma'am. (*Wipes her eyes on a corner of her shawl.*)

CLARA BARTON. Mothers all over the country will bless you, Mrs. Reed.

ROSE (*chuckles*). You used to be such a fraid-cat, Clara. But if you can stand it—(*Sighs.*)—I reckon I can.

CLARA BARTON (*with a beaming smile*). I counted on you right from the beginning, Aunt Rose.

ROSE. Huh? (*Confused.*) What? You mean I've talked myself into going? Good gracious!

[*Rose sits down heavily on nearest box. This time it breaks down. Granny laughs, Amy, Clara Barton and Mrs. Hamilton smile. Even Martha smiles tremulously. Clara and Amy help her to her feet.*

CLARA (*still smiling*). I have my first army. The supply lines —(*Goes to Granny and kisses her on the cheek.*)—without which there is no army. The finances. (*Holds out her hand to Mrs. Hamilton, who takes it and suddenly leans forward and kisses Clara on the cheek.*) The mother of soldiers. (*Puts both hands on Martha's shoulders.*) And the symbol of the sweetheart they left behind. (*Kisses Amy's forehead.*)

ROSE. And me. (*Ruefully rubs her elbow where she skinned it in falling.*)

CLARA BARTON. And Aunt Rose, who symbolizes the kind friend of the soldier. (*Rose takes her in her arms and hugs her.*)

[*Clara Barton steps forward, facing audience. She spreads out her arms in the pose made famous by the Red Cross nurse on the posters.*

CLARA BARTON. At last my great dream is becoming a reality. We have made a start. Now our work of relieving the suffering has begun in earnest. And please, God, may it not end when the war ends. My army is gathering; a great army that will grow and grow and gather as it marches down through the years. We will be mighty in our millions. Our banner will be the red cross of courage on the white field of mercy—our uniform, the garb of our profession. (*Her voice becomes low and deep with feeling.*) I see our army marching down through the generations. (*Slowly.*) And when the Angel of Death walks among men, an Angel of Mercy will walk before him to soften the dread of his coming.

MARTHA (*takes her hand and kneels at her side, looking up into her face. She says simply.*) Clara Barton, you are a good woman.

[*Martha kisses Clara Barton's hand reverently as . . .*

CURTAIN

GIRLS *MUST* TALK

A Comedy

BY PAUL T. GANTT

THE GIRLS

MISS DEEDEE, *a window-dresser.*
MISS MARIE, *her assistant.*
GERTIE, *who has seen darker days.*
RUTH, *who has seen better days.*
BETTY, *a good girl, in trouble.*
ANNIE, *just an old girl.*

PLACE. New York City.
TIME. A morning in spring.

THE LADIES DRESSE SHOPPE *has a very nice front window filled with some very pretty dummies. The "window" is a slightly raised platform running the width of the stage. The opening has a frame; the effect of the stage is a large framed picture—without glass, of course. A dark curtain extends across the whole back of the stage. There is an opening between the curtains over at left. There is no furniture. The window faces the street which is the audience.*

As the play opens, there is a length of three-foot-wide cloth extended across the platform at bottom. This is the cloth that covers the window, presumably, when the window is being dressed. There are four pretty mannequins or dummies on the stage. Their makeup is identical; bright pink base, rose-red rouge, cupid-bow mouths and arched black eyebrows. (If modish wigs of blond, auburn, etc. hair can be obtained, it will add to the effectiveness of the mannequins. Otherwise, let their hair be curled and waved in the latest beauty shop style.) Their arms and legs are rigidly still. When they talk to each other, they roll their eyes in the direction of the person addressed. When the window-dressers are about, the mannequins talk to each other staring straight ahead. It is extremely important that neither Miss Deedee nor Miss Marie should react in any visible way to the talk of the mannequins. The mannequins wear very good-looking outfits of the season's most extreme styles. Miss Deedee and Miss Marie are putting the finishing touches on the dummies. The dressers wear plain black dresses.

MISS DEEDEE (*taking a purse off Annie's rigidly extended forearm*). I think this is going to be all right, Miss Marie. (*Turns Annie's arm down and steps off to survey models.*) Too much is—well—too much, if you know what I mean.

MISS MARIE (*eager to agree with her superior*). That's right. Too much *is* too much.

MISS DEEDEE (*surprised*). But that's what I just said. (*Goes to left.*) Well—I'll be back in a few minutes for a last look, so you hurry and put on the finishing touches.

MISS MARIE. Yes, Miss Deedee. (*Deedee leaves. Marie checks over the dummies, straightening a fold here, turning a foot there, tilting a head here and straightening a stocking seam on the last one. She talks to them as she goes from one to the other.*) You girls don't know how lucky you are with nothing to do all day long but stand in this window and be admired. (*Dummies stare blankly ahead.*) Everybody calls you dummies, but you aren't, really. Not to me, anyway. (*Wistfully.*) I often wish you could talk to me. I like to think of each of you as having a name and a personality. (*She looks them over as a group, then starts working on them, beginning at right. She yanks Ruth's skirt around to get the kick pleat in center.*) Ruth—(*Yanks*)—you're a lady. (*Kneels and makes Betty's foot point out more.*) You're nervous, Betty. (*Goes to Annie and tilts her head.*) Annie! You're the careless one. You don't seem to care.

(*Goes to Gertie and straightens her stocking seam.*) I know your seams don't show from the street, Gertie, but I had better fix this one. You've got a queer look in your eyes, Gertie. I can't make you out. (*Backs off and looks at them.*) There! (*Goes downstage, right.*) Now, I guess I'd better take this curtain off. (*Hums a tune as she detaches it, folding it as she walks along. She goes off left.*)

GERTIE. So today I look queer and she calls me Gertie. Huh! Last week she called me Pocahontas.

BETTY. Don't be downhearted, Gert. That queer look comes from the way the sun shines on you. I'm supposed to be *nervous.*

RUTH. Girls! Please! Don't let that silly Miss Marie affect you. Remember, we have another day during which we must be ready to do our best.

ANNIE. Too bad she can't hear us, Ruthie. I'd give her another name for *you.* (*Sighs.*) Oh, well! Another day, another deed!

BETTY. I wish I *could* feel ready for the day, but I just *know* something is wrong with me. I can't see why that girl never gets these things hung straight on me.

RUTH. I'm sure you will be all right, Betty. Just relax and you will do a good job.

GERTIE. Good heavens, you girls act as if you were on the payroll—along with Miss Marie and Miss Deedee.

BETTY. Aren't they lucky that we're not on their payroll! The things *I* know about this place! They would pay me plenty.

ANNIE. What gives me a big laugh is that they call us dummies.

RUTH. After all, though, we do get paid. We get polished and painted and waxed, and if we weren't here, we might have to—

ANNIE. Don't even *think* it. Remember, you're Miss Marie's little lady.

BETTY. Never a dull moment! Here comes the boss back to see that every little thing is all right.

GERTIE. Hi-ho! Here's where we get our regular pushing around. *She* doesn't think we're even names.

BETTY. I hope she pushes me into a better position so I'll look decent. After all, I do have some pride.

ANNIE. We all have our pride, dearie, so don't start bragging about yours.

GERTIE (*with a bit of sarcasm*). *You* should have the pride of an old employee, Annie. You've been here quite a long time, haven't you, dear?

ANNIE. You needn't be so wise. I saw you the first day you came. Sure, you've only been here a couple of months, but, sister, if you weren't stored in a cellar for a lifetime before that, then I certainly don't know my mildew.

BETTY. Shut up, both of you, and do a good job, or this smarty boss will have you made into kindling.

[*Miss Deedee enters, followed by Miss Marie.*

ANNIE. They'd have a tough time getting any heat out of Gertie's old timber.

GERTIE. Don't be so cute. Just be your plain varnished self and you'll be more popular.

MISS DEEDEE (*looking around*). Miss Marie, you must arrange our displays more smartly. The first lesson in window-dressing is never to do a careless job. You must realize that many people look into our windows each day and judge our merchandise accordingly. Never give anyone a chance to say that our mannequins are carelessly dressed.

BETTY (*staring blankly ahead*). Believe me, sister, if she doesn't look at my dress, I'll be carelessly *un*dressed.

MISS MARIE (*over at right*). I do the best I can, Miss Deedee, but I have such a terrible time getting the things I want. Some of the departments simply won't co-operate.

GERTIE (*staring straight ahead*). Here's where the department heads get one hung on their chins.

MISS DEEDEE. You must remember that the departments have their problems, too.

ANNIE (*staring straight ahead*). Of which the two biggest are these dopes they call window-dressers.

MISS MARIE. Maybe so, but they don't have to hold back their stock on us. You'd think they had to preserve it for future generations.

MISS DEEDEE. They are held accountable for everything they

send down. It has to go back into stock again, you know, to sell.

GERTIE (*looking straight ahead*). And what a headache for the hosiery department. My legs are full of splinters and you know what *that* does to hose.

MISS DEEDEE (*just for the sake of complaining*). Oh, dear, I wish they'd take this month out of the calendar. It's such a difficult month to dress.

MISS MARIE (*wistfully*). I love June. I like to dress them in bridal gowns and bridesmaids' outfits.

RUTH (*dreamily*). I make the sweetest bride—

GERTIE. Pipe down.

MISS DEEDEE. Well, it isn't June, so we'll just have to do the best we can with this month.

BETTY (*staring straight ahead*). Try doing something about this dress of mine. I *know* something's wrong.

MISS MARIE (*walking up and down before the mannequins*). Don't you think we might change the position of a couple of the mannequins? They look so stiff.

GERTIE (*staring straight ahead*). She should try standing around all day in the sun. *She'd* be stiff, too.

MISS DEEDEE (*going right*). Yes, that might help. But do be careful. Some of them aren't very new.

ANNIE (*straight ahead*). Miss Deedee certainly knows her dummies.

MISS MARIE. You're right. Especially that one on the outside. Sometimes she reminds me of someone who's kind of lost interest.

ANNIE (*straight ahead*). My hat's off to you, Miss Marie. You're smarter than I thought you were.

MISS DEEDEE. From here, I'd say you should show a side angle on that third one. (*Marie goes to Betty.*) Just a lee-e-e-tle more to the right. (*She makes gestures for the moving while Marie works.*) There! There—a little more. That will do, I guess.

BETTY. If she'd only stop fussing and take a good look and see what's wrong with me.

MISS DEEDEE. That's better. Now I think there is only one thing more that we need—hats.

MARIE. Heavens, yes! We can't let them stand there without hats. (*Starts for exit.*) And they insist on giving me the most awful things in that hat department. I like to pick them myself.

ANNIE (*straight ahead*). Yeah! Last week she picked them herself and that female who writes the "Tell You Where" shopper's column took us all for a ride.

MISS DEEDEE. If possible, get something more attractive than last week.

BETTY (*straight ahead*). I'll say so! I was never so *ashamed.*

GERTIE. You and me both. That woman in green stood out front and read that column to us. Remember?

RUTH (*straight ahead*). She had a perfect right to read it. She was the one who wrote it.

MISS DEEDEE (*as she and assistant leave window*). You tell them that I asked for a brim, a brimless, a turban and— (*Thinks.*) Oh, yes! A sailor. (*They are gone.*)

ANNIE. I hope I draw a brim. That sun!

RUTH. Bet I get that snarly turban again.

GERTIE. What I say is—a hat's a hat.

BETTY. I *know* a hat won't fix up what's wrong with me.

[*Miss Marie enters with a turban which she sets on Ruth's head.*

RUTH (*straight ahead*). I knew it. I just *knew* it.

BETTY (*straight ahead*). I wish I knew—

[*Miss Deedee enters with three hats. She puts the sailor on Betty, the brimmed hat on Gertie and the brimless one on Annie. The dressers stand off and survey their work.*

MISS DEEDEE. That's better.

MISS MARIE. The hats *do* something to them.

ANNIE (*straight ahead*). Not saying what.

MISS MARIE. They still look stiff.

MISS DEEDEE. Maybe we ought to put the chair back in and let one of them sit down.

MISS MARIE. A good idea. The chair's still here. (*They go off left.*)

GERTIE. I wish they'd feature night gowns and put *me* in a *bed.* I could use a rest.

BETTY (*in agony*). Why don't they look me over? I'll just die.

[*Miss Deedee and Miss Marie come back lugging an arm-chair.*

MISS DEEDEE (*indicating Annie*). Put her in it.

ANNIE (*straight ahead*). A break at last. My feet are killing me.

[*They seat Annie on the edge of the chair, cross her ankles, pull her legs to one side so that she sits sideways.*

MISS DEEDEE (*standing off*). *Much* better.

MISS MARIE. Couldn't we perch one of the others on the arm?

MISS DEEDEE. We might try it. Get that one. (*Indicates Gertie. The dressers perch her on the arm, her ankles crossed and legs stuck out straight.*) Now turn those others so that it seems more like a group.

[*They set to work. In the pushing around, the hat has fallen and now covers Gertie's face.*

GERTIE (*through her hat*). Hey! Who turned the lights off?

ANNIE. Nobody, you fool.

GERTIE. It's dark.

BETTY. The sun's shining.

GERTIE. But I can't see a thing.

MISS DEEDEE (*turns suddenly and sees hat on Gertie's face*). Miss Marie! (*Points to Gertie.*) If you must be whimsical, do it on your own time.

MISS MARIE (*flustered*). I'm sorry. (*Straightens hat.*)

MISS DEEDEE. Don't quote me but I do think she looks better wearing it on her face instead of on her head.

GERTIE (*indignantly*). Say!

MISS DEEDEE. Now! Turn that one just a lee-tle more.

[*Miss Marie turns Betty.*

BETTY (*straight ahead*). They better stop pushing me around and look me over. I *know* there's something wrong.

[*Indeed, Betty is correct. Now that she has been turned, left side to audience, it may be seen that the long zipper fastener on the side of her dress is wide open. The dressers do not see this.*

MISS DEEDEE (*not seeing opened zipper*). Something's still wrong with her.

BETTY (*straight ahead*). You're getting warm, sister.

MISS DEEDEE. Perhaps a little costume jewelry—

MISS MARIE (*going off*). I'll get a junk bracelet.

MISS DEEDEE (*following her*). I think I'll put that handbag back on.

BETTY. What *is* the matter with me? I'm sure I feel a draft.

RUTH. Don't look now, dear, but your zipper is open and you are showing your—you know—

BETTY (*stands rigid and screams at top of her voice*). Ohhhh! Help! Help! You fools! Can't you see— Help! Help! Zipper me! Ohhhhhh, shut me up!

ANNIE. Shut yourself up. You know darn well she can't hear you. There's nothing you can do.

ANNIE. Now that the curtain is down maybe someone will come along on the outside and run in the store and tell about you.

BETTY. I'll get another paragraph in that awful shopping column again. Why can't the store hire efficient girls? Dummies! That's what they are. Dummies!

GERTIE. You should talk, honey.

RUTH. Well, thank goodness there isn't anybody out front right now.

ANNIE. You're wrong, Ruthie. There's a man who's been standing out there since before they started to dress us.

GERTIE. Yeah, I saw the guy. He just stands there as though he were listening and then he makes notes in a little book. I think he's wacky.

RUTH. I hope he hasn't noticed me. I simply don't feel dressed in this turban. I'm just not "right."

GERTIE. You always worry about being *exactly* right, don't you, Ruthie? You never forget you're a model.

RUTH. I used to be the best-dressed woman in any window in town. My gowns were always the. . . .

GERTIE. So the gal wore gowns in those days!

ANNIE. She's right, Gertie, so don't be so skeptical. She was just what she says she was. I was there with her. That was when she had that handsome man for a dresser.

GERTIE. That's what I always wanted—a man to dress me.

ANNIE. Well, this beautiful Charlie used to keep saying that she was his girl. And did she get a flock of attention! He put his real girl's name on her.

RUTH (*in a tone of regret*). Those were the days of real romance.

ANNIE. I didn't think so. He named *me* after the best girl of his worst enemy. You girls should have seen what I had to stand there and wear.

BETTY. Couldn't the boss of the store do anything about that?

ANNIE. Heavens, no! That Charlie man was too sharp. He had the ad boys make a sign that read, "How would you like *your* girl to *look* like *this?*" and stood it in front of me.

GERTIE. Pretty smart lad, I'd say.

ANNIE. Yeah, it worked all right until my boy-friend got wise to the whole thing. Then the handsome one got a slug in him—and that was that.

RUTH. Those boys really were *so* romantic.

GERTIE. Well, it takes all kinds. Here come the accessories.

[*Marie enters with bracelet and handbag. Fastens bracelet on Betty's arm.*

BETTY (*staring straight ahead*). How about a yank on my zipper?

RUTH (*straight ahead*). There's the woman in the green dress. Maybe she'll see your split zipper and tell them.

GERTIE. She'll never tell. She has a column to write. Tough luck, Betty.

[*Marie hangs purse on Ruth's arm.*

BETTY (*straight ahead*). I hope the old man who just came up will see it first. He has a kind look on his face. He *does* see it! Look at him making signs! Marie, you dope, look at him, will you? Look at him, I say—look at him. I don't know who's the dumber, you or I.

MISS DEEDEE (*at entrance*). Miss Marie, something is wrong. What is it? Don't look around, but that old man is making frantic signs and trying to tell us. That's very nice of him. Oh, dear, there's that woman who writes a column. Find out what's wrong quickly, before *she* sees anything.

BETTY (*straight ahead*). Here it is—the zipper on this dress.

[*But Miss Marie has moved over to the right as she looks for the trouble. All the girls attempt to help her by shouting simultaneously.*

GERTIE. Over this way, you dummy.

ANNIE. Back up, Marie. It isn't here.

RUTH. For goodness' sake, look where the old gentleman is pointing.

BETTY. MARIE!

MARIE (*finally finds it*). Here it is.

GERTIE. What a bright little girl.

MARIE. The zipper on this dress. (*She shuts it.*) Is the old boy happy now?

[*Miss Deedee nods.*

BETTY. Listen to her ask, "Is *he* happy?" Am I happy! Now I can face the world again. Thanks, Pop.

GERTIE. That's what I've always said. What we need around here is a man's touch.

[*Miss Marie and Miss Deedee leave the window.*

RUTH. Will you girls stop your clamoring and pay some attention to me! There is more to this job than meets the eye and although those people standing out there may never know it, still *we* must realize that we have something to give them and we must not fail in our duty.

ANNIE. It's the old applesauce, but that "Tell You Where" woman is still out there, so stick together, girls, and may the best dressed win.

BETTY. Why don't the good-looking *single* men come around here sometimes? Why don't they, Gert?

GERTIE. If I had *my* way, they would. All I say is, I hope they put us in bathing suits tomorrow, I hope, indeed I do.

CURTAIN

THE BLUE TIE

A Drama

BY BEULAH JACKSON CHARMLEY

CHARACTERS

MRS. KNAPP, *the mother.*
DORA, *her daughter.*
MRS. JOHNSON, *a neighbor.*

PLACE. A small town in Wisconsin.
TIME. A winter morning. The present.

MRS. KNAPP *passes her hours sitting in the morris chair before the big bay window of the dining room. This dining room is used as an informal living room, the "front room" being reserved for special occasions such as weddings and funerals. There are two doors at either end of the rear wall. The left door opens into the kitchen and the door at extreme right end opens on to a side porch. Another door, downstage left, opens on to the "front room." In center of right wall is a large bay window banked with begonias, fuchsias and geraniums. The windowpanes are frosty and the cross bars are loaded with snow. However, the sun streams in. There is a family portrait or two and a calendar on the wall. The floor is laid with a hand-woven rag carpet. An oak extension table in the middle of the room is partially set for lunch. There are four tall, golden-oak chairs around it. A vase of artificial flowers stands in the center. Back of table, on real wall, is a cupboard for china which goes through the wall to the kitchen and can be opened from either room. Left wall center, is a hard-coal base-*

burner stove. Warm lights from the glowing coals are reflected in the shining nickel griffins that trim either side. A scuttle of coal stands near by. Downstage right, is a combination desk and bookcase. A morris chair, upholstered in green velour and embellished with a crochet doily, stands near the bay window. There is a carpeted hassock in front of it.

As the play opens, Mrs. Knapp is seated in the morris chair reading from her Bible. Her feet rest on the hassock. She is sixty years old and wears a long-sleeved gray flannel dress of her own making. Her iron-gray hair is parted in the middle and coiled neatly at the back of her head. Beneath black, shaggy brows, her blue-gray eyes look out from time to time on the hard Wisconsin winter. She is badly crippled by rheumatism. She whispers the words as she reads. She turns a page. A telegram in a yellow envelope slips from the leaves. She darts a quick glance at the kitchen door. Then slowly and painfully she leans over and retrieves the telegram. She slips it back between the pages of the Bible, closes the book and sits staring out of the window. There is a knock on door leading to side porch. Mrs. Knapp becomes visibly excited. She makes an effort to rise but the pain prevents her. She calls.

MRS. KNAPP. Dora! Dora!

[*Dora enters from kitchen. She is a pretty girl of eighteen with her chestnut hair done in a coronet braid. She wears a becoming short-sleeved green percale dress and a white bib-apron. She carries a plate of biscuits which she sets on the table.*

DORA. What is it, Mother?

MRS. KNAPP. There's someone at the door.

DORA (*crossing to door*). Now who could that be just before dinner?

MRS. KNAPP. Dora, has the twelve-forty come in from Chicago yet?

DORA. It's too early. Besides, you'd hear the whistle.

MRS. KNAPP. Yes, that's right. (*Knock is repeated.*)

DORA (*opening door*). Why, good morning, Mrs. Johnson. It's Mrs. Johnson, Mother.

[*Mrs. Johnson, a neighbor, comes in. She is a small, thin woman of Norwegian descent. Her sandy hair is thin, and wisps of it show around her forehead from under her old black coat, which she has thrown over her head in the manner of a shawl.*

MRS. JOHNSON. Good morning, Dora. Wait a minute till I leave my rubbers on the porch.

DORA. Here, give them to me. I'll put them under the stove. (*She takes rubbers and closes door. She places rubbers on zinc mat under stove.*)

MRS. JOHNSON (*going to stove to warm her hands*). Good morning, Miz Knapp.

MRS. KNAPP. Oh! (*Seems slightly absent-minded.*) Good morning.

MRS. JOHNSON (*smiling*). You sound like you expected someone else instead of me.

MRS. KNAPP (*after hesitating slightly*). No-o-o.

MRS. JOHNSON. It's quite wintry out this morning.

MRS. KNAPP (*as though aware of it for the first time*). Why, so it is.

MRS. JOHNSON (*going to her*). How are you this morning, Miz Knapp?

MRS. KNAPP (*taking shawl from her knees*). This spell of rheumatism hangs on longer than usual. See, my knees are real swollen. (*Straightens one leg painfully, then the other, to show how stiff she is. She is wearing woolen stockings and red felt slippers.*)

MRS. JOHNSON. So they are. (*Replaces shawl.*) But you'll probably get better, now that the days are getting longer. The sun is real bright today even through it is cold. I says to Ole just this morning, we'll all feel all right, come spring.

DORA. Let me take your coat, Mrs. Johnson.

MRS. JOHNSON. I can't stay but a minute. (*Slips out of coat.*) I just run in to see what kind of a night your mother had.

[*Dora hangs coat on a hook behind the stove and then goes back into the kitchen.*

MRS. KNAPP. Just draw up a chair for yourself and make

yourself comfortable. (*As Mrs. Johnson pulls one of the dining chairs over.*) I was just reading my chapter. (*Touches the Bible on her lap.*) And looking over my Christmas cards once more. (*Takes out few cards from Bible.*)

MRS. JOHNSON (*sitting down*). I don't suppose you heard from your boy, Maurice, at Christmastime?

MRS. KNAPP (*proudly*). Yes, I did! (*Calls.*) Dora?

DORA (*appearing in doorway, patiently*). Yes, Mother?

MRS. KNAPP. Dora, get that letter of Maurice's out of the desk.

DORA (*a little impatiently, as she crosses to desk*). Oh, Mother. (*Gets letter and brings it to her mother.*) Here it is.

MRS. KNAPP. And, Dora, while you're here, get that tie box out of the top drawer there. I want to show Miz Johnson what I got Maurice for Christmas.

[*Dora rolls her eyes impatiently, looks at her mother as if to say something. Instead, she sighs and gets box. It is done up in Christmas wrappings. After handing it to her mother, she completes setting table with dishes from the china closet. She sets three places.*

MRS. JOHNSON. Where's Maurice now? I says to Ole, yesterday, it's quite a spell since Miz Knapp heard from her son. It is, too, isn't it?

MRS. KNAPP. He was on the West Coast—San Francisco. No, we hadn't heard from him for over a year. He's been moving around, here and there, you know.

MRS. JOHNSON. He likes to travel, don't he? Well, he comes honestly by that. His father was always one to be moving around, too, in his young days.

MRS. KNAPP (*slowly*). They were both rolling stones. (*She holds the letter and stares out of the window.*)

MRS. JOHNSON. He'll probably settle down when he gets a little older. I never am quite sure where he is, but I remember him in my prayers. Now, if he could find a good girl. . . .

MRS. KNAPP (*still staring out window*). Yes, he's coming back soon to settle down.

MRS. JOHNSON. You were saying . . . about the letter. . . .

MRS. KNAPP (*takes it from envelope, unfolds it to reveal a pressed flower*). See, he sent me a pressed flower.

MRS. JOHNSON (*examining it*). It's real sweet, ain't it? Must be one of those California flowers they tell about.

MRS. KNAPP. Maurice always was a great one for flowers. The other children would play with cats or dogs, but he'd have a dandelion ring on his curly blond head and come home lugging cowslips or blue flags or whatever else was in season.

MRS. JOHNSON (*indicating tie box*). And he sent you that Christmas box, did he?

MRS. KNAPP (*as she opens box and takes out a bright blue tie*). No. I was going to send it to him for his Christmas present. But I didn't know where he was. I didn't get his letter till after Christmas.

MRS. JOHNSON (*examining tie*). My, it's real nice, ain't it? A right pretty blue.

MRS. KNAPP. Yes, Maurice was awful partial to blue. He'll like it.

MRS. JOHNSON. But you didn't give it to him— Oh, you mean the next time he comes home.

MRS. KNAPP. He'll wear it then.

[*During above, Dora has been setting food on table, going back and forth.*

MRS. JOHNSON. I suppose you heard from your other girl, Mertie?

MRS. KNAPP. Oh, yes. Mertie sent us a big box of things—mostly clothes.

MRS. JOHNSON. She still nursing in Milwaukee?

MRS. KNAPP. Yes. She even worked on Christmas day. Mertie's as steady as a clock. Never misses a day.

MRS. JOHNSON. She's different from Maurice, now. I always think girls are such a comfort.

MRS. KNAPP. Maurice was always a comfort to me.

[*Dore comes in with a covered casserole. Mrs. Johnson observes this and rises as Dora places it on the table.*

MRS. JOHNSON. Well, I must be running along. I see it's most dinnertime.

MRS. KNAPP. I'd like for you to stay and eat with us today.

MRS. JOHNSON (*smiling*). You make it sound like a special day. But. . . .

MRS. KNAPP. Ole isn't coming home for dinner, is he?

MRS. JOHNSON. No. He's carrying a dinner pail these cold days.

MRS. KNAPP. I know you don't like to eat alone.

MRS. JOHNSON. Well, if you won't look on me as company and fuss—(*Looks at table, is visibly pleased.*) Why, Dora's already put on a plate for me!

MRS. KNAPP. No, that's for Maurice. We always set a place for him.

DORA. I'll set another place.

MRS. KNAPP (*slowly*). No. Don't set another place. Maurice won't be home to eat today.

DORA (*pleased*). There! See how much good you've done Mother, Mrs. Johnson? Every day she has me set a place . . . every meal. I tell her it's silly. At last she sees I'm right. (*Mrs. Knapp says nothing.*) Come on, Mother. (*Mrs. Knapp struggles to rise. Mrs. Johnson goes to help her. Mrs. Knapp seems to suffer pain.*) Mother, just let me bring your plate to you, and you eat it there.

MRS. JOHNSON. That's sensible. (*Takes tie from her lap, places it on table.*)

DORA. You sit here, Mrs. Johnson.

[*Mrs. Johnson takes the indicated chair. Dora fills a plate with food and hands it and a fork to Mrs. Knapp. Then she sits at table, passes food to Mrs. Johnson and helps herself.*

MRS. KNAPP. Miz Johnson, will you ask the blessing?

MRS. JOHNSON (*clasps her hands and lowers her head*). We thank Thee, Father, for this food. Bless it to our use and us to Thy service. We ask it in His name. Amen. (*They begin to eat.*)

MRS. KNAPP. Dora's practicing cooking and this is the one meal she can make all by herself.

DORA. I learned it in the cookery class at high school.

MRS. JOHNSON (*helping herself to a biscuit*). Seems almost like a party, eating in the dining room—and hot biscuits.

DORA. There's just Mother and I. We usually eat in the

kitchen. But Mother took a notion to eat here today. She had me put on the best cloth.

MRS. JOHNSON. Now if Maurice happened to walk in, he'd be that pleased. (*Looking suddenly at Mrs. Knapp.*) Did I understand you to say you expected him home today?

DORA (*laughs*). Why no. What made you think that?

MRS. JOHNSON (*puzzled*). I don't know. But somehow I got the idea—I don't know from where—that your ma was expecting him.

DORA. Of course he has a way of showing up at the most unexpected times. Two years ago, when we were all ready to sit down to Thanksgiving dinner, we came into the dining room and who was sitting there smiling at the turkey but Maurice.

MRS. KNAPP (*with quiet anguish*). Maurice.

MRS. JOHNSON. It's strange, isn't it, but the one that's away, like Maurice, is the one you think the most of, isn't it? (*As Dora holds out her hand for her plate to replenish it.*) No, thanks, Dora. No more. But that casserole is first-rate. Real bride-like.

MRS. KNAPP (*still with the quiet anguish in her voice*). He was my first baby.

MRS. JOHNSON. And with George being in the sanatorium and your husband dead, I suppose you lean on Maurice more, too, being he's the only man you have left.

MRS. KNAPP. Somehow, I always think of him as he was when he was a little boy. (*She has stopped eating.*) He had yellow curly hair and the merriest blue eyes. (*Sighs.*) Yes. Maurice had the brightest eyes. He was never like other children. He was always more lively and unexpected. He was meant for great things.

MRS. JOHNSON. And now he's grown up.

MRS. KNAPP. Twenty-four come next May. (*She sighs.*)

[*Suddenly a train whistle sounds. It is low at first, then rises in a crescendo. Mrs. Knapp tries to rise. The plate and fork clatter to the floor.*

DORA (*running to her*). Mother!

MRS. JOHNSON (*going to her*). That whistle gave you a start, didn't it? I'm so used to it, I never notice it. (*Picks up plate and fork and places them on table.*)

DORA. Are you all right, Mother?

MRS. KNAPP. I'm all right. Now I want you to get the table cleared and things straightened.

MRS. JOHNSON. I'll help you, Dora.

MRS. KNAPP. Dora can do it herself. (*Dora starts to stack dishes.*)

MRS. JOHNSON. I only thought. . . .

MRS. KNAPP (*with a new dignity*). I would like for you, Miz Johnson, to go in the front room and raise the curtains. Let the light in. Put a match to the stove. The fire's all laid. And please see that all the things are dusted.

MRS. JOHNSON (*excited*). You do expect Maurice home then. I know. You got word he was coming on that twelve-forty from Chicago.

DORA (*coming forward. She seems angry*). No, she doesn't, Mrs. Johnson. She has me clean up and dust in there every single day. There's always a fire laid. She always keeps it ready for company—ever since Maurice went away.

MRS. JOHNSON. I guess it's all cleaned up then.

MRS. KNAPP (*with authority*). I would like for you to do this for me, Miz Johnson.

MRS. JOHNSON (*awed*). Why, yes. If you say so—I'll be glad— (*Goes to door leading into "front room." Turns back once to look in perplexity at Mrs. Knapp. At door.*) Your dinner was real good, Dora.

DORA. Thank you. (*The door closes after Mrs. Johnson. Dora goes to her mother. She is angry.*) Mother, couldn't you talk about anything but Maurice, Maurice, Maurice, all through dinner?

MRS. KNAPP. Folks like to hear about Maurice.

DORA. You mean you like to talk about him. (*Pleadingly.*) Mother, you *know* Mrs. Johnson knows all about him.

MRS. KNAPP. All our neighbors know that Maurice was always a good boy.

DORA (*heatedly*). They know he's the black sheep of the family. That's what they know.

MRS. KNAPP. You shouldn't talk that way about your brother, Dora.

DORA. My brother! What did my brother do for me? Nothing. Only disgrace me in the Village—make me ashamed that I have the same name.

MRS. KNAPP. He never did anything wrong.

DORA. He started out—that curly-haired tot of yours—by stealing watermelons and apples from Old Man Canby.

MRS. KNAPP. All little boys are mischievous. They all go through those stages. They're like young colts. Just too full of life.

DORA. Then, when he was in high school, he got himself talked about on account of that Claire Gordon.

MRS. KNAPP. Folks always talked about Claire Gordon. They talked about Maurice because he tried to befriend her. He was always so kind.

DORA (*bitterly*). That's not the story that went around.

MRS. KNAPP. That was all gossip—gossip of jealous women who were jealous that I had such a fine son.

DORA. Oh, Mother, how blind you are. Maurice is no good. Everybody knows he's a thief or worse. And you sit there and pretend. . . .

MRS. KNAPP. It is not for you to pass judgment on your brother. God will do that when the time comes.

DORA. And while I'm waiting for that great Judgment Day, where can I go hide my head when people point at me and whisper, "She's his sister."

MRS. KNAPP. You were always too hard on Maurice. Just because he was fun-loving. . . .

DORA. Fun-loving! Was that fun the night he got fighting in the Boylesville Tavern—when he came home bleeding?

MRS. KNAPP. He was set upon by some boys looking for trouble. (*Sighs.*) Poor Maurice!

DORA. Poor Maurice, indeed! That's all I hear from morning to night. I'm tired of the sound of his name. Mother, be sensible. What has he ever done for you? He never writes except to ask you for money. He only comes home when he's dead broke. Then he sticks around and eats you out of house and home as long as he wants. Then he's off again without even a goodbye.

MRS. KNAPP. You never understand him. Of all my children, he was the best-hearted.

DORA. What about Mertie and me?

MRS. KNAPP (*tense*). Dora, did you hear a truck drive up to the door?

DORA. I'm not interested in trucks. You just don't want to hear about all that Mertie and I do. Mertie bought two tons of coal for Christmas and sent all those things. And I got this room papered, didn't I, with the money I earned at the Fair Store after school nights?

MRS. KNAPP (*not listening*). Yes, that was the truck and it stopped here. (*Smiles at her.*) Don't worry, dear, about Maurice. He's all right now.

DORA. Mother, how can you stick up for him so? What did he send you for Christmas? Nothing but a pressed flower.

MRS. KNAPP. Yes, that was so like him—so thoughtful. To think of me and send me that flower all the way from California.

DORA. He probably stole it from somewhere.

[*Front door bell rings piercingly. Dora jumps.*

DORA. Now who—everybody comes around this way.

MRS. KNAPP (*quietly*). It's your brother.

DORA. You know Maurice woudn't take the trouble to ring.

MRS. JOHNSON (*appearing in door*). Miz Knapp, there's someone at the front door. Should I. . . .

MRS. KNAPP. My daughter will go to the door.

MRS. JOHNSON. I'd just as soon. . . .

MRS. KNAPP. My daughter will open the door to her brother.

DORA. I won't. Let him come around the back like we all do.

MRS. KNAPP (*trying to rise*). Dora!

DORA (*sulkily*). All right. I'll go. (*Exits sullenly.*)

MRS. JOHNSON (*excited*). Then you knew all the while he was coming home today.

MRS. KNAPP (*quietly*). I expected him on the Chicago train. (*Pause.*) I'd take it as a favor, if you'd go in there with Dora. She'll be needing help.

MRS. JOHNSON. Of course. (*Goes into "front room."*)

[*Mrs. Knapp waits, facing the "front room" door. There is a sudden high scream from Dora. Mrs. Knapp seems to slump in her chair. Dora comes running in sobbing.*

DORA. Mother! Mother! It's Maurice!

MRS. KNAPP (*quietly*). I know.

DORA. They brought him home . . . dead!

MRS. KNAPP. I know. I got the wire last night from Chicago.

DORA. Oh, Mother! (*Throws herself on her knees beside her mother.*) You knew and you let me talk about him.

MRS. KNAPP. I asked you not to judge him.

DORA (*weeping*). I'm sorry, Mommy, so sorry for what I said about him. I shouldn't have said such things. But I've always been a little jealous of Maurice. He was so good-looking and. . . .

MRS. KNAPP. Yes.

DORA. And he was sweet as a youngster. We used to play together—Maurice and me. . . .

MRS. JOHNSON (*appears in doorway. She too, is weeping*). Miz Knapp, some men. . . .

MRS. KNAPP. Yes. I know. I got the wire last night when Dora was at the library. Mr. Farmouth came over and said he'd meet the train and bring him here.

DORA. A wire? What did it say?

[*Mrs. Knapp takes telegram from her Bible and hands it to her. Dora takes it but she is weeping so much, she cannot see.*

MRS. JOHNSON. I'll read it for you, dear. (*Reads.*) *Regret inform you Maurice Knapp, member notorious Loop gang, shot in fight with rival gang at Golden State Night Club. Shipping body from Chicago. Will arrive 12:40. Signed. . . .* (*Mrs. Johnson places wire on table.*) It's signed by the Commissioner.

MRS. KNAPP. Poor Maurice! I guess he was there and he saw some boys in trouble and he tried to help. . . . Maurice, always so good, always. . . . (*Breaks down and weeps.*)

[*Dora and Mrs. Johnson exchange looks.*

DORA. Yes, Mother. Maurice was always so good.

MRS. JOHNSON. Yes. Ole always said that Maurice Knapp may have been a little wild, but he had a good heart.

MRS. KNAPP (*through her tears*). He was *really* a good boy. He was the most promising of the lot—the best-looking, the brightest, and the kindest-hearted.

DORA. Yes. Yes.

MRS. JOHNSON (*gently*). Wouldn't you like to see him, Miz Knapp?

MRS. KNAPP. How does he look, Dora? Does it show where. . . ?

DORA. No, Mother. He looks nice. There's a piece of adhesive tape on his forehead. You can't see the place. He's wearing that old gray suit he had on the last time he came home.

MRS. KNAPP. Has he . . . has he got a tie on?

DORA. No, Mother.

MRS. KNAPP. Hand me that blue tie that I bought for his Christmas.

DORA. Yes, Mother. (*Hands her the tie which is on the table.*)

MRS. KNAPP. Help me up. (*They do so. She stands on her feet, trembling. She starts to go towards the "front room." They go to either side of her to help her. She motions them to go away.*) No. I want to go in there alone. I want to be alone with him.

[*They step aside. Painfully, step by step, the bright blue tie in her hand, she makes her way to the door leading into the "front room" and to Maurice as . . .*

THE CURTAIN FALLS

THE PROJECT

A Satirical Comedy

BY LORRAINE BAGLEY

THE EARTHWORMS

MYRTLE.
DELIA.
LUCILLE.
GERTRUDE.
BELINDA.
EMOGENE.
RADIO VOICES.

PLACE. In the earth.
TIME. Yet to come.

THE EARTHWORMS *are trying to manufacture the good life in a strictly underground way. They have had to scurry into the earth so many times to avoid bombings, that they have decided to make the best of it and live underground and make it good. The scene could be called Myrtle's living room. It is not fully excavated as yet, but the project is in full swing. A beginning has been made under Myrtle's backyard. Entrances and exits are all over the place. They have a sofa down there and armchairs and a radio and a telephone. They also have a short-wave set with earphones and mouthpiece. Of course, the roots of a large tree interfere with the interior decorating. However, a large blueprint and map are tacked to the roots, so they serve some purpose after all. There is a low bench somewhere on which are six tin lunchboxes and three flashlight lanterns.*

The play does not open. It has been going on before the audience assembles. It will continue after the audience leaves. This is a big project, you know. The excavation is dark. There are no curtains. As the audience assembles, they may see figures moving in and out of the darkness. When the audience is all settled, the house lights go out. A voice comes from the dark stage.

WOMAN'S VOICE. I told you and told you. We have to scurry underground so much to avoid falling bombs, that we practically live underground. Naturally, we still want to live the good life. So why not make the inside of the earth as luxurious and comfortable as possible? Myself, I've gotten so that I *like* to live underground. . . .

[*Beams of light illuminate the stage and show three women in overalls, studying the blueprint.*

MYRTLE. We need to pack it harder underneath.

DELIA. Yes, and it needs to have more room for food.

MYRTLE. And seats.

LUCILLE. It should be longer and more wiggly.

DELIA. We might be able to cut holes in the end and stack canned goods.

MYRTLE. I think we'll need mouse traps. They *lived* here before we did, you know.

LUCILLE. If it were wigglier, the bombs would have less chance of hitting it, and if it were longer, we could keep rushing back and forth when parts of it fell in.

DELIA. Look, see where we have to detour around this sewer pipe. Why couldn't we branch off and make an extra shelter?

MYRTLE. What for?

DELIA. Mrs. O'Reilly and her nine children.

LUCILLE. Mrs. O'Reilly could never get through that opening. I told her to diet before it was too late.

MYRTLE. We could widen the whole business. (*She moves and stumbles over one of the prongs of the roots.*)

LUCILLE. Wonderful how trees can grow such big roots.

MYRTLE. You would too, if you had to sit in the ground all your life.

DELIA. I wonder will our children's children have roots instead of feet?

MYRTLE. We need a new wagon on the 3:30 shift. Do you suppose Mrs. Stanley's little boy would rent us his Demon Coaster?

LUCILLE. He doesn't like dirt hauled in it.

DELIA. I don't like it. It has four wheels.

MYRTLE. What about it?

DELIA. That kind climbs up on you when you go downhill.

[*Three women enter wearing overalls and miners' caps with lighted miners' lamps on them.*

GERTRUDE. We mustn't tell anyone of our discovery.

BELINDA. No, because they're needed for defense.

EMOGENE. Besides, there weren't many of them.

MYRTLE. Many of what?

BELINDA. Myrtle, we've struck radishes!

DELIA. Huh! Yesterday, it was Mr. Stravinsky's garbage dump.

EMOGENE. Think of it, Myrtle, we'll have fresh vegetables for some time to come.

MYRTLE. What happens when the owner pulls them up and finds they aren't there?

EMOGENE. He'll just think the worms ate them.

BELINDA. Speaking of worms, I ran into Mr. Tonio this morning. It seems that Mrs. Ditty's funeral is tomorrow and he wants to know if he can use a section of our project.

DELIA. How much?

BELINDA. About six feet. They're going to bury Mr. Bellinger day after tomorrow and Mr. Tonio thinks there'll be room enough for both of them.

MYRTLE. All right, providing he seals our end up so we won't be running into them by mistake.

EMOGENE. He suggests we empty the wagons there in front of the opening for a week and then he'd pound it down.

DELIA. I think he's taking advantage of us.

LUCILLE. We *won't* empty the dirt there. Let him dig up his own dirt.

BELINDA. I *know*. But we've got so *much*.

GERTRUDE. If we emptied the dirt there it would save a twenty-minute walk to the place where we now dump it.

EMOGENE. Why should we convenience him? What has he ever done for us?

GERTRUDE. My dear, it's not what he has done for us, but what he'll have to do for us someday.

MYRTLE. All those in favor of giving Mr. Tonio dirt, say aye.

GERTRUDE. Aye.

MYRTLE. The nays have it. Mark off six feet for Mr. Tonio without dirt.

GERTRUDE. But. . . .

MYRTLE. We've voted. Now! Did you girls remember to prop up that last telephone pole?

BELINDA. We've run out of boxes, Myrtle, so we had to use one of the little wagons.

EMOGENE. There's not a single box in town. We got the last one Tuesday.

MYRTLE. I don't know what we're going to do. Every day for the last month we've run into telephone poles.

DELIA. Well, once we find a road, we can work directly under it in a straight line. Once we find a road.

BELINDA. We took the corner off somebody's basement just before you came in.

MYRTLE. I told you to be careful and not interfere with anybody's property.

BELINDA. But there was no other way around. There was a whole bunch of pipes next to it. We've *tried* removing them.

GERTRUDE. The people didn't mind after we explained what we were doing. In fact, they asked us to come up and have a cup of tea.

EMOGENE. The man was very happy. He's going to put a door over the hole and invite his wife's relatives to drop in some time.

BELINDA. He was nicer than that man last week.

DELIA. The one who keeps money in the basement?

BELINDA. Yes, the one with the printing press.

GERTRUDE. I didn't know he was a publisher.

EMOGENE. Say, girls, remember that nice basement we got into three weeks ago? It had the best-equipped recreation room!

LUCILLE. I remember. All kinds of radios—even in suitcases. And hundreds of maps.

GERTRUDE. And a beautiful collection of cameras.

[*Telephone rings. Myrtle goes to answer it.*

EMOGENE. I'm going to eat my lunch. (*Gets lunchbox from bench. Gertrude and Belinda do the same. They sit on the floor to eat.*)

MYRTLE (*into phone*). Speak! (*Listens.*) Mrs. who? Oh, *Mister* Sturges. Yes, I know, the contractor. (*Listens.*) Yes we own it. What about it? (*Listens.*) Yes—yes—yes—you want to—Oh! You want to build a resort on it. No, I don't exactly *own* that portion. It belongs to most of the people in town. I'm only in charge of the project.

BELINDA (*cracking open an egg which runs*). Oh! I forgot to hardboil my egg.

MYRTLE (*in phone*). No, I'm afraid not. Yes, all right, Mr. Sturges. Goodbye, Mr. Sturges.

EMOGENE. Did he want to buy our dump?

MYRTLE. He offered us ten thousand dollars.

LUCILLE. In a couple of months it will be worth fifteen.

BELINDA (*eating*). Why did I make sardine sandwiches? I hate sardines.

GERTRUDE. I'm glad we decided on a public golf course. That way, most of the people who own it can enjoy it. Mr. Sturges' project would give too many outsiders the benefit.

DELIA. Well, I'll go on with the wagons. (*She exits.*)

LUCILLE (*stretching, the way laborers do when they are about to resume work*). Where's the pick, Emogene?

EMOGENE. I left it stuck in the concrete where we were working this morning.

GERTRUDE. If you use Billy's wagon, watch that front wheel. It's ready to snap off.

MYRTLE. All right. Ready, Lucille?

LUCILLE. Right.

MYRTLE. We'll be back. (*Exits.*)

LUCILLE. If we remember to make a left turn at number three fork. (*Exits.*)

GERTRUDE. The first shift is back on the job again.

BELINDA. I hope they don't miss that left turn.

EMOGENE (*after a long pause*). You know, we never *did* find Mrs. Parker.

[*There is another pause. Each is thinking. Finally the three resume eating.*

BELINDA. You girls indulging in onion?

GERTRUDE. Are you?

BELINDA (*affirmatively*). Uh-huh.

EMOGENE. Then we will. (*Each nibbles on a scallion stalk.*)

GERTRUDE (*passing her box to other two*). Tomato? (*Each takes a small tomato.*)

EMOGENE (*passing a stalk of celery*). Celery? (*Each strips off a leaf.*)

BELINDA. I love celery. (*They munch.*)

EMOGENE. You have a smudge on your cheek, Gertrude.

GERTRUDE (*rubbing*). Is it off? (*Emogene nods.*)

BELINDA. My little girl won't wash her face any more. She says I never do.

[*There is a pause. Each takes thermos bottle from lunch-box and pours coffee. This is done in unison.*

EMOGENE. Do you know how I got here this morning?

GERTRUDE. The milkman?

EMOGENE. That's right.

BELINDA. Have you seen the sweaters the girls in the knitting circle are sending to Camp Richardson?

GERTRUDE. No.

BELINDA. They're very nice except they ran out of brown yarn and had to make the sleeves with red.

EMOGENE. I understand Mrs. Andrews has knitted fourteen pairs of gloves.

BELINDA. They can't send them because they all have six fingers.

GERTRUDE. You know, the church is having a bandage-rolling contest next Friday. (*Confidentially.*) Now don't quote me, but Mrs. Demming has been practicing on her husband's roll-your-own-cigarettes machine.

EMOGENE. Did I tell you what happened when Parson Filbert saw me in my overalls pulling Billy's wagon?

BOTH (*avidly*). No!

EMOGENE. He said, "Going my way?"

BELINDA. His wife is a very lovely person.

GERTRUDE. She doesn't like it because we haven't been to "Loyal Ladies" so long.

EMOGENE. I do miss the group. We left when we were on the verge of finding out where Genevieve got her new dishes.

BELINDA. I still think she *bought* them.

GERTRUDE. Is that so! Then why do they have "Acme Theatre" on the dessert plates?

BELINDA. It was only on one of them.

EMOGENE. It's hard to buy dishes with foreign names these days.

GERTRUDE. Mrs. Sydney writes "Haviland" on the bottom of hers.

BELINDA (*passing slices of cake*). Would you care for a piece of cake?

BOTH. Thank you. (*Help themselves to cake.*)

GERTRUDE (*taking a bite*). What kind is it?

BELINDA. It's one John composed. It's a combination apricot and banana layer cake. He told me how he made it. You have to be sure to keep the apricots and bananas separated.

GERTRUDE. It tastes interesting.

EMOGENE. Mine are never like this.

BELINDA. John always puts all the sugar in the bottom layer because that's the part you eat first. The icing takes care of the top and you only use the middle layer to separate the top from the bottom.

GERTRUDE (*with a start*). Oh! We forgot to tell Myrtle about the short cut under the baseball park.

BELINDA. Say, wasn't it nice of Coach Sigs to let us use the dugout? That makes a finished room.

[*Delia and Lucille come back.*

DELIA. It must be raining above ground.

LUCILLE. The project is leaking a little.
GERTRUDE. Maybe it's somebody watering the lawn where the roof is thin.
DELIA. No. Somebody's rainspout is right over us.
BELINDA. Couldn't you stop it with something?
LUCILLE. We tried to, with our handkerchiefs.
DELIA. Myrtle thinks we may have to use umbrellas in section B 5. The top is getting so thin.
LUCILLE. We'll have to remove that "free dirt" sign on the top. Most of the roof has been carted away.
EMOGENE. It'll be dry under the Federal Building.
BELINDA. Where *is* Myrtle?
DELIA. Tightening pipes in the central tunnel.
GERTRUDE. Suppose these showers keep up all winter?
LUCILLE. Then they won't be showers any more.
EMOGENE. Does Myrtle want to run the 3:30 shift?
DELIA. She told us to wait until she came in. Then, if the leaking stops, we'll all work while the ground's soft.
GERTRUDE. Let's play something then.
EMOGENE. What? *Dig* or *Peter Rabbit's Progress?*
BELINDA. Why don't we mend the tools now? Then we won't have to do it Sunday.
GERTRUDE. Good! I'll get the tools out of the kitchen. (*She and Lucille exit.*)
EMOGENE. I'll finish the shovel.
BELINDA. I'll take the grubbing hoe.
DELIA. I want to put the handle on the pick.
EMOGENE. *If* you can remember what handle the pick goes on.

[*Gertrude and Lucille return with broken picks, shovels and hoes. Emogene grabs shovel. Others grab objects of their choice. They set to work.*

LUCILLE. Emogene, when you finish monograming your shovel, will you monogram my initials on the grubbing hoe?
EMOGENE. I will if I don't have to make your middle initial. I can't do B's yet.
GERTRUDE. I don't think we ought to use scotch tape any more.

DELIA. No. It didn't hold the pick handle together at all.

LUCILLE. I still don't think we should use adhesive tape. The Red Cross should have it.

EMOGENE. Scotch tape is all right if you put enough on.

BELINDA (*goes out to the kitchen and calls*). Where's the axle grease?

EMOGENE. On the shelf next to the mayonnaise.—They're not using scotch tape for defense?

GERTRUDE. Don't forget what happened to the last pick we mended with it.

DELIA. It went up and came down on my head.

GERTRUDE. She was in the hospital for two weeks.

EMOGENE. I'll use the broken pick, then.

LUCILLE. Emogene, you're being noble.

EMOGENE. I'm willing to make sacrifices.

BELINDA (*enters, pulling a child's express wagon which lacks a front wheel. Wagon is piled with wheels of assorted sizes, hammers, pliers, etc.*). It's still raining.

[*She is about to distribute the small tools when all the lights go out and there is a great crash. There is complete silence.*

LUCILLE (*from dark*). You're sitting on me, Belinda.

BELINDA (*from dark*). Turn on the lights.

LUCILLE. I can't find them.

EMOGENE. Where's the fuse box?

GERTRUDE. Under here, in the basement. But you can't go down there. Myrtle's husband keeps it locked.

LUCILLE. Yes. He lives down there now.

EMOGENE. We haven't any quarter to screw in anyhow.

BELINDA. I'll turn on the lanterns.

[*She does so, one by one. This motivates stage lighting. As lights come on, Lucille is lying with the wagon upturned on her and the tools scattered. The women get her to her feet.*

DELIA. Goodness, it's dark down here.

LUCILLE (*explaining*). The lights have gone off.

[*The women get to work. Delia tapes a pick handle. Emogene whittles on a shovel handle. Lucille is fixing a hoe handle. Gertrude helps Belinda with the wagon. They are trying to fit a wheel on it.*

EMOGENE. This place has very bad wiring.

BELINDA. I used my curling iron the other day and the lights went off and on all down the block until I got my hair curled.

EMOGENE. Last week when all the lights went out, they blew the siren.

GERTRUDE. And didn't this place crowd up.

BELINDA. But it was a mistake—something about the siren being off-key and trying out new notes.

LUCILLE. I read in the paper that they finally decided on E flat.

BELINDA (*hammering loudly*). This wheel won't fit.

GERTRUDE. Try the one I took off the wheelchair.

BELINDA (*picking up a wheel*). This one?

GERTRUDE. That's the wheelbarrow. (*Hands her another.*) This one.

DELIA. After we dedicate our project, all the people can come down here instead of into their basements. (*Walks to exit and looks off.*) The lights are off all over.

LUCILLE. This reminds me of the time Huey proposed to me.

EMOGENE. Was he bashful?

LUCILLE. No, we were eating at the time and he spilled gravy on his vest.

DELIA. Oh, I forgot to order anything for dinner. Bill usually does but he didn't feel well this morning. (*Goes to phone, dials and listens.*)

GERTRUDE. We're having spare ribs, I *think*.

LUCILLE. I'd rather not think what we're having. Huey hasn't learned to cook very well, yet.

BELINDA. Myrtle's having spanish rice and halibut.

[*Women are working all during this dialogue.*

EMOGENE. That's not so bad as her Thursday dinners.

BELINDA. Is that when her husband takes all the left-overs of the week and makes them into little balls and fries them in cream?

EMOGENE. Yes.

LUCILLE. Throw your knife this way a minute, Emogene.

EMOGENE. Have you got a chisel? (*They exchange.*)

DELIA. I can't get my number.

EMOGENE. Have you tried the operator?

DELIA. Yes. I've got to order *something*. Bill won't have anything to cook for dinner.

LUCILLE. We'd better call Myrtle and let her know what's happening.

BELINDA (*consulting map*). She ought to be somewhere between the Third Avenue sewer and the Second and Main manhole.

GERTRUDE. Try all the third quarter of the tunnel.

[*Lucille goes to short wave set, adjusts earphones and dials and begins broadcasting.*

LUCILLE. Calling section C-3 or 4, D-3, B-5 and 6. First wing, second wing and third wing. Calling third quarter of tunnel A. Calling Myrtle. Calling Myrtle. Come in, Myrtle. Come in, Myrtle. (*Pause, fretfully.*) Myrtle just won't come in.

GERTRUDE. Where could she be?

LUCILLE. Wait! I hear something. Hello! Who are *you?* (*To others.*) It's a man.

DELIA (*who has given up on phone*). How in the world did he get in there?

LUCILLE (*into radio mouthpiece*). Where's Myrtle? Myrtle! Where is she? (*Listens, then to others.*) He says, how the devil should he know.

BELINDA. Ask him how he likes our project.

LUCILLE (*into mouthpiece*). How do you like our project? (*Listens. To others.*) He says, oh, is that what it is?

[*By now all the women are crowded around the radio.*

EMOGENE. Ask him how he found the entrance.

LUCILLE. How did you find the entrance? (*Listens; to others.*) He was walking along 23rd Street, tending to his own business, see? When he stepped off a curb and fell in. Now he's lost. (*Into radio.*) You'll have to wait until we send our squad in after you. (*To others.*) Quick! Find out where he is. 23rd Street.

EMOGENE (*consulting map*). That's section D-3.

LUCILLE (*to Emogene*). Where's the nearest cache?

EMOGENE. Under the grocery store.

LUCILLE (*into radio*). Follow the tunnel downward till you

come to a slight turn. Then turn and you'll come to some boxes of sandwiches. They're part of our emergency rations and should last you a couple of days. If you see Myrtle, tell her the lights are off. That is all.

DELIA (*again removes phone receiver*). I can't get even eh—eh—eh—eh—eh—eh—eh on the phone.

BELINDA. Maybe it's disconnected.

GERTRUDE. Myrtle was always a little slow about paying her bill.

BELINDA. Try calling Myrtle again.

LUCILLE (*into radio*). Calling Myrtle. Calling Myrtle. Yoohoo, Myrtle. Do you hear me, Myrtle? If you hear me, your lights are out. Your telephone is dead. (*All this in a monotone.*) Have you paid your bill? Have you paid your bill? Watch out for man in D-3. D-3. He is eating sandwiches. That is all.

BELINDA. What if there should be an air raid?

DELIA. I'll try the radio. (*Turns it on.*)

BELINDA. Myrtle must be lost.

LUCILLE. What about the radio?

DELIA. Nothing. Not even static.

GERTRUDE. Myrtle must have taken the Dayton Street underpass by mistake.

EMOGENE. May I have my knife back? (*Exchange tools.*)

GERTRUDE. This little screw won't fit.

BELINDA. You've got the whatcher-call-it in upside down.

[*Lights come on suddenly. Delia rushes to phone. Radio warms up. Women stop work in amazement.*

DELIA (*in phone*). Hello, how's your asparagus?

RADIO VOICE (*may be man or woman*). There is no cause for alarm.

DELIA (*in phone*). No? How much is lettuce, then?

RADIO VOICE. Citizens are requested to stay indoors.

DELIA (*in phone*). Send me five beets, then.

RADIO VOICE. This is not an air raid. This is not a blackout. This is not a test.

EMOGENE. Then what's happening?

RADIO VOICE. Be calm. The power facilities have failed and some telephone poles are down.

DELIA (*in phone*). That's all. (*Hangs up.*)

[*Myrtle enters with her arms full of a khaki uniform and soldier's cap and a rifle.*

MYRTLE. Goodbye, girls. (*She crosses and exits.*)

EMOGENE. That was Myrtle.

DELIA. She was in an awful hurry.

LUCILLE. Maybe she has an inspiration about the project.

BELINDA. We'd better get back on the job.

[*They gather up tools and resume work.*

EMOGENE. I wonder what's on Myrtle's mind?

GERTRUDE. I bet she found that water main we busted yesterday. (*All gasp.*)

BELINDA. Impossible! We covered that up pretty well.

DELIA. Anyhow, she's not lost.

RADIO VOICE. An unusually hard rainfall has undermined a large number of buildings. The undermining seems to have run along a central line with various branchings off. (*The women look at each other and then run to map and blueprint.*) The heavy rains have exposed deep holes in some areas and whole tunnels have been revealed in others.

GERTRUDE. We dug too near the surface.

RADIO VOICE. Authorities are now investigating.

BELINDA. Oh, dear!

RADIO VOICE. Many buildings have collapsed in the North section. Those still intact are: Molly's Ice Creamery, The Experimental Theatre and the public library.

LUCILLE (*who has traced all on map*). That's right along Section F.

DELIA. We would have had it all finished in a week more.

RADIO VOICE. Part of the Order of Elks has slid into the Masonic Temple. We have another bulletin: A group of foreign agents was taken into custody when the contents of their cellar were exposed by the collapse of a tunnel leading into their hideout.

LUCILLE. I *knew* it was too good for a recreation basement.

RADIO VOICE. We will now continue with the program originally scheduled for this time.

RADIO GIRL. You can't leave me. I won't let you.

RADIO BOY. You can't stop me.

RADIO GIRL. Is this what our love has come to?

LUCILLE (*at map*). Masonic Temple. Elks. . . . That's just above section C-2.

RADIO GIRL. Don't! Don't go.

RADIO BOY. I already have my ticket for Kansas. (*Sobbing comes over radio.*)

[*Myrtle enters in army uniform and cap, with the rifle over her shoulder. She starts to cross. Delia runs after her.*

MYRTLE (*to Delia*). Where are you going?

DELIA. Where are *you* going?

MYRTLE. I've got to see a man about a war.

GERTRUDE. What about the project?

MYRTLE. I'm leaving you girls in complete charge. Make the shelter bigger and better and wider and longer. Girls, you *too* are serving. Carry on.

LUCILLE. But where are you going?

MYRTLE. *I* have been called. (*Salutes smartly.*)

GERTRUDE. Who called you?

MYRTLE. As I was walking along section C-3, I came to a wide door and opened it. There was a flight of steps. I walked up and into a room. There was a huge crowd of beautiful young men in line. I stood in line with them. When my turn came, I signed. The man at the desk said, "Buddy, you're in the army now." So I got a uniform, a gun and two pairs of long woolen underwear.

LUCILLE. But you have dependents. What about your husband?

MYRTLE. He worked before I married him. He can get his old job back. Do him good. Sitting around the house makes him neurotic. He hates housework anyhow. (*At exit.*) Goodbye, good luck. I'll send you a card. (*Salutes and marches off.*)

RADIO VOICE. Will she follow him to Kansas? Tune in tomorrow, same time, same station and try to find out.

[*Sad organ music comes over the radio.*

DELIA (*sighs*). Well, guess we've got to carry on, like Myrtle said.

LUCILLE. We can't do any carrying-on till we fix these tools.

EMOGENE. What are we waiting for?

[All go to work. There is hammering and banging, and slowly the lights on stage dim out. The house lights come on, but the banging and hammering and organ music go right on, continuing from the dark stage as. . . .

THE AUDIENCE GOES HOME

GANDER SAUCE

A Comedy

BY BETTY SMITH

CHARACTERS

MARY.
HOLLY HOLMES.
DI TRENT.

PLACE. Detroit, Michigan.
TIME. The present. Late afternoon.

MARY *is sweeping up the living room. It's not a pleasant room. It is furnished merely for utility. The windows, left, are hung with unimaginative curtains. A door, rear, leads to hallway. Another door, right, to bedroom. The essential furnishings are a library table with a commodious drawer, a straight chair near by, a dull divan, two dreary armchairs, all of a suite, a wall telephone and a nondescript rug. This room plainly indicates that it is a furnished apartment meant for transient tenants.*

As the play opens, Mary gives up sweeping and stands broom in the corner. It is hard to tell whether she is pretty. She has a towel around her head and wears a shapeless house dress and run-down pumps. She is in her early twenties. The phone rings.

MARY (*answering phone*). Yes? (*Listens.*) Oh! Holly Holmes. (*Dully.*) Yes, I'm expecting you. Come right up. (*Hangs up, goes to window, draws curtain aside and looks out for a moment. Goes to table, opens drawer, takes out a small revolver, looks at it and tosses it back contemptuously. There is a knock at the door. She closes table drawer hurriedly and stands with her back to it.*) Come in?

[*Door opens and Holly Holmes enters with some timidity. She is a pretty girl of twenty. She is dressed very prettily and carries a large leather purse which she holds tightly in both hands. She seems frightened, yet desperate.*

HOLLY. Mrs. Brown?

MARY. Yes.

HOLLY. You see I came here—(*She wets her lips and tries again.*) I mean, it was awfully nice of you to consent to see me.

MARY. And why not? Won't you sit down?

HOLLY. Thank you. (*Sits stiffly in middle of divan.*)

MARY. The note you sent me sounded so agitated. You said I could help you—(*She waits.*)

HOLLY. It's so hard to tell you why I've come.

MARY. Nonsense. I'm no monster. I'm just a girl like you. Well—maybe not as young, and surely not as pretty. (*She smiles.*)

HOLLY (*smiling back tremulously*). You're so kind, you're making it very difficult for me to tell you—

MARY. I've found that bluntness is often the best policy.

HOLLY (*drawing herself up*). Very well, Mrs. Brown. I'll be blunt. (*Takes a deep breath.*) I came here to ask you to give up your husband.

MARY (*flabbergasted, sinks into chair*). Give up my—*what?*

HOLLY. Harry.

MARY (*coldly*). You mean, Mr. Brown?

HOLLY (*defiantly*). I mean Harry. (*Shyly.*) *My* Harry.

MARY. I beg your pardon! *My* Harry.

HOLLY (*stubbornly*). *My* Harry.

MARY. Let's break this deadlock and say *our* Harry.

[*Suddenly the girl puts her hands up to her face and sobs quietly and bitterly. Mary goes to her, sits next to her and puts an arm about her shoulder.*

MARY. Forgive me, my dear. I had not realized you were so close to the breaking point. You got up all your nerve to come here to ask me to give up my husband to you and things haven't started off right, have they?

HOLLY. You—you. . . .

MARY. I know. You came up here to tell me what to do. You had all the answers ready when I would plead with you not to break up my home. And now you're crying because I'm not playing right.

HOLLY (*standing up*). There's something cold and calculating about you, Mrs. Brown. My conscience *had* bothered me, but now that you're treating it all as a joke, I'll tell you frankly that Harry and I love each other; we are happy together. I have a right to be happy and I'll fight for my happiness.

MARY. It isn't worth it if you have to fight for it. Love should be a strong, sure thing. It shouldn't be something that puts you at the mercy of a—well, a cold, calculating person like me.

HOLLY. I don't know what I expected when I met you. I expected an unattractive woman—yes.

MARY. Why?

HOLLY. Because Harry told—no, that isn't fair. I expected a shrew, a nagging wife. . . .

MARY. As Harry told you.

HOLLY. But this cold-bloodedness! If you'd only show some emotion. . . .

MARY. Such as weeping?

HOLLY. It would at least show you were human.

MARY (*moving away from her. She speaks sombrely*). My dear, I cried my eyes out—the first time.

HOLLY (*sinking back on the divan*). The *first* time?

MARY. The second time, I got mad and threw the woman downstairs. The third time. . . .

HOLLY (*holding up her hand as though to ward off a blow*). No!

MARY. You wouldn't be interested. It's happened so often that it's become dull and monotonous.

HOLLY. You're lying. I don't believe you. You know that Harry loves me. Oh, you're a clever woman, Mrs. Brown.

MARY (*going to her again. She speaks gently*). Look. Suppose we forget all about the coldness and the cleverness—and—the others. Please tell me. I'll try not to hurt you. Please believe me.

HOLLY. Well, here it is. Harry doesn't love you any more. He loves me. You are keeping us apart. He wants you to divorce him so that he can marry me.

MARY. Why didn't he come to me?

HOLLY. He couldn't bear to hurt you.

MARY. And you—you don't mind—hurting me?

HOLLY (*ill at ease*). Well, I thought it would be kinder to come and tell you, rather than have you find it out through some other source. I feel that in telling you the honest truth I am doing the right thing.

MARY. I see. The right thing. If I were a happy wife, knowing nothing of my husband's unfaithfulness, you'd still feel that it was right to disillusion me this way?

HOLLY (*doubtfully*). Yes, I would. (*Pleadingly.*) Don't you want to—*won't* you do the right thing too, Mrs. Brown?

MARY (*slowly*). If I wanted to do the right thing—what any woman would feel was the right thing—I'd go to this table drawer—(*She does so.*)—where I keep a gun. (*She opens drawer, takes out the gun and whirls suddenly.*) And I'd kill you! (*Holly puts her hand over her mouth to hold back a scream. But Mary returns the gun to drawer and slams drawer shut.*) *That* would be the right thing to do according to my instincts. But what purpose would be served? Who would gain anything?

HOLLY (*slowly*). That is true. (*Sincerely.*) But I wouldn't blame you if you wanted to kill me. I'd kill any other woman that tried to take him away from me.

MARY. Oh, my dear. You *do* love him, then.

HOLLY. I'm so glad you understand at last. (*Eagerly.*) You wouldn't want for anything. I'd make Harry support you. I wouldn't want you to be deprived of anything.

MARY. Of course not. You just want to be happy.

HOLLY. Yes. I just want to be happy.

MARY. I don't want to be facetious or anything, but what do you women see in the man? He's getting on to middle age, he's unfaithful. But there must be something. The other women. . . .

HOLLY. Please! Please don't torture me so. I can't stand it—your hinting that there were others. (*Defiantly.*) There were no others!

MARY. That's what the *others* said, too.

HOLLY. Anyhow, what he did before he knew me is his own business. He's changed now.

MARY (*sighs deeply*). Oh, how I hope you're right. Look! You're such a sweet child. Harry's just an old rounder. Now I happen to love him. I know all his faults. I know he's a first-class heel and I could kill him when he does things like this to a nice girl like you. But, in spite of all that, I really love him.

HOLLY (*piteously*). But I love him too. I see no faults in him.

MARY. You're so darn sweet and pretty and so young. You have your whole life before you. There are lots of splendid young men in the world. Somewhere is a man you'll love someday. Someone young and clean—who'll live only for you. Don't throw away your chances because of some other woman's two-timing husband.

HOLLY (*bravely*). You're painting a black picture. You want to discourage me.

MARY (*gently*). I'll have to tell you the truth. I had hoped it wouldn't be necessary. I hate to hurt you.

HOLLY. You can't shake my faith in Harry.

MARY. Why do you think I was so agreeable about having you come to see me?

HOLLY. I—er—I—why, I don't know.

MARY (*sitting next to her*). Yesterday morning, Harry came to me and said, "Mary, I've done it again." "What?" I asked him. "Oh, I'm involved with another sentimental fool." (*Holly draws in her breath sharply.*) "She mistook a kiss or two for an undying passion." (*The girl winces.*) "She's coming to see you," he told me, "to ask you to release me for her own special benefit."

HOLLY (*in a whisper*). No. No! He couldn't. . . .

MARY. And he finished up by saying, "Get rid of the little

fool for me and, Mary, I swear I'll never get into another mess again."

HOLLY (*piteously*). You're not lying?

MARY. I wouldn't lie to such a cruel extent. (*Paces.*) This is the last time I'll do his dirty work for him. (*Passionately.*) I didn't mind the others. I didn't mind telling them off, but you—you're different. (*Contemptuously.*) Harry! (*Holly weeps quietly and heart-brokenly.*) Don't—don't break your heart so. (*Puts her arms around her.*) If you *must* have him, I'll give him up to you. But don't cry so.

HOLLY (*brokenly*). Please don't pity me. Despise me for being such a fool—to be taken in so. . . .

MARY (*bitterly*). You weren't the only one, if that's any comfort.

HOLLY. I can't believe it! I can't!

MARY. But, dear child, he told me how you chased him—called him up at the office. How you wrote him. Why, he even insisted on reading the letters you wrote him, to me.

HOLLY (*shocked*). He didn't! Of all the unscrupulous. . . .

MARY (*takes small packet of letters from table drawer and hands them to Holly*). You know your own handwriting?

[*Holly takes them with trembling fingers.*

HOLLY (*in a low voice*). Yes, they're mine.

MARY (*passing a tired hand across her eyes*). Now you believe me?

HOLLY (*low whisper*). Yes. (*She lets Mary take letters from her nerveless hand.*) I—guess—I'll go. (*Gets up and stumbles blindly to door.*)

MARY. Wait! Don't you want your letters?

HOLLY. Oh, yes. (*Holds out her hand for them.*)

MARY. Let's exchange. Give me the letters Harry wrote to *you.*

HOLLY. I haven't. . . . (*Holding her purse tighter.*) How did you know I brought them?

MARY (*with a smile*). You had planned to quote from them to show me how much Harry loved you.

HOLLY (*pulling packet of letters from her purse*). You know everything. (*The exchange is made.*)

MARY. I'm sorry for everything.

HOLLY. *I'm* sorry.

MARY. Goodbye. (*Holds out her hand. On an impulse, Holly kisses her cheek.*)

HOLLY. Forgive me. (*She hurries out.*)

[*Left alone, Mary sighs deeply. Looks at girl's letters ruefully. Places them in desk drawer under gun. Then she goes to window, draws curtain aside and waves once. She lets curtain fall. She pulls towel from her head. Her hair is smartly dressed. She unzips and discards the ugly house dress, and underneath she is wearing a smart tailored frock. She kicks off her run-down shoes and gets a pair of high-heeled slippers from under divan and slips them on. There is a rap on the door, it opens and Di Trent enters. Di is nearly thirty, a vivid blond, very flashily dressed, and with heavy makeup. She enters eagerly.*

DI. Did it work?

MARY (*tired*). Yes.

DI. Did she give you any trouble?

MARY. Not much. Poor kid.

DI. Poor? Nonsense! The little fool.

MARY. Yet I felt sorry for her.

DI (*worried*). But you did get the letters, didn't you?

MARY (*after a pause, slowly*). Yes. I got the letters.

DI. Good! (*Holds out her hand.*) I'll take them, please.

MARY. Just a moment. I'd like to know what you're going to do with them?

DI. That's none of your business.

MARY. I did a thorough job of disillusioning that poor girl. I sort of got interested in the whole thing.

DI. I paid you to get the letters. You're not supposed to be interested. (*Holding out her hand.*) The letters.

MARY. I haven't been paid.

DI. Oh. (*Opens her purse and counts out ten dollars.*) Ten dollars. Is that right?

MARY. That's right.

DI. Well, here's your money. Now—(*Holds out her hand.*)

MARY. It's not enough.

DI. What do you mean? That was our agreement. You answered my personal in the *News* for a woman to perform a confidential mission. We met. You agreed on the price. I—er—got someone to get that girl to write to this address, to you, the fake wife. I paid a week's rent on this dump. Your part was easy.

MARY. But my woman's curiosity. I've got to know why you want Holly Holmes' letters so badly.

DI. It's none of your business. But if you must know, I need them for evidence.

MARY. Evidence for what?

DI. I'm going to show them to Harry Brown's wife. She'll have to divorce him, then. This girl will turn the trick.

MARY. You'd use that poor thing. . . .

DI. That poor fool.

MARY. Why do want the Browns divorced?

DI. So he can marry me, you simpleton.

MARY. But you're already married.

DI (*startled*). How do you. . . . What's it to you? I'm getting a divorce too.

MARY. Mr. Trent's a very decent person. If he knew of your affair with Harry Brown. . . .

DI. Say! How come you know so much?

MARY. You'll find out.

DI. Let's rise above all this. There's your money. And. . . .

MARY. I know. You want the letters. One more question. Why in the world do you want this Harry Brown? He's unfaithful to his wife. He was unfaithful to you and to little Holly Trent. *Why* don't you let his wife keep him and you keep your husband?

DI. Why don't you mind your own business?

MARY (*steadily*). Why do you want him?

DI (*astonished*). I don't know. Do I have to have a reason?

MARY. He'll be unfaithful to you if you marry him.

DI (*sinisterly*). Not if he knows what's good for him.

MARY (*sighs*). Well, I guess I have to turn the letters over to you. (*Opens drawer and takes letters out.*)

DI. Now you're talking sense. (*Her relief makes her generous.*) And I'm gong to give you an extra five dollars for your trouble. (*Puts five dollars more on table.*)

MARY (*pleased*). Oh, thank you.

DI. That's all right. I'll get it back from Harry. (*Again holds out her hand. Mary is about to hand them to her, but at the last moment withdraws them.*)

MARY. No!

DI (*exasperated*). *Now* what?

MARY. This is a very serious matter. How do I know whether these are Mr. Brown's letters? They may be some high government official's. You want to blackmail him.

DI. Don't talk nonsense.

MARY. Maybe they are military secrets. (*In horror.*) You may be a Nazi spy. I'm just a tool—a pawn. (*Hysterically.*) I'll be killed! I'll be killed!

DI. I never saw anything . . . wait! (*Opens her purse and takes out a thick packet of letters and thrusts them at her.*) Here! Here are letters Harry Brown wrote *me*. Compare the handwriting.

MARY (*takes letters and compares handwriting carefully. Finally looks up slowly*). Yes. I'm convinced. The handwriting is the same.

DI (*rolling her eyes in relief*). At last. (*Thrusts out her hand.*) For the last time. . . .

MARY. I believe I'll just keep your letters as well as Miss Holmes'.

DI (*almost jumping out of her skin*). For Pete's sake! Why? *Why?*

MARY (*slowly*). Because *I happen to be Mrs. Harry Brown.*

DI (*laughing loudly*). What a gag!

MARY (*quietly*). No gag. I can prove it. Who told you to put that personal in the *News?*

DI. Why . . . why . . . Harry, of course.

MARY. Of course. He hatched the whole scheme. I was in on it from the beginning. He asked me to get rid of you for him.

DI (*complacently*). Harry wouldn't want to get rid of this baby.

MARY. I hate to be unnecessarily cruel. But Harry made me read the letters *you* wrote *him*.

DI (*explosively*). He did not!

MARY. He said if you wouldn't listen to reason, I was to take them to your husband.

DI. You wouldn't dare! (*In terror.*) Why, he'd divorce me!

MARY. Isn't that what you want?

DI. If there's any divorcing to be done, I'm doing it. (*Laughing.*) What am I wasting my time for? You're not Harry's wife and you haven't my letters.

MARY. I have them right here. (*Opens drawer, fumbles in it.*) Now what did I do with them? (*Pulls out a modish crushable hat, a pair of gloves, places them on table, absentmindedly takes out gun, places it on hat. When Di sees gun, a look of terror comes into her eyes and she backs towards the door.*) Ah! Here they are. (*Pulls packet out and carelessly tosses gun, Holly's letters and Di's letters back into drawer. Holds up packet.*) Do you believe me now?

DI (*comes closer to examine them. Sighs*). They're mine. And frankly, sister, I don't mind telling you they're dynamite.

MARY (*demurely*). I know. I read them.

DI (*humbly*). Look. I'd like awfully much to have them back, Mrs. Brown.

MARY. And so you shall, if you promise to keep away from Mr. Brown in the future.

DI. You don't have to tell me. After all, John Trent is a pretty decent person—as you said.

MARY. See that he never finds out about you. (*Hands her the letters.*) Here are the letters you wrote my husband. I'd advise you to destroy them.

DI. You telling me? (*A thought strikes her.*) But the letters Harry wrote to me. If my husband. . . .

MARY. You'll have to trust me. I'll take good care of them.

DI (*afraid*). Aren't you going to burn them?

MARY. I'll keep them a while. Just to hold them over your head and keep you in line.

DI (*admiringly*). You know all the angles, don't you?

MARY. I've had experience before, getting Harry out of messes like these.

DI. I'd like to ask a question if you don't mind.

MARY. Your turn.

DI. What in the world do you see in an unmitigated heel like Harry Brown?

MARY. A fair question.

DI. You have proof that he's a philanderer and. . . .

MARY. I know what kind of a heel he is. The answer is, I love him.

DI. Why?

MARY. Why did you?

DI (*astonished*). I don't know.

MARY. I have ten of the best years of my life invested in him —not to mention a few girlish dreams. He was just twenty-one when I married him. He was so good-looking, so darn decent, so . . . well, I know all his faults and I'm still in love with that boy I knew.

DI (*wistfully*). It must be wonderful to love somebody that way.

MARY. You try it. Remember John Trent as he was when you first fell in love with him.

DI (*rapturously*). He played fullback on the football team. He had the curliest hair—(*Stops. Slowly.*) I see what you mean. (*Looking at her wrist watch.*) He'll be coming home from the office. Oh! I must get dinner. (*Holding out her hand.*) Goodbye. (*They shake hands.*) No hard feelings?

MARY (*sincerely*). No hard feelings.

DI. Goodbye again. (*Goes out.*)

[*Mary sighs, sits down wearily and passes her hand across her eyes. Gets up. Sees money on table. Picks it up, turns and starts towards door. Stops. Shrugs shoulders philosophically and thrusts bills into her purse. Also puts gun and the two packets of letters in purse. Goes to phone, dials a number.*

MARY (*in phone*). Mr. Brown? Yes, I wish to speak to Mr. Harry Brown. (*Waits.*) Oh, hello, Mr. Brown. This is Mary Melaney of the Central Theatrical Bureau reporting. Yes, indeed. I was able to obtain your letters from both Miss Holmes and Mrs. Trent. Yes, I ascertained they were yours. You have nothing to worry about now. (*Screams.*) What? (*Lets receiver fall and backs away from phone in sheer astonishment. Goes back and picks up receiver.*)

What did you say? (*Listens.*) That's what I *thought* you said. (*Bitterly mimicking him.*) *Am I doing anything tonight!* (*Takes a deep breath.*) *Mister* Brown! I just got you out of two entanglements. And now you're ready to step right into a new one. What about your wife? (*Listens. Drily.*) Yes, I reasoned as much—that your wife is a very understanding woman. For your information, I wouldn't go out with you if you were. . . . (*Listens.*) No. I've changed my mind. I'm going to keep those letters. No, it isn't the price. Your offer to pay me twenty-five dollars to get them was very generous. But I'm going to keep them. Go ahead. Report me to the Bureau. I'll get fired but *I'll still have your letters.* What am I going to do with them? Well, I impersonated your wife on two different occasions this afternoon. I put my heart in it. I *was* her for the time being. And you know, I got to feeling sorry for the poor lady being married to a heel like you. (*Listens.*) *Mister* Brown! Your language! (*Holds receiver away from her ear a moment. Back to phoning.*) I don't know why in the world she wants you. But I think us women should stick more together. I'm going to keep you safe for her. Now! I have these incriminating letters. I know where you work, who you are and where you live. If I ever hear of you—just once—stepping off the straight and narrow—I am going to deliver those letters to Mrs. Brown. Be good now. That is my message to you. (*Slams up receiver. Stares at phone a minute. Mumbles under her breath.*) Am I doing anything tonight! (*Explosively.*) Well!

[*She goes to table, puts on her hat, picks up her gloves and purse and with a farewell grimace about the room, she goes out as . . .*

CURTAIN

THE WOMAN ALONG THE ROAD

A Holy Week Drama

BY E. HARRIETT DONLEVY

WOMEN OF JERUSALEM

AISA, *wife of a High Priest.*
MIRIAM, *wife of a young Priest.*
REBA, *wife of a successful merchant.*
MICHAL, *wife of a young teacher.*
THE WOMAN.

PLACE. Jerusalem.
TIME. The first Good Friday.

MIRIAM'S *house is on one of the main thoroughfares of Jerusalem. On this day of days, Miriam and three of her friends have gathered in the courtyard of her home. There is a high wall running across the rear of stage. In the wall is a heavy wooden door. The door has a small open square covered with iron grillwork, about head-high from the ground. The furnishings are simple: a long, crude table on which stand a water jug and some cups; some crudely made benches drawn up to the table; and a few crude stools around the courtyard.*

As the play opens, Aisa, an attractive matron dressed in a rose-colored robe and blue head-covering, is pacing about restlessly. Miriam, young and vivacious, wearing a pale yellow robe and a deeper yellow head-covering, is seated at the table. Reba, thoughtful and lovely, wearing a deep blue robe and a violet head-covering, is sitting opposite Miriam. She is busy with her weaving. Also occupied with weaving is Michal, who sits apart on a low stool. She wears a deep green robe and a lighter green head-covering. She is quiet and pensive.

AISA (*peering through the grill*). I confess that I have been most uneasy since dawn. (*Turning.*) This is a strange day, Miriam.

MIRIAM. Aye. (*Pause.*) I thought it strange, Aisa, that my husband left at daybreak for the Temple, and without donning his priestly robes.

AISA. My husband, also, went in his everyday garments.

MIRIAM. I heard him tell another that he and all the Priests had been summoned hurriedly to the Palace of Pilate.

AISA (*standing on tiptoe to peer through the grill down the road*). It would seem from here that the whole of Jerusalem—(*Ironically.*)—excepting the wives of the important citizens—have gather by summons at Pilate's Palace.

REBA (*looking up from her weaving*). But why, Aisa? Why is our ancient City so disturbed? Why have so many strange visitors flocked here? (*Looks at Miriam.*) Miriam, do you know why all the markets were closed this morning, as though it were a Roman holiday? Even my husband, who is wont to keep his bazaar open at all times, keeps it closed on this day.

AISA (*going to her*). Reba, could you not have asked him?

REBA (*shrugs*). It would be of little good. He will not speak of his affairs with me. (*Tearfully.*) He treats me as a child, not as a wife.

MIRIAM (*sighing*). They are all like that. They do not desire us to know what happens in the world outside these walls. Oh, these husbands! Myself, I only know what I overhear. And that is little.

AISA (*going to her confidentially*). I know this: At dawn my husband and my elder brother were holding speech with each other. They did say that King Herod, the Roman governor, was making a visit to Jerusalem.

MICHAL. We of Jerusalem despise the Romans. Herod would not dare set foot in the City were it not of great import.

MIRIAM. Why comes he here? He, a hated Roman, daring to come when we celebrate our Feast of the Passover? Why, Michal?

MICHAL. It is said that there is grave trouble concerning this young Prophet in our midst.

REBA. The same who is causing unrest?

AISA. Aye, the false Messiah.

MIRIAM (*dreamily*). I heard this young Prophet once, at the Temple. There is something about Him that is not soon forgotten. I wished to hear Him speak His Parables again. But the men in my household said it was not fitting that I go. They said He was a false Prophet.

MICHAL. Tamar, she who is my handmaiden, knows of one who had been blind from birth. And this one went to see the Man and, lo! his blindness fell from him. And all this came to pass when he but touched the hem of the Man's robe. His name . . . Jesus, I think.

MIRIAM. His deeds set him apart—as though he came of the ancient Prophets.

MICHAL. It is said that he has defiled our laws and mocked our faith. My husband is but a teacher of young boys, not a Priest. Therefore, he knew not the whole story.

AISA. How blessed you are, Michal, to be told *that* much.

REBA. If the Romans arrest such a Man, his death is a verity. Know you that the Romans think that we of Jerusalem are slaves and fit only for crucifying?

MICHAL. I do not hold with His teachings. But He is a Jew as we are. Therefore, I would not wish Him harmed.

MIRIAM. Crucifixion! (*She shudders.*) A word to make the blood run cold.

[*Very dimly, as if from far away, come muffled shouts and cries.*

REBA (*rising*). Hark! Listen! You may hear the cries and shouts from Pilate's Palace.

[*The other women stop their work and rise slowly to their*

feet. In the silence, the noises come up louder. Miriam hurries to the door in the wall. The other women follow after her.

AISA (*excited*). Do you open the door, Miriam, that we may look down the road. Mayhap. . . .

[*Miriam pulls open the thick door. All gasp and fall back as a woman half falls, half stumbles into the courtyard. She had been leaning against the door. She wears a gray robe and a white head-covering.*

WOMAN (*imploringly*). Please—please to let me come in a moment. Let me sit down.

MIRIAM. But—but we know not who you are.

WOMAN. It does not matter. I am hurt. (*Holds out her left arm.*)

AISA. Please, Miriam, give her sanctuary. She is ill.

[*Aisa and Michal help Woman to bench. Aisa rolls back Woman's left sleeve.*

WOMAN. Aye, my arm. . . .

MICHAL (*gasps in pity at the bruises*). How did it happen?

AISA. The arm is badly bruised. Miriam, do you get some cool water and clean linen.

[*Reluctantly, Miriam goes off R.*

REBA (*going to Woman*). If you would but tell us of the happenings in the City. (*Apologetically.*) We know so little —here in our walled garden.

MIRIAM (*returning with a bowl and a linen napkin*). There was no cloth to hand save this square of my finest damask. (*Pours water into bowl from jug on table.*)

AISA (*takes cloth and dips edge of it in water*). It is of no matter.

[*Miriam holds bowl while Aisa bathes the arm. Michal puts her arm about Woman, who rests her head against Michal. Reba stands a little apart.*

REBA. If you will but tell us. We would know.

WOMAN (*between spasms of pain*). I was down by Pilate's Palace. Verily, the crowd was great there. I desired to know what was happening. But I was caught within the crowd. I could not get out of the way. It was no place for a woman. . . .

REBA (*eagerly*). But you saw—you saw!

WOMAN (*staring ahead*). Aye, I saw.

REBA (*passionately*). Tell us! Tell us!

WOMAN (*rising to her feet. Speaks slowly*). I saw the Man—He whom they call in mockery, King of the Jews. (*The other women look at each other, troubled, and draw away from Woman.*) His eyes were sad and His voice was of a great gentleness. I heard the populace shouting. I saw people throw stones at Him. They protested not when Pilate condemned Him to death.

REBA (*in a tense whisper*). Death! For a Jew, that means crucifixion!

AISA (*with intense hatred*). Those Romans!

WOMAN. Death! Aye, by crucifixion. (*In horror.*) I saw the cross.

MIRIAM (*gives a low gasp of horror, the bowl falls from her hands and shatters on the floor*). The cross!

[*Woman sways as though she would fall. Aisa and Reba support her.*

MIRIAM (*coming forward*). May I give you bread and drink? You seem ill.

WOMAN. My gratitude goes out to you. But I am not ill. I'm just—weary. (*Sits down again.*) I have walked many miles this day and there is much on my mind.

MIRIAM. I will call one of the men servants to help you home. (*Starts to go R.*)

WOMAN. No! (*Miriam comes back.*) I have no home. (*The women look at each other in astonishment.*) Ah, I see by your faces that you are astounded. You are good women—protected, loved, sheltered. . . .

REBA (*gently*). We would hear your story.

WOMAN. I am one who must labor for my bread. I go from city to city. I work where I can—in the homes, the fields—honest work, but very hard. My strength is not great. . . . (*Shrugs.*) Now you are sorry you took me in.

MIRIAM (*ashamed*). No. We welcome you. After all, you are a woman—even as we.

WOMAN. No, I am not like unto you. I am a woman who is alone. Between you and me lies a wide, strange world.

You are protected—not even permitted to go into the streets alone. For me, there is only myself—unto myself.

MIRIAM. But was it always thus? Your hands—forgive me—are not those of one who has always labored.

WOMAN (*painfully remembering*). I remember once, when I was but a child, I lived in the far-off hills. My mother had once been a rich merchant's daughter. But she married with my father, a shepherd. They were happy in the hills. (*The others draw nearer, in interest. They sit on the benches near her.*) One night, my brothers and I were in the hills, keeping watch with our father over the sheep. And we saw a star. It was of wondrous beauty, this star. We wanted to follow it, my brothers and I.

MICHAL (*all attention*). Dared you?

WOMAN (*rising*). No, you would not believe.

MIRIAM (*puts her hand on Woman's hand. Woman sits again*). Nay, tell us. We would hear your story.

AISA. Aye, by coming here you are helping us get through this strange, dark, lonely day.

WOMAN. There was this star. We wondered about it. There was much talk. But in the end we followed it. We came at length to a shabby inn and thence to the innkeeper's stable, where we thought to find but cattle and sheep. And behold there was a man there, and a gentle lady, and with them a tiny Babe. (*She passes a hand across her eyes.*) It was so long ago. I was a small child. It is hard to remember all. But there were many shepherds there in that stable, and there were others who wore shimmering robes and who bore gifts worth a king's ransom. I was very young. Mayhap I dreamed all this. But there was the star. That I did not dream.

MICHAL. That star. You saw it again?

WOMAN. I have never seen it again. (*Miriam pours out a cup of water and hands it to Woman. She drinks it gratefully.*) But the star stayed in my heart. (*Sets the cup aside.*) When I grew older, I again journeyed to that inn. I worked as handmaiden to the old woman there. I thought to see the star again. (*Sighs.*) But it never returned. The woman died and so I went up into Bethany to seek work. In time I forgot the star. Now, sometimes, it is as though I may have dreamed that too.

MIRIAM (*touching her hand affectionately and reassuringly*). Methinks it was no dream.

REBA. I too have heard tell of the star.

MICHAL. It is a legend among the people.

WOMAN. So? I am glad. (*She puts her hand to her heart.*) Of late I am sick in my heart. If I could but find it again —that star—I would be well again. I would once more believe . . . believe. . . .

AISA. Yours is a strange and a moving story.

MIRIAM. We would help you. . . .

REBA. Hush! (*She rises, holding up her hand for silence.*)

[*From far away, may be heard the sullen and angry roar of the crowd. Reba runs to the door, opens it and looks off L.*

REBA. There is a strange sight coming along the roadway. Look, all of you! (*All but Woman crowd around her.*) There are soldiers . . . mobs . . . a Man. . . . (*Silence.*)

MICHAL. The mob is strangely silent now.

REBA. I cannot see. . . .

MIRIAM. My eyes are very sharp. Let me see. . . .

[*They make way for her.*

AISA. But I cannot see over your head.

REBA. Miriam, tell us what you see.

MIRIAM. It is that Prophet. I recall Him. I have never forgotten His face.

MICHAL. But do they come this way?

MIRIAM. They have paused . . . to. . . . (*She stops, then continues.*) They make Him kneel. They are putting the cross on His shoulder. They would have Him carry it. Oh! (*She gasps in horror.*) A soldier runs forward and presses a crown of thorns on His head. The blood flows. A Roman soldier goads Him to His feet. They laugh. . . .

WOMAN (*to herself*). It is wicked. Wicked to take life— wicked to inflict such agony when life is agony enough. There is great suffering in the world—without this cross.

[*Reba turns and sees the Woman's pain. She goes to her, places an arm about her and leads her to the door.*

WOMAN (*with a strange, new dignity*). I would see for myself.

(Looking at her, the others slowly back away from the door. The Woman stands alone, looking down the road.) He is frail and ill. The thorns have pierced His head. The blood runs down into His eyes. (*Turning to the others.*) Lady of the house. . . .

MIRIAM (*stepping forward*). Yes?

WOMAN. Give me that cloth—the square of damask with which you did bathe my wound.

[*As in a dream, Miriam picks up the cloth and hands it to her.*

AISA (*in awe*). What would you . . . with the damask. . . ?

WOMAN. I go to wipe the blood from His eyes.

REBA (*terrified*). They'll never let you through to Him. They will kill you.

WOMAN (*with authority*). They will let me through. (*She goes out of the door and off L.*)

MIRIAM (*wailing*). My best linen! It will be stained. I'll never get it cleaned.

REBA (*at the door*). She is running down the road.

AISA (*looking over her shoulder*). She does not seem ill and weak now.

MIRIAM (*sitting at table*). We have been fooled by her wild story.

REBA. Oh, wonder of wonders, the Romans give way to her! They are letting her through.

AISA. The crowd surrounds her. I cannot see. . . . I cannot see. (*Long pause.*)

MICHAL (*pacing up and down*). This silence! This silence!

REBA. And now they are coming this way—coming this way.

AISA. They will pass this way.

REBA. They come in silence. I wonder. . . .

MIRIAM (*frantically*). Close the door, close the door! The Romans will kill us all! (*Reba and Aisa close the door. All huddle near table, backs to audience, staring at the grill. Nothing is seen for a while.*)

[*The helmet of a Roman soldier is seen passing the opening. Nothing for a while. Then a row of helmets march past. Nothing for a while. Then the heads of the populace are seen going past. After this, nothing for a long, long time. Then the Cross, the top of it visible through the grill, comes by. It pauses at the grill for a moment, then it dips as though He who carried it had stumbled from the weight of it. After a moment it rises and passes out of sight. Now there is nothing at the door. The women fall to their knees and bury their faces in their veils and weep silently. After a long while, there is a firm knock on the door.*

WOMAN (*from outside*). Open the door unto me! (*Dazed, Miriam gets to her feet and opens the door. Others rise as the Woman enters. Woman comes in slowly. She is wonderfully dignified. Her illness has left her. She holds the damask close to her.*)

MIRIAM. You . . . you wiped His face?

WOMAN. Aye.

REBA. They came past here. . . .

WOMAN. On their way to Golgotha, where they are even now nailing that good Man to the cross.

[*The courtyard suddenly grows dark. There is a distant low rumble of thunder.*

WOMAN. Even now the nails pierce His flesh.

AISA (*putting her hands over her ears*). We would hear no more.

MIRIAM (*going to Woman*). There is a great change in you, as though—as though—

WOMAN (*quietly*). When I wiped His suffering face, I saw my star again—the one I saw more than thirty years ago in the hills. It was the same star—blindingly silver—only now, there were drops of blood on it. (*She holds the cloth to her heart. She seems entranced.*)

MIRIAM. My square of damask—there will be stains on it. . . .

[*The Woman holds out the cloth. The others gasp and back away in awe. On the linen is imprinted a perfect likeness of the face of Jesus with its crown of thorns.*

REBA (*under her breath*). A miracle!

MIRIAM. God have pity on all men. This is He, the Messiah our prophets said would come among us in the shape of a mortal man.

AISA. He has come among us but to be put to death.

MICHAL. Even as it was prophesied.

MIRIAM (*wringing her hands*). What a blind, blind people we are.

REBA. Yet in the Temples they called Him an impostor.

MICHAL. It is given to us to know the truth.

AISA. In my heart I felt this might be so . . . that He was the One for whom our people waited.

MIRIAM. We had no right to stay within our sheltered garden, blind to everything about us, while our City committed this crime. We are women. We know things in our heart that it is not given men to understand. We should have spoken for this Man—spoken up to our fathers and husbands and sons.

WOMAN (*from out of her thoughts*). And I found the star again. I wandered far—

MIRIAM. I beg of you to sit down with us. Let me give you food and drink.

WOMAN. No, I must go forth now.

MIRIAM (*pleading*). Don't leave us.

AISA. We know not your name even.

WOMAN. I am known only as Veronica.

REBA. Abide with us, Veronica.

MICHAL. We would have you stay with us always.

WOMAN. I will return someday. (*Goes to door.*) But now I go to Golgotha—to behold with my own eyes. Then I will travel up and down the wide land, telling other women of what has happened in your City this day. (*As if foretelling.*) And all shall believe. (*Gives linen cloth to Miriam.*) And do you guard this well for me. (*Miriam takes cloth reverently.*) Remember! I shall come back among you again. (*She goes. Regretfully, Miriam slowly closes the door after her.*)

AISA. It grows late. The men of my household will be returning.

REBA. Aye, I must start toward my house. (*Sighs.*)

MICHAL. The woman told us very little about herself.

AISA. Shall we tell our men of her—and the face on the damask?

MIRIAM (*shaking her head*). They will not believe.

MICHAL. But in time to come—

MIRIAM (*slowly*). Aye, in time to come all will believe.

AISA (*as if to herself*). She was a strange woman.

MICHAL (*staring at the door*). I dare not believe that my eyes beheld her. Think you that we dreamed she came among us?

REBA. We dreamed not.

MICHAL. Think you she will come this way again?

MIRIAM (*folding the cloth reverently*). Aye, she will return. We must treasure the miracle of this cloth and keep it safe for her. Her name, she said, was Veronica. (*Dreamily.*) It's a good name—Veronica.

THE CURTAIN FALLS

THE THREE-TIMER

A Farce

BY JAMES F. STONE

THE LADIES

VERONA VALE, *a novelist and bride-to-be.*
PAULA, *her best friend.*
GERTIE, *a manicurist.*
MAXINE MANNING, *an acquaintance.*
TESSIE, *a chambermaid.*
YVONNE, *a lady from the dress shop.*

PLACE. New York City.
TIME. Afternoon. The present.

VERONA VALE *is a successful novelist. She can afford a very luxurious suite at the Ritz-Astor Hotel in New York. Her living room is elaborately furnished with an ornate desk, chairs upholstered in silk brocade, and an expensive-looking chaise longue. There are flowers about the room. In the left wall is a door which leads to the bedroom and bath. Downstage of this door is a closet door. Long French windows, prettily curtained and leading out to a balcony, are in center of back wall. Door in right wall leads to hall.*

As the play opens, Gertie is manicuring Verona Vale's toenails. Verona, in a pretty negligee, is reclining on the chaise longue. Gertie sits on a low chair at her feet. Verona is young and beautiful; Gertie is young and pert. Paula, Verona's friend, is packing dainty lingerie in Verona's overnight bag. Paula is young, attractive and smartly gowned.

GERTIE (*turning to look at Paula*). Don't you wish you were getting married, Miss Paula?

PAULA (*folding a lacy slip*). What woman doesn't? (*Sighs.*) But the next best thing is packing the bride's honeymoon bag.

VERONA (*smiling at Paula*). You are a darling, Paula. I don't know how I'd get through the day without you.

GERTIE (*to Verona*). I declare, Miss Vale, you're not excited at all . . . this being your wedding day and. . . .

VERONA. I'll have a nervous breakdown as soon as I have a free moment.

GERTIE. And you're going to be married right here? In this very room?

PAULA (*snapping overnight bag shut*). That's how the blueprints read.

GERTIE. I think it's simply wonderful, really I do. Married to a famous aviator.

PAULA. Verona Vale is famous in her own right. She writes books, you know. (*Picks up bag, carries it to door left, places it in bedroom and returns.*)

GERTIE. An aviator and a love-story writer. (*Sighs.*) That makes it so romantic. Don't you love romance?

PAULA. I'll settle for security and serenity.

VERONA. Don't be a cynic, darling.

PAULA. You're different, Verona. You live in a dream world. My, my, how aesthetic you are.

GERTIE (*to Verona*). Are you? I used to play tennis myself, but I don't have time any more. When are you going to be married?

VERONA. In half an hour, I hope.

GERTIE (*dropping her file*). Oh, my goodness!

VERONA. If we can locate the groom.

GERTIE (*picking up file*). Have you tried phoning?

PAULA. For the last two hours, we've been phoning at ten-minute intervals.

GERTIE. Don't worry, Miss Vale. He'll show up. They always

do. You can't keep a bee away from the honey. (*Laughs lightly.*)

PAULA. You've got something there, Gertie.

GERTIE. I know. My boy-friend says man was not made to live alone. (*Chuckles.*) And *he* won't, if I can help it.

VERONA (*amused*). You seem to know men.

GERTIE. That I do. That I do. (*Accidentally jabs her with nail file.*)

VERONA. Ouch!

GERTIE. Oh, excuse me. I was thinking of an experience I once had with a man and it made me so *mad.*

PAULA (*sitting at desk to look over some letters*). Make the next recollection pleasant and sentimental.

GERTIE (*uncapping bottle of nail enamel*). I'm not the dumb type, really I'm not. (*Applies polish carefully to Verona's toenails. It is almost black-red in color.*) I know how to handle men. Sometimes you got to leave them have their own way. (*Complacently.*) You take my boy-friend.

PAULA (*over her shoulder*). No. You take *mine.*

GERTIE (*no sense of humor*). I mean—he never wants to go out. Says sitting home is better.

PAULA. It *is* cheaper.

GERTIE. But I don't mind because he isn't exactly the type a girl would show off. So we sit home and get along fine.

VERONA (*jumping*). Oh, Paula, *have* you called the desk to see whether my gown has arrived?

PAULA. Just five minutes ago. *Nothing* has arrived.

VERONA (*squirming*). What a day! If Steve only knew what I was going through.

PAULA (*going to her*). *Don't* try to calm yourself, dear. It's a woman's inherent privilege to worry on her wedding day.

GERTIE. And after, too, if you ask me. (*Leans back to survey her work.*)

VERONA (*drawing her feet away*). Thank you, Gertie.

GERTIE. But the second coat. . . .

VERONA. This will do.

GERTIE. Being that you're getting married you *ought* to have two coats on your toenails.

VERONA (*waves her away and reaches for the phone*). No, no.

(*To Paula as she removes receiver.*) I'm going to call his club again. He simply can't do this to me.

PAULA. You don't suppose he's had another spell?

VERONA. The Lord forbid!

GERTIE (*curiously*). Spell?

VERONA (*phoning*). Culver 1235.

PAULA (*to Gertie*). A hangover from a plane accident. Dizzy spells. Loss of memory.

GERTIE. That ought to come in handy after he's married.

VERONA (*phoning*). Is Mr. Stevens there?

GERTIE. Will that be all, Miss Vale?

VERONA. Yes, thanks. (*Gertie rolls up her implements in the towel.*) Not there? Thank you. (*Hangs up and glances at her wrist watch.*) Half an hour to go. Something *must* have happened to him.

PAULA. It's just an informal wedding. Even if he is a little late it won't matter.

VERONA (*stands up and slips into her mules*). Oh, no! What about the minister? What can I tell *him?*

PAULA. Decide when he gets here. Besides, your gown hasn't arrived.

VERONA (*pacing*). I'm going to get married on time even if I have nothing to wear.

GERTIE (*chuckles*). That's the idea.

VERONA. Paula, you know how irresponsible Steve is.

PAULA. Just like all flyers.

GERTIE. If you want my opinion of those high-flyers. . . .

PAULA. Gertie, please go. You're making Miss Vale nervous.

GERTIE. Okay. And congratulations, Miss Vale. I'm sure you'll be very happy.

VERONA. Thank you.

[*Gertie goes off left, forgetting her implements.*

PAULA. She's an optimist.

[*Phone rings.*

PAULA. I'll take it. You relax. (*Into phone as Verona listens eagerly.*) Who? On her way up? Oh! thank you! (*Hangs up.*)

VERONA. Who is it?

PAULA. Maxine Manning.

VERONA. Of all people! She'll drive me to distraction with her inane chattering.

PAULA. And what a brain. She's so dumb she thinks a vice-president is a gang leader.

VERONA. Get rid of her.

PAULA. What can I tell her?

VERONA. Anything. But keep her out from under my feet.

PAULA. I'll tell her you're resting up for the wedding.

VERONA. She's so suspicious, she'll never believe that.

PAULA. Oh, wouldn't I like to get my hands in her cheap permanent!

[*Knock on door.*

VERONA. There she is. (*Goes to door right.*) Tell her I'm bathing. (*Goes.*)

PAULA (*opens door left. Very sweetly*). Maxine darling! What a pleasant surprise!

MAXINE (*enters breathlessly*). Where is she? Where is the darling? (*Maxine is fluttery and very smartly dressed in too-young clothes. She is well over thirty but thinks she conceals it by her vivacious manner.*) I could hardly believe my eyes when I heard about it. Who is he? Do I know him? What does he look like? What does he do for a living?

PAULA. Please! One question at a time. But who told you about it? It was supposed to be a secret.

MAXINE. I know. But Verona told Mrs. Crew and Mrs. Crew told Anne Sutherland and Anne told Betty Bruce and Betty told. . . .

PAULA. That's enough. I haven't time for serial stories.

MAXINE. Where *is* Verona? I must see her at once. I want to congratulate her. I always said she's get a man. But what kind of a man is he? Where did she meet him? Oh, never mind, I'll ask her myself. Where is she?

PAULA. She's—she's lying down. Resting.

MAXINE. What! How can she lie still at a time like this? Why, if I were in her shoes, I'd be goose pimples all over. (*Giggles.*)

PAULA. Let's not disturb her now, Maxine. Why can't you come back later?

MAXINE. And miss the wedding? I should say not! What time does it take place? And where? Who's going to be there? And you haven't told me the man's name. Maybe I know him. Maybe. . . .

PAULA. I'm quite sure you don't know him. He's been in South America for years. He's an aviator.

MAXINE. Oh, how romantic! Does he fly an airplane?

PAULA (*impatiently*). Yes, yes.

VERONA (*calls from off right*). Paula?

PAULA (*going right*). Yes, dear?

MAXINE (*starts for right*). I must see what the bride looks like.

PAULA (*stopping her*). Wait a minute, Maxine. Give the girl a break. You wait here. I'll tell you all about it. (*Hand on knob.*) Read a book.

MAXINE. At a time like this? Don't be silly.

PAULA. Sit down and rest your feet.

MAXINE. They're not tired.

PAULA. Sit down and rest your brain, then.

MAXINE. My brain isn't tired.

PAULA. That's right. It's just a little lame. (*Goes off right.*)

MAXINE (*following quickly*). But Paula. . . . (*Door shuts in her face.*) Well!

[*Tessie knocks at door left.*

MAXINE. Come in.

TESSIE (*the chambermaid, enters with towels*). Excuse me. I brought some towels. (*She is fat and homely, wears a striped dress, apron and unbecoming cap.*) Say, are you the bride?

MAXINE (*pleased*). Oh, no. I'm a guest.

TESSIE. I thought you was. I wanted to talk with you.

MAXINE. Miss Vale's the bride.

TESSIE. Her and me both. I'm going to be a bride tomorrow.

MAXINE. Really? What a coincidence.

TESSIE. No, just love. I'd sure like to get a look at the other victim.

MAXINE. You mean Miss Vale?

TESSIE. I'm just kidding. Yep, I'm takin' the fatal step tomorrow. And I been waitin' a long time.

MAXINE. I can hardly believe it.

TESSIE. Me, too. My arm is sore from pinchin' myself.

MAXINE. Do you think you'll feel any different after you're married?

TESSIE. Yeah. Relieved. It's different with Miss Vale. She knows what she's getting.

MAXINE. Surely you do. . . .

TESSIE. Nope. I ain't got no idea what he looks like . . . I mean, in real life. Met him through the Lonely Hearts Correspondence Club. But he's sure a handsome cuss. I'll show you his picture. (*Takes photo from her apron pocket.*) Ain't he a scrumptious-lookin' creature?

MAXINE (*taking picture*). He *is* good-looking. I'm surprised.

TESSIE. Surprised? I'm *numb.*

MAXINE. But what's that on his chin?

TESSIE. His lip, I guess. I heard Miss Vale is goin' to be married right here in this room.

MAXINE (*absently placing photo on table*). Is she? I just heard about it and rushed right over. I haven't seen her yet. (*Sighs longingly.*) I wonder how it feels to be on the brink of matrimony.

TESSIE. Like waitin' for a blitzkrieg to strike. Especially after waitin' all these years.

MAXINE. How many?

TESSIE. I'm twenty-five and never been kissed.

MAXINE. I can understand that.

TESSIE. That doesn't mean that a whole lot haven't tried.

MAXINE. And given up in disgust, I presume.

TESSIE (*fussed*). Yes. I mean no. (*Looks around vaguely.*) I got to get on the job. This is my last day and I'm breakin' in a new girl. (*Again the vague look, then the dawn.*) Oh, yes. The towels. (*Puts them on chair and goes out door left.*)

[*Maxine turns to table, picks up photo, hurries to door as if to call Tessie. Shrugs, changes her mind. Sets photo up on table. Then goes to door right.*

MAXINE. Verona! I simply must see you. I. . . . (*Gertie knocks on door left.*) Oh, come in again.

GERTIE (*entering*). I forgot my tools.

MAXINE (*exasperated*). Here! (*Picks up pile of towels and hands them to her.*)

GERTIE. *Tools.* I'm the manicurist.

MAXINE (*throwing down towels*). Help yourself. (*Knocks at door right. Without waiting for an answer, she suddenly opens it and walks in.*) Verona, I think it's perfectly horrid the way you're treating me. You know. . . . (*But the door is closed and her voice is cut off.*)

[*Gertie gathers her manicure things. Yvonne knocks on door left. Gertie doesn't answer. The door opens and Yvonne enters. She carries a large dress box. Yvonne is thin, acidulous and past her first youth. She has a hungry look.*

YVONNE. Excuse me. Is this Miss Vale's suite?

GERTIE. Yes, but I think she's dressing.

YVONNE (*placing box on table*). I'm from the gown shop.

GERTIE. She's waiting for you.

YVONNE. We've been so rushed and she allowed us so little time and what with the altera—(*Stops dead as she sees photo.*) Good heavens!

GERTIE. What's the matter?

YVONNE. Jimmy!

GERTIE (*looking around*). Where?

YVONNE. What's he doing here?

GERTIE. I don't see anybody.

YVONNE. What do you know about this?

GERTIE. Not a thing. I'm just the manicurist.

YVONNE (*picking up photo*). What's this picture doing here?

GERTIE (*looks at it*). I guess that must be the groom.

YVONNE (*almost screaming*). The groom?

GERTIE. Not bad-looking, is he?

YVONNE. You're telling me! Do you know who this is?

GERTIE. I told you. I think he's Miss Vale's fiancé.

YVONNE. He's *my* fiancé.

GERTIE. No!

YVONNE (*reads inscription on back of photo*). "Eternally yours." This is my Jimmy.

GERTIE. You mean he *was* your Jimmy.

YVONNE (*turns picture, reads*). "To my Dream Angel." That's *me*. That's what he always called me.

GERTIE. Maybe you were yesterday's dream. Men are all alike. You can't trust them.

YVONNE. Just wait till I see him. I'll dream-angel him.

GERTIE. Miss Vale can't find the Dream. I mean, he's lost.

YVONNE. He's what?

GERTIE. She's nearly crazy trying to locate him. She's afraid she's being left in the lurch.

YVONNE. You mean at the church.

GERTIE. Anyway, he can't be located.

YVONNE. That's your story. Well, I'm going to stay right here and have this out with him. He can't do this to me. What time is the wedding?

GERTIE. It won't be long now. I just did her toenails.

YVONNE (*glaring at the photo*). The beast! Something told me he was no good. He's got a wicked eye. Well, she can have him. She can marry him. But someone will have to hold him up for her when I get finished with him.

GERTIE. What are you going to do?

YVONNE. I'm going to turn this wedding into a funeral. You just wait and see.

GERTIE. I'd love to, but I'm not invited.

YVONNE. You can come as my guest. This is my party. (*Starts left.*) She can spend her honeymoon picking lead out of him. (*Pats her pocketbook fondly.*)

GERTIE. You . . . er . . . haven't got a gun?

YVONNE. I collect large sums of money. The store makes me carry a gun. (*Again pats her pocketbook.*)

GERTIE. But if you shoot him, think of the scandal. Your picture will be in all the papers.

YVONNE. Good! Then I'll get in the movies. (*Sees window, looks out.*) Ah—a balcony.

GERTIE. Yeah. You can go right in the main hall from it. That is, if you want a quick getaway after the murder.

YVONNE. I can use that. (*Sees book on table.*) What's this?

GERTIE. Oh—that's Verona Vale's latest book.

YVONNE (*picks it up, reads title*). *How to Make a Man Happy.*

GERTIE (*giggling*). No wonder he left you.

YVONNE. Happy! I'll write one—all over his face. *How to Make a Man Miserable.* (*Throws book down.*) The deceitful wretch! (*Starts left.*) I can't wait to get my hands on him. (*Turns.*) Don't you dare say anything about this. If you do. . . . (*Pats her pocketbook fondly.*)

GERTIE (*eyeing pocketbook*). I—I—won't.

MAXINE (*from off*). All right, dear. I'll see.

GERTIE. Someone's coming.

YVONNE. I'm going. (*Picks up box.*)

GERTIE. Don't take her dress. She's been waiting. . . .

YVONNE. She won't need it now. (*Exits left door suddenly.*)

MAXINE (*entering from right door*). Oh! We thought maybe the groom had arrived. Miss Vale is so worried.

GERTIE (*with meaning*). She should be.

MAXINE. Whatever do you mean?

GERTIE. She's got an awful ordeal to face.

MAXINE. You mean you've *seen* him?

GERTIE. No. Only his picture. (*Indicates photo on table.*)

MAXINE (*picking it up*). That isn't his picture.

GERTIE. You mean—that isn't Miss Vale's fiancé?

MAXINE. Oh, no. The poor girl! She forgot her sweetheart's picture. But I suppose she'll be back.

GERTIE. Who are you talking about?

MAXINE. The chambermaid. She left this picture here.

GERTIE. It—it belongs to her?

MAXINE. Yes. It's her future husband. They're going to marry tomorrow.

GERTIE (*collapsing into chair*). Oh, my gosh!

MAXINE. What's the matter? What has happened?

GERTIE. Oh, I hate to think of what *is going to happen.*

MAXINE. Are you ill?

GERTIE (*jumping up*). I've got to find that girl.

MAXINE. Do you know what you're talking about?

GERTIE. No—yes—no. Oh, I don't know. (*Rushing to door right.*) Give me air . . . air. . . . (*Exits wildly.*)

TESSIE (*screams off right, then enters, limping*). Oh! Oh, my sore toe!

MAXINE. What in the world!

TESSIE. What's eatin' that manicurist? She run right over me.

MAXINE. She must have had an hallucination.

TESSIE. Must have been powerful. How many did she drink?

MAXINE. It's not a drink. It's a vision.

TESSIE. She's no vision. I came back after my picture. I forgot it. Golly, I wouldn't want to *lose* him. (*Gazes adoringly at picture.*) Not with that pretty puss.

MAXINE. Pretty is for a woman—handsome for a man.

TESSIE. Pretty or handsome, he's good-looking.

MAXINE. I forgot. Here I stand talking and Miss Vale wants to know if her gown has come. (*Exits into bedroom.*)

TESSIE (*raising her voice to talk after her*). There's only one thing worrying me. (*Looks at picture*). How much will this honeymoon cost me?

PAULA (*sticking her head out of bedroom door*). Girl?

TESSIE. Certainly I'm a girl. Do I look like a horse?

PAULA. Will you please come help us straighten this room?

TESSIE. Sure, sure. (*As she goes into bedroom.*) Anything to get my mind off what's going to happen tomorrow.

[*Yvonne opens French window slowly from outside. Enters carefully and looks around cautiously.*

VERONA (*from bedroom*). I'll just try again, Paula. (*Enters calling back over her shoulder.*) Perhaps I'd better phone again. (*Yvonne is partially concealed by draperies.*) I've simply *got* to know. . . .

YVONNE (*stepping forward*). Hello.

VERONA (*startled*). Oh!

YVONNE. I'm from the gown shop.

VERONA. Thank goodness! But where is my gown?

YVONNE. You won't be needing it.

VERONA. What do you mean?

YVONNE. I mean the man you think you're going to marry is my fiancé.

VERONA. You're crazy. You don't know what you're talking about.

YVONNE. Oh, don't I? I suppose you're going to play the heroine and stand by to the bitter end. Ha! That's a laugh.

VERONA. I refuse to listen to you. Please go.

YVONNE (*taking small revolver from bag*). This says I'm staying.

VERONA (*choking off scream*). No!

YVONNE. Don't scream. Just answer my questions. What time do you *think* you're going to marry him?

VERONA (*nervously*). It's almost time now. The minister should be here any moment.

YVONNE. Good. I'll head the reception committee. (*Indicating closet door.*) What's in there?

VERONA. It's a clothes closet.

YVONNE. Get in there and keep quiet. (*Forces her to door.*)

VERONA. But I'll smother.

YVONNE. What a pleasant thought. Get in there. (*Opens door and forces her in.*)

VERONA. Please!

YVONNE. Keep quiet, I said. (*Closes door and turns key.*)

TESSIE (*from bedroom*). I'll get a clean bedspread.

[*Yvonne just has time to get to draperies. Tessie enters, on way to hall door, stops to pick up photo. Starts for hall door with it.*

YVONNE (*stepping forward*). Just a minute.

TESSIE (*turns*). Huh?

YVONNE (*holding out her hand*). I'll take that.

TESSIE. You will? (*Stares at photo.*) What's the matter? Kinda like his looks?

YVONNE. Kinda. And you?

TESSIE. I ought to. We're goin' to get hitched. (*Taps photo.*) Him and me.

YVONNE (*startled*). Good Lord! What a man.

TESSIE. I'll say.

YVONNE. You—you're supposed to be the bride, too?

TESSIE. It won't be long now.

YVONNE. All I can say is, you don't look it.

TESSIE. Well, I ain't had much experience.

YVONNE. It can't be that *you're* "Dream Angel"?

TESSIE (*simpering*). Does it show that plain?

YVONNE (*pointing to photo*). Do you know what that man is?

TESSIE. What?

YVONNE. He's a polygamist.

TESSIE. What? (*Looks at photo.*) He wrote me he was a Baptist.

YVONNE. I'm going to stay right here and meet him face to face when he arrives.

TESSIE. He ain't comin' here. He can't come here.

YVONNE. Don't try to stall. I know all about the wedding plans. But I want to find out how he operates. You can forget all about getting married today.

TESSIE. But I don't want to get married today.

YVONNE (*taking out gun*). Come here. (*Nods to closet door.*) I'm going to put you on ice until I need you.

TESSIE. But that ain't no icebox.

YVONNE. Get in there. I'm making a collection of brides.

TESSIE. That's a clothes closet.

YVONNE. Get in. I'm going to greet the minister and the groom. I'll let you both out in time for the wedding march.

TESSIE (*sees Verona*). Say, what's she doin' in there?

YVONNE. Get in!

TESSIE (*as Yvonne pushes her in*). But this's taken. It's goin' to be crowded.

YVONNE (*turning key*). Quiet, or I'll shoot through the door.

TESSIE (*muffled from closet*). Oh, she's goin' to shoot us through. . . .

VERONA (*the same*). Sh! Don't talk.

TESSIE (*the same*). I can't breathe—

PAULA (*coming from bedroom*). Verona, what's keeping you? (*Yvonne steps back to draperies.*) Where. . . .

MAXINE (*who has followed her out*). She's gone.

PAULA. But where?

MAXINE. How should I know? But why?

PAULA. You don't suppose anything happened to her?

MAXINE. I bet she jumped out of the window!

PAULA. Don't be silly. Why should she?

MAXINE. Maybe she couldn't stand the strain—I mean, the suspense.

PAULA. Oh, talk sense.

MAXINE. But you know what happened to that girl that was about to be married in Verona's latest book.

PAULA. Nonsense! But where could she go in her dressing gown?

GERTIE (*knocks, then enters breathlessly from hall door*). Excuse me for coming right in. Have you seen her?

PAULA. No. We're looking for her, too.

MAXINE. She's wandering around in her negligee.

GERTIE. Has she really got a gun?

PAULA. What *are* you talking about?

GERTIE. That girl. (*Points vaguely.*)

MAXINE. I don't see any girl.

PAULA. What girl?

GERTIE. I should have warned you before. She's going to break up the wedding.

PAULA (*to Maxine*). Can you understand what she's saying?

GERTIE. She says Verona Vale stole her boy-friend.

PAULA. What *is* all this?

GERTIE. I'll tell you.

YVONNE (*stepping out with gun in her hand*). Never mind. I'll tell them.

GERTIE. She *has* got a gun.

PAULA. Who are you and what does this mean?

GERTIE. She's. . . .

YVONNE (*to Gertie*). You keep out of this.

GERTIE (*gulps*). All right.

YVONNE. I'll show you exactly what this means. (*Pulls open closet door.*) All right, ladies. All out for roll call.

GERTIE. But it's all a mistake.

VERONA (*staggering out*). I think I'm going to faint. (*Indicating Tessie.*) She used up all the air.

TESSIE. It was gone before I went in.

PAULA (*supporting her*). What happened, dear?

VERONA. I . . . I. . . . (*Gasps.*)

YVONNE. Somebody explain.

PAULA. That's up to you, young woman.

YVONNE. I'll start with a few questions. (*To Tessie and Verona.*) Are you going to get married today?

VERONA. I don't think I am.

TESSIE. I *know* I ain't.

GERTIE. Let me talk.

YVONNE. Shut up.

TESSIE. She's got to talk. She's a manicurist and they're like barbers.

YVONNE. Are you all nuts?

TESSIE. I'm all right. (*Doubtfully.*) I guess.

[*All the women start talking at once.*

YVONNE. One at a time. Who is supposed to get married today?

VERONA. I am—if I can find my fiancé.

YVONNE. Ladies, we've all been double-crossed. The three of us. And I'm going to stop this wedding if I have to put a bullet through everybody.

VERONA. Oh! (*Screams and faints on chaise longue.*)

ALL. She's fainted!

MAXINE. Throw some water on her—like they do—

TESSIE (*collapsing weakly into chair*). Throw some on me too.

YVONNE. And wait until I get my hands on that double-crossing Don Juan.

TESSIE. That ain't the name he gave me.

PAULA. That's the reason you can't locate him, Verona. He knows and he's hiding out.

MAXINE (*slapping Verona's wrists*). Say something, darling.

GERTIE (*to Yvonne*). If you'll listen to me for just a moment. . . .

YVONNE. Another word out of you and you'll go in that closet.

[*Gertie rolls her eyes and gulps.*

PAULA (*to Yvonne*). What do you mean by saying Miss Vale's fiancé is your fiancé?

YVONNE. Where's that photo?

TESSIE (*holding it to her*). I got it.

YVONNE. Give it to me.

TESSIE. I will not!

YVONNE (*points gun*). Give!

TESSIE. Yes, ma'am. (*Thrusts it at her.*)

YVONNE (*holding it to Tessie's face*). Take a good look.

TESSIE. Why? I've seen it before.

YVONNE. Is that your fiancé?

TESSIE. Yeah. But I don't know him well enough to fight over him.

YVONNE (*showing photo to Paula*). Is this the man Miss Vale is engaged to?

PAULA. That? (*Laughs.*) Certainly not.

YVONNE (*nonplussed*). You're sure?

PAULA. Wait! (*Runs into bedroom, returns with framed photo of man in uniform.*) This is Miss Vale's fiancé.

YVONNE. Gosh! (*Gun wavers.*) I guess I made a mistake. (*Puts gun back in purse.*) I'm sorry I frightened Miss Vale. (*Takes gun out again and turns furiously on Tessie.*) But I'll have this out with you.

TESSIE (*her hands over her head*). I give up.

YVONNE. Where did you meet Jimmy?

TESSIE. Through a correspondence school.

ALL. What?

TESSIE. I mean, through the Lonely Hearts Club.

YVONNE. That dirty double-crosser has never been lonely in his life. We've both been taken for a ride.

TESSIE. He never took me anywhere. I've never met him.

YVONNE. I'll tell him a thing or two. . . .

TESSIE. Want me to help you?

YVONNE. You keep out of this. You don't know when you're well off. (*Suddenly.*) Did you send him any money?

TESSIE. No. But I sent the Lonely Hearts two bucks.

VERONA (*reviving*). Paula. . . .

MAXINE. She's coming to.

VERONA. Where . . . what. . . .

PAULA. It's all right, dear. Everything has been explained.

YVONNE. I'm awfully sorry I upset you, Miss Vale.

VERONA (*sitting up*). Oh, now I remember. Steve. . . . (*She starts to weep.*)

PAULA. It's all a mistake, Verona. This girl thought her fiancé was two-timing her with you. But he wasn't.

TESSIE. He was. But with me.

PAULA. This maid met her fiancé through a Lonely Hearts Club and she left his picture in this room.

GERTIE (*at last getting to talk. She is so excited, she quivers*). And when this girl—(*Points to Yvonne.*)—found his picture here, she naturally thought Miss Vale was marrying him today.

YVONNE. And he's still a stinker!

VERONA. What else can happen today?

YVONNE. I have your gown. . . .

VERONA. I'll never get to use it. I can't find Steve.

[*Phone rings. All rush to it. Paula gets there first.*

PAULA (*phoning*). Yes? (*Listens.*) Oh! (*To Verona.*) It's him!

VERONA (*grabbing phone*). I'll tell him a thing or two. (*Phoning.*) Hello? (*Sweetly.*) Darling! What in the world happened to you? (*Listens. Sighs in relief. Sways.*) Oh. . . . Oh. . . .

TESSIE. She's goin' to pass out again.

PAULA. What is it, darling?

OTHERS. What's the matter?

VERONA (*weakly dropping receiver*). He—he fell asleep! (*Collapses in chair.*)

PAULA (*taking receiver*). Fell asleep? Where?

VERONA. Home. In bed.

MAXINE. Asleep? At a time like this?

GERTIE. What a man!

TESSIE. I'd like to get a peek at him.

PAULA. But, Verona, at the very moment of his wedding. How *could* he?

VERONA. He was reading my book *How to Make a Man Happy.*

GERTIE. Well!

VERONA (*rushing back to phone, into receiver*). Hurry, darling. I'm waiting. (*Hangs up.*) Oh, what a relief. (*Girls all laugh and start talking at once.*) And now—if I may have my wedding gown—

YVONNE (*going to window*). One wedding gown, coming up. (*Hauls in a string. The box is attached to it.*) I had to hide it someplace. (*All laugh. Yvonne puts box on table and opens it.*)

VERONA (*takes gown out of tissues*). It's lovely!

[*She slips out of her negligee. Paula and Yvonne slip wedding gown over her head. Maxine zips it up the back.*

ALL (*in admiration*). Ah-h-h-h!

VERONA (*graciously*). And you're all invited to stay for the wedding.

TESSIE. Excuse me. I got to go.

VERONA. Where, Tessie?

TESSIE. To get my job back. I resigned, you know.

PAULA. Oh, I'll fix that for you. I'll speak to the hotel manager.

TESSIE (*going to hall door*). I still got to go.

GERTIE. But Miss Paula told you. . . .

TESSIE. I got to see a lawyer.

YVONNE. Why?

TESSIE. I'm goin' to sue the Lonely Hearts and get my two bucks back. (*Goes out, slamming door. All laugh.*)

[*There is a knock on the hall door.*

VERONA (*electrified*). The minister.

[*All grow sober. All but Verona take out their handkerchiefs and begin dabbing at their eyes.*

PAULA (*throwing her arms around Verona*). Be brave, darling.

[*Head high, a smile of triumph on her lovely face, Verona moves slowly to door to meet her fate as . . .*

QUICK CURTAIN

A HINT OF LILACS

A Social Drama

BY RUTH WELTY

THE WOMEN

JULE, *a scrubwoman with a police record.*
ANNIE, *an Irish scrubwoman.*
MRS. ROSS, *the boss of the scrubwomen.*
BESSIE, *who remembers a better way of life.*
MARGARET, *a young working mother.*
MRS. VANDEVER, *a lady customer.*

PLACE. New York City.
TIME. The present. Night.

MRS. ROSS *and her corps of scrubwomen have charge of cleaning up a large office building. They are working at present in the ladies' board room of a large brokerage office. It is a small, well-fitted room where ladies come to watch the stock ticker. Covering most of the back wall is the conventional board, with its columns of closing prices of railroads, industrials, oils, motors, foods, and so on. Down left, near the wall, is a hooded arrangement which is the illuminated ticker, now at peace. The room has about two dozen chairs placed in rows, facing the ticker. These are substantial chairs, designed for the comfort of the lady stock-manipulators. At least one is upholstered with removable cushions. Along front of stage, parallel with the "fourth wall," are presumably two windows which are made brief use of during the play. There are two low benches along this in-*

visible wall. It is about nine o'clock at night and the lights are on.

As the play opens, Jule is scrubbing the floor with a brush. She has a can of scouring powder and a bucket. She is a middle-aged, gray-haired, grim-visaged, hard-lipped scrub-woman—an old-time police-blotter registrant who is now going straight and is proud of her job. Annie, who is kneeling beside one of the front chairs, is looking over a newspaper which she has found. Annie is nearing middle age, is stout, easy-going, Irish and good-natured. She holds a dusting cloth which rarely sees vigorous use.

ANNIE (*flipping paper so she can read it more easily*). Ha! Would you believe it, Jule!

JULE (*not stopping her work*). What?

ANNIE. There do be a sale on at Macy's!

JULE. Now, Annie, what's sales to us?

ANNIE. Fruit cake, sixty cents the pound. An' smoked turkey —terrible expensive.

JULE. You'd do better gettin' to work.

ANNIE (*unconcernedly*). I'm a-workin'.

JULE. Yeah!

ANNIE. I *am*. (*Dusts with one hand, still reading.*) It's doin' me best, I am, heavens knows. Considerin' I'm tied to a growlin' crone with the devil to work in her. A body's knees gives out onct in a while.

JULE. *All* the while.

ANNIE. Anyway, it's most time for lunch. Though it's a quare thing to be eatin' victuals at nine o'clock at night.

JULE. Work!

ANNIE. Aw, Jule, it's eatin' we are in a minute.

JULE. If you had the fear o' God in you, you'd be doin' your job, 'stead o' thinkin' 'bout victuals.

ANNIE. I got all the fear o' God I can be comfortable with. And if it's wishin' you are to be rid o' me, speak up. I'll be askin' the boss to let me work with Bessie. Bessie's a good girl. We get along—the pair of us.

JULE. Bessie! That puny trollop.

ANNIE (*angrily—she is ever ready to lash out*). Don't you—I'll be forgettin' your gray hairs and givin' you a slap.

JULE. Bessie's sick. Sick all over.

ANNIE. It's grievin' she is after the country. An' no wonder—that dark hole she lives in with that sick man o' hers. An' never a breath o' sweet air.

JULE. She's no worse off, Annie, than the rest of us.

ANNIE. Sure an' she's worse off! Didn't she see the light o' day far off in a valley? An' didn't her mother raise flowers for a livin' before the pains took her off? Sure she knows different. You an' me—we're rats. It's dark holes we've crawled into all our lives.

[*Mrs. Ross, the boss of the scrubwomen, pauses in the doorway, clears her throat loudly. Annie looks up with a start and falls to work vigorously until Mrs. Ross passes on. Then she stops to read the paper.*

ANNIE. Oh, an' it's perfumery they're havin' a sale on, too. Imported odors. One eighty-four. See the picture?

JULE. I don't want to see no picture.

ANNIE. Ain't that sweet, now. Bessie'll be wantin' to see this. (*Tears picture out slowly, carefully.*) When she comes in for her bite o' lunch, she can be lookin' at it.

MRS. ROSS (*enters suddenly, displeased at Annie's fooling*). Well, Annie? You got time to read the paper?

ANNIE. Just puttin' it in the basket I was, Miz Ross. (*Rises, puts paper in waste basket, managing to finish tearing out advertisement and to place it in her bosom.*)

MRS. ROSS. You ain't half done this room yet. And here it is nine o'clock! What's the matter with you two?

JULE. 'Tain't me. I work hard, Miz Ross.

MRS. ROSS. Look at that dirt.

JULE. That's Annie's dirt.

ANNIE. I'm gettin' to it, ma'am. My knees ain't so good like they was.

MRS. ROSS. You better shake a leg, Annie, or it's the sack for you. I'm warnin' you now. I ain't havin' no triflers in my outfit.

ANNIE. No, ma'am. Yis, ma'am. (*Dusts energetically.*)

Mrs. Ross. How many stories in this office building? Seventeen! This broker's office ain't the only one. It's all got to be cleaned between six at night and three in the morning. And it will be, or I'll know the reason why.

Annie *and* Jule. Yes, Miz Ross.

Mrs. Ross. Mind now!

Both. Yes'm.

Mrs. Ross (*muttering as she goes to door*). Guess I'll have to get me some Negroes. Whites ain't good no more. (*She goes.*)

[*A gong sounds offstage.*

Annie (*stopping work at once*). Lunch!

Jule. Now see what you done! Got us bawled out.

Annie (*goes to corner, gets her sack of lunch, proceeds to spread it out comfortably on chair in front of her as she seats herself on bench*). Ach! Don't ye be mindin' her. Talk's her job, it is. I ought to be washin' me hands, I'm thinkin'. But my stomick—it says no. So I ain't.

Jule. Well, *I'm* washin'. My three boys may be jail-birds, but their mother was never a slattern. (*Stalks out left.*)

[*After a moment, Bessie comes in. She is a slender, harassed-looking woman past her first youth. She has more refinement than the others. She is nervous and strained. She carries an apple.*

Bessie. Can I eat with you, Annie?

Annie. Sure thing, Bessie. I was waitin' for you, dearie.

Bessie. It's close, isn't it? And the air—do you care if I raise the window?

Annie. Sure, make it like ye want it, dearie.

[*Bessie comes down to front of stage, pantomimes opening of window. Sits on bench, staring out over audience, breathing deep as though she were at the window.*

Annie. It's the night air ye be takin' into your lungs. An' it ain't fer the likes o' you, I'm thinkin'.

Bessie. It's good. Clean and good!

Annie. How's *your* partner, dearie?

Bessie (*still engrossed with the night*). Margaret? All right.

Annie. Doin' her share o' the work?

BESSIE. Almost. She will when she gets her strength back. . . . How cool and fresh the air is tonight. Almost like where I used to live.

ANNIE. It'll do. (*Pause.*) Margaret still grievin' 'bout leavin' her baby at home?

BESSIE. Yes. He's all alone—and only four months old. (*She shivers.*) Oh, Annie! Why do women like us go on living?

ANNIE (*in the middle of a bite*). Eh? What's that?

BESSIE. I mean it! What's the use?

ANNIE. Now, Bessie, me darlin', that's a hell of a way fer a girl still in her twenties to be talkin'. What are you doin' with that apple? No wonder you got the blues. Here, take this. (*Takes apple from Bessie and forces half her big sandwich into the girl's hand.*) Pork, it is. Give ye somethin' to go on. (*Softly, after a moment.*) I know. It's young ye are an' a heart full o' love fer your man. How is he, dearie?

BESSIE. Last night—he had to sit in the chair all night. Couldn't breathe, somehow. I wanted to get a doctor. But you got to have money to pay for a personal visit. (*Desperately.*) Sometimes, Annie, I—I just can't— (*Controls herself; then lifts her head rapturously.*) Oh! Smell!

ANNIE. What?

BESSIE (*turning back into room*). Like spring. It is, Annie. All at once it's like flowers.

ANNIE. It's winter yet, dearie.

BESSIE. Don't you smell it?

ANNIE. No-o. All I do be smellin' is the cleanin' stuff on me hands.

BESSIE. A minute ago, when I came in, I was sick. I was like him—couldn't get my breath. (*Tries to catch the elusive odor; can't find it.*) Oh, it's gone! I don't smell it!

ANNIE. You're wore out, poor dear. Set ye down, an' get somethin' inside ye.

BESSIE (*sitting on edge of chair*). Everywhere the bad smells. At home it's dark and stifling. The fever smell all through our room. Those tenement stairs—I stumble up them, holding my breath. Then I let myself into our room. It's worse than the stairs. I hate the air with only dying in it. I hate it, Annie.

ANNIE. Try puttin' a bit o' bread in ye, darlin'. (*Bessie slowly takes a bite and chews it.*) That's better, hm?

BESSIE. For a minute just now, I thought I was back in Fairways. It's a nice name, ain't it—Fairways? And I thought my mother was just coming in the door, with a big basket of flowers she'd cut fresh for the market. They was all wet with the dew, and sweet. Life was pretty good then, Annie. (*Takes another bite.*)

ANNIE. Sure, it was that! An' it will be again, when your worry with your man gets over.

BESSIE (*sniffing, making a discovery*). There it is! I know where it is!

ANNIE. What?

BESSIE. That lady customer who smells so good. She always sits in this chair. (*Goes to one of the cushioned chairs and brings her face close to the back cushion.*) Yes—it's strong now. It fills the room. Flowers, Annie.

ANNIE. Dearie, that reminds me. (*Brings out her clipping and shows it to Bessie.*) I saved it fer ye.

BESSIE (*reading*). Perfume!

ANNIE. A sale on it.

BESSIE. Rose, hyacinth, while lilac—a dollar eighty-four an ounce.

[*Margaret enters from left. She is young, quiet, pretty in a stolid sort of way, not quite sure what life is all about.*

BESSIE. Margaret! They're selling good perfume—cheap—down at Macy's!

MARGARET. I wish they was sellin' baby clothes cheap. (*Seats herself on floor near benches with her lunch.*) His blanket's thin, an' it's cold in the room these nights.

JULE (*enters, washed, with her packet of lunch*). Well, Margaret, settin' on the floor, are you? (*Seats herself comfortably with her lunch.*)

BESSIE (*to Margaret*). Here's a newspaper for you, Margaret. (*Hands her a copy of* Wall Street Journal.) Maybe I got a blanket somewhere. I'll wash it up for you. (*Goes back to chair next to cushioned one.*)

MARGARET. Would you, Bessie? He's so little—and me not there to warm him. (*Looking at paper.*) "The Wall Street

Journal." Wonder why they print a paper like that—all figures. (*She sits on it.*)

JULE. Some folks knows what figures is all about.

ANNIE. Sure, they's folks comes here an' sits all day watchin' figures that go by up there. (*Indicates board.*) They're cracked in the head, I'm thinkin'.

JULE. They ain't honest, that's what. Work like what we do's honest. Nothin' else.

BESSIE. Women make money watching the figures. It must be wonderful to sit all day watching figures and making money. All the smell of the soap and the cleaning powder is gone by then. Why must this stuff smell so bad?

JULE. There's things that's worse, a whole lot.

ANNIE. It's jail, she means.

JULE. Yes, jail! (*Turns on Annie.*) I may a-went to jail onct or twict, but I got enough sense now not to be bawled out by no boss.

ANNIE. Indeed, an' ye needn't be castin' no slurs at me!

JULE. It's you that's castin' the slurs.

ANNIE. Indeed, an' I only said ye'd went to jail, an' it's the truth.

JULE. An' I won't be called a jail-bird! By you nor nobody!

BESSIE. Please! Don't talk like that. Don't it make you kind of sick?

JULE. But she called me. . . .

ANNIE. Shut up!

MARGARET. Everybody!

[*There is a moment of silence. They eat.*

BESSIE (*tremulously*). It's like the fever, and the tenement—that gets into you and eats your soul out. At home—here—you never get away from it! Oh, I can't stand it any more! (*Beats cushions of the chair, burrowing under them. Suddenly, she springs to her feet with a shock of surprise.*) Oh! *Oh!* (*With a cry, she kneels down and snatches out a rich purse from under the cushions.*) Look what I found!

ANNIE. A purse! Fer the love o' Gourd!

MARGARET. Somebody's left it. Open it quick, Bessie.

[*All the women crowd around Bessie while she opens the purse. It contains a folded certificate of stock, a vial of ex-*

pensive perfume, a twenty-five-cent piece, and a handkerchief.

ANNIE (*as Bessie hands her the certificate*). An' what might this be?

BESSIE. I don't know.

JULE. Where's the money?

BESSIE. There is only this! (*Holds up the quarter.*)

JULE. Two bits! Gourd! There's *got* to be more than that! (*Snatches purse, explores it eagerly.*) Nothin'! (*To Bessie, pointing to the perfume.*) What's that you got?

BESSIE. Nothing. Just a little bottle.

JULE. Give it here. (*Snatches it, examines, smells it, thrusts it back.*) Stink water!

ANNIE (*fingering the purse*). It's a pretty price some man has paid for this. Maybe we could be sellin' it somewheres.

JULE. Not me. I don't fool around no fence. Cops is watchin' the fences.

MARGARET (*pointing to certificate in Annie's hand*). What *is* that thing? (*As Annie turns it over to her.*) "Certificate of stock. One hundred shares."

JULE. Looks like the paper that money's made out of.

MARGARET. New money before it's old and dirty.

ANNIE. Could we be a-sellin' that, do ye think?

MARGARET. There's some names wrote on it—here.

JULE. Uh-oh! If there's names, we don't try nothin'. Names in writin' can land you in jail.

MARGARET. But what will twenty-five cents buy? When we all want so much?

JULE. I ain't sayin' I wouldn't carry the purse. Now look. You, Margaret, take the handkerchief. See? It's elegant. Cost a lot of money.

ANNIE (*to Jule, bridling*). An' who might ye be, sayin' who shall have which?

JULE. It's my room, ain't it, the purse was found in?

ANNIE. It's my room too. And 'twas Bessie did the findin'. Here, Bessie. Here's your property. (*Grabs purse, handkerchief, stock certificate and gives them all to Bessie.*)

JULE (*to Annie*). What do you think you're doin', you Irish mick?

ANNIE. It ain't yourn. It's Bessie's. She found it.

JULE. But we're all in on this. We'd better be. 'Cause if *I* ain't, I'll snitch on you, that's what I'll do.

ANNIE. Well, gray-haired though ye be, I've a mind to knock yer bloomin' teeth out! (*Annie advances threateningly on Jule, who takes a fighting stance. Bessie runs between them.*)

BESSIE. Here, take it. Take everything. Only stop fighting.

[*Shamefacedly, the women part.*

JULE. Do I get my share or do I go to Miz Ross?

BESSIE. Listen to me, both of you. Jule, you take the purse. You don't mind, really, do you Annie?

ANNIE. Think I want to go on carryin' my ten-cent-store purse?

BESSIE. Then *you* take it.

JULE (*gives a possessive cry*). Yi-ah!

MARGARET. Can't we sell it and divide the money? It's made of fine material. Somebody will buy it.

JULE. Who?

MARGARET. I don't know. Someone. I seen one like it, in a store window marked twenty-seven dollars.

JULE. Just the kind I been wantin'. Hand it over, Bessie.

ANNIE. Don't you do it!

JULE. Hand it over or I'll make you wish— (*There is a sound just outside the door.*)

MARGARET (*giving a little scream*). Oh! Wait! Somebody's comin'!

JULE. O, Gourd!

[*Quick as a flash she thrusts the purse back into Bessie's hands and drops down to her work with the brush, swishing her lunch out of the way. Bessie has only time to hide the articles behind her back when Mrs. Vandever, a richly dressed, spoiled, shallow, petulant society woman enters quickly.*

MRS. VANDEVER (*disappointed*). Oh, you've started on this room already. (*Comes down front.*) Which one of you has been cleaning here? (*No one answers. Annie and Margaret start desultorily to work.*) Apparently all of you have. Well? Did one of you see a purse? A black purse with silver mountings?

ANNIE. Silver, is it!

MRS. VANDEVER. Did *you?*

ANNIE (*glibly*). No, ma'am. Niver a bit of it, ma'am, an' praise the saints.

MRS. VANDEVER (*to Jule*). You?

JULE. Naw.

MRS. VANDEVER. You're sure?

JULE (*suddenly flashing a little coin purse from her bosom*). That's my purse. That. And it carries all I got. And what I got's honest.

MRS. VANDEVER (*looks around and under the cushioned chair. To Margaret*). How about you? Have you seen my purse?

MARGARET. No—n-o, ma'am.

MRS. VANDEVER (*to Bessie*). And you?

BESSIE (*backing away a little*). I—I don't understand, ma'am. I'm only one of the cleaning women.

MRS. VANDEVER. You can understand that I've lost my purse. I didn't take it out of here. It must still be here. (*Continues her search.*)

ANNIE. There's plenty o' folks uses this room, ma'am.

MRS. VANDEVER. During the day, yes. But I was the last customer to leave. I had to see the closing prices. Steel was behaving very badly. (*Suspiciously.*) There is something very queer about this.

ANNIE. It's you that's the queer one, Miss, with your talk about steel.

MRS. VANDEVER (*to Bessie*). May I ask what you have behind your back?

BESSIE. It's only—my dirty cleaning rag. You—you're a lady, you wouldn't like to—

JULE (*to Bessie*). Aw, shut up! What are you tryin' to talk to her kind for?

ANNIE (*to Jule*). *You* shut up!

MRS. VANDEVER. Where is your boss? You have one, I suppose?

ANNIE. Oh, yis, ma'am.

MRS. VANDEVER. Well? One of you go get her.

ANNIE. She won't do you no good, ma'am. She don't know no more'n us. Even less, you might say.

MRS. VANDEVER. I prefer to speak to her myself. (*To Bessie.*) Young woman! You go and tell your boss a lady wishes to speak to her right away.

BESSIE (*knowing she cannot turn without the articles showing*). Me?

MRS. VANDEVER. Certainly. You're not working. (*Bessie gulps, sways a little.*)

MARGARET. I'll go get her.

MRS. VANDEVER. Wait! You might hide it somewhere, if you've found it. Oh, dear! How does one deal with such women? Call her! Call your boss!

ANNIE (*yelling in a sing-song tone*). Miz Ross! Yoo-hoo! (*Mrs. Ross appears in the doorway.*) This lady is wantin' to see ye.

MRS. VANDEVER (*to Mrs. Ross*). My good woman, are you in charge of these charwomen?

MRS. ROSS. I am. What have they done now?

MRS. VANDEVER. They don't seem to want to talk about something I've lost. I'm Mrs. Allen Vandever. I come to this brokerage office nearly every day.

MRS. ROSS. And what have you lost?

MRS. VANDEVER. My purse. I'm positive I left it here. Yet they say they haven't seen it.

MRS. ROSS. Did it have much money in it?

MRS. VANDEVER. No money at all. But a valuable certificate of stock. I'm almost sure I left it in this very chair.

[*Mrs. Ross goes to chair, pounds the cushions, feels around it.*

MRS. ROSS. It's not here.

MRS. VANDEVER. But I was the last person here. They were closing up the office when I left. I don't want to accuse anybody, but—

MRS. ROSS. Maybe the tenant found it an' is keeping it for you.

MRS. VANDEVER. No, I called up the board-room manager half an hour ago. He hadn't seen the purse.

MRS. ROSS (*bluntly to the women*). Which one o' you got it?

MARGARET, JULE *and* ANNIE. I ain't.

BESSIE (*more slowly*). Nor I.

MRS. ROSS. Which one o' you knows anything about it? Come! Speak up!

ALL FOUR. Nobody. Not I!

MRS. ROSS. You're lyin' to me. If you are—

JULE. What'd we want with a purse? We ain't got nothin' to put in it.

MRS. ROSS (*to Mrs. Vandever*). Shall I search 'em?

JULE. You won't frisk me. I'm a decent, God-fearin' woman, I am.

MRS. ROSS (*to Mrs. Vandever*). Say the word!

MRS. VANDEVER. Do whatever you have to do to get it. My aunt will never forgive me. It's her stock certificate.

MRS. ROSS (*narrowly*). Bessie, come here. (*Bessie slowly comes forward two or three steps.*) What you got behind your back?

BESSIE (*scared but holding her ground*). Nothing.

MRS. ROSS. Let's see if it's nothin'!

BESSIE. It's nothing, I tell you. Only a—dirty cloth.

[*Mrs. Ross starts towards Bessie, but Annie quickly gets between the two.*

ANNIE. Don't ye be layin' hands on Bessie. Boss or no boss, I'll—

MRS. ROSS. Get out of my way!

ANNIE. Ask her from here what you want. (*To Mrs. Vandever.*) It's a poor sick thing she is, stayin' up all the day with her dyin' man an' workin' all night. (*To Mrs. Ross.*) You keep your distance or I'll be lettin' one o' me dirty fists fly in your clean face, ma'am.

MRS. ROSS. So! Gettin' fresh, are you? Well, we'll see if you hand the police this same line o' gab. (*Turning away. To Mrs. Vandever.*) I'm callin' headquarters, lady. It's the only way to handle a bunch o' toughs like these.

MRS. VANDEVER (*flustered*). Oh dear! I suppose you must.

MARGARET (*alarmed, hurrying after Mrs. Ross*). Don't call the cops, Miz Ross.

ANNIE (*at the same time Margaret speaks*). Go on! Yell for the bulls, ye rat!

MRS. ROSS. Keep 'em in sight, lady, and don't let 'em out o' this room, I'll be back in a minute. (*She hurries off.*)

MARGARET. Don't let her do that! I can't go to jail! I got to go home to my baby! I *got* to! (*Calls.*) Miz Ross! Miz Ross! (*Tries to leave.*)

MRS. VANDEVER (*barring exit*). I'm sorry, you can't leave this room. She told you that.

MARGARET. Don't let her get the cops on us. My baby's all alone. He'll starve! He'll die! Oh, you'll let *me* off, won't you lady?

MRS. VANDEVER. You wouldn't talk. It's in the hands of the police now.

MARGARET. But I can't go to jail. Don't you see that I can't? God have mercy on me, I'll talk. I'll tell you the truth. I got to. It's *her* has got it. (*Points to Bessie. Annie gives a cry and lunges towards Margaret but Jule catches her.*) She found it in the chair like you said. An' she's hidin' it from you. I ain't got nothin' to do with it. It's Bessie that has it. Oh, let me go home to my baby when quittin' time comes.

MRS. VANDEVER (*to Bessie*). So, it's you after all!

BESSIE (*her eyes blazing with indignation, but her hands still behind her back*). Yes, it's me.

MRS. VANDEVER. Give me my property. The law will make you.

MARGARET (*imploringly*). Hand it over, Bessie. You can't hold out on her now.

BESSIE (*suddenly hurls the certificate, handkerchief, quarter and finally the purse at Mrs. Vandever's feet*). There's your damn property and I hope it chokes you.

MRS. VANDEVER (*quickly retrieving the certificate and examining it*). Thank goodness! It's a pity you couldn't have been honest in the first place. (*Gets rest of things.*)

MARGARET. You'll call off the cops now, won't you? If they do come, you'll tell 'em I got to go home to my baby?

MRS. VANDEVER (*to Margaret*). My good woman, why are you working like this at night, if you've a young baby? There's some kind of maternity law that helps mothers.

BESSIE. There ain't no law for Margaret or for us. 'Ceptin' the law that beats us down. And you know it, damn you. That's why you're so keen on getting the cops. You want to see us all in jail, where there's no air—no life, even. That's what you want!

MRS. VANDEVER. That's absurd. I only wanted my property. You wouldn't give it to me.

BESSIE. Because you got plenty more where that came from. And we ain't got nothing. Not even air to breathe that's clean and sweet.

MRS. VANDEVER. I'm sure everyone has air. After all, I *am* entitled to my property.

ANNIE (*in her sharp chuckle*). 'Tain't yours! It's yer aunt's an' ye stole it, an' yer a-feared she'll be findin' ye out afore ye can put it back.

MRS. VANDEVER. Why, you common woman!

ANNIE. I guess it's us that ought to be callin' the cops.

MARGARET. Oh, dry up, Annie, please!

JULE. Yeah, don't make no more trouble.

MARGARET. She's got her property.

BESSIE. All excepting one thing. (*Shows the vial of perfume.*) And I'm going to have that! I don't care a lot what happens to me. You can't have *that* back! (*Opens vial, touches her hair, her neck, the lobes of her ears with the perfume.*) Oh—oh! Now I smell sweet! (*Takes long breaths, rapturously.*) Now I don't know there's any yellow soap or vile cleaning powder or horrible fever smells on the earth.

ANNIE. There, now, dearie—

BESSIE. I don't know there's anything but—but flowers blooming everywhere. I never thought I could feel like this again. You can take me to jail if you want to, lady. It can't do anything further to me—nothing that ain't already happened to me since I left Fairways. I ain't caring—'cause I won't be smelling it. I won't ever smell nothing bad again.

ANNIE (*caustically to Mrs. Vandever*). It's kind o' puzzled ye're lookin'. Maybe ye'd like to know what Bessie's talkin' about?

MRS. VANDEVER. It's hardly necessary. I have what I came for.

ANNIE. But ye haven't had yer nose rubbed on a cake o' yellow soap.

MARGARET. Annie, don't!

MRS. VANDEVER. You are insulting.

ANNIE. Indeed, an' I'm showin' ye life as it's lived in tall office buildin's at night.

JULE (*falling to, on her brush*). Aw, dry up! We'll all be gettin' the sack.

MARGARET. We all ought to be gettin' to work. Unless the cops come. (*Humbly to Bessie.*) You ain't sore at me, Bessie? I couldn't help it, honest.

BESSIE. Forget it, Margaret. (*To Mrs. Vandever.*) Here's your perfume, lady. I was forgetting it lasted only a little while. There's life I got to go back to.

MRS. VANDEVER. I don't want it. That is, you can have the perfume. I buy it fresh every few days.

MRS. ROSS (*entering*). Well, I got the cops at last. They'll be right up.

MARGARET (*screams and wrings her hands*). How could you! How could you!

MRS. VANDEVER (*lamely*). You see, I have my property.

MRS. ROSS. Oh, your purse. Is everything o.k.?

MRS. VANDEVER. It is intact.

MRS. ROSS. You're sure? (*Mrs. Vandever nods. Mrs. Ross turns to the women.*) An' which one o' you had it? Come! Speak up! I'm waitin'! (*A tense pause, full of suspense, broken only by Margaret's weeping.*)

MRS. VANDEVER. Just a minute, Mrs.—what's your name?

MRS. ROSS. Ross.

MRS. VANDEVER. You see, Mrs. Ross, no one had it.

MRS. ROSS. Nobody?

MRS. VANDEVER. No. I found it over in this other chair, where I moved to speak to a friend. It was under the cushion. (*Margaret darts to her, kneeling and kissing her hand.*) Oh, don't come near me, please. I feel—that is, you remind me— Oh, go away, please!

MRS. ROSS. Is she the one?

MRS. VANDEVER. Oh, no! No! Can't you understand? It was no one here.

MRS. ROSS. Well, in that case I'd better be headin' off the cops. The Lord knows I ain't courtin' trouble in my outfit.

MRS. VANDEVER. I'll be leaving, too. Goodbye, Mrs. Ross, and I do thank you.

MRS. ROSS. Good night to you. I guess my outfit's pretty honest after all. (*She hurries out.*)

MRS. VANDEVER (*pauses in the door, embarrassed*). You make me very uncomfortable. I wish I could—but no, I wouldn't know how to begin. I—I don't even know how to talk to you. My own perfume is stifling me. I wish you could all go home, but—maybe that would be worse still. Oh dear! You have me all confused. (*She goes out.*)

BESSIE (*taking another whiff of the vial*). Ain't it sweet? Seems like my mother just come in that door with her basket—and I was burying my face in the blooms—all wet —and cool—and sweet—sweet—

THE CURTAIN FALLS

SQUAW WINTER *

A New England Tragedy

BY FRANCES LANGSDORF FOX

CHARACTERS

EFFIE HALE, *a farm woman.*
ANN, *her daughter.*
SARA, *her sister.*
ORPHA, *an Indian woman.*
ALICE, *a neighbor woman.*

PLACE. A small farming community in Maine.
TIME. Late afternoon. Early winter. The present.

EFFIE HALE'S *farmhouse is neat and spare. There is a bare expanse of wall across the back of the room, broken in the center by a closed and barred door. There is a heavy table which stands upstage, right of center. It is covered with a clean white cloth and holds a lighted oil lamp, a large medicine bottle and a spoon. A door leading to kitchen is upstage, right. A door leading to outside is in left wall. The corner, left back, is cut off by a window lighted by the last wan glow of a cold, gray late afternoon. Well forward in the left wall, which advances obliquely, is a fireplace. The mantel is neatly decorated with clean white tidies and holds nothing but a clock. A rocker is drawn up to the lighted fireplace and turned towards center, downstage. A low stool stands before it. The room gives the impression of extreme order in barrenness.*

* First produced by the Carolina Playmakers.

As the play opens, Effie Hale is sitting limply in rocker, asleep, with a patchwork quilt covering her knees. She is fifty, and is dressed in clothes too long and too full for today. Her thin, iron-gray hair is drawn tightly behind her ears and pinned in a firm knot. Her mouth gives the same impression. Her face is thin, pale and wasted from illness. Orpha, the Indian woman, comes in from left. She is stocky, clumsy and untidily dressed in a long, dirty cloth dress and a large Indian blanket thrown about her like a shawl. She carries a large basket on her back. Seeing Effie sleeping, she closes door noiselessly. She advances stealthily into the room, her eyes searching every corner of it.

ORPHA (*in a low, guttural whisper*). Ann? Ann? (*No answer. She makes a gesture of impatience and glides over to Effie, peering at her.*) Huh! Pretty sick! (*Her eyes take in the bare mantel, the empty table. She fingers tablecloth, examines spoon closely and grunts again contemptuously.*) Nothing here! (*Goes to window, looks out in both directions and shakes her head. She whispers suspiciously.*) Ann! (*Anger passes over her stolid face. She goes to door left, opens it, and then looks back menacingly.*) Orpha will come back. (*Fingering a corner of a rug that is sticking out of her basket.*) She make you pay! She make you pay or she tell!

[*Orpha goes out silently, but the door slips from her hand when nearly closed and shuts smartly. Effie awakens with a start, her hands involuntarily going to her heart, though she lowers them at once to her lap.*

EFFIE (*sharply*). Who's there? (*Waits for an answer.*) I thought I heard the door—who's there? (*In disgust tries to pull herself together.*) Asleep again and the lamp not lit a half an hour. I declare. . . .

[*With a gesture of determination incongruous with her weak weariness, she throws aside the cover and slowly and painfully pulls herself up from the chair. Supporting herself first by the chair and then by the mantel, she moves unsteadily to the fireplace and feebly but doggedly, with set lips, begins sweeping hearth with fireplace broom standing in corner. Ann, her daughter, comes in hurriedly from left. Ann is eighteen, attractive, but pale and worried looking. She is dressed simply. Her hair is drawn back like her mother's, but escapes in curling wisps about her face. She speaks as she comes in.*

ANN. I though I saw Orpha on the road. (*Sees what her mother is doing.*) Mother! That's for me to do.

EFFIE (*straightening, one hand on rocker to steady herself*). A little honest work won't hurt anybody, Ann. Seems if I couldn't sit here a day longer without lifting a finger. (*She sways. Ann grabs her.*)

ANN. There! You see? The doctor said you'd have those weak spells if you didn't stay perfectly still for a month or so. Here, sit down. (*Pushes her gently into the rocker and wraps the quilt about her.*) No one came while I was gone, did they?

EFFIE. No one.

ANN. I declare, you've no more sense about yourself than a baby.

EFFIE (*sitting back wearily, breathing hard*). But the hearth dirts up so quick with all the wood you use to keep me warm. It's a person's duty to do her own rightful chores.

ANN (*taking broom and sweeping hearth*). It's your duty to rest and get well. Aunt Sara and I can attend to the chores well enough.

EFFIE. It's not natural just to set, with my hands as idle as Satan would like, and let you two do all the work. It's not fair to you.

ANN (*desperately*). It's all we *can* do! Other things. . . .

EFFIE (*sharply*). What's to be done?

ANN (*controlling herself*). Nothing. I guess Satan won't bother with you for a while. Remember you were sick for near four months, Mother.

EFFIE. I'm not likely to forget it soon. Lying there without even enough life to lift my Bible, and seeing death as close as that pine tree out of my window, always waiting . . . waiting. . . .

ANN (*shuddering*). Waiting! (*She goes to window and stands looking out, then pulls herself up with a start.*) I know. (*Impulsively.*) It's an awful thing to be helpless, Mother.

EFFIE (*flatly*). There's always help for the good. (*Ann looks at her in curious terror, then turns again to window.*) And whether you're sick or well doesn't. . . .

ANN (*going to rocker*). You'd set more stock on gettin' well if you'd felt what we felt for you. It was like you were locked up in that room—(*Inclines her head to door upstage center.*)—away from us, And for all that we wished and prayed—(*Effie moves impatiently.*)—yes, prayed—we couldn't get to you, or do for you. It was like a thick door between us—as if you were locked up in there like *he* used to be, in that empty part of the house. (*Stares at bolted door.*)

EFFIE. There's no sense in takin' on. It's over now.

ANN (*very low*). No, it's not.

EFFIE (*not hearing*). You're too young and pretty to take things so hard. I should like to see you lively and singing, like you used to be.

ANN. I've no heart for singing.

EFFIE (*anxiously*). You look tuckered out. I declare, Ann, you're as nervous as a cat. And always standin' at that window. . . .

ANN (*turns away from window guiltily*). I'm sorry, Mother.

EFFIE. Like folks used to do when they were expectin' an Indian raid.

ANN (*startled*). There'll be no Indian coming into this house if I can help it.

EFFIE. I don't know what's got into you.

ANN (*impulsively, as she sits at the stool at her mother's feet*). I would have died if you died, Mother.

EFFIE. If I had died, it would have been Providence.

ANN. I'd fight anything that took you away from me!

EFFIE. Aye, child, I think you would. You've always been a loving one, that's certain. But you'd learn 'twas no use to fight Providence.

ANN. Wouldn't *you* care if *I* died?

EFFIE. Certainly, I'd care. But no matter how much stock you set by a person, there's your duty to Heaven first.

ANN (*rebelliously*). A person could talk that way in meetin' but not really believe it.

EFFIE. Yes. They could. I learned that when your father died. (*She pauses but Ann is questioningly quiet.*) You freeze your mind and heart inside of you. Nothing is ever the same. But you don't die. You memorize the meanings of things, get used to being frozen. Then you take hold and you see that you're not dead. (*She thinks.*) It's like that time of year we call squaw winter. It isn't real winter at all, but just that first cold time before Indian summer comes.

ANN. Sometimes squaw winter's so cold, you think it's real winter sure.

EFFIE. That's foolishness. There's always bound to be a warmer time. Time goes on and you go on with it. That's all. (*Suddenly.*) Ann, I want no takin' on when I go, beyond sorrow that's decent and proper. Too much feeling's an abomination to the Lord.

ANN. That's not human.

EFFIE. It's right. Mind you remember.

ANN. It may be right, but it's too hard to live by. (*Sharply, as she rises.*) Did you take your medicine? (*Effie looks away and does not answer.*) *Did* you? (*Goes to table and takes up bottle.*) Mother, you haven't touched your medicine since yesterday forenoon!

EFFIE (*suddenly pleading*). I'm better, Ann. I wanted to save it.

ANN. I could just take and shake you! (*Shakes bottle and opens it.*)

EFFIE. A bottle like that costs a heap of money, doesn't it?

ANN (*about to pour, looks up, answers hastily*). I wouldn't worry about that now.

EFFIE (*wistfully*). Thought to get you a new dress, good shoes and a string of beads from Orpha, the Indian woman.

ANN (*starts at last words, chokes back a protesting "no." Holds out the filled spoon*). Here!

EFFIE (*carefully, not noticing Ann*). I wish Sara would tell me where the money came from. We sold off everything worth selling, when your father's poor brother was locked up in there—(*Indicating door in upstage wall.*)—sick.

ANN (*bending over her with the spoon*). Sara's taken care of everything this long. Now you take this medicine.

EFFIE. How did you and Sara get enough money for the medicine and that other doctor and all? I can't help wonderin' if Sara's in debt, for we've no more than a church mouse, as it is.

ANN. I can't pour this medicine back. If you don't take it, I shall hold your nose like they do babies'.

EFFIE. You'll spill it.

ANN (*putting spoon to Effie's lips*). Then take it! (*Pushes it into Effie's mouth. Effie makes a wry face.*)

EFFIE. You've been good to me, Ann. Awful good. I've been a hindrance and you've done more'n common for me.

ANN (*really touched, places her hand on Effie's shoulder*). Anyone'll do all they can for their own. You've always said that. (*Intensely.*) Life would be too lonely to bear if there wasn't someone to love and to do for.

EFFIE. If I could only get at my garden again, I could make it up to you.

ANN (*indignantly*). You can't do that yet. Plowing in the damp and joltin' over those rocks and hollows—seeding and keepin' things fit in all weather. Breakin' your neck to bring in what's growin'. . . .

EFFIE (*bitterly*). There's been little enough to bring in these years past.

ANN. Just because last year wasn't good. . . .

EFFIE. Nor the year before and the one before that. Back before your father died, it was beginning. Time was when the earth worked with you. Now you give it all you have and 'twon't bear unless it's a mind it. (*Ann tries to interrupt.*) We're losin' hold. You can't hide it. We're losin' hold. Seems like the land's too tired to bear.

[*During last part of speech, Alice has entered at left unnoticed by Effie or Ann. Alice is nearly thirty, sturdy, but worn and worried looking. She answers the last part of Effie's speech.*

ALICE. That's true enough, heavens knows!

ANN (*startled*). Land o' livin', Alice! (*Laughs hysterically. They stare at her in astonishment. She pulls herself together.*) You gave me an awful turn, comin' in like that!

ALICE (*in confusion*). You didn't hear me come in?

ANN (*shortly*). No.

ALICE. I declare, I'm so turned around, I don't know where I be. (*Silence.*) Seems like I always get started on the wrong track. . . . (*Stops as she notices the women staring at her intently.*)

EFFIE. What ails you, Alice?

ALICE. I've got something to ask you. (*Waits.*) Maybe I shouldn't—maybe you'll think. . . . (*No help from other two.*) I'm goin' to speak right out, Mrs. Hale, before I get afraid of what I'm goin' to say. This isn't my way of doing things, but. . . . (*She takes a deep breath.*) I've come to ask you to loan me some money.

[*Ann's laugh rings out harshly in the silence. Alice looks at her in hurt anger, turns and begins to stalk out. Ann goes after her, catching her by the arm.*

ANN. Alice! Alice! I wasn't mockin' at you. I swear it! (*Alice comes back sullenly in questioning silence.*) It's just that there's no money here. Not for you nor for us either.

ALICE. It's no laughing matter. Johnny's run out of his shoes again, and there are things I need in the city I can't trade for. Mel won't have his job till the city people come back in the summer again, and it's just turnin' winter now. You have *no* money? None, you say?

EFFIE (*pleadingly*). Ann, 'tisn't true we can't help her?

ANN. If we could, would I hide it? If we had it, 'twould be hers. You know that, don't you, Alice?

ALICE. I know if you had it, you'd lend it to me without lettin' on to the others. (*Miserably.*) It's the same as beggin', almost.

EFFIE. Ann, go look in the box and make sure.

ANN (*in exasperation*). Mother, I know! It's no use. (*Turns. During next speech, walks slowly and dejectedly to upstage bolted door, leans facing it, her palms against it.*)

ALICE. Aye. No use. (*Passionately.*) I told Mel 'twould be

like this if he didn't keep hold of what he had. I told him no use takin' jobs from summer people if you had to lie slack all winter waitin' for them. Every June before he'd go off to work for them, I'd tell him, you'll ruin us—tryin' to make us better. (*Sits in chair, left of table.*) Now the farm's runnin' down from no care. It won't bear any more, like you said. We're losin' hold—all of us. (*Sharply.*) Are you really as bad off as you said?

ANN (*shortly, as she turns*). Yes.

ALICE. Aye, it does look different here. It's so bare. Your things. . . .

ANN. They're sold. Did you have to ask? (*An embarrassed silence. Ann turns to go to Effie, then steps backward quickly towards bolted door.*) Lands, Mother, it feels like all the winds of winter comin' through that door. Don't you want me to hang something over it?

EFFIE. Let that door alone and keep away from it. I don't like your standing around it all the time.

ALICE (*eager to please*). You could take off the inside lock and open up that part of the house for boarders.

EFFIE. Never in this world.

ALICE. It would be a way to help yourself out. It's been empty since years ago, when your husband's brother died in there. What's in there now?

ANN. The dark and the cold and days best forgotten. (*Goes to Effie.*)

EFFIE (*looking at her keenly*). You sound like a woman worn. And you ought to be still glad—like a child. (*Moves impatiently.*) Oh, I wish. . . .

ALICE (*bitterly*). You can lose being a child quickly, I can tell you. (*Rises.*) I'd better be goin 'on. It's a long way over and longer back, and I don't want Mel to know I've been here.

ANN. You've only been here a minute. Did you come all the way up here just to ask and then. . . .

ALICE (*at door*). I'd go further than that on the chance. I can't talk up for a loan now that I know how it is with you, but I can tell you I'd do almost anything. (*Thoughtfully.*) Anything. (*Turns back with new interest.*) They say down at the village how someone's stolen a rug from one of the summer folk's cottages. One of those small, expensive ones.

EFFIE. From where? Which one? Not the Goodals!

ANN (*passionately*). No! No! It isn't true! They didn't *steal* it. They didn't!

ALICE (*looking at her strangely*). Stealing goes against you, doesn't it? Time was I'd have felt dreadful like that too. But now—I swear I don't know. That thief was mighty smart.

EFFIE. How dare you talk so about such wickedness?

ALICE. The Day of Judgment's a long way off. In the meantime, that thief has something to live on.

ANN (*still passionately and coming near Alice*). But it wasn't stealing. Don't say such things till you know they're true.

ALICE. You're fair as wrought up as if you were the guilty one yourself.

ANN (*close to her*). No. I'm not. Why, I'm not at all!

ALICE. There's no sense in such takin' on over the bad luck of folks you don't know. There's enough in a body's own dish these days. Goodbye. (*Goes out abruptly but turns in the doorway.*) I'm dreadful sorry about your trouble. (*Goes, closing door behind her.*)

EFFIE (*calling after her*). I hope things'll be better with you. (*To Ann.*) But I never did hear such talk from a decent, God-respectin' woman! Seems like folks are lettin' slip everything these days—land, and their goodness and all.

ANN (*intensely, as she moves towards Effie*). You can't help thinkin' that way sometimes. Some things can happen that can change what you used to think was right. It isn't bad in you but just that you see things like they are.

EFFIE. The thief was a smart one, was he?

ANN. You do things not on your own power sometimes. When the time comes, there's something that pushes you—pushes and forces and drags you. And you go.

EFFIE (*quietly*). It would kill me if my daughter took up like that Alice is doin'.

ANN (*dully*). Don't think of such dreadful things. It'll tire you.

EFFIE. I declare, all you and Sara do is tell me to stop thinkin'. I never saw two people so close about things to their own kin. (*Ann, impatient with the familiar complaint, turns to window.*) It would be good if Sara didn't think for a while either. She's been lookin' dreadful worried lately.

ANN (*staring out of window*). Oh, no. Perhaps she's just catchin' a cold. I hope she put on enough warm clothes today.

EFFIE. Are you watchin' for Sara? What are you doin' at that window? Who do you expect to come?

ANN (*fervently*). I don't want anyone to come.

[*The Indian, Orpha, comes in silently from left. Effie, turning to door, notices her first. She speaks in sharp alarm.*

EFFIE. Orpha, what do you want here?

ANN (*turns in terror, sees Orpha*). You get out. What right have you to come trackin' dirt into folks' houses?

ORPHA. Orpha come before.

ANN. Then she *was* here.

ORPHA. Orpha will talk to you.

ANN (*pleadingly, as she goes to her*). You promised. . . . (*Orpha thumps basket down on table. Ann quickly fingers some beads in basket.*) What handsome beads, Orpha. (*With increasing nervousness.*) They're the handsomest I've ever seen.

ORPHA. I will talk to you.

ANN. Have you any more in your basket?

ORPHA. I want you to buy. . . .

ANN (*tugging at her arm*). Come out in the kitchen where it's warm. You can show me the beads out there.

ORPHA. Warmer here. (*Pause.*) I want you to buy back rug.

ANN. No, I don't want to buy a rug. I want those lovely beads. Do come out and set and let me see them.

ORPHA. No one will buy rug from me. They say rug too good. They say I stole. You buy rug back. (*Her eyes move shiftily to Ann, who stands petrified. With a sudden jerk she pulls a valuable small rug from her basket and holds it out.*) Here! (*Ann, in speechless panic, looks from Orpha to Effie.*)

EFFIE (*excited*). That's the rug from the Goodal's summer cottage, the one they told Sara and me to clean careful because it was worth a lot of money. How did you come by that? Speak out!

ANN. It's too long a story now, Mother. It'd tucker you out for certain. Orpha had better be off before it's too dark for her to see her way.

ORPHA. No. I stay.

[*As Ann stands helpless, Sara enters briskly from left. Sara is younger and stockier than Effie, more determined and surer than Ann. When she sees Orpha, she draws back in terror. But self-possession and anger at once cover her first start of fear.*

ANN (*eagerly turning to her*). Oh, Aunt Sara! (*Grasping her arm.*) Do something!

SARA (*furiously to Orpha*). Go away at once.

EFFIE (*leaning forward*). She's stolen the rug from the Goodal's summer cottage, Sara. You know, that expensive rug they trusted us to keep an eye on?

ORPHA (*not moving, to Sara*). I give you money for rug. Now I can't sell rug. They say I steal rug. They say they will not buy from an Indian not honest. You must buy it back.

SARA. I can't. I spent the money. I needed that money, else I wouldn't have come to you in the first place. You can be sure of that. Now go away.

ORPHA. I lose my money. You must buy.

EFFIE (*aghast*). Sara, you took money from her? You spent it? You? You. . . .

[*Sara looks at her in terror. Ann goes to Orpha and tries to lead her to door.*

ORPHA (*motionless*). You buy back rug or I tell people how I get rug.

SARA. You can't. You promised. . . .

ORPHA. If you do not pay me back, everyone in village will know why I am poor.

SARA (*glancing furtively at Effie*). Be still! You'll excite my sister. I'll keep the rug for you and pay you as soon as I get money.

ORPHA. If I give you rug, you never bring money.

SARA (*outraged*). Certainly I will!

ORPHA. You tell me wrong when you say people will buy. Maybe you lie again. I keep rug till you pay. If you do not pay, I tell.

SARA (*lowering her voice and glancing furtively at Effie*). Keep it hidden then. And keep quiet. I'll get the money somehow.

EFFIE (*holding chair arms and straining forward*). Sara! You're not admitting.

SARA (*interrupting*). It won't be this month or even this year perhaps, but I'll pay you back if it's the last thing I do. I'm honest—in spite of this. I can keep my word even if you can't. (*Intensely.*) Now you get out of here and never come back.

ORPHA (*stolidly*). You pay.

SARA (*holding on to her self-control*). Yes, yes, I'll pay! Keep quiet until tomorrow. I'll do something about this, somehow. (*Her voice rising.*) And I'll tell you something you're not likely to forget till Judgment Day. (*Raising her hand as if to strike her.*) Now go!

[*Orpha cringes and shuffles to door. At door, she turns and holds out rug.*

ORPHA (*ironically wheedling*). *Good* rug! You buy?

SARA (*screaming*). Get out!

[*Orpha shuffles out, leaving door open. Sara rushes to door and closes it violently and stands with her back to it, breathing hard. There is a dazed pause. Ann starts to go to Sara but stops when she sees Effie straining forward in chair.*

EFFIE (*faintly*). Sara . . . Ann. . . . (*Piteously.*) You *didn't* do it?

[*Ann turns away and stares at bolted door.*

SARA (*her figure drooping, steps nearer Effie*). I guess we've got to tell you, Effie. We hadn't aimed to, but there's no undoing what we done. (*Pleadingly.*) There wasn't any other way, Effie. There wasn't any money and no way to get it. We had to pay the doctors and buy your medicine.

EFFIE (*firmly.*) No!

SARA. We thought you were dying. I'd noticed that rug when I cleaned there this summer. After the Goodals went back to the city, they asked me to go over there from time to time to see if it was safe. I remembered how much they said it was worth.

EFFIE (*in despair*). So you stole. . . .

ANN (*turning fiercely*). We didn't steal, Mother. We took it because we had to have the money for you.

SARA. I was going to buy it back—somehow—before the Goodals came back.

EFFIE (*inflexibly*). How?

SARA. As soon as the cannery opened, I was going to work there with the Canucks and Polacks and raise the money.

ANN (*eagerly*). We didn't think the Indian had enough gumption to try and sell it in the winter and get us into trouble. We thought she would hold it until we could pay her back. Then we would have returned the rug.

SARA. We went and came back a dozen times before we could bring ourselves to touch it.

ANN. Don't think it came easy, Mother. It was like making yourself pick up a red-hot poker. But you might have died. . . .

EFFIE. You stole! Like a common, dirty Indian woman. You stole!

ANN (*recoiling*). Mother!

EFFIE. You stole. You broke the Lord's commandment. We can never dare go to Meetin' again.

SARA. That's nonsense. (*Firmly, as Effie tries to interrupt.*) Don't you think there's a sight of people in Meetin' who've acted against the letter of the law because they've been driven against all belief? (*Effie bows her head.*) The Lord won't judge too harsh when you've done something with your hands and still kept a faithful heart.

ANN. That's so. (*Going to her.*) Oh, Aunt Sara. . . .

SARA. What we did wasn't right by the Word, but it was the only thing we could do. (*Turning away.*) Oh, it's harder than you can tell—when you're in dreadful need—to think of heaven and earth at once.

ANN (*sitting on stool and looking up pleadingly at Effie*). And we did need. We didn't know sickness cost so much.

SARA (*eagerly*). It wasn't meant as stealing. Just borrowing.

We'll put it back in the Goodal cottage. We *had* to get you well.

EFFIE. Do you think that getting me well in that way is right with heaven? Do you think you can break a commandment of the Lord's and have good come of it? (*Her eyes are intent on something beyond and a little above the rest of them.*) It was sin. It was sin.

SARA. It's not sin when you save a life by it.

EFFIE (*so intently that Ann jumps up from stool*). It's not a right life any more when it's saved by sin. (*Looks at mantel, rises suddenly from chair.*) No! (*She stands rigid. Ann and Sara stand petrified with apprehension. Suddenly Effie seizes medicine bottle and dashes it against the hearth, where it shatters.*) I'll take no more of it! It's bought from the Devil!

SARA (*putting her hands over her eyes as though she could not bear the sight*). You fool! You fool! (*Ann kneels before the hearth, trying to scoop up some of the medicine with the spoon. Sara, unnerved, turns to Effie.*) It's gone! And we can't get you any more and you can't make out without it. Can't you see that we did it just to save you—to make you better? And now that you're in a fair way to get well, you throw everything away again. You fool! (*Slumps into chair by table.*)

EFFIE. Ann, get up. Don't go down on your knees for such wickedness.

ANN (*rising bleakly with a bit of the bottle in her hand*). It's lost.

EFFIE. Every night I used to thank Providence for savin' me. (*Dully.*) Now I know it wasn't Providence but thievery.

ANN (*shaken and speaking unconvincingly, stands behind Effie's chair*). We'll make it up to them. (*Puts her hand on her mother's shoulder.*) If we can't do it now, when I get my school. . . .

EFFIE (*shaking off her touch*). When you get your school! How'll you ever get to the Academy, even, when all the money we've had, and a sight that we haven't, has been spent on me?

ANN. I'll get there somehow.

EFFIE. And who'll let you teach their children when they know you come of stealin' folk? (*Sara looks up.*) And that you stole yourself?

ANN. No one will know. We would say nothing and Orpha *won't* tell.

EFFIE (*bitterly*). It's likely that she won't tell. And those city folks won't miss their rug, I suppose. People find out everything in this village. And when they once start talkin', they won't let you have peace anywhere. My own sister made my daughter steal!

SARA (*springing to her feet*). Stop it! Do you think I *wanted* to do it? Ain't I bent over backwards all my life to be good—nigh as much as you have? Don't you think it killed me—almost—to go breakin' into someone's house and takin' something I'd no right to? But it had to be done. (*Pleadingly.*) Don't you see that?

EFFIE. It was sin.

SARA. You keep sayin' that and sayin' it like a church bell caught in the wind. Be human for a minute, Effie, and look at it clear. I'm your sister. I couldn't let you die. I didn't know you had no more heart than was in a prayer book. Aren't you glad I saved your life?

EFFIE. No, I'm not. I'd rather die honest! I'd rather go crazy and be shut up in the other side of the house, like my poor husband's brother. (*The eyes of all three go to bolted door. Effie, arrested by a sudden thought, draws herself erect.*) Yes—I'd rather. . . .

ANN (*going to her*). Mother, you mustn't talk so.

EFFIE (*in a strange, intent tone*). Yes—I'd rather. . . . (*Pause.*) I will. . . .

ANN (*frightened*). Mother!

EFFIE (*as if talking to herself*). It's locked from the other side —locked safe.

ANN. Stop! Mother, stop!

EFFIE. Locked away from the world—closed up—alone with repentance.

ANN (*desperately*). Stop talkin' so wild. Listen to us!

EFFIE (*with sudden, terrible calm*). You're daughter of mine no longer; Ann. You've put a wall between us with your sinnin'. I'm goin' away and live in repentance and you'll have to shift for yourself.

ANN. Mother, what are you sayin'?

EFFIE. You and Sara can live on your robbin's, I've no doubt. But I see no need to live with those as have sold their soul to the Devil.

ANN. You've no call to repent.

EFFIE. Your souls are your own and I guess it's your right to go to perdition if you've a mind to. But you've brought me back to life with stolen goods, and I'll not live with sinners while I make my peace with God.

SARA. You're apt to die before you make your peace, with all your foolishness about throwing away that medicine.

EFFIE (*shortly*). Then I'll die alone without you to hinder.

SARA (*coming forward*). If anyone goes, it's *my* soul will be damned for your sake. Won't you see past what you've learned and what you've made up your mind to, for anything at all?

EFFIE. You didn't have to do it. I don't see it that way.

SARA. You look through meetin'house windows instead of eyes. That's your holiness. Things is either right or wrong. Never love or charity or faith. Just stubbornness like a mule. You've always been that way, Effie. But when you tell your own sister, who's gone against her nature to save you, that she's so wicked that she's not good enough to live with—it's the last straw.

ANN (*gently easing her mother into her chair*). Don't rile her, Aunt Sara. (*Pleadingly, to Effie.*) Mother, don't listen.

EFFIE (*with grim determination*). I'm goin' over.

ANN. You're not goin' anywhere.

EFFIE (*getting to her feet*). I'm goin' over into the other half of this house. (*Ann stares at her mother in terror and backs away until she is standing against the center, bolted door, her hands behind her, pressing on door as if keeping it away from her mother.*) Your father never thought when he walled it off for his poor brother that. . . .

SARA. Effie, that's dead and gone.

EFFIE (*taking a step forward*). I'm goin' over there and bolt the door between there and this part of the house. I'm never comin' back to this wickedness—never again in this world.

SARA (*grimly*). It's a good idea and just the right place for anyone so unnatural she can't forgive her own sister. But it's kind of foolish, for nothin's to stop me from comin' round to your front door to find out how you are.

EFFIE. There's nothin' more than a gun to stop you. I tell you, Sara, and you too, Ann. If I find either of you comin' over tryin' to bring me to the Devil again, I shall take my husband's old rifle that's in there. . . .

ANN (*screaming*). No! No!

EFFIE. You've no need to be afraid, Ann. I shan't hurt you. But I shall shoot myself, just as sure as I smashed that medicine bottle, and for the same reason. Mind that.

ANN (*hysterically, as she goes to Sara*). We're sendin' her away. We're makin' her crazy. Do something, Aunt Sara. Do something! (*She grabs Sara's arm and shakes her.*)

SARA (*pulling away*). Stop your carryin' on. 'Twon't get anything done that way.

ANN. But do something! We aren't savin' her. Everything's so wrong! So wrong!

SARA. Let go! Are you all crazy here but me?

[*She shakes loose from Ann. Effie, after resting both hands on the table, takes the lighted lamp and goes to barred door. Steadying the lamp against the wall, she manages to pull back the bar. As Ann is pushed away from Sara, the door stiffly pulls open. All is black and cold beyond it.*

SARA. Effie, stop that nonsense. You can't think of doin' a thing like that. You've got too much sense, even if you've no heart.

ANN (*running to Effie*). You can't mean it! You can't! (*Tries to cling to her mother.*)

[*At her touch, Effie seems to draw all her strength together. Raising the lamp menacingly, as if to throw it at them, she pushes Ann away with her free hand. Ann falls at Sara's feet. Before Sara can free herself from Ann, who clings to her knees, Effie pulls the door open wide and exhaustedly slips, like a fading light, behind it, bringing it shut after her. The room is left in darkness except for the light from the dying fire. In the breathless pause, there is the sound of a heavy bar falling firmly into place, a slight stir of movement, then stillness. Ann, sobbing wildly, throws herself on the locked door and beats her fists against it.*

ANN. Mother! Unlock it! Come back! Come back!

[*Sara has moved to door, but when she hears it being bolted on the other side, she stops short. Hopelessness takes the place of her energy, her arms fall to her sides, her shoulders sag wearily. She turns away from door.*

SARA (*numbly*). Lord deliver us! (*Pause.*) Lord deliver *her.*

ANN (*stops weeping, goes to Sara and speaks wistfully, like a hurt child*). She'll come back?

SARA (*stirs, shivers, speaks tonelessly without looking at Ann*). Get a lamp, Ann. It's dark—and cold. (*Ann does not move.*) Night comes up early, now it's winter.

ANN. She'll come back? Won't she come back, Aunt Sara?

SARA (*tonelessly*). No. She'll never come back.

SLOW CURTAIN

THE BAYFIELD PICTURE

A Drama

BY SPRANGER BARRY

THE CHARACTERS

THE GIRL.
THE ARTIST.
THE WOMAN.

PLACE. Near a large city.
TIME. The present, A spring day. Late afternoon.

THE ARTIST *is forcing the Girl to enter a deserted one-room shack a few hundred feet back from the highway. At back is a window with frayed curtains. At right is a small table on which are a kerosene lamp, a blanket and a length of rope under the blanket. Center is a rough table with two chairs. There is a door at left.*

As the play opens, the stage is empty and silent for a moment. Then. . . .

ARTIST (*off left*). Open the door! (*Door is opened from outside.*) Now walk straight ahead.

[*A Girl walks in with both hands in the air; in one of them is her pocketbook. She is well dressed. She is followed by another woman, the Artist, who is not as well dressed. She carries a pistol.*

ARTIST. Keep your hands high above your head. (*She shuts the door.*)

GIRL. Will you please explain the meaning of this?

ARTIST. Very soon, Miss Bayfield.

GIRL. Ah! You *think* you know me?

ARTIST (*mockingly*). Oh, everyone knows *you,* Miss Bayfield.

GIRL. I flatter myself that I have achieved what may be called a national reputation, then. And I suppose that you have stopped my car and brought me here because you want some of the money which you think that reputation has earned for me?

ARTIST (*still mocking*). You are very clever, Miss Bayfield.

GIRL. So they tell me. But I don't see why you forced me to walk up that wretched hill to this dirty place. I would have given you my purse down there on the highway.

ARTIST (*studying her face*). You *are* Frances Bayfield, aren't you?

GIRL. Here! Take my purse, please, and let me go. You're delaying me for a very important engagement.

ARTIST. Not so fast. (*She indicates a chair by the table.*) Please sit in that chair.

GIRL. Why—what—

ARTIST (*emphasizing with the pistol*). Go ahead. Sit. (*The Girl does so.*) Place your bag on the table and put your hands behind your back. (*The Girl obeys.*) Now hold still or it will be the worse for you.

[*With a rope which she takes from under the blanket, the Artist ties the Girl's hands behind the chair. She is behind the Girl, who doesn't see that she has put the pistol in her pocket.*

GIRL. What—what are you doing? What's the meaning of this?

ARTIST. The less noise you make, the better it'll be for you.

GIRL. I tell you I'm in a hurry. Will you let me go?

ARTIST. There! (*Tying last knot.*) I don't think you can wiggle out of that. (*Steps away from the chair.*) I call that a first-class job of tying-up.

GIRL. This is outrageous! There's my purse—on the table. Why don't you take it and let me go?

ARTIST. I don't want your purse.

GIRL. There's nearly twenty dollars in it.

ARTIST. Not enough.

GIRL. Oh I see! You're out for larger stakes. You intend to hold me for ransom. I assure you, you'll be disappointed. I really haven't anything.

ARTIST. I'm not interested in your money. Do you take me for a thief?

GIRL (*with a sardonic laugh*). Oh, no, you're just a delightful lady who stopped my car and at the point of a gun forced me to leave it and walk up a hill to this shack, where you tied me to a chair. A most charming hostess. When will you serve the tea?

ARTIST. I'm glad to see you have a sense of humor. You're going to need it.

GIRL. I shouldn't be surprised. Now, I think the least you could do, under the circumstances, is to expain why you've done this to me. And will you please make the explanation short? I'd like to reach some agreement with you as soon as possible—I still have a pressing engagement.

ARTIST. I know. I know exactly what that engagement is.

GIRL. Indeed?

ARTIST. Yes, and I know what you have in the rumble-seat of your roadster. A certain large package.

GIRL. That's right. But it isn't a bomb. It's a painting.

ARTIST (*nods*). A painting. But its effect on my life might be exactly the effect of a bomb.

GIRL. Really, I don't understand. And these ropes are chafing my wrists. I do wish you'd come to the point.

ARTIST. I'm sorry that the ropes hurt you, because you're going to be wearing them for three or four hours.

GIRL. Doesn't that money in my bag have any effect on you?

ARTIST. None whatsoever.

GIRL. I'm still in the dark. You don't want money. You say you're not a thief or a kidnapper. Then what *do* you want?

ARTIST. A few hours of your time.

GIRL. But I tell you I've—

ARTIST. I know. You've an important engagement. I know all about it.

GIRL. You do?

ARTIST. You're on your way to the city—to the Metropolitan

Art Club—to the galleries where they're holding their Annual State Competition. And in the rumbleseat of your car is the painting that you wanted to enter in that competition.

GIRL. You seem to be well informed.

ARTIST. I had to be.

GIRL. I still don't understand—

ARTIST. You will. The closing time for entering pictures in the competition is six o'clock this evening.

GIRL. That's right.

ARTIST. And that's why I'm going to keep you here.

GIRL. You mean—

ARTIST (*smiling*). I see that at last you understand.

GIRL. You mean you're going to keep me prisoner here until after six o'clock so that I can't enter my picture in the competition. (*The Artist smiles again.*) Is it—is it some sort of practical joke?

ARTIST. No, not a joke.

GIRL. Then I suppose you realize that you're guilty of a criminal offense.

ARTIST. I know the risks I'm running. But I also know that it will be hard for you to prove anything. This is a lonely stretch of road, and I have friends who will swear that I was miles away from here all this afternoon.

GIRL. Evidently you've planned this very carefully.

ARTIST. Very.

GIRL. And still there's that great question: why.

ARTIST (*smiles*). It's strange, eh?

GIRL. If you don't want me to pay you to release me, what do you gain by keeping my picture out of the competition?

ARTIST. It's very simple, Miss Bayfield. I have a picture of my own entered in the competition.

GIRL. You?

ARTIST. Yes. Why not?

GIRL. You—a painter?

ARTIST (*angrily*). Yes, and a good one! One of the best in this state!

GIRL. Is that so?

ARTIST. As a matter of fact, there's only one artist in this state better than myself. (*Pause.*) That's Frances Bayfield.

GIRL (*graciously*). Thank you. What's your name?

ARTIST (*dully*). You wouldn't know it. I've no reputation. I haven't sold anything to museums or rich collectors. (*Impulsively.*) But I *can* paint. I can prove it in this competition. I can win if you're not entered.

GIRL. Haven't you used a rather melodramatic way of keeping me out of the contest? Isn't it a little bit too much like an old-fashioned movie?

ARTIST. Perhaps. But I'm staking all on this competition. There's a thousand-dollar first prize. And even that isn't the chief consideration.

GIRL. I understand. The publicity.

ARTIST. Let us say—reputation.

GIRL. I see. Well, I admire your courage, but I'm still very angry with you and I warn you that I intend to have you arrested. That is, unless you release me. If I hurry, I can still make the city before six o'clock. Will you let me go?

ARTIST. No.

GIRL (*angrily*). Very well. Get yourself a reputation by winning this contest. Then see what I do to your reputation after you've got it.

ARTIST. I'm not afraid. I don't believe you can harm me. But even if you could, I'd go ahead with it.

GIRL (*still angry*). I think you're a —

ARTIST. Now there's really no sense in your getting angry.

GIRL (*calmly*). You're right. Tell me, how did you know I'd be using this road exactly at this time—and how did you know what I looked like? I never allow myself to be photographed.

ARTIST. It's true I didn't know what you looked like. But I knew where you lived—and I've seen your car before. When I heard this morning that, at the last moment, the great Frances Bayfield had decided to enter the competition, I knew which way you'd have to drive to get to the city. So since nine o'clock this morning I've been sitting down by the road, waiting for a black roadster that had a woman driver and a large package in the back seat. It's been a long wait, but worth it.

GIRL. Well, it looks as if you win. It's getting late. Closing time will soon roll around—and if what you say about your painting is true, you'll probably win the competition.

ARTIST. Thank you. I'm glad you see it sensibly.

GIRL. Only I think I ought to tell you that—

[*Outside the house a woman's voice calls "Hallo!" The Artist leaps to her feet and looks out the window.*

ARTIST (*as she fingers the pistol*). Someone's coming! Don't make a sound or say anything to attract attention. I—I think I told you I'm desperate. Here! (*She throws the blanket over the Girl's shoulders, thus hiding the ropes. She pulls the Girl's hat off, then her own, and places both on the table. She replaces the gun in her pocket*). Now be careful.

WOMAN (*enters. She is pleasant looking, rather plainly dressed and a little older than the other two*). Good afternoon, ladies.

ARTIST. How do you do?

WOMAN. I'm sorry to disturb you, but I'm in rather a difficulty. My car's just run out of gas and I wondered—

ARTIST. We have no phone.

WOMAN. Oh, dear. Well, does that car down there belong to you?

ARTIST (*with a look at the Girl*). Yes.

WOMAN. I wonder whether I might take just enough gas to get me to the next filling-station. I'm in a dreadful hurry or I wouldn't ask it of you.

ARTIST. Well, I—

WOMAN. Oh, I won't need your help. I'll be able to do the job myself. May I—please? I should appreciate it very much.

ARTIST. Very well. Take as much as you need.

WOMAN. Thank you. You are a dear and I'm very much obliged to you. (*She opens her purse.*)

ARTIST. It's quite all right. You needn't pay for it.

WOMAN. I insist. (*Taking out bill.*) Do you have change of five dollars?

ARTIST (*shortly*). No.

WOMAN (*smiling as she takes card and pencil from purse*). I'll write a little I.O.U.

ARTIST (*impatiently*). I tell you it isn't necessary.

WOMAN (*as she jots down something on the card*). I beg to differ. (*Smiles.*) You see, I have a pet theory, and I'm very superstitious about it. I believe that no artist—or any other person—can have any great success without meticulous integrity. And I mean integrity all the way down the line—especially in the little things. (*Gives card to Artist, smiles.*) If you'll drop in at my studio some afternoon, I'll repay you and give you a cup of tea. (*Artist takes card without looking at it.*) Thank you very much. I'm in *such* a hurry. Good day and thank you. (*She hurries out.*)

GIRL (*with a smile*). There goes your alibi. Now you can't prove that you weren't in this shack this afternoon. She saw you—and that makes two of us against your one.

ARTIST. I still don't care. I won't let you go. I'm so tired of struggling and pinching that I won't mind being put in jail if only I win that first prize. They couldn't take that away from me, even—

GIRL (*quietly*). What about what she said—you know, integrity in an artist—all along the line.

ARTIST (*starts*). I wonder who she was?

GIRL. Why don't you look at the card?

ARTIST (*reads*). I.O.U. twenty-five cents.

GIRL. The other side.

ARTIST (*turns card over. Reads silently and then lets card fall to floor*). Oh!

GIRL. Well?

ARTIST (*slowly*). The name on the card is—Frances Bayfield.

GIRL. Frances Bayfield! (*She gives way to a long, almost uncontrolled laugh.*)

ARTIST. Well, is she the impostor or you?

GIRL (*controlling her laugher*). Now—now, my dear, this is going to be hard on you. Try—try to take it calmly. I don't want to be cruel, but *I* am the impostor. And she's the real Frances Bayfield.

ARTIST. And I've kept you here—and let her go—to the city. I even helped her.

GIRL. Yes. I—I believe I'm sorry for you.

ARTIST (*bewildered*). It—it—I—I—But what were you—how did you—

GIRL. Simple enough. No one's ever seen Frances Bayfield. She's a real recluse, so I thought I might as well take advantage of that fact. About five years ago—in the days when I was better off than I am now—I bought one of her pictures. Things have gone badly with me and I've had to sell off my pictures and things. At last I decided to sell my Bayfield. It would have fetched a few hundred at any dealer's. But when I heard of this competition, I said to myself: "Why not get a thousand for it? No one knows Frances Bayfield. You've got a Bayfield picture. Just be Bayfield herself. Take the picture in and take the money out." So I circulated that rumor that you heard this morning. I even hired a car like Bayfield's black one. Then you stopped me.

ARTIST. But why did you keep saying—

GIRL. Oh, I had to keep up my part. Besides, I might have talked you into letting me go. And then—

ARTIST. Then the real one came along.

GIRL. That was really the genteel finishing touch. The real Frances Bayfield evidently decided to enter the contest. You see, I'd have been found out and punished if I'd gone into town. You've saved me from that.

ARTIST. I'd have been punished, too. Now *I'm* saved from that.

GIRL. Seems like we've both been saved. Strange, isn't it? Well, I'll get along without that prize money.

ARTIST. Of course you can still sell your Bayfield.

GIRL (*slowly*). No, I don't think I'll sell it. I'd like to keep it as—well, say a symbol of integrity. I'll get along. There must be a job somewhere.

ARTIST. There must be two jobs somewhere.

GIRL. You mean—

ARTIST. Why not? I think we should stick together.

GIRL. Good girl! (*Laughs.*) You know, you've got plenty of nerve. You'll make it.

ARTIST (*laughs*). Your nerve isn't so bad, either. You know what?

GIRL. What?

ARTIST. I guess I wouldn't have felt right if my picture had won—my way. It might have been the best at the exhibition, but in my heart I would have known there was a better picture in the state.

GIRL. You want to win because your picture is better than the best?

ARTIST. I guess that's it.

GIRL. Maybe it will win in spite of Frances Bayfield.

ARTIST. No. It isn't that good. (*With determination.*) But someday—

GIRL. That's the spirit.

ARTIST. We'll go to the city tonight.

GIRL. I've got twenty dollars. That will keep us a while.

ARTIST. And tomorrow we look for jobs.

GIRL. Good! Only—

ARTIST. Yes?

GIRL. You'll have to untie my arms first.

[*Artist laughs, takes knife from table drawer and cuts ropes.*

GIRL (*rubbing her wrists*). There! That feels better. (*Puts her hat on and takes up her bag.*)

ARTIST (*putting gun in table drawer*). I think I'll leave this here.

GIRL. Was it loaded?

ARTIST. No. (*Both laugh.*)

GIRL. Are we ready? I think there's enough gas left in the car to take us to the city.

ARTIST (*putting on her hat*). I'm ready. You know, some people might call this a coincidence.

GIRL. What?

ARTIST. Miss Bayfield's coming here.

GIRL (*slowly*). It was no coincidence.

ARTIST. Then—

GIRL. Maybe there's a guardian angel who watches over—

ARTIST. Artists—

GIRL (*as they go to the door*). And fools like me—

ARTIST (*as they go out*). I hate to be sentimental, but I believe you're right. (*They are gone.*)

CURTAIN

LITTLE IMMORTAL

A Portrait Play

BY ELISABETH WEHNER

THE FAMILY

HATTIE BEECHER, *who later writes "Uncle Tom's Cabin."*
MARY, *an older sister.*
CATHERINE, *a grown-up sister.*
MRS. LYMAN BEECHER, *the new stepmother.*

PLACE. Litchfield, Connecticut.
TIME. Winter, 1817.

HATTIE BEECHER *and all the Beecher children love to spend rainy afternoons in the attic. The attic is a large, raftered room with gabled windows and doors. Strings of herbs and onions hang in festoons from the rafters. There are a box of apples, a broken-down trunk from which protrudes old greatcoats and beaver hats, a rickety table and some broken chairs, and an old horsehair sofa with its springs hanging on the ground. A ripped, dusty picture of a Beecher ancestor hangs on the wall. There are also four barrels filled with sermons. A cold, drear rain is slanting against the window panes. Upstage, there is a flight of wooden steps which lead up into this attic. A hooded cradle stands in a corner.*

As the play begins, Catherine, a prim-looking girl of sixteen, is writing at the table. She wears a dress of the times and her hair is caught in a snood at the back of her head. Mary, twelve years old, is putting a family of dolls through a do-

mestic routine, dressing, undressing them, sitting them up, etc. Hattie, a serious child of ten, is delving into the barrels of sermons, looking for something to read. Both little girls are dressed in woolen dresses, white woolen stockings, buttoned boots and pinafores. From up the steps come the nostalgic notes of a mouth-organ played by one of the Beecher boys in the living room below. Silence, save for the music, the scratching of Catherine's quill pen and the swish of manuscript sheets as Hattie tosses papers from barrels.

CATHERINE (*looks up in annoyance as mouth-organ grows louder. Finally throws her quill down and goes to head of stairs. Calls*). Edward! Will you stop that dismal music? How can I write?

[*Music stops. She returns to writing.*

HATTIE. Catherine, may I go outdoors and play?

CATHERINE. No. It's raining.

HATTIE. The boys are out.

CATHERINE. That's different.

HATTIE. Why?

CATHERINE. Boys can do things that little girls are not permitted to do.

MARY. Hattie's just as strong as any boy, and brave. She's not afraid of snakes and toads.

CATHERINE. She may not go out.

HATTIE. Henry Ward is out and he's only five years old.

CATHERINE. Once and for all, Hattie, you cannot have your own way. I'm in charge of you until our new mother gets here. I will not permit you to be a hoyden.

[*Hattie goes to window, pushes a box under it, stands on box and throws open window. She leans far out and waves. A rainy gust of wind disturbs Catherine. She looks up in annoyance.*

CATHERINE. Hattie! What are you doing?

HATTIE. I'm just looking to see what the boys are doing.

CATHERINE. Well, what *are* they doing?

HATTIE. William and George are under the shed making a kite.

CATHERINE. Isn't Henry Ward with them?

HATTIE. No.

CATHERINE. Where is *he?*

HATTIE. He's out in the rain digging with his little wooden seaside shovel.

CATHERINE (*rising*). Good gracious! He'll catch the lung sickness. (*Goes to window and calls.*) Henry Ward! Stop that immediately. Boys! Take him into the kitchen right away and dry him out. (*Slams window shut.*)

HATTIE. You should have let me go out. I would have watched him.

CATHERINE. Silence! (*Again sits at table.*) What was he digging for?

HATTIE. When they put Mama in the grave, Henry Ward asked where she was going, and Papa said to Heaven. So he keeps digging down, trying to reach Heaven and Mama.

CATHERINE (*sighs*). Poor little tyke. (*Resumes writing.*)

HATTIE. Catherine. . . .

CATHERINE. Do find something to read, Hattie, and stop bothering me.

HATTIE (*throws more sermons on the floor*). Just barrels and barrels of sermons and nothing to read. (*Examines a manuscript, reads title.*) *An Appeal on the Unlawfulness of a Man Marrying his Wife's Sister.*

CATHERINE (*not looking up from her writing*). You may not read it.

HATTIE. It's one of Pa's best sermons.

CATHERINE. Nevertheless, you may not read it.

HATTIE (*throws it on floor, fishes out another one. Reads title to herself*). Catherine, why do they call Papa "The Great Gun of Calvinism"?

CATHERINE. Don't bother me. (*Writes furiously.*)

HATTIE. But, Catherine. . . .

CATHERINE. Will you stop chattering? How *can* I write?

HATTIE. But I have nothing to do.

CATHERINE. I *told* you to rock the cradle. Baby Charles will start crying again if you don't.

HATTIE. Oh, all right.

[*Hattie rocks cradle once or twice. Looks around. Finally*

gets piece of rope, ties one end to cradle and plays out the rest. She holds an end, giving the cradle a jerk from time to time when she remembers.

CATHERINE. I declare, I'll be glad when Papa gets here with your new mama. She'll make you mind.

HATTIE. When is Pa coming home—(*She gulps.*)—with *her?*

CATHERINE. They should have been here long ago. (*Glances at window.*) The carriage is late on account of the rain. (*Resumes writing.*)

HATTIE (*after a while*). What are you writing, Catherine?

CATHERINE (*exasperated*). A funeral ode for our departed mother and an address of welcome to our new mother.

MARY. I don't want a new mama. I want. . . . (*Starts to sniffle.*)

CATHERINE. I'm afraid Papa isn't asking us what we want. (*Kindly.*) Why don't you put your dolls to bed, Mary? They look so tired.

MARY (*obediently*). Yes, Catherine.

HATTIE. I'm not going to like this new mama—*ever!*

CATHERINE. Oh, do hush up, child. We have to try to like her. They say she's very beautiful.

HATTIE. I don't care.

[*Catherine resumes her writing. After Mary gets her dolls to bed on the couch, she lies down with them and goes to sleep. Hattie resumes her search for reading matter. She finds an almost empty barrel and digs deep down.*

HATTIE (*shouting suddenly*). I got it! I got a book! (*In her excitement, she falls into barrel. Her legs stick up in the air.*)

CATHERINE. Harriet Beecher! (*Pulls her out of the barrel.*)

HATTIE (*comes up beaming, clasping a book*). I found a good book. (*Reading title.*) *The Arabian Nights.*

CATHERINE (*shaking her violently*). Of all the little nuisances! (*As she goes back to her writing.*) I declare, *I'll* never have any children.

HATTIE. I declare, no children will ever have *you*. You're too cross.

CATHERINE. Just for that, Miss Sly-Boots, I won't let you have that book.

HATTIE (*pleadingly*). Please let me have it, Sister.

CATHERINE. You know you can't read big words anyhow. Besides, you wouldn't understand it.

HATTIE. I can read everything. And I learned twenty-seven hymns and two chapters from the Bible by heart.

CATHERINE. When?

HATTIE. When I was living with Grandma Foote.

MARY (*plaintively, coming out of her nap*). I want to go stay with Grandma Foote when my new mama comes.

CATHERINE. Hush.

HATTIE. May I have the book, Catherine?

CATHERINE. If you are very good and let me finish this, you may have it later. Now put it on the table. (*Reluctantly, Hattie places book on table.*)

[*From downstairs comes the wailing of a five-year-old.*

CATHERINE (*throwing both hands into the air*). Heavenly days! What's that?

HATTIE. That's Henry Ward crying for Mama.

CATHERINE (*goes to head of stairs and calls*). Henry Ward! Henry Ward! (*Sobs diminish.*) Now stop crying like a silly baby.

[*Sobs cease. Catherine goes back to table.*

HATTIE (*indignantly*). He is not a silly baby.

CATHERINE. Oh, he is too.

HATTIE. He's a good boy and someday he's going to be a great minister like Papa.

CATHERINE. Yes? I wish he were a minister now. I wish you were all ministers—missionary ministers—far away in darkest Africa. (*Resumes writing.*)

HATTIE (*inspired, goes over and shakes Mary*). Mary! Mary, wake up and let's play ministers.

MARY (*stumbling to her feet*). All right.

HATTIE. I'll be the minister and you be the congregation.

MARY. You're *always* the minister. I want to be the minister for once.

HATTIE. We'll take turns. I'll be the minister first.

[*Hattie takes a bell-shaped beaver hat from one of the trunks and crams it on her head. It rests on her ears. Then she gets a tail-coat and dons that. The tails drag on the floor and the sleeves hang down. Mary dons a similar hat and coat. Hattie thrusts a sheaf of sermons into Mary's hands. Absently gives cradle a yank or two.*

HATTIE. And we'll let baby Charles be a minister, too. (*She sets a beaver hat on the roof of his cradle and throws a batch of sermons into the cradle. She picks out a thick sermon for herself.*)

MARY. Now we're all ministers and there's no congregation and it isn't fun without the amens.

HATTIE. We'll be a conference of ministers addressing each other. I'll start. (*Looks over the top of imaginary spectacles.*) I'm in the pulpit.

[*Catherine has finished writing. Now she sands the paper and leans back in her chair to read her paper to herself.*

HATTIE (*reading from sermon in her hand*). "Calvinism is a mighty giant on the pathway of history."

MARY. Amen.

HATTIE (*reading from another sermon*). "Unbelievers, duelists and—and drinkers are obstructing the revivals and deferring the—" (*Stumbles over next word.*)—"Mil-len-ni-um."

MARY. Yea, Brother.

HATTIE (*turning to third sermon*). Here's a nice juicy one.

MARY (*suddenly*). Do you have conviction of sin, Brother?

HATTIE (*shouting*). Heresy! Heresy!

BABY (*triumphantly from cradle*). Wah-wah!

CATHERINE. Quiet!

HATTIE (*quietly and sternly to Mary*). I'm still minister. (*Glares at her over top of imaginary spectacles and reads.*) "The Unitarians are gaining. Their power of corrupting the youth of the Commonwealth by means of Harvard University is silently putting sentinels in all the churches; leg-is-la-tors in the halls and judges on the bench and. . . ."

MARY (*suddenly interrupting fervently*). Bless His Holy Name. (*Whining.*) It's my turn now.

[*From downstairs comes a woman's silvery laugh. Children stand in petrified silence. Catherine rises to her feet.*

CATHERINE (*in a whisper*). They have arrived.

[*Mary runs to Catherine and clings to her. Hattie stands her ground.*

MRS. BEECHER (*from downstairs*). No, no, Dr. Beecher. You put up the horse and carriage. I've met the boys—now I'll go up to the attic and introduce myself to the girls. I assure you I can handle the situation. Please! (*Again the tinkling laugh.*)

[*The three stand waiting, silent. Soon Mrs. Beecher is seen coming up the stairs. She is a beautiful woman, just past thirty. She has auburn hair and a clear skin. She is becomingly dressed in travel clothes of the period.*

MRS. BEECHER. How do you do? I'm your new mother. (*She smiles at them.*)

HATTIE. My, she is pretty.

MRS. BEECHER (*again the smile*). Thank you, my dear. I have met all your brothers. A fine lot of boys and all are going to be ministers, your pa says.

MARY. Yes, ma'am. Even baby Charles in the cradle there.

MRS. BEECHER (*after a fleeting glance towards cradle*). Of course the little boy—his name is Henry, I believe?

HATTIE. Henry Ward.

MRS. BEECHER. We'll have to find another profession for him. He does stutter dreadfully. A pity—such a beautiful child.

HATTIE. Henry Ward is so going to be a great preacher.

MRS. BEECHER (*with the dazzling smile*). What charming loyalty. But, dear, your little brother *is* handicapped.

HATTIE. Someday Henry Ward Beecher will be the greatest preacher in the whole wide world.

MRS. BEECHER (*to Catherine*). Fiery little thing, isn't she?

CATHERINE (*coming forward*). I'm Catherine, the oldest child.

MRS. BEECHER (*kissing her cheek*). I know. You're the poetess of the family. Your pa told me.

CATHERINE. My profession is teaching school.

HATTIE. But she's very nice just the same. She isn't always cross like she is today. But that was because she was exercised about your coming.

CATHERINE. Sh!

MRS. BEECHER. Frank little thing, isn't she?
CATHERINE. Papa spoils her. He encourages her to speak out like that.
MRS. BEECHER. Harriet! Now let me see—what did Dr. Beecher tell me about her? Oh, yes. He used the word "genius," I believe.
CATHERINE. No, she's just a little tomboy. Papa said he'd give a hundred dollars if she were a boy.
MARY. And Pa says she is as odd as she is intelligent.
MRS. BEECHER (*with an edge to her voice*). Hm. I see. His favorite. (*Looking at Mary.*) And who is the shy little girl?
MARY. Mary.
MRS. BEECHER. Are these all your dolls, dear?
MARY. Yes, ma'am.
MRS. BEECHER. Your destiny is obvious. You'll be a good wife and mother.
MARY. Thank you.
MRS. BEECHER. Harriet, what are you going to be when you grow up? A teacher, also?
HATTIE. No, ma'am. A great writer.
MRS. BEECHER (*laughs*). Dear, dear. I wanted to be a writer, too, when I was your age. But I soon outgrew it.
HATTIE (*fiercely*). But I *am* going to be a writer.
MRS. BEECHER (*soothingly*). Well, if Henry can be a preacher, I'm sure you can be a writer.
HATTIE. What does she mean, Catherine?
CATHERINE. Hush, Harriet.
MRS. BEECHER (*playfully chiding*). Little girl, you have my name.
HATTIE. No. you have *mine*.
MRS. BEECHER. We can't have two Harriet Beechers in the house.
HATTIE. I had my name first.
CATHERINE. Don't be impertinent. (*To Mrs. Beecher.*) We always call her Hattie anyhow. So there will be no conflict. (*To Hattie.*) Now do mind your manners.
HATTIE (*hanging her head*). Yes, Sister.
CATHERINE (*picking up her paper*). I have prepared a speech of welcome to you, Mrs. Beecher.

MRS. BEECHER (*playfully*). Now . . . now.

CATHERINE. I mean—Mother.

MRS. BEECHER. That's splendid. I'll be so pleased to hear it.

CATHERINE (*reading*). *I speak for myself and my brothers and sisters. We promise to make it our constant study to render to you the affection and obedience that we would render our own mother were she restored to us from the grave.* (*Looking up.*) There's more, but I think this is sufficient to show you our feelings. (*She steps forward.*) We welcome you to Litchfield.

MRS. BEECHER. Thank you. To succeed such a wonderful person as your mother, is indeed a momentous responsibility. I shall try to take her place in every possible way.

CATHERINE (*taking ring of keys from her belt*). I turn over the household to you.

MRS. BEECHER (*accepting keys*). I thank you.

HATTIE. Rain's stopped, Catherine. May I go out and play?

CATHERINE. Ask your new mama.

HATTIE (*after a pause*). I—I—don't want to go out.

MRS. BEECHER. Never hesitate to ask my permission. It shall always be granted in a worthy cause.

HATTIE. Yes, ma'am.

MRS. BEECHER (*pulling off her gloves*). I shall start right in being your mother by scolding you a wee bit, dear. I wouldn't be taking care of you in the true, motherly sense if I didn't correct you. Would I, now?

HATTIE. I haven't done anything.

MRS. BEECHER. According to letters which I received from my Litchfield friends, I understand that you have made inseparable companions of a family of Negro children some squares away.

HATTIE. They are my best friends.

MRS. BEECHER. Now, dear, we must be kind to the Negroes, of course. They are most unfortunate. If they are seriously ill, you may bring them some broth. But you may not associate with them any more.

HATTIE. But they're such nice children. I like them.

MRS. BEECHER. A clean, bright little girl like you—a *Beecher* —surely you are exaggerating your feelings?

HATTIE. They're as good as I am.

MRS. BEECHER. No, no, child. You are now my little girl. You don't think these Negroes are as good as *my* little girl? (*Hattie hangs her head and says nothing.*) Come, Hattie. Speak up.

HATTIE. You are my mama now and I must do as you say. I will not play with them any more.

MRS. BEECHER. That's my good girl.

HATTIE (*fiercely*). But I will always love them in my heart.

MRS. BEECHER. No temper, please. This scolding was as unpleasant for me as it was for you. But I have done my duty. (*Takes off her hat.*) Now I want to see that blessed baby. (*Goes to cradle, throws beaver hat off.*) Who put that dirty thing there?

MARY. We were just playing.

MRS. BEECHER. The baby is literally covered with these filthy papers. (*Throws out sermons. Suddenly screams and steps back.*)

CATHERINE (*running to her*). What is it?

MRS. BEECHER. Someone has placed a nest of baby mice at the foot of the cradle!

HATTIE. I did.

MRS. BEECHER. *You?*

HATTIE. They were so cold.

MRS. BEECHER. How revolting!

HATTIE. Old Tom killed their mother. Now there is no one but me to take care of them. I am their mother.

MRS. BEECHER. What utter nonsense. Catherine, have one of the boys drown them. (*Holds out box to Catherine.*)

HATTIE (*snatching box from her*). No, you shall not have them drowned.

MRS. BEECHER (*wheedlingly*). But nice little girls don't like mice. They are very cunning now, but they'll be ugly when they grow up. They won't feel drowning.

HATTIE. They have a right to live.

MRS. BEECHER (*exasperated*). *Why*, for heavens' sake?

HATTIE. Anything that's born has a right to live.

MRS. BEECHER. Now that's very stupid reasoning.

HATTIE. I love them because they have no friends. (*Looking

at her.) When I grow up, I'm going to be friends with all the things that have no friends.

MRS. BEECHER (*smiling again*). Of course, dear. But not mice.

HATTIE. Yes. God made them as carefully as he made you.

MRS. BEECHER. I am tempted to say that you are a most unpleasant child. (*Smiles.*) But I won't.

HATTIE. I'll take them out of the house if they bother you.

CATHERINE. Yes. Gracious, Hattie, such a fuss over mice. Do take them out to the barn.

HATTIE (*radiant*). Yes. A mother mouse might adopt them.

MRS. BEECHER. Of course. Run along now.

[*Hattie starts for the stairs.*

MARY. I'll go along with you, Hattie. Goodbye—Mother. (*Drops a little curtsey.*)

MRS. BEECHER (*smiling warmly*). Goodbye, dear.

HATTIE. Goodbye. (*Curtsies.*)

MRS. BEECHER (*coyly*). Goodbye, what? I'm married to your papa, you know. (*Mary has disappeared down the stairs.*)

HATTIE. I know. (*Steps down one step. Speaks fiercely.*) And because you have come here and married my pa, when I am big enough, I mean to go and marry *your* pa. (*She runs down the stairs with her basket of mice.*)

MRS. BEECHER (*to Catherine*). What an unfeminine child!

CATHERINE. Hattie's much too honest to be feminine. (*Mrs. Beecher gives her a sharp look.*)

MRS. BEECHER. She *is* highly intelligent. It would be dreadful, however, if she grew up to be a woman reformer—you know—dabbling in politics? Getting fierce over public issues?

CATHERINE. Hattie will come out all right. Sometimes she is *trying*, but she has a good heart.

[*Sound of the mouth-organ comes up the stairs.*

MRS. BEECHER. What. . . ?

CATHERINE. That's Edward playing the mouth-organ. He's the musical member of the family.

MRS. BEECHER (*smiling*). What an extraordinary brood I've inherited. (*Putting her hand on Catherine's arm.*) Confidentially, dear, doesn't that sort of music annoy you?

CATHERINE (*raises her head proudly and looks straight into her eyes*). No. I rather like it.

MRS. BEECHER. Oh! Well— (*Smiles winningly at Catherine.*) You're a very sensible young lady, dear. I shall want your help with little Hattie. I think you and I together could change her.

CATHERINE. In what way?

MRS. BEECHER. By tactfully showing her the error of all those foolish ideas she's accumulated.

CATHERINE. I don't know, Mrs. Beecher—I mean, Mother. There's something about Hattie that shouldn't be tampered with. (*Quickly.*) Papa is very proud of her.

MRS. BEECHER (*coldly*). Indeed!

CATHERINE. Papa has a little nickname for her—and—somehow, we all believe in it.

MRS. BEECHER. What does he call her? Little Mouse?

CATHERINE. Oh no. (*Pause.*) He calls her Little Immortal.

MRS. BEECHER (*coldly*). I see. (*Smiles.*) Well, I didn't come a day too soon. (*Going to stairs.*) If you'll excuse me, dear, I must see your father immediately. I wish to have an understanding with him about Hattie.

CATHERINE. Yes, ma'am.

MRS. BEECHER. Little Immortal!

[*Her silvery laugh rings out mockingly as she descends the stairs. The music of the mouth-organ comes up louder as Catherine goes to the cradle and as . . .*

THE CURTAIN FALLS

THE FACES OF DEKA

A Futuristic Play

BY MICHAEL MORGAN

"And in those days, women ruled the world."

THE WOMEN

BERENICE, *matriarch of Vira.*
DORA, *captain of the palace guard.*
HARRIET, *secretary of state.*
THALIA, *minister of propaganda.*
SERVANT, *to His Highness, husband of Berenice.*
ADELAIDE, *ambassador from Kenna.*
MARGARET, *student matriarch of Vira.*
SUSANA, *scientist of Kenna.*
SOLDIER.

PLACE. Claire, capital city of the State of Vira.
TIME. The Moon of Grapes in the year 7762 of the Great Change.

THE MATRIARCH'S *audience room in the palace at Claire, capital of the State of Vira, is a spacious, imposing room, with large windows at the back overlooking the city's great central square. Down left is a door leading to the rest of the palace, while down right is another door leading to Berenice's private rooms. Cater-cornered between the right and back walls is a platform on which stands Berenice's plain, serviceable desk and a chair. Forming a half-moon, more or less center, are three sturdy, uncomfortable arm-chairs. There is no other furniture.*

As the play opens, Berenice, the matriarch of Vira, a tall, Amazon-like creature, is standing by the great windows, staring out into the distance. She wears all white, a very short pleated skirt, a short-sleeved silk blouse, sandals, and a short cape lined with scarlet. Her white hair, which lies heavy on her shoulders, is bound with a narrow gold fillet. She is a mature woman of large gestures, free striding movement, and commanding presence. Young Captain Dora of the palace guard enters. Her costume is much the same as the matriarch, save that the color is yellow, and the much shorter cape is lined with brown. Fastened to her hip is a dress dagger. On her left shoulder is a gold epaulette denoting her rank. Behind her come the middle-aged Thalia, minister of propaganda, and Harriet, the secretary of state. Both of these women wear the same costumes as the captain and the matriarch, but in colors to suit their fancy. All of them are stamped with the same freedom of movement as the matriarch, and all are obviously leaders.

DORA (*saluting in a manner oddly reminiscent of the old Fascist salute*). Excellency.

BERENICE. Well, what is it? What news?

HARRIET. Bad news! The forces of Kenna are advancing rapidly. Our soldiers are retreating in front of them like frightened cattle.

DORA. May I remind the secretary of state that our soldiers have left full payment for every step that they have retreated?

HARRIET. I am not questioning their bravery!

DORA. What did you mean by "frightened cattle"?

BERENICE (*coming to her desk and sitting down*). Stop quarreling! I will not have it.

THALIA. Any news of Margaret?

BERENICE. None. But she'll return. She must return.

DORA. If she can get through the lines. (*She sits on the arm of one of the chairs.*) When she left there was no hint of war. As far as she knows, the women of Kenna are our friends.

HARRIET (*sitting in one of the chairs*). And don't forget that she must pass through the outer boundaries of Kenna.

BERENICE. I'm not forgetting that.

DORA. Did she take any home-flying pigeons with her?

BERENICE. Three.

THALIA (*pacing the floor*). And we've not received one. Not one.

BERENICE. But I have a feeling she is all right. Something tells me she is still safe—that she will get through to us.

DORA. Suppose she has been captured? She will be a great hostage in the hands of Kenna . . . worth many prisoners.

BERENICE. I know that. But no message has come from Kenna—and until that message comes we must suppose that she is still safe.

HARRIET. I wish I could believe that.

BERENICE. Why not?

HARRIET (*going to the desk*). Eileen of Kenna is clever—malicious—sly. It would be very like her to capture Margaret, and then wait, like a spider in a web, until the psychological moment arrives.

BERENICE (*impatiently*). What psychological moment?

HARRIET. Suppose we capture someone Eileen wants—someone we would not be inclined to exchange—such as one of her generals? Or better still, one of her scientists?

BERENICE. How would we capture one of her scientists? She keeps them safe enough in Kenna.

HARRIET. It could be done, you know.

BERENICE. What are you getting at, Harriet?

HARRIET. You tell her, Thalia. The idea was yours.

THALIA. Suppose we sent three women into Kenna with orders to kidnap a scientist and bring her into our lines.

BERENICE. Have you lost your mind? (*A servant, dressed in plain gray and without the cape, enters.*) What is it?

SERVANT. His Highness, the Prince, desires to speak with you, Excellency.

BERENICE. What does he want now?

SERVANT. Well, Excellency, he—he— (*She pauses and looks shamefacedly about her.*)

BERENICE. He what?

SERVANT. He wants an extra egg for his breakfast.

BERENICE. Mother in Heaven! (*Slams her hand down on desk. It is all the other three women can do to keep from laughing.*) Inform His Highness that Vira is at war, and that he must make some small sacrifice for the women who are dying in the battle lines.

SERVANT. Yes, Excellency.

BERENICE. And tell the cook to give him the egg I was supposed to have for tomorrow's breakfast.

SERVANT. Yes, Excellency. (*Bows and goes out.*)

DORA. You spoil that man, Your Excellency.

BERENICE. If I don't happen to like eggs, is that any concern of yours?

DORA (*hastily*). No, Excellency.

BERENICE. Very well, then. Now, what's this stupid kidnapping scheme of yours?

HARRIET. It sounded stupid to us, too . . . at first.

THALIA. I think it only fair to tell you that it was my husband's idea . . . not mine.

DORA (*horrified*). Do you mean to say that you've been feeding me a lot of silly nonsense thought up by a man?

THALIA. Now, Dora, I know that you don't have a very high opinion of men.

DORA. I certainly don't. Men belong in the kitchen, taking care of the children, and worshipping in church. They certainly don't belong in the army.

BERENICE. Do you remember the reports from the battle of Black Cloud Mountain? Men fought side by side with their women in that battle, and fought bravely. You can't deny that, Captain.

DORA. I'm not trying to deny their bravery. But men don't know anything about military strategy, and I'm telling you now, Thalia, the more I think of your scheme, the more scatterbrained I think it is. And I won't have anything to do with it.

THALIA. You liked the idea until you found out my husband thought it up.

DORA. I never said I liked it. I only said I thought it should be submitted to the matriarch.

HARRIET. Stop being so prejudiced on the subject of men, Captain. Why, you're as much of an old fuss-budget as your mother.

DORA. May I remind the secretary of state that my mother was one of the greatest soldiers Vira ever had?

HARRIET. And may I remind the captain of the guard that her mother was one of the most stiff-necked, self-satisfied old war-horses. . . .

DORA. You'll be telling me next that you approve of votes for men!

HARRIET. Yes, I do.

THALIA. Harriet, have you lost your mind? What does a man know about politics?

BERENICE. If you three don't stop squabbling, I'll put you all in prison for disorderly conduct.

HARRIET. I'm sorry, Excellency. (*Trying to contain herself.*) But Dora makes me so mad.

DORA (*contemptuously*). Men!

BERENICE. Captain!

DORA (*quieting down*). Yes, Excellency.

BERENICE. And now will you explain your little scheme—or your husband's little scheme—or whose ever little scheme it is!

THALIA. Well, Phillip had just finished reading a history of Kenna. . . .

DORA (*flinging up her hands*). Mother in Heaven! An intellectual man!

BERENICE (*like an ancient schoolmarm*). Another word out of you, Captain, and I'll ask you to leave this room.

DORA. Very well, Excellency.

THALIA. Phillip was very much impressed with the fact that the entire social system of Kenna was based upon science.

BERENICE. What do you mean?

THALIA. What would you say was the basis of our social system?

BERENICE. Labor.

THALIA. Precisely. Here a woman is judged by the amount of labor credits which she accumulates during her lifetime.

The idle woman, the playgirl type, is despised. The tiller of fields is as much respected as you or I.

HARRIET. But that is not true in Kenna. They have a very large idle class whom they call "The Intellectuals."

THALIA. Here we train the body, and a very small minority of us have what is called a "cultural" education. Our people vote us into office and then expect us to do the thinking for them. We train the matriarchs. We send them off on the great pilgrimage to Deka, just as we sent you, Berenice. Just as we have now sent Margaret.

DORA. None of us knows what happens on the pilgrimage. We know that each of you returns changed, somehow.

BERENICE (*nervously*). That is the secret of the matriarchs. It is not for you to question nor for me to confirm.

DORA. I am not questioning it. But I reserve the right to wonder about it.

BERENICE. That has nothing to do with the problem at hand. Continue, Thalia.

THALIA. But the social system of Kenna is based on the intellect. The people there are soft, indolent, luxury-loving. Their ruling council is called the Committee of Scientists, and their matriarch makes no pilgrimage to Deka. She is elected by the scientists to a life term. She is herself a scientist, although not always the greatest one.

HARRIET. I spent two years at the University of Kenna. Eileen is a brilliant woman, but Susana is the guiding mind of Kenna. Everyone knows that.

THALIA. Phillip asked me, and I think it a fair question: "Why is it that we, the well trained, the hardy, the strong, should lose battle after battle to these lazy, soft-couch people?

BERENICE. And what did you answer him?

THALIA. He answered his own question . . . that the trained mind will always triumph over the trained body.

DORA (*bursting forth*). If I ever heard a stupid sentence, that one is it! For the sake of the Great Mother, surely you're not going to listen to such asinine stupidity, Excellency.

HARRIET. I'm tired of your narrow-mindedness, Captain. Any

idea that does not agree precisely with your own idea is false in your eyes.

DORA. May I remind the secretary of state that she was educated in Kenna, and was poisoned by their stupid propaganda. But my mother knew that our own military college was good enough for her and good enough for me—good enough for any citizen of Vira.

BERENICE (*thoughtfully*). What else did Phillip suggest, Thalia?

THALIA. That we will never triumph until we remove the thinking mind of Kenna's army.

HARRIET. And that mind is Susana.

BERENICE. Your plan is to kidnap Susana—bring her here?

THALIA. Yes.

DORA. Of all the scatterbrained schemes that I've ever heard—

BERENICE. Shut up, Dora. (*Striding up and down.*) It would be instant death for the three if they were caught in Kenna.

THALIA. Of course.

DORA. You're not seriously considering it, are you?

BERENICE. I don't know. Oh, Mother, I wish Margaret were here!

DORA. Margaret is still in her training period. She can't give you the practical advice that we can give you.

BERENICE. You don't understand, Captain. Margaret has visited Deka. It does something to you, that pilgrimage. Something that cuts you off from all the other women in the world—something that gives you a new way of thinking.

DORA. Of course, if we're not good enough for you. . . .

BERENICE (*putting her hand on Dora's shoulder*). I'm sorry, Dora. I didn't mean that—it's something you could never hope to understand. (*Sits on the edge of desk.*) Thalia, it's a foolhardy scheme.

THALIA. I realize that as well as you.

HARRIET. It is terrible to admit that we have reached a point where we must consider foolhardy schemes.

DORA. Berenice, let me take the palace guard and go to the front. I can't stand being penned up here—away from danger—doing nothing. . . .

BERENICE. I know, Dora. I realize how difficult it's been for you, sacrificing your personal glory to protect this palace that needs no protection. But I dare not send you away. As long as the people can see you, they know they are safe. You are their golden soldier—their little warrior-goddess. With you gone, there would be panic. They would know, then, clearer than any words, that Vira stands on the brink of utter defeat. Even if the soldiers of Kenna were at our very gates, I would not send you out.

THALIA (*maliciously*). That is the price one has to pay for popularity, Captain.

DORA (*whirling and pulling out her dagger*). You keep your slithering tongue out of my affairs.

THALIA. I've always hated you—your insolence, your fine body—the way the people love you for your pride. But Phillip was right. The mind can always conquer the body. And my mind will conquer you!

DORA. Why you. . . .

[*She leaps toward Thalia but Harriet springs between them. As she pushes Dora back, Berenice flings Thalia into a chair.*

HARRIET. Are you both mad? Excellency. . . .

BERENICE. Let them clear the air. They'll be no good to you nor me nor Vira as long as this feeling is between them.

DORA. I'm sorry, Excellency. For a moment, I lost control of my temper. I'll be all right in a moment.

[*Thalia slumps back into the chair and tries gaspingly to get her breath.*

BERENICE (*pouring out a glass of water and taking it to her*). Here!

THALIA (*drinks eagerly, then passes the back of her hand across her mouth and hands back glass*). Thank you. My apologies, Excellency.

BERENICE. Each of you is needed in her place. One would be useless without the other. Do you understand that—both of you?

THALIA. Yes, Excellency.

DORA. I'll try and remember.

BERENICE. See that you do. (*Sits behind her desk.*) Now,

about this scheme. It has a merit none of you has mentioned.

THALIA. What is it?

BERENICE. Eileen won't be expecting it. Oh, I know Eileen, yes, and the great Susana, too. They think they know exactly how our minds work. Push forward with an overwhelming number of soldiers—to victory. That's our method. That's been our method in the past, and that will continue to be our method as long as Vira stands an independent state.

HARRIET. It certainly hasn't proved a very good method in this war.

BERENICE. But this is the first time we've ever fought Kenna, don't forget that. We've always fought states that were—shall we say—less intellectual.

DORA. It doesn't seem possible that this Vira—this sacred ground—could even face a possibility of defeat.

THALIA. We're facing more than defeat. We're facing invasion.

HARRIET. It means the end of our state. The end of everything that we have known for a thousand years. Our people will lose their strength, their beauty, their greatness. They will become soft and lazy. Worse than that, they will be slaves. Our freedom, our laughter, our joy in living will be gone!

BERENICE. Eileen is prepared to fight our fine, strong army. She is not prepared, however, for. . . .

THALIA (*softly*). For the kidnapping of her most valuable scientist.

BERENICE. That is the true merit of the scheme. If I were only certain it would work.

DORA. The whole idea is stupid. The way to conquer is to overwhelm. (*A soldier dressed in the gold and brown of the guard, but without Dora's shoulder insignia, enters and salutes.*) What is it?

SOLDIER. A dispatch by pigeon from the front, ma'am.

BERENICE. A message from Margaret?

DORA (*opening dispatch. In a dead voice*). No, not from Margaret. No answer.

SOLDIER. Yes, ma'am. (*Salutes and goes out.*)

HARRIET. Well, don't stand there. What does it say?

DORA (*walks quietly over and puts dispatch on Berenice's desk*). Our army is in flight, with an estimated loss of two thousand women.

BERENICE. Mother in Heaven!

DORA (*sinks down in chair and buries her face in her hands*). I can't stand any more of this. I can't!

HARRIET. In flight!

THALIA. We are very close to the end.

DORA (*looking pleadingly up at Berenice*). Will you let me go now? Will you? You can't ask me to sit here and accept defeat without striking a single blow. You can't!

THALIA. She is our golden soldier, Berenice. The army would follow her into the very face of death. With her to lead them, she might turn the rout. . . .

DORA (*in amazement*). You speak for me, Thalia?

THALIA. I speak for my country.

DORA. I see. (*She turns to the matriarch, who is staring out of the window.*) You haven't answered me, Berenice. May I go?

BERENICE (*turns slowly*). How much is Margaret worth to us?

DORA. What did you say?

THALIA. I don't believe you've heard a word that we've said.

BERENICE. How much is Margaret worth to us?

HARRIET. She is to be our next matriarch after you are gone.

DORA. We are pledged to protect her with our lives.

THALIA. She is our future hope, you know that.

BERENICE. Is she worth Susana?

HARRIET. What are you talking about?

BERENICE (*turning back into the room*). We've had no word from Margaret. None at all. Supposing she was captured.

DORA. She wore the laborer's gray instead of the matriarch's white. If she were captured, the chances are no one of Kenna knows her true importance.

HARRIET. Susana has her fingers on every pulse in Vira. She'd know.

BERENICE. If our wild scheme succeeded, and Eileen refused to exchange Margaret for Susana, what then?

HARRIET (*after a pause*). Then the whole scheme would be worth no more than *that*. (*Snaps her fingers.*)

THALIA. Wait. We could train another matriarch.

DORA (*horrified*). The person of the matriarch is sacred.

THALIA. Only because we make it so.

BERENICE. Is Margaret worth the State of Vira? Is she?

DORA. I never thought about it like that before.

HARRIET. We are making mountains out of molehills. We don't even know that she's a prisoner.

SOLDIER (*entering and saluting*). Adelaide of Kenna under a flag of truce to see Your Excellency.

[*The three women stare at each other in consternation. Then, as though an electric current had passed through them, they draw themselves up.*

BERENICE. Admit her.

[*Soldier salutes and goes out.*

HARRIET (*almost whispering*). What do you think has happened?

BERENICE. Only the Great Mother knows.

SOLDIER (*entering and saluting*). Adelaide of Kenna!

[*Adelaide of Kenna enters. She wears a soft, flowing gown of many colors and a long, diaphanous cape. Her hair is piled on her head in soft curls, and there is a complete femininity about her. Soldier salutes again and goes out. Adelaide drops a deep curtsy.*

ADELAIDE. Hail to Berenice, matriarch of Vira.

BERENICE (*flinging up her arm in salute*). I salute Eileen of Kenna, and her servant Adelaide. Thalia, my minister of propaganda. Harriet, my secretary of state; and Dora, captain of my palace guard.

ADELAIDE (*bowing*). To you all, greetings.

THALIA, HARRIET *and* DORA (*not in concert*). Our greetings.

ADELAIDE. I bring you sad news.

BERENICE. What is it?

ADELAIDE. Your student matriarch is in our hands.

[*The women of Vira glance quickly at each other.*

BERENICE (*slowly*). She was on a pilgrimage to Deka. We consider those on pilgrimage as sacred.

ADELAIDE. We of Kenna do not. You see, we have no pilgrimage to Deka.

BERENICE. Yes, I know. I thought perhaps. . . .

ADELAIDE (*with a superior air*). Idle thinking is stupid thinking—forgive me, Excellency.

BERENICE. I suppose you brought us some terms.

ADELAIDE (*smoothly*). The unconditional surrender of your country and the recognition of Eileen as the supreme matriarch.

HARRIET. Those terms are impossible.

ADELAIDE. Friend Harriet, you and I were at the University of Kenna together. You should know that the word "impossible" is not in our vocabulary.

[*The servant enters and bows.*

BERENICE. What do you want?

SERVANT. His Highness' compliments, and you took away the book he was reading this morning.

BERENICE (*looks at the servant blankly for a moment, then lifts the book from the desk and flings it at her*). Take it and get out.

SERVANT (*clutching the book*). Yes, Excellency. (*She hurries out.*)

ADELAIDE (*in her superior way*). How extraordinary. I didn't know the men of Vira could read.

THALIA. We are not complete barbarians, I can assure you.

DORA (*forcing the words out*). Our men are as unusual as our women. (*She looks around pugnaciously at the startled women of Vira.*) Look how . . . how brave they were . . . at Black Cloud Mountain.

ADELAIDE. Yes, I've heard of that great battle. They fought side by side with your women. How charmingly barbaric.

DORA (*fighting to hold down her temper*). Madam, I can assure you. . . .

BERENICE. Captain, Adelaide of Kenna did not come here to discuss our men!

DORA. Yes, Excellency. (*She sits down.*)

ADELAIDE. But I adore discussing men. I find them such pleasant subjects. And I have always heard that His Highness is unusually handsome.

DORA (*bursting out again*). Vira is famous for her handsome men.

ADELAIDE. So they are. Where do you find them, Excellency? (*Mockingly.*) On your pilgrimages to Deka?

BERENICE. You people of Kenna have always considered yourselves very high and mighty . . . so great, indeed, that there is no necessity for your matriarchs to make the great pilgrimage. What a pity. They might have learned something to their advantage.

ADELAIDE. What type of knowledge is it that leaves you dazed as though you were sick with a drug? That allows you to wander into your enemy's camp as though you were sick with a great fever . . . that makes you scream at the sight of a man . . . much less a woman?

THALIA. Explain your words.

ADELAIDE. That was how your Margaret acted when we captured her . . . how she's been acting ever since. If you want to send her into a case of hysterics, all you have to do is let her look at a man. (*Laughs softly.*) Your great matriarch to be, is, I am afraid, a bit of a coward.

DORA (*leaping on her*). That is a lie! (*Harriet and Thalia drag her off Adelaide, who is white with anger.*) I've known Margaret all my life. We are blood sisters. She is no more a coward than I am, and you know it.

BERENICE (*strides over and slaps Dora across the face*). Silence! (*To Adelaide.*) I . . . I beg your indulgence.

ADELAIDE (*coldly*). Naturally. I have no illusions concerning barbarians.

BERENICE. Then have no illusions about this. I know the reasons behind Margaret's actions. I can assure you that they will not last.

ADELAIDE. You mean her—may I use the word "hysteria"—is a result of her pilgrimage to Deka?

BERENICE. Yes, it is. You think that she is a coward . . . that even a man frightens her. . . . She's not afraid. It's that she's seeing something new. Something that you civilized people have never understood in all of your thousand years of civilization.

SERVANT (*entering again*). Your indulgence, Excellency.

BERENICE (*wearily*). What does His Highness want now?

SERVANT. The seller of hats is here. His Highness wishes you to choose between a blue hat and a pink hat for him.

BERENICE. Great Mother! Does he think I have nothing. . . . (*Stops abruptly and leans her weight on desk as though she were suddenly very tired. When she speaks again her voice is very gentle.*) Tell him I'll be there presently.

SERVANT. Yes, Excellency. (*Goes out.*)

ADELAIDE (*laughing softly*). I have always heard you spoiled His Highness. I did not know that he would take precedence over the surrender of your state.

BERENICE. Madam, you are not here to discuss my conduct. You have stated your terms—the recognition of Eileen as supreme matriarch. I take it from that, I am still to remain governor of the State of Vira. . . .

ADELAIDE. Paying, of course, homage to Eileen.

BERENICE. And in return we get the person of Margaret.

ADELAIDE. The sacred symbol of the perpetuation of your government—yes.

BERENICE. You will have our answer in three days.

ADELAIDE. I cannot wait that long.

BERENICE. You must. This is not a matter which my ministers and I can decide. The vote of the people will give you your answer. We cannot tabulate the final voting in less than three days. During that time you will be the honored guest of Harriet. I have spoken.

ADELAIDE. The last barbarity—the vote of the people. But three days . . . so be it.

HARRIET. Come. I will escort you to my house. (*Turns to Berenice.*) With your permission, Excellency.

BERENICE. With my permission.

[*Harriet and Adelaide go out. The moment they are gone, Dora and Thalia close in on Berenice.*

DORA. What are we to do now?

BERENICE. The only thing we can do.

THALIA. I must go warn the governors to arrange for the voting. (*Starts for the door.*)

BERENICE. There will be no voting.

THALIA. But you just said. . . .

BERENICE. I needed that three days for something else. Dora, didn't you once make a bet to ride from here to the capital of Kenna and return in three days?

DORA. And I did it, too, with twenty minutes to sp— (*She stops short.*) Great Mother! But we don't even know they're holding Margaret at Lexar.

BERENICE. Susana's at Lexar.

THALIA. With Susana in our hands. . . .

DORA. Checkmate!

THALIA. Suppose we fail.

BERENICE. We can lose nothing more than we've lost already.

DORA (*pleadingly*). You'll let me go, Berenice?

BERENICE. Failure is death without mercy.

DORA. Please, Berenice.

THALIA. And I—I know I'm small and frail, but my nerves are steel. And after all, it was my Phillip who thought of the plan.

BERENICE. Yes, your Phillip thought of it.

DORA. Harriet would never forgive us if she were left out.

BERENICE. No, Harriet must stay here. She knows the Kennians well. If we fail, they could not ask for a better governor.

THALIA. Then who is to be the third?

BERENICE (*sitting at desk and writing note*). Am I so transparent a thing that you cannot see me? (*She rings a small bell.*)

THALIA (*horrified*). Not you!

DORA. You're the matriarch. The person of the matriarch is sacred.

SERVANT (*entering*). You rang, Excellency?

BERENICE (*giving her the note she has just written*). Take this note to His Highness and bring me the answer quickly.

SERVANT. Yes, Excellency. (*She goes.*)

THALIA. You said the people would go into a panic if we sent Dora away. Do you not think there would be a greater panic if you were to disappear?

BERENICE. And who said I was to disappear?

DORA. Even you can't be in two places at the same time.

BERENICE (*laughs softly*). Would you like to take a wager on that? (*Servant enters.*) That was quick. Give me the answer. (*Servant hands her a note.*) That's all.

SERVANT. Yes, Excellency. (*Goes out.*)

BERENICE (*reads note and laughs softly*). So I spoil my husband, do I? I think perhaps sometimes it is a very good practice. (*Grins at the two women.*) Tonight I will give a dinner for Adelaide of Kenna. His Highness is suddenly going to want to visit the mountains. I will refuse him. Then he will have a tantrum. Have you even seen His Highness in a tantrum, Thalia?

THALIA. Heaven forbid!

BERENICE. His Highness is too handsome a man to be let out alone, so I will, of course, go with him. And I cannot go without my personal guard, can I, Dora? And naturally I will need someone to help me work out plans for the future. Who could be a better choice than that mistress of psychology, my minister of propaganda?

THALIA. Of course! With one little tantrum you dispose of all of us in a most logical fashion—and arouse no suspicions.

DORA. I'm coming to believe more and more that men do have their uses.

BERENICE. Now go, both of you. I know that you have matters to attend to—and so do I.

DORA. Excellency! (*She salutes and hurries from room.*)

THALIA. All my life I've dreamed of going into action for my state. I never thought the dream would come true. I'll see you at dinner, Excellency.

BERENICE (*already at work on papers*). Yes, at dinner, Thalia.

[*Thalia goes. For a long moment there is silence, while Berenice goes through papers and makes a list. Then through the inner-suite door at the right, staggers a woman dressed in servant gray. It is Margaret. Weak and wounded as she is, she too is a leader.*

MARGARET (*almost without voice*). Berenice! (*Collapses.*)

BERENICE. Yes, what is it? (*Looks around irritably, then, seeing Margaret, she springs to her feet with a startled gasp.*) Margaret! (*She runs over, half pulls, half carries her to a chair, gets a glass of water from desk and holds it to her lips.*) You here! How did you make it? Where did you come from?

MARGARET (*speaking jerkily from fatigue*). Through the forbidden passage—into your bedroom.

BERENICE. How did you escape the Kennian hands?

MARGARET. A man helped me.

BERENICE. Oh! (*Looks toward outer door a second, then goes over and opens it a crack.*) Guard!

GUARD (*outside the room*). Yes, Excellency.

BERENICE. Allow no one in here—regardless of who it is—until further orders.

GUARD (*outside*). Yes, Excellency.

BERENICE (*shutting door and turning to Margaret*). Does anyone know you're back—besides myself?

MARGARET. No one. I had to see you first.

BERENICE. Good. The fewer people who know you're here, the better for all of us. With everyone thinking you are captured—with the incentive that will give to our people—I can force this whole stupid war into a victory for us. And Eileen of Kenna dare not reveal that she no longer holds you captive. Even Dora, Thalia and Harriet must not know you're safe.

MARGARET. I can't make myself invisible.

BERENICE. I'll send you to the mountains tonight with His Highness. He's the only one with brains enough to realize the importance of keeping you hidden from even the loyal eyes of Vira. His Highness—and perhaps, yes, Thalia's husband, Phillip. I'll send him along with you, too. They'll protect you.

MARGARET (*during above, she has sat up and is now smiling wryly at Berenice*). They will protect me.

BERENICE. Can't you forget for once that you're a woman and that they are men?

MARGARET. I learned my lesson well at Deka.

BERENICE. Oh! Oh, yes, Deka. For a moment I was forgetting Deka.

MARGARET (*bursting out with repressed emotion*). Why did you send me without letting me know—without even one hint of what I was to find?

BERENICE. How could I let you know? It is forbidden to speak of Deka. The journey is long and cruel. The chances were that you'd never reach there.

MARGARET. Berenice, how can such things be? To have everything you've ever believed in destroyed in one sweeping moment.

BERENICE. I know, I know. I felt the same when I stood there and saw the things you saw.

MARGARET. And to think that Dora and the other young officers of the guard used to laugh about you. Yes, and I laughed too. The way you jumped whenever His Highness spoke. We used to call you the slave wife of Vira. He had only to express a whim and you granted it quickly—almost as though you were afraid of him.

BERENICE. I know you laughed. Even Adelaide of Kenna laughed today about it. But, Margaret, I can't help it. When I look at him I see the faces of the great black hills of Deka.

MARGARET. It was like a slap across the face. I tell you, when I saw them, it was like a slap. Those mighty faces carved from the mountainside—left there forever by a people who are gone from us—leaving us no record of themselves save those faces—and a number carved on a near-by rock—1942. Berenice, they were the faces of *men!*

BERENICE (*slowly*). You know, Margaret, I think that men must have once ruled this earth.

MARGARET. They must have, for only rulers could leave such a monument.

BERENICE (*more to herself than to Margaret*). But why do women rule the world now?

MARGARET. I don't know, but whenever I see a man now, I feel sick and ashamed. How could they, who were once so godlike, be what they are now?

BERENICE. Because they failed.

MARGARET. Failed?

BERENICE. I think they failed somehow. They failed as we are failing. I don't know. I've thought about it so much, but . . . I don't know.

MARGARET. You mean that finally the women were sick of

their man-made world, and revolted? That the women took power into their own hands and stamped out all that man had done before?

BERENICE. That's what I think—yes. Our history does not begin until after we are already powerful. But I think those people must have been like us. They must have had their years of famine and of plenty, as we do. They must have had their homes, and their laughter, and their ambitions, even as we have them. And I think, perhaps, they too had their wars, to feed the power and the glory of their separate states.

MARGARET. But they were gods, Berenice. Those who could carve such faces must have been gods.

BERENICE. No. One of them had suffering stamped on his face . . . human suffering. Gods don't suffer like that.

MARGARET. Then we are as great as they were.

BERENICE. No, Margaret. We are as small as they were. We stamped them out, but we have provided nothing better, and that is failure. Listen, Margaret.

MARGARET. Yes, Berenice?

BERENICE. Tonight, Dora, Thalia and I ride to Kenna. We plan to bring back the scientist Susana.

MARGARET. You mean—kidnap her?

BERENICE. Wait. Hear me out. With Susana in my hands I can force Kenna into peace. . . .

MARGARET (*quietly*). There is no need of that.

BERENICE. Margaret, you might as well know the entire truth. Our soldiers are retreating. This foolish scheme is our only hope.

MARGARET. I meant there was no need to go to Kenna to kidnap Susana.

BERENICE. Have you a better idea?

MARGARET. No.

BERENICE. Then what. . . ?

MARGARET (*rises, goes to bedroom door, opens it*). You can come in now. (*Susana of Kenna enters. She is a tall, commanding woman, inclined to heaviness. If she had lived in the twentieth century, she might have been president of a girl's school or at least a dean. She wears the flowing dress of her state.*) Berenice, allow me to present Susana of Kenna.

BERENICE (*stepping back in surprise*). Susana . . . of Kenna!

SUSANA (*inclining her head*). I have heard much of the matriarch of Vira.

BERENICE (*not yet recovered from her surprise*). You—here—a prisoner! (*Turns to Margaret.*) Margaret! How did you do it?

MARGARET. I told you a man helped me escape. The man happened to be Susana's husband.

SUSANA (*laughing softly*). Margaret tells me you spoil your husband, Berenice. I wonder if you spoil him as much as I spoil mine?

BERENICE. But I don't understand—what is this all about?

SUSANA. Berenice, surely you did not think I would allow an enemy state to be in possession of knowledge which I did not possess?

MARGARET. She is trying to tell you, Berenice, that she has made the pilgrimage to Deka.

SUSANA (*placidly*). Of course. Years ago. In Kenna our word for Deka is Da-ko-ta, but it is the same place. And I am afraid that it had very much the same effect on me that it had on Margaret.

BERENICE. Then you, too, think that men once ruled the world.

SUSANA. I am certain of it. So certain that I think they should be brought back to their proper place in the world. So certain that I started this war against you, my friend, against all of the states, in order to bring you under my dominion—to enforce what I know to be true.

BERENICE. You started this war because. . . . (*She flings up her hands.*) I am sorry. I am a stupid dolt. I don't understand the words I am hearing.

MARGARET. Listen, Berenice. Why do you think the great pilgrimage has always been reserved for the matriarchs?

BERENICE (*laughing coldly*). Obviously so that the people . . . the little sheep we rule . . . will never learn that once man was as great as woman.

SUSANA. And that is stupid nonsense! Man alone failed.

MARGARET. Woman alone failed.

BERENICE (*catching their spirit*). But man and woman together can climb to reach the stars.

SUSANA. When I started this war I had no idea that you felt the same as I about woman's failure to keep peace in the world. But now, Berenice, let there be peace between our two states.

BERENICE. Peace. (*Burying her face in her hands.*) Peace.

SUSANA. Between us we can begin the new order. It will be slow, of course. We will not see its completion in our time. Perhaps Margaret will not see it in hers. But the time will come. Already it is waiting there across the horizon, like a glory hidden behind a cloud.

BERENICE (*straightens up, extends her hand. Susana grasps it*). We are not carvers in stone, but perhaps we will leave as great a monument to the future as the faces of Deka.

SUSANA (*suddenly laughing softly*). Let us go find Adelaide. I want to see her face when we announce the peace. (*As she and Berenice reach outer door.*) I never did like that woman! (*Both laugh and go out.*)

[*Margaret sinks down in one of the chairs and slumps from weariness.*

SERVANT (*entering*). Your Excellency— (*Recognizes Margaret as the student matriarch raises her head.*) Oh, Your Highness! You've come home to us.

MARGARET. Obviously. What do you want?

SERVANT. I thought to find Her Excellency. His Highness is still waiting for Her Excellency to decide about his hats, and I'm afraid that His Highness is losing his temper.

MARGARET (*laughs, stands up, buckling her thumbs in her belt*). If he goes into a tantrum, throw water on him. A new order has begun. Men are no longer to be treated with tender kindness. And if he objects—(*She throws back her head and lets out a shout of laughter.*)—tell him to take his punishment like a man!

[*Still laughing, she swaggers out, leaving a very startled servant as . . .*

THE CURTAINS CLOSE

LITTLE STRANGERS

A Comedy

By MARY THURMAN PYLE

THE CHARACTERS

Lucy, *a maid.*
Miss White, *a social worker.*
Eve Thornton, *a young matron.*
Mrs. Bartlett, *the Governor's wife.*
Alice, *a child's nurse.*
Dorothy Dean, *an attractive young wife.*

Place. Fairview, U. S. A.
Time. The present. A spring day.

Mrs. Thornton's *living room is very pleasant. It has dormer windows in backstage wall. Upstage in right wall is door leading to front hall. Downstage of it, is door leading to guest room. Another door, up left, leads to kitchen. In center of left wall is a fireplace. Before it, slanted to face audience, is a sofa and armchair. Another armchair downstage of fireplace. Desk against right wall with chair before it. Other chairs about room. Flowers fill the window boxes seen through the opened, prettily curtained windows. Fresh flowers in vases stand about on the various tables.*

As the play opens, the doorbell rings. Lucy enters from kitchen, crosses to hall door and exits. Lucy wears a trim uniform, slightly awry, with wisps of hair escaping under her cap and her big, red hands extending awkwardly from her white cuffs. She re-enters with Miss White, who is tall, angular, but still young. People sometimes make fun of

Miss White, but they do not know the good she does in this world. She wears a dark suit with white collar and cuffs, plain oxfords and a white Panama hat. She wears dark cotton gloves and carries a large plain handbag.

LUCY. Come right in, Miss, and make yourself at home. I'll tell Mrs. Thornton you're here.

MISS WHITE. Thank you. She's expecting me.

MRS. THORNTON (*entering from down right*). Oh, how do you do, Miss White. Do sit down. (*Miss White sits on sofa. Mrs. Thornton sits opposite her. Mrs. Thornton is a pretty and a fluttery young woman, well meaning and friendly. She wears an attractive afternoon dress.*) Lucy, will you bring some hot chocolate. Or do you prefer tea or coffee, Miss White?

MISS WHITE. Hot chocolate will be delightful. It's nice of you to think of it. It's rather cool today, and so windy.

MRS. THORNTON. Lucy, the chocolate, please. And suppose you close the window. (*Lucy does so and goes out.*) I think hot chocolate is really the nicest drink on a cool day, don't you?

MISS WHITE (*firmly*). Now, Mrs. Thornton, you asked me to come about the baby.

MRS. THORNTON. Yes. It certainly was lovely of you to come, as busy as you are.

MISS WHITE. It was a pleasure.

MRS. THORNTON (*protesting*). Oh, but I *know* you're a busy woman! When I think of all that wonderful social-service work you do. Why, of course you're busy.

MISS WHITE. My work is my life, Mrs. Thornton. And we're very busy at the Charities now. But about the baby. . . .

MRS. THORNTON. Oh, yes, the baby. Dear little Paul! I hope Dorothy—that's my friend Mrs. Dean—likes the name. I know the child's mother wanted him to be called Paul. But everyone has his own taste in names, don't you think?

MISS WHITE. We had better review the case history of little Paul. (*Takes typewritten card from her handbag.*)

MRS. THORNTON. Of course.

MISS WHITE. Since you are still interested in little Paul—

MRS. THORNTON. But naturally I'm interested!

MISS WHITE (*reading*). "Born, December 18, 1939, in the free ward of the City Hospital. Father died three months prior to baby's birth. Mother died two weeks after baby's arrival. No near relatives. Mother asked local Charities to care for baby and find home for it."

MRS. THORNTON (*interrupting*). When I called at the Charities to make my Christmas donation and saw that precious baby and heard it needed a home, I decided then and there I'd write Dorothy about it. Dorothy is my *very* dear friend Mrs. Frederick Dean. *You* know. I told you.

MISS WHITE (*getting in a word*). I recall quite well. I only wish you had written to Mrs. Dean sooner.

MRS. THORNTON. But I did. But she and Fred were visiting her mother in Detroit, and with all that delay and everything! And then she couldn't get Fred to agree. Fred is her husband. But now he sees that it's the only thing for Dorothy. I really think he's decided he'd like it himself. It would really be the greatest possible joy to both of them, in my opinion.

MISS WHITE. I'm sure of that. I've seen it happen many times. But you see, in this case—

MRS. THORNTON. In this case, it took a little fixing. I wrote to Fred myself and described that beautiful baby and assured him it came from good, substantial people. You *did* verify that, Miss White?

MISS WHITE. Of course.

[*Lucy enters, upstage left, with tray on which are two cups, saucers, a small plate of wafers and two dainty napkins. She passes tray to Miss White, who takes napkin, cup and saucer, then to Mrs. Thornton, who does the same.*

MISS WHITE. Thank you. (*Sips chocolate.*) This is very refreshing.

MRS. THORNTON. Thank you, Lucy. Please have a pot of chocolate ready when Mrs. Bartlett arrives.

LUCY. Yes, ma'am. (*She goes.*)

MISS WHITE. Are you expecting Mrs. Bartlett?

MRS. THORNTON. I asked her to bring the baby over this afternoon, but I didn't tell her that Dorothy would be here to—to *take* the baby away with her. I thought Mrs. Bartlett would be happily surprised when she learned that dear little Paul was at last provided for.

MISS WHITE. I'm afraid that will be too great a surprise for her. You see, Mrs. Bartlett. . . .

MRS. THORNTON. It was so perfectly wonderful of Mrs. Bartlett to keep Paul in her own home—the Governor's mansion, too—until someone adopted him. When the quarters at the Charities became too crowded with babies, someone had to take him.

MISS WHITE (*asserting herself*). Mrs. Bartlett is a very superior woman, Mrs. Thornton.

MRS. THORNTON. No Governor's wife has been better loved than Mrs. Bartlett. When she took little Paul, with her many duties and her social life, I couldn't help but admire her all the more.

MISS WHITE. She's an admirable woman and a lovely character. In some ways she leads a rather lonely life. She lost her only child some years ago, you know.

MRS. THORNTON. Just like Dorothy Dean. Only, her baby died two years ago, poor darling. But now she and Fred are to have little Paul. Dotty and I both say that the Governor's mansion, even though Paul has lived in it only for a few months, ought to have a lasting effect on his life.

MISS WHITE. Did Mrs. Bartlett say anything about the baby when you last spoke to her?

MRS. THORNTON. Only that he *had* had a cold but was now well and laughing and cooing all the time and was such a darling! She said his hair is definitely going to be dark and curly.

MISS WHITE. Didn't she say anything else?

MRS. THORNTON. What are you driving at? What *would* she have said? Isn't the baby all right?

MISS WHITE. He's quite all right. So altogether all right that Mrs. Bartlett doesn't want to give him up. She wants to keep him herself.

MRS. THORNTON. She can't. The Deans are going to adopt him.

MISS WHITE. Mrs. Bartlett wants to adopt him.

MRS. THORNTON. My friend has already spoken for him. How could she be so mean?

MISS WHITE. You didn't know for sure about the Deans, and so much time has elapsed. . . .

MRS. THORNTON. I explained about the delays.

MISS WHITE. But Mrs. Bartlett didn't know all those things. In the meantime she's grown very much attached to the baby and now she simply can't bear to give him up.

MRS. THORNTON. Just because she's the Governor's wife she thinks *her* wishes will come first.

MISS WHITE. After all, Mrs. Bartlett has given him the most tender care for four months. Something is due her.

MRS. THORNTON. And something is due the Deans, especially poor Dotty. She had to beg and plead with her husband. And then they consulted a lawyer, and they've had all the papers drawn up all ready to sign. I'd be ashamed to tell Dotty she couldn't have him, after I thought I'd arranged everything so beautifully. She's set her heart on that baby.

MISS WHITE. And Mrs. Bartlett has set her heart on him.

[*Doorbell rings.*

MRS. THORNTON. That's Mrs. Bartlett now, probably. Oh, dear, what a mess. But I mean to have that baby for poor Dotty.

[*She rises, takes Miss White's cup and napkin and places them and her own on table as Lucy goes through room on her way to door.*

MISS WHITE. Poor Mrs. Bartlett doesn't dream that she is being asked here to give up the baby!

MRS. THORNTON. She's known all along that Mrs. Dean would eventually get him.

[*Lucy enters, followed by Mrs. Bartlett and Alice, the latter carrying a bundle—the baby. Mrs. Bartlett is middle-aged. She is an important-looking lady who dignifies her position admirably, but who is not lacking in kindly graciousness. She wears a charming costume suitable for a spring afternoon. Alice is the perfect baby nurse—trim, expert, dressed in correct white uniform and short dark cape. The bundle is a costly appearing one, done up in a fine white cashmere shawl in the folds of which one may glimpse a lovely pink cap and coat.*

LUCY. Mrs. Bartlett, ma'am. (*She goes off left.*)

MRS. THORNTON (*going forward*). Oh, Mrs. Bartlett. I'm so glad to see you. It was sweet of you to come.

MRS. BARTLETT. My dear, it was a pleasure. I recall your interest in little Paul and of course you want to see how he is getting along. How do you do, Miss White. (*Miss White smiles at her.*) It's nice to see you again. And now of course you want to see him. Alice, the baby!

[*Alice steps forward. The three women form an admiring circle around her and gaze with absorbed interest as she exhibits her charge.*

MRS. THORNTON. Oh, the darling! What rosy cheeks! And that sweet little brown curl!

MRS. BARTLETT (*proudly*). Isn't he the picture of health? Did you ever see a finer baby?

MISS WHITE. You've done wonders with him, Mrs. Bartlett. (*She glances at Mrs. Thornton with meaning.*) And—

MRS. THORNTON (*hastily*). Does he always sleep so soundly?

MRS. BARTLETT. Until time for him to wake up. He's on a strict schedule, isn't he, Alice?

ALICE. Yes indeed, Mrs. Bartlett.

MRS. BARTLETT. This is Alice, Mrs. Thornton. She's simply wonderful. I've had her ever since I took little Paul. She's very strict with both of us, aren't you, Alice?

ALICE (*smiling professionally*). Oh yes. Mrs. Bartlett would spoil him dreadfully if I didn't take a firm hand.

MRS. BARTLETT (*in a shamefaced but confidential manner*). I can't help wanting to spoil him. I'm not up on all the new wrinkles on the care of babies. (*Wistfully.*) It's been a long time since I had a baby. When I was a young woman, we spoiled them, I suppose.

MISS WHITE. And the results were just as good as those from the newfangled methods.

[*Alice retreats upstage in a dignified manner, feeling that this is a personal affront.*

MRS. THORNTON. You can take him into my guest room if

you like. I am expecting a friend to arrive in a little while, but that's all right.

MRS. BARTLETT. Take him in, Alice. He'll be more comfortable.

MRS. THORNTON. Right in here. (*She leads the way into room downstage right. Alice follows.*)

MRS. BARTLETT (*sinking into easy chair*). Really, Miss White, I could never begin to tell you how I've grown to love that baby. Adopting a child never seemed feasible before I took Paul to care for. But now I know why so many women adopt children. And although I haven't spoken to my husband yet about it, he never denies me anything.

MISS WHITE. Hasn't Mrs. Thornton told you that her friend Mrs. Dean. . . .

MRS. THORNTON (*re-entering*). He's so adorable.

MRS. BARTLETT. I rather thought you'd enjoy seeing him.

[*Doorbell rings.*

MRS. THORNTON (*nervously*). That must be Dorothy.

LUCY (*entering*). The chocolate, ma'am.

MRS. THORNTON (*nervously*). Well, never mind. Answer the door.

LUCY. Yes, ma'am. (*Goes into hall.*)

MISS WHITE. I must be going.

MRS. THORNTON. Oh no! I want you here especially.

MISS WHITE. There is really no need of my being here. In fact, I'd rather not. (*She goes to door upstage left.*) I'll just slip out through the back door if you don't mind. (*Mrs. Thornton makes a protesting gesture.*) It will be less complicated. (*Goes out door upstage left.*)

MRS. BARTLETT. Why, how strange of her to leave so abruptly.

[*Lucy enters from hall carrying Mrs. Dean's suitcase. Dorothy Dean follows, carrying a smaller bag. She is a slender, pretty, wistful girl. She is attractively dressed for traveling. Mrs. Thornton rushes to meet her and they embrace, as Lucy takes the bags into the guest room.*

MRS. THORNTON. Dotty darling!

MRS. DEAN. Oh, Eve, it's heavenly to see you.

MRS. THORNTON. I'm so glad you finally managed to get here.

MRS. DEAN. It's wonderful of you to arrange everything.

MRS. THORNTON (*remembers Mrs. Bartlett and becomes a bit fidgety.*) Oh, Mrs. Bartlett, may I present Mrs. Dean? Dorothy, our Governor's wife, you know.

MRS. BARTLETT. How do you do, my dear.

MRS. DEAN. How do you do, Mrs. Bartlett. I've heard so much about you, and of course I'm personally grateful. . . .

MRS. THORNTON (*interrupting*). Mrs. Bartlett ran over for a call.

MRS. BARTLETT. And to show off little Paul. He's my little charge, Mrs. Dean. A lovely baby I've been caring for.

MRS. DEAN. Eve's written me how wonderful you've been about it all. And where is he, Eve? I can't wait to see him.

MRS. THORNTON (*lamely*). He's in the guest room.

MRS. BARTLETT. With his nurse. I'll have Alice bring him in. (*Goes into guest room.*)

MRS. DEAN (*sitting by Mrs. Thornton affectionately*). Oh, Eve, you have been such a darling. And Fred's as pleased as I am, now that he's finally given in. We have our little porch room all fixed for the baby, with the sweetest furniture you ever saw. Fred says it's very masculine looking. Fred's already trying to decide what prep school to send Paul to.

MRS. THORNTON. Dotty, dear, would you be frightfully disappointed not to have him now?

MRS. DEAN. Of course I would. I've set my heart on it. I can't wait to get my arms around him.

MRS. BARTLETT (*comes back, followed by Alice carrying the baby*). Let Mrs. Dean hold him a minute, Alice.

[*Alice rather grudgingly hands the bundle to Mrs. Dean, then steps back.*

MRS. DEAN. Oh, you little dear! Eve, he's beautiful! You didn't tell me the half of it. Just wait till Fred sees him. Look! He smiled at me.

MRS. BARTLETT (*becoming suspicious at last*). We'll take him now, Mrs. Dean. We really must get him home. So much excitement is bad for him.

[*Lucy appears in door upstage left with tray containing cups, saucers and pot of chocolate. Mrs. Thornton is too per-*

turbed to notice her, so she sets tray on table and stands uncertainly, waiting to be told what to do.

MRS. DEAN. Oh, that's all right. He has to get used to the change sooner or later. I'll keep him here tonight, if you don't mind.

MRS. BARTLETT (*turning to Mrs. Thornton indignantly*). Mrs. Thornton, perhaps you'll tell me what this means? You asked me to call and bring little Paul. But there is something going on of which I am unaware.

MRS. THORNTON. Mrs. Bartlett, I'm afraid there's a dreadful misunderstanding. I told you some months ago that I had a friend who I thought would adopt Paul. Now Mrs. Dean has come and—

MRS. BARTLETT. Adopt him! My dear Mrs. Thornton, I'm afraid Mrs. Dean is too late. You said nothing more about it and in the meantime I've decided to adopt him.

MRS. DEAN. But you can't. Eve wrote me last January and we had a lawyer make out the papers, and we've a room all ready.

MRS. BARTLETT. But who took him from the Charities four months ago and who has given him a home ever since? Here, Alice, take the baby.

[*Alice goes to Mrs. Dean, who only holds the baby tighter.*

MRS. THORNTON. I can't tell you how bad I feel about all this, Mrs. Bartlett. But I thought you understood—

MRS. BARTLETT (*with dignity*). The baby belongs to me and the law will uphold me. Mrs. Dean doesn't even live in this state. The Charities wouldn't dare to refuse the Governor's wife. My yearly donation practically supports them.

MRS. DEAN (*almost crying with anger and chagrin*). That's a mean advantage to take! (*Turning to Mrs. Thornton.*) Eve, you had no right to mislead me this way. I simply can't bear the disappointment. (*She breaks down and cries in earnest, burying her face in the baby's blanket.*)

MRS. THORNTON (*indignant in her turn*). Why, the very idea! I simply worked my head off trying to arrange the whole thing.

MRS. BARTLETT (*anxiously, to Mrs. Dean*). You mustn't mash

him! And please don't cry on him. The poor little fellow will be frightened. Alice! Take the baby.

[*Alice tries to take the bundle from Mrs. Dean but Mrs. Thornton pushes her aside and takes the baby herself from the weakly protesting Mrs. Dean and holds it triumphantly. Lucy watches everything wide-eyed.*

MRS. THORNTON. You haven't a bit of a right to him, Mrs. Bartlett. The Deans have the written consent of the Charities for the adoption and Dorothy has come all this distance to take him home.

MRS. DEAN (*between sobs*). And Fred is coming tomorrow in the car to help me take him home.

MRS. BARTLETT (*breaking down and weeping into her handkerchief*). I simply can't bear to give him up. I've grown to love him so much. My husband says he hasn't seen me so happy in years.

[*She sobs. Lucy, who has been listening with great interest, now slips out upstage left.*

MRS. THORNTON. I'm sorry. Truly I am. (*She weeps into the baby's blanket.*) But it can't be helped. I've arranged for the Deans to have him and they will sign the papers tomorrow.

[*Doorbell rings but everyone is too upset to notice.*

MRS. BARTLETT. I'll get my husband to do something about it.

MRS. THORNTON. Even the Governor can't get Paul away from Dotty. She has a signed paper from the Charities.

MRS. BARTLETT. But I must have him. He's so adorable and I love him so.

MRS. DEAN. I simply couldn't give him up now that I've held him. He's such a darling!

[*Miss White enters from the front door. She is carrying a bundle similar in size and shape to Paul, but wrapped in a drab gray "Charities" blanket.*

MISS WHITE. I rang, but evidently no one heard me.

[*All look at her in astonishment.*

MRS. THORNTON. Why, Miss White! I thought you had left. Whatever have you got?

MISS WHITE. I foresaw a little trouble here, so I decided to offer a solution. I hurried over to the Charities to get it.

MRS. THORNTON. A solution?

MRS. BARTLETT. I want little Paul.

MRS. DEAN. So do I!

MISS WHITE. Mrs. Bartlett, wouldn't another baby do as well?

MRS. BARTLETT. No!

MISS WHITE. I'm afraid Mrs. Dean has first claim on Paul. But there are other little helpless waifs sadly in need of homes and mothers. There are babies enough for all who want them. Now this little fellow—(*Beginning to exhibit the baby with pride and affection*)—is the very nicest baby we have at the Charities. He's healthy, good-natured and fine-looking. A regular darling. Any woman who takes little Billy will never regret it.

MRS. BARTLETT. I wouldn't think of it. I've grown fond of Paul and I'll fight Mrs. Dean every inch of the way for him.

[*Miss White steps back disappointed.*

MRS. DEAN. But I have the first claim. I know I have.

MRS. THORNTON. Of course you have and I'll stand by you.

[*Lucy enters upstage left, carrying, surprisingly enough, a bundle which is unmistakably a baby. It is wrapped in a gaudy red-and-green but clean blanket. She pauses uncertainly in the doorway.*

LUCY. Excuse me, ma'am.

MRS. THORNTON (*turning to stare at Lucy*). Lucy, what in the name of common sense have *you* got?

LUCY. Please, ma'am, a baby.

MRS. THORNTON (*horrified*). Your baby?

LUCY (*on her dignity*). Course not. My youngest is going on seven and me a widow these three years.

MRS. THORNTON. Then whose is it?

LUCY. It's my cousin's baby, ma'am. My cousin died when it was born and its grandmother's been trying to raise it. But she's old and not very well and it was too much of a job. So last month I took it.

MRS. THORNTON (*accusingly*). But you never told me a thing about it. Where do you keep it?

LUCY. At home. But Jane, my oldest girl, rolled it over here this morning in the baby buggy and left it in the sun on the back porch. I hope you don't mind, ma'am.

MRS. THORNTON. Of course I don't mind, Lucy, if you don't neglect your work. But why are you bringing it in here, may I ask? (*Her tone implies that there are enough babies in room already.*)

LUCY (*coming forward in humble eagerness*). Please, ma'am, excuse me, but I thought as maybe one of the ladies would like to take it. I ain't really able to bring it up, being a widow with four of my own. I took it because I couldn't bear for the little thing to go to an orphanage. My cousin was a nice, well-brought-up girl, and she would have liked nice things for her baby. (*She waits. There is silence. She continues with less hope, embarrassed and faltering now.*) I wouldn't have dared come in like this, but I'm that desperate! And I thought, being as how both these ladies wants to adopt a baby, that maybe one of 'em might like to take this one and give it a real home. It's a little girl, and pretty as a picture. Rose is her name.

MISS WHITE. We both had the same idea, Lucy. But it didn't work. We'd better take our babies back to where we got them.

LUCY. Yes, ma'am.

MRS. BARTLETT (*suddenly*). Did you say that was a little boy, Miss White?

MISS WHITE (*eagerly, as she shows baby to Mrs. Bartlett*). Yes. Isn't he handsome? And so good! See? I think his hair is definitely going to be curly.

MRS. BARTLETT. He *is* nice. Why can't Mrs. Dean take *him?* She hasn't become attached to Paul as I have.

MRS. DEAN. I won't have any baby but Paul. It was hard enough to persuade Fred to take *him.*

MRS. BARTLETT. The child is all right, isn't he, Miss White?

MISS WHITE. Oh yes. Naturally he doesn't present as fine an appearance as Paul. You have done such wonders with him, Mrs. Bartlett, that I had rather depended on your taking little Billy and giving him the same splendid care. They were saying at the Charities only yesterday that, with a wife like Mrs. Bartlett, nothing could stop our Governor. Now little Billy needs you and—

MRS. BARTLETT. I get the point. Babies enough for all who want them. (*Wistfully.*) Do you really think I'd learn to love this one as much as I love Paul?

MISS WHITE (*gently*). I'm sure of it.

MRS. BARTLETT (*looking at baby*). Well! Did you see him smile at me? Positively grinned. Billy, did you say his name was? (*Pleased.*) Why, that's my husband's name! William, that is.

MRS. THORNTON (*as Lucy starts out*). Let me see the baby, Lucy.

LUCY (*beaming*). Yes, ma'am.

MRS. THORNTON. Here, Dotty, take Paul. He's yours. I know you're going to love him. (*Dorothy takes Paul and clasps him with ecstatic gurgles. Mrs. Thornton takes baby from Lucy.*) Why, she's precious, Lucy. Don't you worry about her. I'll help you with her. Just sun her on my back porch all you like.

LUCY. Thank you very *much,* ma'am.

MRS. THORNTON. I believe you're about due a raise in wages, Lucy.

LUCY. Oh, ma'am! *Thank* you.

MRS. THORNTON. And I'll take care of her for the rest of the afternoon.

LUCY. Thank you very much, ma'am. (*She goes out upstage left, smiling widely.*)

MRS. BARTLETT. Alice, take little Billy. I'll be keeping you on.

ALICE. Yes, Mrs. Bartlett.

MRS. BARTLETT. But let me hold him a minute first. (*Takes baby from Miss White and holds it fondly, woman-fashion. Miss White, after an appraising look at the ladies, smiles with satisfaction and leaves, center right.*)

MISS WHITE (*as she goes*). Goodbye. Call me if you need me for anything. (*But no one hears her.*)

MRS. BARTLETT. Come, Alice, we must get little Billy home at once. Goodbye, Mrs. Thornton, Mrs. Dean.

MRS. DEAN (*absently*). Goodbye.

MRS. THORNTON (*absently*). Do come again, Mrs. Bartlett.

[*Mrs. Bartlett leaves, center right, carrying the baby and followed by Alice.*

MRS. DEAN (*bending adoringly over her bundle*). What is there *about* a baby—

MRS. THORNTON (*bending over her bundle*). Dotty, let's take them in the guest room and put them to bed for their naps.

MRS. DEAN. Let's!

MRS. THORNTON (*calling*). Lucy! Two bottles, please.

[*They go off, downstage right, cooing and gurgling over their respective bundles as . . .*

CURTAIN

CULCHA

A Negro Comedy

BY WALTER CARROLL

THE SISTERS

JANE WILBUR, *president of the Lodge.*
MRS. DORSEY, *a prominent member.*
BEULA, *another prominent member.*
MRS. LINCOLN, *who reads a report.*
TESSIE, *a member.*
MALLIE, *a member.*
JEWEL, *a member who runs errands.*
ELLA JONES, *an upstart.*
LILY PONSENSON, *famous singer and visiting speaker.*
OTHER LODGE MEMBERS.

PLACE. Rural North Carolina.
TIME. Early evening. The present.

THE CULTURE SEEKERS *have a clubroom over a vacant store. It had been used as a storeroom, but now it is called "the lodge room." It is equipped with a dozen chairs donated by a funeral parlor. The paint is scraped off most of them, but a few bear the legend:* This was stolen from the Brotherly Love Funeral Home. *The chairs are arranged in rows. At right, is a large, square table with three chairs in back of it. Large, inaccurately done showcards, indicating past campaigns for church and charity funds are tacked at random about the walls. There is a door, leading to the hall, at left. Upstage are two large windows, curtained in the brightest turkey-red muslin imaginable. The room is lighted by two bulbs with yellow tin shades suspended by a cord from the ceiling at either end of the room. Green and red paper Christmas decorations still hang from the lights. They are relics of a Christmas party and were considered too lovely to be removed.*

As the play opens, rapid footsteps are heard running up the stairs. The door opens to admit Beula. She is a very black Negro woman. She wears a wide-brimmed black hat, a yellow coat, black stockings and light tan shoes. Her face is very black but her stubborn feminine instinct forces her to wear a black lace veil as a hat accessory. She carries a showcard, hammer and tacks. She collides with a chair and kicks it aside in a sudden flare of temper. After a few clumsy attempts with the hammer, she succeeds in tacking card to wall. The card displays the features of a dignified, well-dressed young Negro woman. Above picture, in large red letters, is the statement: Lily Ponsenson Sings! *Beula sets hammer aside and dusts off her hands. Mrs. Dorsey enters. Her complexion is lighter and her attire more conventional.*

MRS. DORSEY (*entering*). Beula, what are we s'posed t' be up hea' so ea'ly faw? Lily Ponsenson won't be hea' fo' 'nuther 'owa yet.

BEULA. Miz' Doa'sy, it's dis hea' way: Jane Wilbur, who done put herself in cha'ge o' dis hea' lec-cha, wants we should all be hea' fo' practice 'foah Miss Ponsenson gets hea', to make sure dat no one makes any faulty contributions to dis af-fiah [affair].

MRS. DORSEY. Ah jus' cain't wait to see her.

BEULA. Ah cain't, eitha. Lily Ponsenson is a mighty fine singer. She is got culcha. She gonna make a speech 'bout how we 'uns kin git mo' culcha.

MRS. DORSEY. An' culcha is what us niggers ain't got—I read someplace.

BEULA. White folks tells us, we 'uns got to rise up an' claim ah hea'tage [heritage]. We ain't got no right to be happy an' contented like we is. We got to get dis hea' culcha into us no matter how misser'ble it make us. (*Goes around straightening chairs while Mrs. Dorsey pulls a red bandana handkerchief from her pocket and dusts off the table.*)

MRS. DORSEY. Beula, what is dis hea' hea'tage we all is s'posed to have?

BEULA. It's de singin' de young bucks do to wase' 'way de time. It's de lyin' stories folks pass 'round.

MRS. DORSEY. Seems lak hit's all de no-count doin's no-count, low-down niggers do to pass de time 'way.

BEULA. Stompin' in de chu'ch when de sperit is on us, is hea'tage, too.

MRS. DORSEY. Then we is *got* it. Why mus' we *git* it?

BEULA. Seems like we got to *know* we is doin' hea'tages and not jus' 'joyin' ever'thing.

MRS. DORSEY. Culcha mean den, dat we do lak we do, on'y dey ain't no moah fun 'nnected wid it. Dat's w'at Ah figgers out f'om de way dat Ella Jones is always talkin' 'bout culcha.

BEULA. Is Ella Jones goin' to make de speech per-ducin' Lily Ponsenson?

MRS. DORSEY. I reckin. She was ova t' my house las' night askin' me dis an' askin' me dat 'bout de way she speak an' stan's, 'til ah was nea' daid. (*Mimicking, as she minces around the room with one hand on her hip.*) Is dis de way ah oughtta hol' m'seff up? An', do yo' think mah ice-blue satin dat Ah got f'um de Lovely Shop will go 'long wid m' talk? (*Sits down disgustedly.*)

BEULA. Ella Jones open her big mouf, she gonna mess us all up. Ah think some'un else ought to make dat per-ducin' speech. (*Sits down and relaxes.*)

MRS. DORSEY. Ole' Miz Jane Wil-bah comin' hea. She keep Ella Jones doin' right.

[*Slow footsteps are heard coming up the stairs.*

BEULA. Speakin' o' de debbil—(*Hastily corrects herself.*) I mean—angels, Ah think Ah hea' Ole Miz Jane now.

[*Jane Wilbur enters. She is an elderly Negro woman with a wizened black face and kinky white hair. She wears a small, ridiculous red hat perched on her forehead, a bright green coat, black stockings and run-down white shoes. Nevertheless, she has an air of authority and she commands the respect of all the women.*

JANE (*sternly*). Guls! Guls! Why ain't dis place in o'dah? (*Fussily rearranges chairs. The two women get to their feet respectfully.*) Come big 'ccasion lak dis, Ah got t' do all de wu'k.

MRS. DORSEY (*following her and unstraightening all the chairs. Beula follows her and straightens them again*). Miz Jane, how come yo' lettin' Ella Jones make dat talk? It don' seem t' me lak she's capable.

JANE (*stops and faces Mrs. Dorsey defensively*). Miz Doa'sy, Ella Jones is got talent. Didn't she win dat tu'ky fo' singin' at de chu'ch?

MRS. DORSEY. Ah knows dat, but . . .

JANE (*cutting her short*). Ella Jones is goin' to make a great singer 'fore long an', 'sides, it take a singer to talk 'bout a singer. Dis hea's Ella's big chance an' she gonna do it.

BEULA. Ah thinks Miz Doa'sy's right. Ella ain't got no culcha. 'Sides. . . .

JANE (*cutting her short, too*). 'Sides, nuthing, gul. Yo' ain't got no culcha yo'seff. Betta hush up 'bout it.

BEULA (*hurt*). Dat is de mos' unkindest slice o' all. Ah'll remin' yo' dat mah husband's principal o' Washington Consolidated School fo' de Backwards.

JANE. An' dat's de on'y reason yo' is in de Lodge. (*Takes her place behind the table and raps on it with the hammer in lieu of a gavel.*) Guls, please don' let's have no fussin'. S'posin' Lily Ponsenson was t' walk in hea' an' find us fightin' ova sumpin' lak dat? Dat would rate us as a basement lodge.

[*Four women enter. Mrs. Lincoln is black, swarthy, fat and middle-aged. Jewel is younger, lighter in color. Tessie is short and good-natured. Mallie is long and skinny. They are dressed as their fancy and the cast-off clothes of the white women they work for, dictate. All are happy and excited and chatter loudly as they barge in and find seats.*

MRS. LINCOLN. I'se so 'cited!

JEWEL. Yo' dress is gaw'jus, Mallie. How's mine?

MALLIE. Even gaw-jusser. (*To Tessie.*) Dat's a right sma't hat yo' is got, Tessie.

TESSIE. The lady Ah wu'ks fo' 'lows me to tote home all her ole clo'es.

[*Jane Wilbur raps for order. Women quiet down and take seats. During following dialogue, other women may filter in to take remaining seats.*

JANE (*in a matronly and complimentary tone*). Ah'm so glad dat yo' is hea' so ea'ly. Dat shows yo' observes directions an' dat's what it take to make a pow'ful o'ganization. Le's hurry ovah de stuff so's we kin rehuse what we got to do. (*Hauls out a nickel Ingersoll watch, which is attached to a long black string, from her bosom.*) My, my, Ella Jones ought to be hea' right now.

BEULA (*taking advantage to slam Ella*). Maybe her husband beat her up agin.

[*Women titter. Jane glares at Beula.*

JANE (*sternly*). Beula, will yo' please reframe fum donatin' yo' two cents wuth eva' two minutes or else wrop yo'seff up an' go home. (*Beula sniffs. Jane addresses Jewel.*) Miss Jewel, would yo' run ova' to Ella's house an' see iff'n yo' kin find her? (*Jewel leaves. Jane addresses the sisters.*) Sisters, we's got a repo't to git fum Miz Lincoln. After which, owa hon'ed visitor will be per-duced by Miz Jones. Miz Lincoln! Iff'n yo' pleases. (*Sits down.*)

MRS. LINCOLN (*goes to stand behind table. She reads from a paper*). On de'—(*She mumbles indistinctly.*)

JANE. Would yo' min' readin' dat fust pawt ova' agin? An' dis time be a little loudah.

MRS. LINCOLN (*very loud*). De campaign t' raise money fo' de new chu'ch was 'riginally stah'ted by Miz Clayton Lincoln. Miz Clay Lincoln was long wid othah ladies who raise' de fust money befo' de money Ah has mentioned was raised. But as owa presidint, Miz Jane, needed de money fo' a Christian Crusade, de money went on an unknown cruise. (*Jane shifts uneasily.*) We is had repo'ts dat she use dis money fo' 'nothah pu'pus. O' cause, we won't let dis vulgah slandah mess her up—uh—Ah means mess up owa faith in her. (*Jane glares at her, but when she *notices the sisters are staring at her, she smiles weakly.*) Now come de histo'y o' Miz Jane. (*Clears her throat.*) Jane Wil-bah was bawn—(*Pauses, scowls at paper.*)—in Wake County, No'th Ca'lina. When she reach de age o' twenty-two, she gradu'wated fum high school an' gained a position in de Laundry Depawt-ment whea' she. . . .

Jane (*stopping her*). Dat's fine, Miz Lincoln. All but de gramma. Betta fix dat up 'fore yo' reads de res'. Iff'n yo'll step 'cross de hall wid me, Ah'll he'p yo'. 'Twon't take long. (*Grabs her arm and tows reluctant speaker to exit. To sisters.*) Guls, while me an' Miz Lincoln is makin' a few 'justments, yo' all be practicin' what yo' is gonna say to Lily Ponsenson. When Ella Jones gits hea', somebody step cross de hall an' fotch me. (*Yanks Mrs. Lincoln out.*)

Beula (*tossing her head*). Ella Jones! Ella Jones! Who dat ole Miz Jane to push Ella Jones ovah on us all de time.

Mallie. Miz Jane say ole Ella, she got de culcha.

Beula. Culcha! Culcha! She ain't got 'nuff culchur to wear a shimmy to chu'ch. (*Stands on chair to better address the sisters.*) I says dis 'bout Ella Jones. She ain't nuthin' but a sack o' meal tied in de middle. She always talkin' 'bout how she got two brothers wu'kin' fo' de gov'mint. She got two wuk'in fo' gov-mint all right. (*Dramatic pause.*) Dey is convicts on de state faw'm!

Tessie. Beula, Ah b'lieves yo' jus' tryin' to wuk a way fo' yo'seff. 'Sides, what Ella Jones' brothers got to do wid the culcha she gettin' fo' herseff?

[*Jane Wilbur enters by herself. Her hair is pulled down and her hat is askew. But she has a happy smile on her face and a crumpled paper, Mrs. Lincoln's speech, in her hand.*

Jane (*smiling*). Guls. . . . (*Frowns at Beula. Shamefacedly, Beula climbs down from chair.*) Ah regrets dat Miz Lincoln had a se'ous stroke an' had to go home. De paper won' be read today. Nex' meetin' it will be read off wid some changes.

[*Ella Jones enters importantly. She is a portly, buxom, well-corseted woman. She wears an outfit, more in the fashion. It is evident she wears no cast-off clothes. Her air is superior. She uses less dialect than the others.*

ELLA. Ladies, Ah am deeply shocked at the conditions Ah withhold in our Lodge meetin' room. Ah am a-shamed to have this great lady, Miss Lily Ponsenson, come here. But if yo' all will sit still an' not open yo' big mouths, maybe de lack o' culcha 'mongst yo' all will pass her by.

MRS. DORSEY. How come yo' talk lak dat to us 'uns, Ella Jones? Ah is jus' befo' kickin' yo' culcha'ell backgroun' out'n dis windah.

ELLA (*backing up nervously*). Now yo' look hea'. Yo' wouldn't mess wid yo' chairwoman, would yo'?

JANE (*ineffectually*). Guls—guls.

BEULA (*on fire*). Iff'n she was a mess lak yo', *Ah* would. Watch yo' sides, Washtub! Hea' Ah come! (*Lowers her head and runs at Ella, preparing to ram her. Ella screams and makes a break for the door. But Beula tackles her. There are excited screams as the sisters form a tight group about the fighters. Jane pounds on table, ineffectually, with the hammer.*)

MRS. DORSEY (*after a while*). Pull her girdle off'n her, Beula.

BEULA (*screams after a pause*). Hea' yo' is, guls!

[*A compromising girdle flies over their heads and lands in Lily Ponsenson's face. Lily is just entering with Jewel. No one observes them.*

JEWEL. Ladies, hea' is Miz Ponsenson.

[*The fighting continues furiously. Jane pounds with the hammer. Lily is very light skinned and dressed smartly. Jewel puts both hands to her mouth and yells.*

JEWEL. De guest o' honah is come.

[*The group breaks up. Ella Jones is seen crawling on her hands and knees. When she sees Lily, she gets to her feet.*

ELLA (*going to Lily*). How-chu-do, Miz Ponsenson. We was jus' practicin' fo' de chu'ch basketball-game proceeds. (*Escorting her to table.*) We is so flattered to have yo'. (*To the sisters.*) Let's all be seated.

[*All take seats. Lily, Ella and Jane sit behind table.*

JANE (*rising and hitting table three times with hammer*). De meetin' will now come to o'dah. 'Spendin' wid de usual repo'ts, roll call an' so on, Ah now per-duces Miz Ella Jones, who will per-duce Miz Ponsenson, who we is so happy to have wid us. (*Sits. There is perfunctory applause.*)

ELLA. Yo' all is not 'spected to hea' Miz Ponsenson sing. Dat privilege is reserve 'fo' better-class folk dan yo'. (*Murmurings of discontent.*) Miz Ponsenson has 'greed to talk to yo' 'gainst her bettah jedgemint. Ah hopes yo' all is prop'ly thankful fo' dis hea' priv'lege 'mongst yo'. (*Graciously.*) Ah now has de hon-uh to intra-duce Miz Lily Ponsenson, famous singer o' stage an' radio.

[*All but Beula and Mrs. Dorsey applaud.*

LILY (*rises and bows. Looks over group disdainfully before she speaks. She does not use dialect. Her voice has a spurious culture*). Ladies—(*Pauses.*) Yes, I *will* address you as ladies. (*Beula and Mrs. Dorsey stare at each other in amazement.*) I hope you will forgive me if I seem a bit apart from you. I am of the same race and color, I admit.

BEULA (*in astonishment*). Yo' don' say!

[*Jane glares at her and raps with hammer.*

LILY. But there the resemblance ceases. You see in me one who has pulled herself up by her own bootstraps.

MRS. DORSEY (*sotto voce*). She kin hardly talk English! Culcha!

LILY. I am not used to speaking to folks of your class; you realize it is quite a strain on a sensitive artist to do this sort of thing. (*Smiling wistfully.*) But that is one of the bitter prices we artists pay for our fame. We cannot deny ourselves to the people. By the way, do not ask for my autograph. To protect myself, I must make a nominal charge of twenty-five cents. To continue: I am appearing here tonight, only because your chairman, Miss Ella Jones, persuaded me. However, I do not regret the sacrifice. For I know that even you have a love for the great gift that I possess.

BEULA. Is dis hea' all 'bout culcha?

LILY. I am coming to that, my good woman. I sincerely believe that culture can be obtained only from culture. In all society there are two classes: those that disseminate culture and those who may only reverence it as an unattainable thing. Your class, it grieves me to say, is destined to carry on as you have always carried on. The torch of culture must be carried by the artists of the race. May its glow ever warm you as you go your humble ways. (*She sits down. The sisters are dazed. Two applaud feebly. Lily holds up a languid hand.*) No ovation, please!

MALLIE (*stunned*). What do she all say?

ELLA (*rising quickly*). I will now pass among yo' an' receive contributions to defray in pa'ht Miz Ponsenson's expenses in meetin' wid us tonight. (*Looks around for something to collect money in. Jane removes her hat and gives it to Ella. Ella starts passing the hat, beginning with the last row.*)

BEULA (*staring at Lily from the front row*). Pawdon me, Miz Ponsenson, but ain't yo' got a brother name o' Wilbur?

LILY (*nervously*). Why, yes! I—er—mean—No! Of course not!

BEULA. An' didn't yo' use' to be coh-ted by a boy name o' Saul?

LILY (*more nervous*). Why ye— Of course not. What is the meaning of these stupid insinuations?

BEULA. Miz Doh-sy, is yo' eva' seed that face befo'?

ELLA (*now working the front row*). O' cawse. Eva'body has. Her face is on ever' telephone pole in town.

BEULA. Ah means 'fore dat. Look good, Miz Doh-sy.

MRS. DORSEY. Ah's lookin' good an' beginnin' to 'member.

BEULA. Don' yo' 'member when yo' an' me is wu'kin in de ladies' prison, doin' washin' an' cookin' fo' de boss-man dea?

[*Beula and Mrs. Dorsey rise and lean across the table staring at Lily. Lily is ill at ease and takes out her compact and bravely repairs her makeup.*

MRS. DORSEY (*triumphantly*). Ah 'members now! Ah rec'lects dat face!

BEULA (*slowly and solidly*). 'Member Lily Bell Robin?

MRS. DORSEY (*in excitement*). That high-falutin'-talkin' bright-skin gul! Ah 'members now! (*All the sisters rise to their feet.*) She was in de pen fo'. . . . (*Thinks.*)

BEULA (*turning to the sisters*). Guls, do yo' know what dis baby was in steel heaven fo'?

SISTERS (*not in concert*). No. What fo'? Give out an' tell us, Beula.

BEULA. She stab her husban' in—in—de night. Five yeahs 'go. (*Lily's eyes roll toward the exit.*)

MRS. DORSEY. Yea', she stab him with a fawk while de po' man was eatin'.

BEULA. But they done let her out fo' good 'havior.

[*Lily makes a desperate run for the door. But the sisters are too quick for her. Two of them grab her and bring her back to the table.*

TESSIE. An' now we 'uns would be 'bliged iff'n yo'd make us 'nother talk on culcha.

[*Women cackle in delight.*

BEULA. Tawk fas'.

LILY. I'm sure I don't know what you are talking about. (*Attempting to make a break.*) I must be going.

MRS. DORSEY (*picking up hammer and fingering it casually.*) Ain't no call t' hurry. We ain't got culcha yit.

TESSIE (*suddenly*). Ah wants mah dime back.

[*Other women murmur in agreement.*

BEULA (*dumping contents of hat on table*). He'p yo'seff, sisters, but 'member it ain't culcha t' take mo'h'n yo' put in.

[*Sisters scramble for money.*

LILY. Look here. I have an important broadcast tonight. You've no right to delay me. You've no right.

MALLIE. What do we 'uns know what am right? We's jus' fit to follow de tawch yo' carries.

TESSIE. An' we follows it easiah iff'n yo' stays hea' whea' we kin see it.

LILY. Very well. I admit that I have a brother named Wilbur. Now will you release me?

BEULA. Now yo' is tawkin'. What about Saul?

LILY. Yes, yes. I knew such a person.

JEWEL. Ah craves t' hea' 'bout dat fawk-stabbin' in her highfalutin' wu'ds.

MRS. DORSEY. Tawk!

LILY. This is absurd. (*Looking around.*) Miss Jones, as chairwoman—

BEULA. As chiah'oman she don' coun' no mo'.

MRS. DORSEY (*weighing hammer ominously*). Is yo' tawkin' or is yo' ain't?

Ella (*falsely*). Ah 'vises yo' to th'ow yo'seff on de muh'cy o' dese good sisters.

Lily (*after a pause*). Very well. The past cannot hurt me now. I am an artist in my own right. I was the daughter of a sharecropper. I was anxious for better things. I educated myself and . . .

Tessie. But how come yo' stab yo' man?

Lily. To be frank, I couldn't stand the way he sopped up pork gravy with a bit of crumbly corn bread. I *had* to jab him with that fork. It didn't hurt him—(*Pause.*)—much.

Tessie. She got somepun' thea'. Ah hates a soppin' man.

Lily. I throw myself on your mercy. Now you know all. I trust to your inherent kindness of heart not to expose me.

Mrs. Dorsey (*laying down hammer*). Well, guls, what we do now?

Beula. Well, she say we git wah'm followin' tawch in her han'. Seems lak we git wah'mer wit' stove in owa Lodge Room. Maybe Miz Lily donate us a stove.

Lily (*sitting down and taking checkbook from purse*). Very well. What's the amount of the blackmail?

Beula. Le's see . . .

Mrs. Dorsey (*warningly*). No secon'-han' heatah, now.

Beula. Twenty dollahs.

Mrs. Dorsey (*as Lily starts to write*). Wait. We need kindlin' an' coal, too.

Beula. Make it foh'ty dollahs.

Jewel. How 'bout some limoleum fo' de floah?

Beula. Sixty dollahs.

Mallie. Dem cuh'tains ain't got no culcha. We need us some white ones.

Beula. Write out sixty-two dollahs.

Jane (*coming forward*). Make it hundred dollah even. Den cruise money is 'counted fo'. Den Miz Lincoln ain't got no call to read dat repoht which is full o' mistakes.

Mrs. Dorsey (*coldly*). We do dat. Not fo' yo' but fo' de good name of de sisters.

Beula (*to Lily*). Hundred dollahs even.

Tessie. We spen's it, sales tax come in.

Beula. Hundred and th'ee dollahs.

LILY (*writes furiously and then throws check at women*). There's your hush money. Now, if I may go. . . .

BEULA (*blowing on check*). Yo' bettah hurry. Lots o' po'ah folk settin' 'round waitin' fo' yo' to come bring culcha. Miss Ella Jones will escoht yo' t' bus station.

ELLA. Come 'long, Miz Ponsenson.

[*They go to door.*

LILY (*at door, turns*). I must say—(*They stare at her.*)

MRS. DORSEY. Seems lak we needs a new book fo' to keep meetin' minutes in.

LILY (*hastily*). Goodbye.

[*They go. Jane turns to slink out after them.*

MRS. DORSEY. Miz Jane, seein's yo' is oldest membah o' de Lodge, yo' is po'mitted to stay. (*Beaming, Jane goes to take her place behind table.*) Po'vidin' yo' set on de moa'ner's bench. (*Meekly, Jane sits in first row. Beula and Mrs. Dorsey stand behind speaker's table.*)

MRS. DORSEY. De time has come fo' 'lection o' new awf-ce's. (*Pause.*) Ah hea'by nominates Beula fo' presi-dint.

JANE (*leaping to her feet*). Ah objects! (*Mrs. Dorsey reaches for hammer.*) Ah means Ah secon' de notion.

MRS. DORSEY. All in favah, say aye.

ALL. Aye.

BEULA. An' Ah 'pints Miz Doah-sy chiahwoman.

ALL. Aye.

MRS. DORSEY. An' now Ah moves that Beula give we 'uns de tawk on culcha we didn't git. (*She sits down.*)

BEULA (*leans forward and clears her throat*). Culcha. Culcha means—(*Curtains begin to close.*) Culcha am lak dis. When yo' missus say, "Beula, you may take home some o' de ham we had fo' dinner," culcha means dat yo' don' tote it all home. Yo' leaves some in missus' ice-box fo' nex' day. Culcha means yo'. . . .

[*But the curtains are closed.*

THE END

TOMORROW IS THE DAY

A Tragedy

BY JAMESON BUNN

CHARACTERS

PEGGY STEWART, *a bride-to-be.*
MRS. STEWART, *her mother.*
JEAN BASCOM, *her best friend.*
GRACE, *another friend.*
KITTY, *another friend.*
DELIA, *the colored maid.*

PLACE. A small town in North Carolina.
TIME. The present. An afternoon in April.

PEGGY STEWART'S *bedroom has the same young-girl freshness as the April day. The door leading to the hall is in right wall downstage of center. Upstage of door is a slim-posted mahogany bed with a curved tester draped in soft white voile edged with ball fringe. Beside the bad is a handsome table with phone, lamp, magazines, etc., on it. Upstage center is a walnut highboy with a comfortable wing chair of flowered chintz near by. Closet door is right of highboy. Two windows in left wall are curtained in the same material as the bed. A small dressing table and chair stand between them. Downstage left is a chaise longue covered in rose moire. The walls are covered with a Colonial wallpaper, and there are several framed prints and photographs on the wall. A large silver-framed picture of a handsome young man occupies the place of honor on the dressing table. There are snapshots of him stuck in the edges of the mirror. Standing in the middle of the room is an opened, brand-new wardrobe trunk, partially packed, and an opened hatbox, both proudly bearing the initials P. S. W. On the bed are several neat piles of lingerie, folds of white tissue paper, a pair of new blue satin mules, a bottle of sachet and various toilet articles.*

As the play opens, Mrs. Stewart, a sweet-faced middle-aged woman, is folding a fluffy pink negligee. She does this painstakingly and lovingly. Finally, after many gentle pats, she places it on a hanger and carefully hangs it in trunk. Phone rings.

MRS. STEWART (*calling*). Delia? Delia! Answer the phone. (*Steps back, surveys negligee. Not satisfied, removes it, refolds it and with a last motherly pat, as if to say, "There now," she leaves it. Phone rings again.*) Delia!

DELIA (*off*). Yes'm?

MRS. STEWART. Oh, never mind. (*As phone rings again.*) Oh dear! All right! (*Into phone.*) Hello? Oh, hello Philip. How's the prospective bridegroom on his wedding eve? (*Listens.*) The bank examiners? That's too bad! Today of all days too. No, Peg's still at the luncheon. She was *so* counting on seeing you this afternoon. (*Sound of car stopping outside.*) Wait! I hear a car. It might be Peg. (*Goes to window, looks out, returns to phone.*) I'm sorry. It's only the florist. (*Listens.*) No, I haven't seen Jean Bascom all day. If she comes by, I'll tell her you want to see her at the bank. (*Listens, then tremulously.*) Don't you think "Mrs. Stewart" is a bit formal—now? That's better. Goodbye—son. (*Hangs up, looks around vaguely, trying to hold back the tears. Pulls out a trunk drawer, lines it with tissue and sprinkles dabs of sachet on it. Trunk initials catch her eye. She traces them with a finger.*) Peggy—Stewart—Wilson. (*She buries her face in her hands and starts crying.*)

JEAN (*appears in doorway with daintily tied package under her arm*). I was afraid I'd find you doing that, Mrs. Stewart. (*Although Jean is carelessly dressed in a loose-fitting polo coat, sweater, skirt and plain brown felt hat, she is the type who can wear the same clothes day after day and still look nice. With a little careful grooming and the right kind of expensive sport clothes, she would look lovely. As it is, she is the type that would pass in a crowd but never be singled out for attention.*)

MRS. STEWART. Oh, Jean! (*Jean puts her arms around her.*) I thought I was alone. How'd you get here?

JEAN. The florist stopped by my house to leave the flowers for the wedding breakfast. He said he was making a delivery here so I hopped a ride with him. (*Holding Mrs. Stewart at arm's length and looking at her.*) You've been indulging in a good old fit of sentimentality. (*Drawing her close again.*) Well, I feel the same way. We'll have a good cry together.

MRS. STEWART (*drying her eyes*). We'll do no such thing. Please don't tell Peg what a fool I am. Oh dear, I'll have to run down and tell Delia to put the flowers in water.

JEAN. Sit down and rest. I told Delia about the flowers.

MRS. STEWART. You're always so thoughtful.

JEAN (*thrusting package at her*). Here! Stick this in Peg's trunk.

MRS. STEWART. Now, Jean! The wedding breakfast is enough. You'll spoil her.

JEAN. She's like you. Nothing can spoil her.

MRS. STEWART (*putting package on bed and resuming packing*). You're full of blarney, Jean Bascom, but I like it. Yes, Peg does pretty well for an only child. But, Jean, you shouldn't spend so much money on her. You'll need it in New York.

JEAN (*lighting a cigarette*). I may not go. (*Stuffs pack of cigarettes carelessly back in left pocket.*) I can't bear to leave Father. (*Bitterly.*) *She* won't take care of him.

MRS. STEWART. It's a great pity your mother died when you were so young. Your life hasn't been easy.

JEAN. I'm not complaining.

MRS. STEWART. You're very loyal to your father and I admire you for it. But he ought to get a job so you wouldn't be so tied down.

JEAN. He'll never get a job as long as *she's* around. I hate her. Sometimes I could. . . .

MRS. STEWART. Jean, she's your father's wife.

JEAN (*crushing out her cigarette*). How can I ever forget it?

MRS. STEWART. Let's get our minds on more pleasant things. (*Holds out an armful of clothes.*) Put these in the second drawer. (*Jean throws her hat on foot of bed, takes folded clothes and dumps them in drawer.*) No, no, dear! Don't throw them in. Fold them. Like this. (*Illustrates.*)

JEAN. I haven't had much experience in packing. I never go anyplace.

MRS. STEWART. Why, Jean, you've taken some lovely trips with Peg. You two were in Charleston last year this time.

JEAN. And this year she marries Philip.

MRS. STEWART. You'll be marrying soon. I'll be packing your things. I feel that you belong to me. You and Peg really should be sisters. Put some sachet in here, dear.

JEAN. You do it. I'm all thumbs today.

MRS. STEWART (*as she sprinkles sachet in drawer*). All these wedding parties wear you girls out. (*Jean moves over the blue satin mules, sits on bed, then picks up mules and sits holding them.*) I hate to keep bringing it up, Jean, but aren't you undertaking too much, entertaining the whole bridal party at the country club? Peg will love it, I know, but. . . .

JEAN. I want tomorrow to be the happiest day in her life. I want to contribute a little to that happiness.

MRS. STEWART. You're a fine, unselfish girl.

JEAN. When do you expect Peg back?

MRS. STEWART. I haven't the faintest idea. You know how these luncheons are. But, Jean, weren't you supposed to have lunch with Peg and the girls?

JEAN. Yes. But since I got a day off from the bank, I decided I needed the time to get things ready for the breakfast.

MRS. STEWART (*clapping her hand over her mouth*). Oh my goodness! I forgot! Philip wants you to call the bank right away.

JEAN. But his father said it was perfectly all right for me to be off today and tomorrow.

MRS. STEWART. But the bank examiners came in this morning. (*Jean stands up suddenly. The mules fall to the floor.*)

Wouldn't you *know* they'd pick a time like this? Phil says they need you, dear. (*Jean stoops and picks up the mules and carefully stands them side by side on the bed.*) It's a shame. You and Philip having to work the day before the wedding. He sounded upset. (*Jokingly.*) I hope his books are in order. (*Very carefully, Jean moves the mules to another part of the bed.*) I'm only joking. But just thinking of those examiners makes me nervous. How you folks keep all that money straight is beyond me. I can't even keep my checkbook balanced.

JEAN (*crossing to trunk, puts mules in drawer very carefully, and closes drawer with equal care*). Oh, you get used to it.

MRS. STEWART. I'd hate to work in a bank. You hear so much about holdups.

JEAN. There's a burglar alarm in each cage and a pistol in every cash drawer.

MRS. STEWART. I'd be too frightened to use them. (*Sorting things out on the bed.*) Now where are those slippers? She'll want those in her bag and. . . . Oh dear, I must have packed them. . . . (*Goes to trunk and starts to pull out drawers.*)

JEAN. Mrs. Stewart?

MRS. STEWART (*absent-mindedly*). Yes, dear?

JEAN. I've got something to tell you. You're the only person who. . . .

[*On cue "you're," Delia enters, holding high above her head and draped over her shiny black arm a white wedding dress and veil. She edges in sideways—so precious is her burden, she must not muss it.*

DELIA. Here 'tis, Miss Lucy. I got all dem wrinkles out. Evenin', Miss Jean. (*But Jean is staring at the dress.*)

MRS. STEWART (*breathlessly*). It's beautiful! (*Jean walks blindly towards the dress. Mrs. Stewart's face begins breaking up.*) Oh, I just can't take it in.

DELIA. Now, Miss Lucy. . . .

MRS. STEWART. I can't realize that tomorrow is the day. It seems like yesterday we were packing her things to take her to boarding school. She was so little and cunning. I thought I just couldn't let her go. Well, I don't feel a bit differently today. (*Laughing and crying at the same time.*) It sound silly. Philip is such a nice boy, and I like all the Wilsons very much, but I. . . . (*She cries softly.*)

JEAN (*putting out her hand and stroking the dress*). So soft and white. . . .

DELIA. 'Twon't be white long wid y'all weepin' all over it. Y'all act mo' lak a funeral dan a weddin'.

MRS. STEWART. Can't we be a little sentimental without you fussing at us?

DELIA. I don' see nothin' to take on so 'bout. Want dis hung in de closet?

MRS. STEWART. No. I'm going to hang it in my room.

DELIA. So's you kin look at it 'n cry all night.

MRS. STEWART. No such thing. Straighten out the train. (*Phone rings.*) Answer the phone, please, Jean. Come on, Delia.

DELIA. Wait a minute, Miss Lucy, de veil's hung. (*Adjusts it.*) Now you kin manage.

[*They leave the room. Jean stares at phone as it rings again. She starts to back out of the room. Stops. Squares her shoulders, comes back and picks up the phone.*

JEAN. Hello? Jean. Yes, Philip. Mrs. Stewart said you were trying to locate me. The examiners? Philip . . . they're quite right. I can tell you the exact shortage. One thousand two hundred and seventy-eight dollars. . . . I'll come right over. Philip . . . please . . . does Peg have to know? I don't want to spoil tomorrow for her. Thank you, Philip. . . . (*As she replaces receiver very slowly.*) Thank you very much. (*She looks around the room as if memorizing each part of it. She hears Mrs. Stewart talking and quickly slips out.*)

MRS. STEWART (*off*). Did you press Peggy's blue chiffon?

DELIA. Yes'm. It's hanging in her closet.

MRS. STEWART (*as they enter*). You can finish what you were doing downstairs, Delia. Jean will help me finish. . . . (*Looking around.*) Jean. . . . Why, she's gone. The phone! Do you suppose her father's sick?

DELIA. I declare, Miss Lucy, you worries 'bout everything.

MRS. STEWART. She probably went down to the bank.

DELIA. Look!

MRS. STEWART. What's the matter with you?

DELIA (*pointing to the bed*). Dat dere hat on de bed. It's bad luck.

MRS. STEWART. That's just a silly superstition.

DELIA. Poor Miss Peggy.

MRS. STEWART. But it's Jean's hat. Not Peggy's.

DELIA. Don' make no difference. 'Twas on Miss Peg's bed. (*Going to closet.*) I'll hang it up. (*Does so.*)

[*Girls are heard laughing and chattering as they come upstairs.*

DELIA (*smiling as she closes the closet door*). Speakin' of angels, dere she is.

MRS. STEWART. Now don't go upsetting her with your superstitious nonsense.

DELIA. No'm.

PEGGY (*off*). Mother! Mother, where are you?

MRS. STEWART (*calling*). In your room, dear. (*As Delia is leaving.*) Delia, can you tell I've been crying?

DELIA. Cose I kin. I *knows.* (*She goes out, and while she is greeting girls in hall, Mrs. Stewart runs to dressing table and rubs a powder puff across her nose.*)

[*Grace, Kitty and Peggy, laughing and talking, pour into the room.*

GRACE. Hello, Mrs. Stewart.

KITTY. How is the bride's mother?

MRS. STEWART. Hello, Kitty. And Grace! Isn't that a new dress?

GRACE. Uh-huh.

MRS. STEWART. How sweet you both look. (*In a special voice.*) Hello, Peg dear.

PEGGY. Mother, look what Kit gave me. Isn't it lovely?

[*Proudly she displays a handsome silver platter. She is so radiantly happy, she seems to glow. Everything about her fairly shouts, "I'm young! I'm in love. I'm getting married tomorrow!"*

MRS. STEWART. It's lovely.

PEGGY (*pulling at her mother*). Sit down, darling. I want to tell you about the luncheon. It was marvelous!

GRACE. And the cutest place-card holders. Here's one. See?

MRS. STEWART (*looks and admires*). Lovely!

KITTY. I ordered them from Richmond.

PEGGY. I wish you could have seen the salad. It was molded like a lily and. . . .

MRS. STEWART. I wish I could stay and hear all about it, but I've simply got to go over to the church and see about the flowers.

KITTY. Let us help you.

MRS. STEWART. No. I'll take Delia. I know your luncheon was exquisite, Kitty. You inherited your mother's good taste. (*Turning to Peggy.*) I'll put the platter with your other presents. Remember, there's another party tonight and you all want to look pretty and fresh tomorrow. Do rest a bit.

PEGGY. I couldn't. I'm too excited. Has Phil been by?

MRS. STEWART. No, dear. He and Jean have to work. The bank examiners are here.

PEGGY. Oh, Mother, not really?

MRS. STEWART. But he'll be through in time for the dinner. (*She kisses Peggy lightly on the forehead.*) I'll be at the church if anyone calls. Oh! Jean came by but she had to go back to work. (*She goes.*)

KITTY. Poor Jean. I declare, she has to work all the time.

PEGGY. So does Phil.

GRACE. Brace up, Peggy. You'll see plenty of him from tomorrow on.

PEGGY. But tomorrow isn't today. I want to see him now. (*Laughing.*) Aren't I silly?

KITTY. Young is the word.

[*The girls laugh and get comfortable, pulling off their hats. Kitty sits in front of the dressing table, putting on lipstick. Grace pushes things aside and stretches out on the bed. Peggy stands in the middle of the room, running a comb through her hair.*

GRACE (*kicking off her shoes*). There! That's better. Wasn't Elinor's dress stunning?

PEGGY. She always looks nice.

KITTY (*busy with lipstick*). Uh-huh.

GRACE. Why y'all getting so beautiful?

KITTY. Habit.

GRACE. Somebody throw me a cig.

PEGGY. Here, lazybones. (*Throws pack on bed.*) There're matches on the table.

GRACE. Thanks. (*Takes last cigarette from pack and tosses pack on table.*) Last one. (*Lights it.*) Where're you going on your honeymoon, Peg?

PEGGY. Wouldn't you like to know! (*Grace giggles.*)

KITTY (*picks up picture on dressing table and looks at it closely*). Phil's awfully good-looking, Peg.

PEGGY. I think so. But of course I'm prejudiced.

GRACE. Well, I'm impartial and I say he'll pass. (*Breathing deeply.*) Whew! I *never* ate so *much*. That wasn't a luncheon, Kit. It was a five-course banquet.

PEGGY. It was swell, Kit. You've all been so sweet to me.

KITTY. You're only a bride once, little one.

PEGGY. Thank goodness for the *once*. I'd hate to be an old maid.

GRACE. Speaking of old maids, Jean is showing suspicious symptoms—quickening of the temper, few lines around the mouth.

PEGGY. Don't talk like that about Jean.

DELIA (*hat and coat on, sticks her head in the door*). Miss Peg, we'se gittin' ready to go 'n' Miss Lucy said to tell you to pick out whut you wants in de suitcase so's we kin finish packin' yo trunk tonight.

PEGGY. All right, Delia.

DELIA. I cooked a good chocolate cake dis mornin'. If y'all wants a piece, it's in de cake box.

GRACE. Oh Lawd, Delia, I've done nothing but eat since Peg got engaged.

DELIA. It sho ain't hurt yo' looks none, Miss Grace. You'se prettier'n ever.

GRACE. Delia, you're my friend for life.

[*An automobile horn sounds outside.*

PEGGY. Mother's blowing for you, Delia.

DELIA. Yes'm, 'n' she mean fer me to come too. Bye, y'all, 'n' dere's coca-colas in de ice box. (*She leaves to a chorus of "goodbyes."*)

GRACE. Delia's a bird in this world. You're going to miss her. I bet you can't cook an egg.

PEGGY. I can so!

GRACE. Are there any questions you'd like to ask about the culinary arts?

KITTY. Or about life and love?

PEGGY. You've enlightened me enough already. (*She stretches out on the chaise longue.*)

GRACE. Surely there is some very important question you want to ask?

KITTY. Like how to be glamorous and still be cold-creamed? Or how to have curls and not sleep in a hair net?

GRACE. The answer is a good permanent.

PEGGY. My hair's naturally curly.

KITTY. Lucky dog. Throw me a cigarette, Grace.

GRACE. Sorry, but I smoked the last.

KITTY. Oh, you did, did you? (*Goes over to bed and pushes her playfully.*)

GRACE. Go 'way. (*Kitty tickles her foot.*) Kit, stop tickling my foot! Make her stop, Peg.

PEGGY. Huh? (*Her thoughts are far away.*)

KITTY. Peg's in a fog. She doesn't even hear you. (*Picks up package that Jean had left.*) Peg, here's another present. *Peg!* Come out of your dream. (*Tosses the package to Peggy.*)

GRACE. I never saw so many presents. Well, it proves that it pays to have a big wedding.

PEGGY. Wonder who it's from?

KITTY. Open it and see, crazy. (*Crosses to Peggy.*)

GRACE. Hurry up! I'm dying of curiosity.

[*Peggy opens package and holds up an exquisite silk and lace slip. The card drops unnoticed to the floor.*

PEGGY. Oh!

KITTY (*examining it closely*). It's exquisite. It must have cost a fortune.

GRACE. Who sent it?

PEGGY (*rummaging through the paper*). I can't find the card.

KITTY (*picking it up*). Here it is. Why, it's from Jean!

PEGGY. Jean?

GRACE. That girl must have discovered a gold mine, the way she's spending money.

KITTY. Look, Peg, there's a verse on the card.

GRACE. Read it out loud.

PEGGY (*reading*).

Mindful of you the sodden earth in spring.
And all the flowers that in the springtime grow,
And dusty roads, and thistles, and the slow
Rising of the round moon. . . .

GRACE. The girl's nuts. Just plain nuts. What sense does that make?

KITTY. I think it's beautiful.

PEGGY. It's one of Edna Vincent Millay's poems. My favorite. (*Folding the tissue back around the gift.*) But I wish she hadn't done this. She needs the money at home. Giving me the breakfast is too much, and now this. It's almost embarrassing.

GRACE. I wish someone would embarrass me like that.

KITTY. You've known Jean a long time, haven't you, Peg?

PEGGY. We played together as children.

GRACE. And you roomed together in college. You took trips together. You've been her closest friend. What will she do when you're married?

[*Peggy goes to trunk slowly and carefully puts gift away in drawer.*

PEGGY. Jean has a lot of character. She worked her way through college waiting on tables, and she's slaved ever since in the bank. I've been afraid for a long time she might have a nervous breakdown.

GRACE. She might at that. No money, no boy-friend and a disgusting family to put up with. Why in heck doesn't her father get a job?

PEGGY. He's ill, Grace. Please, let's talk about something else.

GRACE. Ill, my eye. He suffers from a perpetual hangover. He hasn't drawn a sober breath since he married that . . . that creature.

KITTY. She'd drive anybody to drink. I wonder what on earth she uses on her hair? It's the ghastliest brass color.

GRACE. Ye Gods! Think of spending your days cooped up in a bank cage and every night cooped up in a cage with her! I'd blow my brains out.

PEGGY. It's all so wrong—my having so much and Jean having so little.

KITTY. But, darling, she'll be out of it in a little while. She's going to New York and make a new life for herself.

PEGGY. You all don't know what's in Jean. She used to write such marvelous things in college. Verses as good as these. But now she never has time to write except at night and then she's too tired.

GRACE. Going to New York won't do her any good. She'll still have to work and send money home.

KITTY. At least she won't have to look at that woman.

GRACE. She'd make some man a swell wife. She ought to get married.

KITTY. And, pray, to whom? Since Peg's captured Phil, there just aren't any eligible men here.

[*They are so busy talking, they do not notice that Jean has entered quietly and is standing in the doorway.*

GRACE. There's always Tommy.

KITTY. Who'd have him? He's prissy as an old maid. And fifty if he's a day.

GRACE. When you've reached Jean's age, you can't be too particular.

KITTY. Oh, I've got a swell idea. There'll be a lot of Phil's college friends at the wedding tomorrow. Maybe we can do a little matchmaking for Jean.

GRACE. Swell! Peg, you make her get her hair set and Kit and I will see what we can do. Because Jean really needs. . . .

JEAN (*quietly on cue "Jean"*). I hate to interrupt this most interesting conversation, but I left my hat here.

[*The girls look up startled. Peggy runs to Jean.*

PEGGY. Jean!

GRACE. Why . . . er . . . hello, Jean.

KITTY. We were just talking about you.

JEAN. Yes, I heard you. (*Looking around.*) I thought I put it on the bed. But. . . .

PEGGY. Jean, your present was lovely.

JEAN. I'm glad you liked it. (*Starting out.*) I guess I didn't wear a hat.

PEGGY. Don't go. Come and sit down.

GRACE. Yeah. We're having a regular bull session . . . settling all the world's problems.

JEAN. Including mine?

KITTY. Come on, Jean. This is the last time we'll be together like this in heavens knows how long.

JEAN. That's true enough.

PEGGY. Let me take your coat.

JEAN. No, I can't stay. I only stopped by . . . because I have something to tell you.

GRACE. If it's private, we'll leave.

JEAN. Oh well. It can wait. (*Sitting down.*) Tell me more about what you were discussing when I came in.

GRACE. Oh, that. We were just talking.

JEAN. Your plan for getting me married was very interesting. I never knew I was that important to you.

KITTY. Oh, you know how we run on. But I do honestly think you'd be happier married.

JEAN. Why?

KITTY. It's fun being the center of your own little world, having your own home and family. You feel that there's some object in your being here after all and. . . . Oh, I can't put it in words.

JEAN. You're doing very well. (*Pause.*) You're mighty quiet, Peg. What do you think about me?

PEGGY. I wish you could be as happy as I am. The only thing that worries me is that you're unhappy.

JEAN (*smiling*). Then you have no worries. How was the luncheon?

GRACE. Swell. But we missed you.

KITTY. What a shame the bank examiners had to come in and make you miss everything.

GRACE. We had an awfully good time.

JEAN. I'm sure you did. Kit's parties are always nice.

KITTY. Coming from you, that really is a compliment.

PEGGY. Was Phil at the bank when you left?

JEAN. I don't know. (*Confused.*) Yes, yes, he was there.

GRACE. I bet his father's giving him pointers on how to treat a wife.

KITTY. A banker's son should know all the answers

PEGGY. Do you feel all right, Jean?

JEAN. Sure I do. Why?

PEGGY. Nothing. Only I thought you were working too hard or. . . .

KITTY. I know you *said* ten o'clock, Jean, but what time do you really want us to get to the breakfast?

JEAN. I'm not going to give the breakfast. (*Murmur from girls.*) That's what I really came by to tell you, Peggy.

PEGGY. What's happened? Is your father worse?

JEAN. Oh no. Nothing like that. But Phil's father and I had a talk this afternoon. It seems he had wanted all along to give it. He said, being the bridegroom's father and all. . . . Well, it did seem more appropriate. So. . . .

GRACE (*indignantly*). I think he had a nerve waiting till this late to pull a stunt like that. *I'd* tell him off.

KITTY. She can't, Grace. He's her boss. But I think myself it was pretty poor taste.

JEAN. You understand, don't you, Peg?

PEGGY. Of course I do. You've done too much for me already.

JEAN. I do want to give it, I do. But I guess Mr. Wilson does have a prior right.

PEGGY. But he shouldn't have let you go to all the trouble of planning it. Why didn't he say something in the beginning?

JEAN (*lamely*). I guess he just didn't think about it before.

GRACE (*jumping up and shoving her feet into her shoes*). It makes me boil! Just because he runs the bank and you work for him is no reason he can run everything. If I were you, Peg, I'd call Phil right now and. . . .

JEAN (*in a panic*). No! No, don't do that. It's all settled.

KITTY. Can I help you phone the guests about the change?

JEAN. Thank you. But Mrs. Wilson is attending to it.

GRACE (*going to Jean*). Well, of all the high-handed manipulating! This beats all. Excuse me for talking about your in-laws, Peg. (*She casually reaches into Jean's pocket.*) Give me a cigarette.

JEAN (*jerking away*). What are you trying to do?

GRACE. Find a cigarette. Got one?

JEAN (*searches in her other pocket, pulls out a crumpled package*). Here.

GRACE. Thanks. (*As she lights her cigarette.*) What've you got in that other pocket, Jean?

JEAN (*quickly, as she puts her hand into the pocket*). Nothing.

GRACE (*as she tosses pack back to Jean*). I bet it's another present.

KITTY (*rising*). I declare, you've got more curiosity than any girl I've ever seen. Leave Jean alone and come on. I've got to get a manicure.

PEGGY (*rising*). Don't you all go.

KITTY. I'd better, Peg. I'm late already. See you later, Jean.

JEAN. Sure.

KITTY (*as she and Peggy go to door*). Come on, Grace, if you want to ride with me.

GRACE (*gathering up her things*). You don't think I want to walk home, do you?

KITTY (*to Peggy. In the hall*). Don't bother to come down, Peg.

GRACE (*to Jean, as she leaves*). Bye, Jean. You're a better sport than I'd be about the breakfast.

PEGGY (*in the hall*). Kit, I can't thank you enough for the luncheon and the gorgeous silver platter. Grace, I've already told you how much I appreciate the dinner and. . . .

[*The voices fade away. Jean gropes in her pocket and with a shudder draws out a small revolver. She looks at it intently, turning it over and over. Then she hears Peggy returning and hastily stuffs it back into her pocket. She rises, sticks a cigarette in her mouth and pretends to be looking for a match.*

PEGGY (*sighing deeply*). Whew!

JEAN. Tired?

PEGGY. A little. (*Sinks on chaise longue.*) There're matches on that table right in front of you.

JEAN. I must be going blind.

[*She takes a match and, crossing to Peggy, holds out the pack of cigarettes to her.*

PEGGY (*taking one*). Thanks. (*Jean strikes the match but her hand trembles so, that Peggy has to catch hold of her wrist and steady it for them to get a light. Peggy blows out the match and holds Jean's arm out, watching it quiver.*) Jean, what's the matter?

JEAN (*sitting in chair*). Nothing, Peg. I guess I inherited it. Dad's hands are the same way.

PEGGY. Is he . . . ill again?

JEAN. No, Peg. No! You're imagining things.

PEGGY. You can't lie to me. I know you too well. Are you worried about the breakfast?

JEAN. You're being ridiculous. There's nothing the matter with me. (*Attempting to speak lightly.*) Of course, I was a little cross when I heard you all discussing me, but. . . .

PEGGY. I'm surprised at you taking that seriously.

JEAN. The truth does hurt. But what's the good of talking about it? Did you really like the present?

PEGGY. Oh yes. You're so good to me, Jean. You've given me so many nice things. You're quite right to give up the idea of the breakfast. It would have been too much.

JEAN (*rising*). Peg! You don't think that I. . . . Listen! Of all the things I ever wanted to do, it was to give that breakfast. I *wanted* to do it.

PEGGY. But the expense. . . .

JEAN (*hysterically*). Oh, Peg, what difference does expense make now? (*Crushing out her cigarette.*) Goodbye, Peg. (*She starts out. Peggy runs after her.*)

PEGGY. Jean! Come back here.

JEAN. Goodbye. I'll see you tonight. (*She is crying.*)

PEGGY. You can't go home like this. Tell me what's. . . . (*Turning Jean around.*) Why, you're crying! Oh, Jean, please don't cry. Please!

JEAN (*trying to pull herself together*). I'm just . . . as . . . sorry as I can be. I didn't . . . mean . . . to make such a fool of myself. I'm going home.

PEGGY. You're not going anywhere until you tell me what's wrong.

JEAN (*crying more bitterly*). You wouldn't understand. You've had everything a girl could want—a lovely family, clothes, dates—everything. Everyone loves you. I've never had anything.

PEGGY. Everyone admires you and likes you, Jean.

JEAN (*not listening*). And now for the rest of my life, I'll be shut up in. . . . (*Coming to her senses.*) Oh, Peg, I didn't mean that. Don't listen. Don't pay any attention to me. I'm just tired. I wish you all the happiness in the world. You know that, don't you, Peg? Don't you?

PEGGY. Of course I do.

JEAN. I'm so ashamed of acting like this—spoiling what should be the happiest day of your life.

PEGGY. You couldn't spoil anything for me. You're the best friend I have in the world. (*Jean is crying quietly. Peggy makes her sit on the chaise lounge.*) Your troubles are my troubles. I want to share them with you just as I want to share my happiness with you.

JEAN. I want to go home. I can't talk any more now.

PEGGY. All right. But you can't go out with your eyes all red and swollen. People will think something awful has happened to you.

JEAN. I'll go wash my face.

PEGGY. You just relax. I'll fix you up. (*Wearily, Jean puts her head back on the pillows.*) That's better. (*Gets handkerchief from drawer, wets it with skin freshener*). Close your eyes. (*She rubs Jean's forehead and talks in a low, soothing voice.*) Now doesn't that feel good? You shouldn't be so unhappy on such a lovely day.

JEAN (*with an effort.*) It is a nice day. Just like Charleston was last time this year.

PEGGY. Yes. Remember the little darky who took our bags and lisped like thith, "Yeath, ma'am"? That was the afternoon we took that dreamy ride in the boat through the cypress gardens. All the flowers seemed so sleepy and still. The paddles lapping was the only sound.

JEAN. I remember. Remember Cape Cod?

PEGGY (*laughing*). Cape Cod? I'll never forget that old Cadillac. You had to crank it. How about that day we ran out of gas and you went back for more while I minded the car, and I got scared when I saw a man coming and picked up a stick. He was the state forester. And was he mad! "Madam," he said, "I'll have you know that women are safe in our woods."

JEAN. I remember how I laughed when you told me.

PEGGY. Oh, Jean, we had such good times together. We'll go on trips again and read books together and do all those things. My home will always be your home.

JEAN. Your home will be Phil's home.

PEGGY. His or mine, it's the same thing. We both love you.

JEAN (*sitting up and looking at her*). No, Peg. It's not the same thing. Tomorrow is the end. You'll never be free again. (*The words startle her.*) Never be free again. (*Recovering and resuming her train of thought.*) There'll be Phil and your house, yes, and babies. They'll come first, and rightly so.

PEGGY. There'll always be room for you.

JEAN. I won't be here.

PEGGY. What do you mean?

JEAN. I mean. . . . (*She hesitates.*) Oh, I'll be an executive in a New York office, drawing a huge salary, and when you come to see me, you'll have to go through a whole line of secretaries, and then I'll probably be much too busy to see you.

PEGGY (*playfully roughing her hair*). You better not be.

JEAN (*catching her hand*). Peg, no matter what happens, you must never worry about me. When I'm gone to . . . to . . . New York, don't remember today. Just remember the fun we had together.

[*The phone rings. Jean springs to her feet. Peggy's face lights up. She runs to answer it.*

PEGGY. That's Phil!

JEAN (*tensely*). Don't answer it!

PEGGY. Why, Jean, he should have called hours ago.

JEAN. Please, please don't answer it.

PEGGY (*laughing as she takes off receiver*). Don't be silly, Jean. (*Into phone.*) Hello? Oh, hello, darling. Oh yes! It was a lovely luncheon. And Kit. . . . (*Stops suddenly and listens intently.*) What? Yes. (*She looks at Jean questioningly.*) She's here now.

JEAN. Hang up!

PEGGY. What, Phil? What! No! Oh no, Phil! *No!* There's a terrible mistake. . . .

[*Jean wrenches the phone from her and slams it back.*

JEAN (*moaning*). He promised not to tell. He promised. . . .

PEGGY (*looking at Jean horror-stricken*). I don't believe it. It's not true. Jean, it's not true.

JEAN (*dully*). It's true.

PEGGY (*unbelievingly*). But why, Jean? Why?

JEAN. Rent, food, coal . . . trips. . . .

PEGGY (*in a whisper*). No.

JEAN (*with a twisted smile*). Do you think I took those trips on my salary? (*Quietly.*) Yes, I stole the money.

PEGGY. If you needed money so desperately, why didn't you come to me, your friend?

JEAN. I'm not a beggar. I have some pride. *Don't* stand there pitying me.

PEGGY. You couldn't have known what you were doing.

JEAN. I knew. And I knew the price I'd have to pay. The only thing I regret is that you had to find it out . . . today. He promised not to tell you. (*Pleadingly.*) You can't marry him, Peg. You can't. He doesn't love you. If he had, he'd never have told you.

PEGGY. His father made him.

JEAN. That's a lie. Phil wanted to be the one to let you know. I never liked him. Now I hate him.

PEGGY. It's not his fault. If he hadn't phoned, his mother would have. The newspaper phoned her and. . . .

JEAN (*in resignation*). Now everybody knows. (*Her hand closes over the pistol in her pocket.*) There's no need of waiting, then, until after tomorrow.

PEGGY (*grabbing her by the arm*). What have you got in your pocket?

JEAN. Nothing that concerns you.

PEGGY. It's a pistol! You've got a pistol. Jean! You're not going to kill Philip?

JEAN. Philip? (*Wheels around, utterly astonished.*) Him? (*The pistol in her hand now.*) I'm the one going to prison and you're thinking of *him?* (*Coldly.*) Don't worry. I'm not going to shoot your beloved. This pistol is meant for people who rob banks. (*She starts to go out.*)

PEGGY (*blocking the doorway*). I won't let you leave with that gun.

JEAN (*quietly*). Don't try to interfere, Peggy.

PEGGY. Give me that pistol!

JEAN. Get out of my way!

PEGGY. No!

JEAN. All right. (*Sadly.*) I didn't mean to have it happen here. (*Raises the pistol to shoot herself.*)

PEGGY (*throws herself on Jean and attempts to take the pistol from her*). Je—

[*The pistol goes off. The word hangs suspended. For a moment the two girls stare at each other. Then Peggy crumples and falls.*

JEAN (*in a whisper*). Peg! (*The pistol falls to the floor. She screams.*) Peg!

[*With a moan she falls to her knees. Clumsily she gathers the body to her and holds it close, rocking it gently to and fro like a mother with a child as . . .*

THE CURTAIN FALLS

CAKES FOR THE QUEEN

A Pantomimic Comedy

BY LEALON JONES

THE FIGURES

HEAD BAKER.
TASTER.
SMELLER.
MIXER.
MEASURER.
QUEEN'S SECRETARY.
HOBOETTE.
QUEEN.

PLACE. Kingdom of the Queen of Hearts.
TIME. Eight o'clock and the moments that come after.

WHAT THEY LOOK LIKE. The Head Baker, the Taster, the Smeller and the Measurer are all the same height. All wear short, white pleated dresses, tiny, red, round aprons and jaunty white caps. Each has a small circle of bright rouge, about the size of a quarter, on each cheek. Their lips are bright scarlet exaggerated cupid's bows. All are young and pretty and oh, so vivacious.

The Secretary wears a dress of domino cloth of just the right length. Her shining dark hair is severely dressed. She is chunky. She may even be plain fat, if you wish. She wears seven large medals on her dress.

The Hoboette wears a crazy old tattered straw hat filched from a scarecrow. Her hair is a shock of bright red wired yarn. Some of it sticks out through the holes in her hat. Over her shoulder is a crooked stick with a red bandana bundle swinging from the end. She wears a slouchy green dress, decrepit shoes and no stockings. Her coat also came from the scarecrow. One sleeve is gone; the coat is torn up the back and the hem is uneven and ragged. But she's fixed it up with green, red and yellow square patches. She is brown from the sun, and freckles are sprinkled generously over her face. Black out one of her front teeth and you have an artistic mess, but very charming.

The Queen! Oh, what a queen! She is tall, slender, regal and pretty. She wears a long, flowing gown of pure white satin. (All right then, *sateen*!) Her blue silk cape has a scarlet silk inner lining. On her dress are pinned numerous lovely, shining medals with red and blue ribbons. Among them is a tiny dull one about the size of a dime. She has awarded herself these medals for bravery and fortitude on various occasions. There was the time when she sat for a whole hour without yawning, listening to the Prime Minister's speech on taxes. Another time—but we won't go into *that*. And there was the time she didn't scream when a mouse ran under her bed. On her head—well, what would you expect to see on a Queen's head anyway? A crown, of course, silly. This one is a lovely tiara studded with ever so many jewels.

WHAT THE QUEEN'S BAKERY LOOKS LIKE. In the back, it's seven feet high. But the two sides slant down to three feet. It is painted bright yellow, with six rows of red six-inch squares along the bottom. There is a double door in the middle of the back. A neat sign above the door reads QUEEN'S BAKERY. In the middle of the right wall is an opened casement window daintily hung with white ruffled curtains generously sprinkled with red polka dots. Under the window is a cooling table. It is a cooling table because a sign swinging from it says so. In the middle of the left wall are two white doors, shoulder high, with orange rings to open and shut them. This is the oven because it says so right on the doors. A large work table stands near by. (Don't forget to put a swinging sign on, so that people will know what it is.) Underneath the table is a white can, coyly labeled TRASH. And, oh, yes! There is a large clock face painted over the oven door. It does not speak—nevertheless, it says, "eight o'clock." There are a couple of red shelves next to the big door. Large white containers, one labeled SUGAR, another FLOUR, another SPICES, another ICING, two large bowls labeled BUTTER and a pretty bottle labeled VANILLA, stand on these shelves.

THE KIND OF MUSIC YOU SHOULD USE. Percy Grainger's *Shepherd's Hey* is a very good choice. An orchestra would be nice, but a single piano will do. The tune should be sprightly and should cease each time words are spoken. The movements of the figures are completely in rhythm with the music, of course.

A WORD OR TWO ABOUT THE PANTOMIME. All figures except the Secretary and the Hoboette should use light, dainty movements. Broader, more humorously grotesque movements should be used by the Secretary and Hoboette. Instead of using tiny, running steps and delicate movements, they should use broader steps and more vigorous movements so that they become pantomimic foils for the others. The Queen's pantomime is very dainty. Do you think you could get a dance director to help you out with this production? If so, it is quite possible to make the dance element of equal importance to the play itself. You could make a pretty good ballet out of this, you know.

NOW WE GET INTO THE PLAY. Clock offstage strikes eight. Four dainty figures trip in lightly from stage right, keeping time to the music. They pause stage center and face audience. One carries an atomizer, another an eye-dropper, a third a measuring cup, and the fourth a measuring spoon. With military precision, they place right hand on right hip and do eyes right.

Head Baker enters from stage left. She carries a large wooden mixing bowl. She trips in, pauses even with others, faces audience, does eyes right to others, trips downstage, stops, does right face, bows and smiles to her assistants. They bow and smile in unison. She straightens, places mixing bowl on table and claps her hands three times. The assistants hurry to their work. The Taster sprays Smeller's face with atomizer. Smeller does the same for Taster. The Mixer and Measurer polish their utensils and the Head Baker examines the oven.

A knock on center door! Head Baker claps her hands thrice. Assistants come to attention in front of door, two on a side, somewhat downstage. Head Baker stands a little apart.

Secretary enters in a grand fashion with pompous strides. She pauses near door. She bows to bakery force. They return bow. She carries a large scroll from which she now removes large blue ribbon. Scroll unrolls to a three-foot length. As her lips move exaggeratedly in seeming speech, seeming always to say, *ba, ba, ba,* an off-stage feminine voice speaks. The music stops.

VOICE. *Hear ye, hear ye, hear ye! First order of the day from Her Charming Majesty the Queen. To the Head Baker:* (Bows to Head Baker who bows back.) *You are commanded to bake four small tea cakes for Her Majesty's visitors who are coming this morning. Let the cakes be as light as the down of Her Majesty's white swans, and as tasty as Persian melons. You are ordered to use recipe number four-eight-three B, with only seven-eighths teaspoon of vanilla. I, Her Majesty's Chief Secretary, do hereby leave this command with you.*

Music starts up again as, with a flourish, Secretary rolls up scroll, presents it to Head Baker and bows. The bakery force bow to her. She does an about-face and struts from the room.

Now there is a great hustle and excitement. Head Baker goes to shelves, puts scroll away and brings flour can to mixing table, where the Measurer measures the needed amount with meticulous care. Then Head Baker brings two bottles of milk from shelf and places them on table. She opens one with ceremony. Brandishing a teaspoon, she stands before the Taster and Smeller, who are stage center, the Taster being stage left. With the Mixer hovering expectantly near, she extends a spoonful of milk for the

Taster to sample. The Taster tastes, makes a wry face and nods *No!* The Smeller smells the spoonful and does the same. Head Baker throws bottle into trash can. Second bottle is opened. Same process. This time, both nod *Yes!*

The milk is given to the Measurer, who measures a cupful with great care, using a medicine dropper at the last to get it correct. The milk is given to the Mixer, who spills a little while conveying it to the mixing bowl. The Measurer fills it again with the dropper. Again the Mixer spills a little and again the dropper is used. At last the Mixer reaches the bowl and the milk is poured in.

Head Baker brings basket of eggs from shelf, breaks one into cup and has Taster taste it from spoon. Taster makes wry face. Smeller smells egg. Same business. Egg is thrown into trash can. Another egg is offered. Taster makes a wry face at it but smeller nods approval. Head Baker silently counts *eeny-meeny* on the two to determine who is out. The smeller wins. The egg is dumped into the mixing bowl and the Mixer gets to work.

Head Baker brings two bowls of butter from shelf to table. Taster samples bit from first bowl, makes a terrible face and chokes. Smeller smells butter, holds her nose and runs for atomizer while Head Baker throws this bowl of butter into the trash can. Atomizer is used on the Taster's mouth and the Smeller's nose and they become happy again. The second dish of butter proves to be heavenly. Both accept it ecstatically. Head Baker takes butter to Measurer, who carefully measures three tablespoons which she puts in the mixing bowl.

Now the red head of the Hoboette is seen at the window. She looks in, laughs in silent glee, then disappears.

Sugar, flour, vanilla and baking powder are tested in the same manner. All are enthusiastically received. The following amounts are put into the mixing bowl: a cup each of sugar and flour, a teaspoon of vanilla and one of baking powder. With the others gathered round, the Mixer vigorously mixes (all in time to the music, of course)—then the final test! Head Baker dips out a spoonful of batter and offers it to Taster, who tastes seriously, ponders and tastes again. The others show their feeling of suspense. She nods *Yes!* All but the Smeller clap their hands gleefully. Smeller smells and also approves. Again gleeful applause. Now the Head Baker pours the batter into four small baking pans. She claps her hands thrice. The force, except the Mixer, assembles in front of the oven. The Head Baker procures a velvet cushion of a royal purple color from the table drawer and holds it while the Mixer places the pans on it. Holding the cushion at arm's length, she carries it to the oven between the two lines of assistants, who smilingly extend their hands towards the oven. The Mixer opens the oven and the Mixer and Measurer place the pans inside. The Mixer closes the oven and the Head Baker places the cushion on the table. All stand at attention facing clock, whose minute hand starts to move joltingly from minute to minute. All count slowly to twelve, using right forefinger to emphasize. At twelve, clock stops turning. Head Baker looks mysterious and pantomimes *Sh-h-h!* Others do the same, fingers to lips. The Head Baker claps her hands three times and the Mixer opens the oven.

The Head Baker looks inside and turns around to beam and nod. The cakes have been baked successfully and the force is ecstatic. (How, you ask, could that be in just twelve counts? It could be that props of four baked cakes were put in just before curtain and these are the ones that the Mixer and Measurer take from the oven.)

The bakery force gathers round the oven to behold the magnificence of its newest creation. It resumes its former position. The Head Baker takes the cushion, holds it at arm's length and the Mixer and Measurer daintily place pans on it. The pans are carried to the cooling table by the Head Baker and are placed on it by the Mixer and Measurer. All step back to admire their art, much the same as feminine visitors would admire new twins. One can almost see the words *Cunning! Darling! Too cute for words! Adorable!* and other absolutely feminine derivatives, gushing from them.

The force then withdraw to stage left and, with their backs

to cooling table and window, go about various jobs. The Head Baker replaces ingredients on shelves. The Taster and Smeller use the atomizer and the Mixer and Measurer clean their utensils.

While this is going on, the Hoboette again appears at the window. She grins broadly, licks her lips, puts her arm inside and steals one cake after the other! Her hair brushes against the curtain. Why? Ah, just wait! Our great drama now becomes more intense.

The Secretary appears at the door. The Head Baker claps her hands three times and the bakery force comes to attention as before. The Secretary unties a big blue ribbon from another large scroll, unrolls it and pantomimes reading. The music stops.

VOICE. *Hear ye, hear ye, hear ye! Second order of the day from Her Charming Majesty, the Queen! To the Head Baker: You are commanded to allow me, Chief Secretary to Her Lovely Majesty, to inspect the cakes baked according to the first order of the day.*

With a bow, the Secretary hands scroll to Head Baker. The bakery force bows to the Secretary. Head Baker goes to place this scroll with the other and to get cushion. She beckons Taster to assist her. Both go to the cooling table. Consternation! The cakes are gone! While the Head Baker looks under the table, the Taster spreads the alarm. To the mixing table they come to help look for the cakes. Forsooth, such a commotion! They are in quite a dither.

The Head Baker runs to the Secretary and motions to her to come to the cooling table. She does so with pompous strides. The Head Baker points to the table with both hands and shakes her head. Drawing herself up to a pose of outraged dignity, the Secretary points an accusing finger at the force and stalks out.

Trouble? Oh dear! The poor bakery force is up in the air. Such sniffling on each other's shoulders one never saw before in all one's life. All save the Head Baker. She alone remains adamant. She comes silently to stage right and assumes a thinking attitude. The force crowds around her, watching her every expression breathlessly. She goes to the cooling table and examines it minutely. Then she examines the curtain. Ah! She has found it! She pulls a piece of red yarny hair off the left curtain and examines it. (We told you how the Hoboette's head brushed against the curtain, didn't we?) Of course the force is there looking on. The Head Baker holds up the piece of red stuff. She nods grimly to them. They nod grimly to each other.

The Head Baker claps her hands thrice. They come to attention, two lines facing each other. The Head Baker goes to mixing table and motions them to follow. They do so in single file. She opens table drawer, takes out a rolling pin and gives it to the first in line, doing it grimly, thrusting her arm out quickly. The recipient takes it grimly. To the next two she gives two big spoons. She spies a flyswatter on the wall. Number four gets that. She reserves the egg-beater for herself. She claps her hands three times. The force does an about-face and follows Head Baker out. She is still holding the yarny hair daintily between the thumb and finger of her left hand. The stage is empty. The stage waits. The music stops and waits.

The music starts again as the Hoboette appears at the door with the Head Baker leading her by the left ear. She pantomimes yelling each time she is prodded by the rolling pin or something else. They bring her to stage center. She is trying to eat a cake during this time. The Head Baker matches the hair she has with that of the Hoboette. The others help in the matching. They nod grimly to themselves and begin pointing their fingers at her, prodding her anew. Of course she begins yelling again. They examine her coat, finding the three remaining cakes in an inside pocket. The cakes are removed daintily by the Taster while the Smeller holds the coat open. Both hold their noses and make wry faces while handling the coat.

Then comes more trouble in this g-g-g-reat, swift-moving drama. That dratted nemesis, the Secretary, appears in the doorway, strutting her importance. What else can the poor bakery force do but come to attention before the door? As usual, the Secretary bows. As usual, the force bows back.

What's going to happen now? Things are really just, just too bad the way they are. The Secretary's lips move.

VOICE. *Her Charming Majesty, the Queen!*

Dumbfounded, the members of the force exchange looks of despair. This is the payoff! As the Secretary steps aside, the Queen enters. And such a delightful person she is—so lovely and so graceful. Everybody bows of course. And the Queen responds with a nod of her head. Her lips move in pantomimic speech.

VOICE. *What has happened to my cakes?*

Then the Head Baker shows the Queen what has happened. She opens oven and pantomimes taking out the cakes and putting them on the cooling table. The force swings over to stage right, stands in a line, and at intervals nods in unison, trying ever so hard to impress the Queen with the Head Baker's truthfulness. With a sweep of her hands, the Head Baker shows how the cakes were filched through the window. Then she points accusingly at the Hoboette, who is still eating a cake. The force points in unison at the Hoboette, nodding accusingly.

With a light, floating step, the Queen goes over to the window, points at the Hoboette and motions from the cooling table to the window as if to say: *Did you steal the cakes?* Gleefully, the Hoboette nods, pantomiming a hearty laugh. What does she care? Didn't she get something good to eat?

But now the Queen's face freezes to sternness. Across the stage she sweeps to the main table, where she picks up a big mixing spoon. As she motions the force to bring the Hoboette to her, the culprit tries to sneak away. But it's too late! With a rush, the bakery force is upon her, pushing her over to the Queen and making her bend over. Daintily, the Queen paddles the pilferer, who pantomimes a loud squawk every time she is hit. Then the Queen discards the spoon, which is promptly sprayed with the atomizer by the Smeller. Noticing the cakes, the Queen picks one up and smells it. Such a look of distaste she shows. She looks at the Head Baker.

VOICE. *I cannot stand these cakes. They have ONE teaspoon of vanilla instead of SEVEN-EIGHTHS of a teaspoon.*

This startling news makes the force look terribly downcast. Then the Queen picks up the cakes, goes to the Hoboette and motions her to hold open her coat pocket. With a show of delicate repugnance, she daintily drops the cakes into the pocket. Then she takes stage center and speaks. (*Or at least moves her mouth as though speaking.*)

VOICE. *My dearly beloved subjects, it is now my great pleasure to bestow medals upon six of you in recognition of valiant service to your Queen. First a medal to each member of the bakery force for the daring capture of a culprit.*

Such a happy flurry of excitement in the bakery force! But now the Queen is perplexed. Where shall she get medals? She glances unwillingly at the gorgeous array of medals on her own dress. No, no, she can't bear the thought of giving up her own precious medals. Then she sees those on the Secretary's dress. Quickly, she takes five medals off the Secretary, who tries—oh, so hard!—to smile bravely. But the minute the Queen's back is turned she just has to boo-hoo like a big cry-baby. (In dumb show, of course.) The Queen pins a medal on each one of the bakery force. And she kisses each one on the cheek, too! Then she speaks.

VOICE. *And for taking these impossible cakes out of my sight, I present a medal to the culprit.*

Once more the Secretary's dress furnishes a medal which the Queen gingerly pins on the Hoboette's scarecrow coat. With a wide grin, chest out and arms akimbo, the Hoboette revels in her great moment. Now the Queen is puzzled. How can she kiss that ugly phiz? An inspiration! She holds up her handkerchief and kisses the Hoboette through it. Whereupon the Hoboette strides jauntily to the door, treats everyone to a dashing wave of her hand and is off! The Queen speaks again.

VOICE. *And to Her Majesty I present a medal for having such a delicate sense of smell regarding cakes.*

Off the Secretary's dress comes her very last medal. Onto the Queen's dress it goes. Then the Queen kisses a fingertip and touches it to her own cheek. She, too, is kissed by the Queen.

The Queen notices that the Secretary is bawling like a three-year-old that just lost its lollipop. Touched by such profound grief, the Queen desires to know what is wrong. The Secretary points to her medal-less self. Soothingly, the Queen chucks her under the chin. No use. The Queen tries it again, ever so sweetly and smilingly. Still no use. Something's got to be done. Regretfully the Queen looks at her own medals. She's got to give one up. So, she chooses the tiny dull one, pins it on the Secretary and kisses her cheek. What a change! The Secretary is all smiles. The Queen goes to the doorway, then turns and speaks to the Head Baker.

VOICE. *Bake me four small cakes at once, recipe number four-eight-three B with SEVEN-EIGHTHS of a teaspoon of vanilla.*

The bakery force bows happily. The Queen glides out of the room. The Secretary goes to the door and turns. She casts one tearful look at her medals now being proudly worn by the baking force. Then she looks down at the minute medal on her own dress and looks cheerful. After all, did not the Queen pin it there with her own dear hands and with a kiss? She bows, the force bows. She leaves.

There is a happy rush as the force pounces upon the Head Baker and hugs her for her achievement. Naturally, she receives the homage with delight.

Then the Head Baker brings her force to attention by clapping her hands three times. Happily, everyone starts the business of mixing more batter and—

THE PLAY'S OVER

CONSTANTIA *

A Romantic Drama

BY CHARLES STEARNS

DRAMATIS PERSONAE

CONSTANTIA, *mother of Constantine the Great.*

EUDOCIA, *her sister, who has suffered persecution.*

METRODORA, *a fine lady of the Court, bigoted to Paganism, and favoring the rival of Constantine.*

APHRODITE, *a fine lady of the Court, inclining to Paganism, from the love of dissipation.*

ARPASIA, *sister to Constantine.*

THALIA, *a very sensible young lady of the Court, inclined to Christianity.*

LAUTERIA, *handmaid of the Palace.*

PLACE. The ladies' apartment in the Palace of the Caesars at Rome.†

TIME. When Paganism was slowly giving way to Christianity.

SCENE I: EUDOCIA AND CONSTANTIA

[*Eudocia is represented sitting; Constantia enters, and Eudocia rises to receive her. Constantia seats herself, and Eudocia looks at her some moments with concern, and then speaks.*

---

* From *Dramatic Dialogues,* published in 1798.

† No setting is required save a painted backdrop on which are painted large marble columns and vistas of richly carpeted halls. The only furniture required is a regal-looking chair standing on a low, carpeted dais, and two benches of simulated marble. Rich scarves may be thrown over the benches. Characters enter and exit via wings left and right.—EDITOR.

EUDOCIA. My dear sister! Why are you so sorrowful today? I always love to see you cheerful. This cloud which seems settled on your brow gives me serious concern.

CONSTANTIA. Dear Eudocia, you may imagine, but you cannot fully comprehend, the sensibility of a mother. The condition of marriage commonly increases the tenderness of the human heart, but the parental relation much more. Were you a mother, you might possibly comprehend my present anguish of heart.

EUDOCIA. Tho you have lost your husband, you have everything else in your situation to make you happy. He left you seated on the throne of the greatest empire of the world—caressed and almost adored by the Court. You were exceedingly beloved by your husband while alive, and he has left you in the height of honor and public esteem.

CONSTANTIA. My husband is gone, and that were enough to make me extremely sorrowful—but it is by no means the whole of my present pain. The wives of Emperors are always to be pitied. I have a thousand times, in the midst of the noblest scenes of magnificence, wished that I had been the wife of some shepherd, or simple swain, whose ideas corresponded with mine. Differences of sentiment may produce much unhappiness between married persons of the best tempers in the world.

EUDOCIA. What difference could there be between your husband and you? He always treated you with extreme tenderness.

CONSTANTIA. He did—and he was naturally kind and generous. He suffered me to do very much as I pleased. He even permitted me to educate my son according to my own opinions. He is gone; and tho he was a most pleasing husband, when I think of him I am filled with horror— Had he been a Christian, and could I now believe him to be rejoicing among the Saints, I should have great consolation. But he always worshipped those gods which are vanity and a lie.

EUDOCIA. But you have a son, accomplished in genius, and in every virtue. If your sensibility be as great as you affirm, you must have joy of him.

CONSTANTIA. I have a son. He is dearer to me than life. Heaven knows how I love him. I watched with raptures of tenderness over his infant years. I have often bedewed his cheeks with the tears of delight. He grew up before me like a beautiful plant. His manners corresponded to my wishes. Early I seasoned his mind with the sublime truths of Christianity. I taught him to adore one everliving GOD—the Creator and Preserver of all—and the Mediator, the Messenger of God to man—and that he should love his neighbor as himself. Strange doctrines to us, till of late. I have endeavored strongly to impress it upon his mind that he was born not for himself but for the world.

EUDOCIA. And has not the event fully answered your expectations? Who can be more virtuous or more agreeable than the young prince? Extremely agreeable in his person and equally amiable in his manners. His genius is brilliant and his morals truly sublime. Lost to self-indulgence, he flies from public spectacles and scenes of wantonness, and public entertainments, to seek the society of the discreet and virtuous. And he abides the company of such ladies alone as exceed in honest fame the Lucretias and Porcias of ancient Rome. Even now he is composing a system of laws to establish equal rights and liberty among the people on the benevolent principles of Christianity.

CONSTANTIA. I know and feel what you say of him to be true. But this day must decide his fate to reign or die—for his advancement to the imperial throne, or his execution by torture.

EUDOCIA. Then I wonder no longer at your extreme concern. But who can oppose so amiable a prince?

CONSTANTIA. There is yet a powerful party in the Senate in favor of the ancient religion, who only want an opportunity to kindle the flames on the altars of perfection, in which so many Christians have smoked as victims to false gods. If they can get the army in their favor, they hope to succeed. Marentius, my son's rival, is at their head.

EUDOCIA. But by whose influence does this party move? There is scarcely a man about the Court in their favor.

CONSTANTIA. Women have often determined the fate of

nations. You know that enchantress, the beautiful Metrodora. Tho she affects so much tenderness for us, she is deeply engaged in the opposite interest. She is the soul of the party. Her influence, or mine, prevails on this day. But she is coming. It is most for our interest that I should meet her alone.
[*Eudocia withdraws.*

Scene II: Constantia and Metrodora

Metrodora. Sublime Empress, let me approach you with that humility which becomes your august presence.

Constantia (*laying her hand with a forbidding air on Metrodora's arm.*) Metrodora, for heaven's sake, desist. I am a poor, weak woman, pained to the heart. And I have no appetite for flattery. Never, since I had the splendid finery of being an empress, did I feel pain as I feel it this moment. O my son! This day it will be decreed that he must reign or die.

Metrodora. Well then, since you deny me the pleasure of addressing you as an empress, let me talk with you as a friend. My fears for your son are not less than yours. He is the idol of the Court and the favorite of my own heart. But I find the party in the Senate and in the army strong against him. I am afraid there is no way to support the young prince or even to preserve his life, but one.

Constantia. And what is that one?

Metrodora. You will accuse me, my friend Constantia! I have always wondered that you and your son, rejecting the religion of your own godlike Romans, should worship a crucified Jew—an honest man, perhaps, but a very unfortunate one. You laugh at Gentilism, but do you think there is anything in Gentilism so absurd?

Constantia. You say we worship a crucified Jew. This is wholly an error. No Christian ever worshipped a crucified Jew, but one God, the Creator and Preserver of all, whom the Christians call by the endearing name of Father. They reverence Jesus not as a man but as the word and wisdom of God, and to promote the glory of the Father. For the word and wisdom of God dwelt in him. The Christians adore not men but God.

METRODORA. And how do you know that the wisdom of God dwelt in him? Can you depend on witnesses who were dead nearly two thousand years ago and who, if living, would be three thousand miles distant?*

CONSTANTIA. Who among us doubt the main events of the wars of Troy! Or that Aeneas founded the Roman nation? We believe witnesses incomparably more distant and more remote in time. And this we know is perfectly reasonable. Yet this is not my present object. I ask you, Metrodora, if you can trust your ears to discern sounds, your eyes to be judge of colors, or your mouth to taste its meat?

METRODORA. Certainly, we should know nothing if we could not trust our senses as being naturally true.

CONSTANTIA. And your understanding to judge of truth?

METRODORA. Most certainly.

CONSTANTIA. Then I know most certainly that the wisdom of God dwelt in Jesus of Nazareth, because, in opposition to the darkness of the world sunk in vice and superstition, he taught us to adore one God, in whom we live, move and have our being—to love him sincerely and to obey him from the heart—that we should love one another, and in love serve one another—and that God is most just and will reward all human beings according to their works.

METRODORA. According to their works, do you say? I should not think that to be a very comfortable doctrine for you and me.

CONSTANTIA. Besides, it teaches us to pursue all things which are excellent. That whatsoever things are true, whatsoever things are honest, just, pure—whatsoever things are of good report, if there be any virtue, if there be any praise—that we should think on those things. Now, I know most certainly that all this is right. Let our priests or philoso-

---

* The author, a Massachusetts clergyman writing at the end of the eighteenth century, evidently substituted his own time and place—roughly speaking. The text should be altered for production purposes.—EDITOR.

phers say what they will. What then shall I do? Shall I believe or shall I not believe? Indeed, I must believe or do violence to my own mind.

METRODORA. And so you will expose yourself and your son to death by this hopeful system. I am astonished at your obstinacy. I never thought of these things much, but I know the danger of them. Have regard to the life of the young prince, whom you expose to immediate death, if, by you, he retains Christianity.

CONSTANTIA. You are now acting on the vicious principles of your own worship. You adore Laverna, Goddess of Deceit. You pretend concern for me and my son—but you mean to destroy us both! If your plans succeed, tomorrow we die in torments. But I hope soon to baffle you and all your designs. You have nothing to fear from me. Should I prevail, you still live as ever. But I must see my sister, Eudocia, this moment. The young ladies will wait on you. (*Constantia withdraws.*)

METRODORA (*alone*). Why, if that be the case, and the matter goes ill, I will contrive some way to deny the whole affair and throw the blame on the Senate.

SCENE III: THALIA AND ARPASIA.

[*In the beginning of this scene, the young ladies enter and pay their respects to Metrodora, who pauses a moment and then withdraws.*

ARPASIA. O my heart! How much I fear for the fate of my brother!

THALIA. I have better hopes than you concerning him. I believe that he will have success.

ARPASIA. And what reason have you for such a hope?

THALIA. I cannot imagine that such virtue should not meet success. Most sincerely do I wish that he may maintain his principles, nor give up his conscience for the splendor of a crown.

ARPASIA. I know not what to think. Sometimes my fears for him are so great that they almost make me wish that he would renounce the cross of the Nazarenes.

THALIA. But how can you wish such a thing? You surprise me!

ARPASIA. I never listened to discourses on this subject like my brother. My mother used to instruct us both. Constantine was always a serious youth. My mother would read for hours together out of the Bible, as the Christians call their Sacred Book, and Constantine would devour every word. But my mind was much more upon balls, assemblies, and other parties of pleasure.

THALIA. But do you not wish your brother to succeed?

ARPASIA. I hardly know what to think. I wish he may succeed as a Christian, or renounce the Christian faith and be happy.

THALIA. I should be unhappy to have him do that.

ARPASIA. Why? Cannot one be happy without being a Christian?

THALIA. Not so well as with it, I believe. One thing I clearly perceive—that it will be greatly for the interest of our sex to have Christianity prevail. *It is a matter of great consequence to our sex to have it prevail.*

ARPASIA. What say you? Can that be?

THALIA. No system treats our sex with so much tenderness and respect.

ARPASIA. How can you make that appear?

THALIA. By a fair comparison of facts. You know that women have been abused in various parts of the globe. The Christians say this was predicted from the time that Eve stole the forbidden apples of Paradise. Except in Greece, which has always been the seat of learning and politeness, women have been subjected to the arbitrary disposal of the men. And even among them [the Greeks] they are by no means as free as among the Christians.

ARPASIA. Are they [the Greeks] more generous in their principles than our noble Romans?

THALIA. Certainly. The noblest of our Romans claim the right of arbitrary divorce. In Germany and other northern nations, they [women] are treated as slaves and subjected to the scourge. In Asia, they are sold like common animals in the market.

ARPASIA. And how do you know that it is not even so amongst the Christians?

THALIA. There are several ladies of my acquaintance who have married Christian husbands. They appear very happy. This led me to enquire into their principles and customs.

ARPASIA. And did you find anything worthy of notice?

THALIA. I found what I thought worthy of notice. They maintain it as a principle that woman was created from the substance of man and therefore it must be unnatural to abuse her. That marriage is no human law, but a divine ordinance previous to all human laws.

ARPASIA. This certainly deserves our attention. A revolution in religion will be for the interest of our sex. It will be greatly in their favor. That is always good which does good. I will try my influence over some of the young senators. But are you fully informed of that matter?

THALIA. You may rest assured that I am. I have spared no pains for information. And I find that the more a Christian is attached to his religion, the more kind he is to his wife.

ARPASIA. Then this shall be the ladies' religion. It will be the happiest of all events for society, and prove to great advantage to our sex till the latest period of time.

SCENE IV: APHRODITE ENTERS TO THALIA AND ARPASIA.

APHRODITE. Ladies, I am glad to meet you. I hope you will comfort me a little for I am most seriously out of humor.

ARPASIA. Is that the reason that you come to us? When I am out of humor, I generally tarry at home till I feel better.

APHRODITE. But my mortification is inexpressible. I thought your brother had not been so much a dunce.

ARPASIA. How is my brother a dunce?

APHRODITE. It is said that he openly avows that he is a Christian—that he lives as one, and will not accept the empire unless he can retain his religion.

ARPASIA. And how will that affect you?

APHRODITE. Why, then the fashion of the whole Court must be altered, and all modes must receive a new model.

ARPASIA. I should suppose that you would only like it the more. As you are a very fashionable woman, the more new fashions, the better for you.

APHRODITE. But only consider what a dilemma I shall be in. My clothes are all ready for the dances at the Feast of Diana. It cost me thirty thousand sesterces to the mantua-makers. Besides, the cloth, which was brought from Sardis, cost more than its weight in gold. And now to think that your brother— I have no patience with him!

ARPASIA. And what, madam, has he to do with your dress? His attention is, I trust, engrossed by affairs of mightier consequence.

APHRODITE. If he be advanced to the empire today and retain his Christian principles, then the Dances of Diana, which are to be held on the Ides of next month, are to be put by.

ARPASIA. And what if they should be?

APHRODITE. Why, do you not see? The whole cost of my dress will be sunk, and I shall lose the opportunity of engaging the notice of the public.

ARPASIA. And is that all? Must the interests of the Roman empire, co-extensive with half the world, be set aside on account of your dress, and to give you an opportunity of dancing before a large company?

APHRODITE. I am mortified to death!

ARPASIA. This is extravagance indeed! Why, my dear Aphrodite, have you no reflection? Thalia has been summing up, together with me, the advantages which Christianity will bring to our sex. Speak, Thalia, if you please.

THALIA. In our researches, we found that, of all systems of religion, that of the Christians is most favorable to our sex, and best adapted to secure the good treatment of women.

APHRODITE. That is *something,* it is true. But what will become, in the meantime, of my dress and the Dance?

ARPASIA. Never mind that, Aphrodite. If my brother fails, he will be executed in the extremest tortures, and your dance will go on.

APHRODITE. That's true. So it will.

ARPASIA. And if he succeed, there will be great rejoicings on the occasion. Now, to accommodate you, Aphrodite, the moment that I hear of it, I will send you a Christian mantua-maker, and you may have your clothes altered. Then be the first lady who appears at the emperor's inauguration. Come forward in your rich dress, imported from Sardis, to pay your respects to the new emperor. This will secure you favor, make you popular with the new government. Your name shall be sounded through the Roman empire.

APHRODITE. The admiration of a whole empire is better than that of a ballroom. Yes! Let Constantine prevail! From henceforth I will be a Christian, since that is to be the prevailing fashion.

SCENE V: CONSTANTIA ENTERS WITH EUDOCIA.

EUDOCIA. Well, young ladies, how do you stand affected to the good cause? Are you willing to be Christians—all of you?

ALL. Yes—yes—yes, madam.

EUDOCIA. A noble resolution! I hope you will have the constancy to maintain it.

[*Lauteria enters suddenly, distracted with fear.*

LAUTERIA. O madam, madam, madam, all is ruined! Constantine's head is not worth so much as my pincushion. Metrodora carries all before her policy. She has gained the orator Helvidius by the promise of a million sesterces. Old Priseus stood out a great while, but she finally gained *him* over by promising to marry him. Poor Master Constantine! He is gone as sure as death. (*She weeps.*)

CONSTANTIA. Ladies, lead me away. I fear I shall faint. O my son! (*To the ladies.*) But do not change your purpose. Remain true to the Christian beliefs.

[*Constantia withdraws, supported by Arpasia and Aphrodite, who soon return.*

EUDOCIA. What pain she feels for her son. But are we not all in as great danger as Constantine?

LAUTERIA. O, madam, to be sure we are. We are all gone, sure enough. (*Weeps again.*)

EUDOCIA. But how do you know these things? From whom do you have your information?

LAUTERIA. From one of Metrodora's spies. He has made love to me and expects that I will marry him. But I told him positively that I would not have him unless he would tell me all I wanted to know.

THALIA. I yet have confidence. Constantia's mind is fruitful in resources.

ARPASIA. I fear that hope or joy is no more for us in this world.

[*Lauteria withdraws, weeping.*

SCENE VI: CONSTANTIA RETURNS.

CONSTANTIA. Ladies, you yet may hope. Tho all Lauteria's information be true, we are not ruined, nevertheless.

EUDOCIA. And how do you expect to prevent the evils which threaten us?

CONSTANTIA. The votes of the thundering legion, who are all Christians, are to be taken for the new emperor. Then those of the troops on Mount Aventine, who are mixed, and will look out to see how others vote; then those of the troops in the field of Mars. If the others have voted in my son's favor, [they] will not dare resist.

EUDOCIA. But what will you do with the Senate?

CONSTANTIA. I have found means to make the Senate's bargains with Metrodora public. If they attempt to speak, they will be perfectly ridiculous

EUDOCIA. My dear sister, you have acted the part of an able politician and general.

CONSTANTIA. Men indeed pretend to rule the world; and I am very well content that they should enjoy the *name*. But women, from a sudden effort of dexterity, will often correct their coarse blunders, and help them out of their mistakes, as you see in this instance.

ARPASIA. You will prove that we had better not have a new emperor, but make the men of Rome submit to us?

CONSTANTIA. You mistake, my daughter. Such offices are unnatural to us. Our constitutions are too delicate, and our feelings too tender.

ARPASIA. O, I hope Constantine will succeed.

CONSTANTIA (*looking out a window*). My dear ladies! The matter will be decided in five minutes. What an interval of anxious suspense! O Heaven grant my son may have success!

[*The ladies all cover their faces and sit in deep silence of fear and expectation. At this moment Lauteria enters suddenly, wild and distracted with joy.*

LAUTERIA. O my sweet mistress, good news! My dear Empress, good news! My dear young ladies, good news! Constantine is elected! He is sitting in the Portico, clothed in imperial purple, and they are going to carry him in triumph to the Capitol!

[*Eudocia rises suddenly and throws her arms about her sister. All the ladies enclose her round with congratulations.*

ALL (*at the same time or in quick succession*). O, my dear sister! Our dear empress! Our noble lady! Dear empress! O, how happy!

CONSTANTIA (*repelling the ladies and bursting from her sister's embrace*). Excuse me, dear ladies. Sister, let me go! Let me fly to embrace my son!

[*She bursts from them and flies out in an ecstasy of joy. Eudocia and the other ladies remain.*

EUDOCIA. O happy event, happy for our sex, happy to Rome and happy to the whole world. The Church has prevailed and idols are no more. Let us hasten to pay our respects to the new emperor.

ALL LEAVE THE STAGE